JONATHAN EDWARDS

Jonathan Edwards at the age of 48, a painting attributed to Joseph Badger (1705-1768). Reproduced by courtesy of Yale University Art Gallery, bequest of Eugene Phelps Edwards.

JONATHAN EDWARDS

A NEW BIOGRAPHY

Iain H. Murray

THE BANNER OF TRUTH TRUST

THE BANNER OF TRUTH TRUST
3 Murrayfield Road, Edinburgh EH12 6EL
PO Box 621, Carlisle, Pennsylvania 17013, USA

*

© Iain H. Murray 1987
First published 1987
Reprinted 1988
Reprinted 1992
ISBN 0 85151 494 4

*

Typeset at The Spartan Press Limited, Lymington, Hants
and printed and bound in Great Britain at
The Bath Press, Avon

To S. M. Houghton

Without whose constant aid, counsel, and
fellowship in the gospel, so very much less of the
work of the Banner of Truth magazine and of
the publications of the Banner of Truth Trust
would have been accomplished in these
thirty-one years, 1955–1986.

'Iron sharpeneth iron; so a man sharpeneth the
countenance of his friend' (Proverbs 27.17).

CONTENTS

ILLUSTRATIONS

COLOUR AND BLACK AND WHITE PLATES

Frontispiece

Jonathan Edwards at the age of 48, a painting attributed to
Joseph Badger (1705–1768). See pages 367–368.

Between pages 160 and 161

Statue of George Whitefield at the University of Pennsylvania

The Housatonic River, about half-a-mile from the site of
Edwards' home at Stockbridge. Photograph by Charles Klotz.

Between pages 192 and 193

Sarah Edwards at the age of 41, a painting attributed to Joseph
Badger.

Map of places relating to Edwards' life

ACKNOWLEDGMENTS

The illustrations on pp. i, 23, 39, 57 and 201 have been taken
from *The Beginnings of Yale*, 1701–1726, E. Oviatt, 1916.

The illustration on the right of page xviii is reproduced by
courtesy of the Edward Mellen Press, New York.

We are indebted to Yale University Press for permission to
quote from *The Journal of Esther Edwards Burr 1754–1757*, edited
by C. F. Karlsen and Laurie Crumpacker, 1984, and to Yale
University Art Gallery for the use of the portraits of Jonathan
and Sarah Edwards.

For the genealogical chart of the Stoddards I am indebted
largely to Patricia J. Tracy, author of *Jonathan Edwards, Pastor*.

The picture on page 249 is reproduced by courtesy of The
Forbes Library, Northampton, Massachusetts, U.S.A.

PREFACE

'Imperfect as it is, it has cost me much time and labor; much more than I thought of when I undertook it,' so Samuel Hopkins wrote on the completion of his *Life and Character of the Late Reverend Jonathan Edwards* in 1761. Subsequent writers on Edwards have probably all experienced similar difficulty. The very extent of Edwards' writings constitutes one problem. Robert Hall, the eminent English Baptist, could 'read Jonathan Edwards's writings with undiminished pleasure for sixty years' but biographers cannot work on such a time scale. It no longer surprises us that some who set out to write a Life of Edwards never saw their hopes fulfilled. In the 1860's, a Presbyterian minister and painstaking editor of the Puritans, Alexander B. Grosart, wrote of the materials he was acquiring for 'a worthy Biography' of Edwards. It was never to appear. Possibly Grosart gave up because he knew that Professor Edwards Amasa Park had the same subject in hand on the other side of the Atlantic. Park, after finishing a successful life of Samuel Hopkins in 1854, seems to have had the Edwards project before him for most of the rest of the century. In 1897 Grosart could write, 'The venerable and venerated theologian and scholar, Professor Park of Andover, has long been engaged on an adequate life of Edwards'. But Park died in 1900 with his Edwards' biography still incomplete and never to be published.

Editors and publishers have faced similar problems with Edwards' works. Yale University Press commenced what was hoped would be the definitive edition of *The Works of Jonathan Edwards* in 1957 but, to date, almost thirty years later, only seven volumes have appeared and these contain less than half of the material to be found in the vast two-volume London edition of Edwards first published in 1834 and currently reprinted by the Banner of Trust Trust. For the foreseeable future this British edition of Edwards is going to be the only one which is readily and economically available to the general Christian public to whom the spiritual wealth of Edwards principally belongs.

[xi]

Our chief purpose in writing this biography has been to further encourage the reading of Edwards himself. For that reason, for ease of reference, we have given in brackets in the text itself the page references to the two-volume edition of Edwards. Those who have yet to begin to read Edwards' writings may find some help in Appendix 1 where I offer guidance on where to start.

As this work at last goes to press, I am conscious of a debt to many people. The Rev. James Shiphardson was a Methodist minister in Durham City, England, whom I never knew personally, but whose copy of the two-volume British edition of Edwards (then a rarity in the second-hand market) I received from his daughter on May 21, 1952. They remain treasured even in the dismembered form into which they have fallen after these many years.

To Dr. George Claghorn of West Chester, Pennyslvania, I owe special thanks for the way in which he helped me – a complete stranger – when we met in the Beinecke Library at Yale, New Haven, in 1967. Our common interest was in the Edwards' manuscripts now stored in that Library. Dr. Claghorn held up his own research to assist me, even to the point of taking me on a memorable visit to East Windsor and Northampton. He has done more than anyone else in locating items of Edwards' scattered correspondence and a few of these letters have appeared in the Yale edition of Edwards. It is certain that if Dr. Claghorn is able to finish his extensive work on Edwards' correspondence it will be a major aid to future biographers.

For counsel at a much later stage I am grateful to Dr. Stuart Piggin of the University of Wollongong, New South Wales, who, while on a visit to Yale in 1985, was able to read my material in typescript and to make valuable suggestions.

My visits to libraries in the United States have been very limited. But I must express appreciation to the Beinecke Library and for the work which others have done as a result of its unique collection of Edwards' manuscripts. In the U.K. I have been principally indebted to The Evangelical Library and the Dr. Williams' Library, London, and to New College Library, Edinburgh. The Fisher Library of the University of Sydney has also been of major help.

Preface

Many, much valued, secretarial assistants have helped me at various stages of this biography, over a period of twenty years, and although I cannot here list all their names I would like them each to know of my abiding appreciation.

Gratitude is due to my friends, James Adams of Mesa, Arizona, James B. Eshelman and Charles and Penny Klotz of Carlisle, for their encouragement. I must thank all my colleagues in the work of the Banner of Truth Trust for their customary, indispensable aid.

We believe that all the truths exemplified in Edwards' life remain relevant today. One of those truths is that a Christian — wife is a man's best and most constant helper. Were it not so these pages could never have been carried through to a conclusion.

We are thankful to have been able to complete this work chiefly because we believe that Edwards' life and writings are so relevant to this present period in the history of the Church. He would not have been surprised had he known of the great advances of the kingdom of Christ in the two centuries which have followed his death. Few Christians have looked to the future with brighter hope than Edwards. He believed, for example, that the age of scientific discovery was only in its beginnings and that there would come new and 'better contrivances for assisting one another through the whole earth by more expedite, easy, and safe communication between distant regions than now'. The vast distances separating the nations of the eighteenth century would disappear, 'the distant extremes of the world shall shake hands together', and this progress would be God-given towards the day when 'the whole earth may be as one community, one body in Christ'. We have often thought of these words in writing the following pages, first in Britain and then in Australia. May God continue to use his servant's testimony to kindle faith in the truth and prayer for revival in generations still to come!

Iain H. Murray, July 21, 1986
3 Murrayfield Rd, Edinburgh, Scotland.

ABBREVIATIONS

J E	*The Works of Jonathan Edwards*, 2 vols., London, 1834 and currently reprinted by the Banner of Truth Trust, Edinburgh.
(1.344)	Such figures in the text refer to the volume and page numbers in the above edition.
J E (Yale)	The Yale edition of *The Works of Jonathan Edwards* (7 vols, 1957–85). For details see p. 479.
Dwight	*The Life of President Edwards*, S. E. Dwight, 1829. A less complete version of this biography, edited by Edward Hickman, is in volume 1 of J E, pp. xi-cxcv, and where this source is used references are given in the text rather than in footnotes.
Travels	*Travels in New England and New York*, Timothy Dwight, 4 vols, 1821–22.
Webster	*A History of the Presbyterian Church in America, from its origin until the year 1760*, Richard Webster, 1857.

Note on Bibliography

Bibliography of and on Edwards is now so extensive that it runs into volumes, notably:

The Printed Writings of Jonathan Edwards, A Bibliography, Thomas H. Johnson, Princeton, 1940.

Jonathan Edwards: Bibliographical Synopses, Nancy Manspeaker, 1981.

Jonathan Edwards, a reference guide, M. X. Lesser, Boston, 1981.

JONATHAN EDWARDS

'That good and sensible man . . . that great man'.
JOHN WESLEY, Works, vol. 10, 1831, pp. 463 and 475

'Mr Edwards is a solid, excellent Christian . . . I think I have not seen his fellow in all New England'.
GEORGE WHITEFIELD Journals, October 17, 1740

'The profoundest reasoner, and the greatest divine, in my opinion, that America ever produced'.
SAMUEL DAVIES in a Farewell Sermon at
Hanover, Virginia, July 1, 1759, Sermons
on Important Subjects, S. Davies, 1824,
Vol. 4, pp. 456–7

'He was, in the estimation of the writer, one of the most holy, humble and heavenly minded men, that the world has seen, since the apostolic age'.
ASHBEL GREEN, President of the College of
New Jersey, in Discourses Delivered in the
College of New Jersey, 1822, p. 317

'The British Isles have produced no such writers on divinity in the eighteenth century as Dickinson and Edwards'.
JOHN ERSKINE, quoted in The Biblical
Repertory and Princeton Review, 1871, p. 98

'The greatest, wisest, humblest and holiest of uninspired men'.
A note in John Collett Ryland's copy of
Hopkins' Life of Edwards, quoted in The
Three Rylands, James Culross, 1897, p. 96 fn

'Jonathan Edwards unites comprehensiveness of view, with minuteness of investigation, beyond any writer I am acquainted with. He was the greatest of the sons of men. He has none of the graces of writing, I admit: he was acquainted with no *grace* but *divine*.'

ROBERT HALL, *Works*, Vol. I, 1866, p. 175

'We cannot take leave of Edwards, without testifying the whole extent of the reverence that we bear him. The American divine affords, perhaps, the most wondrous example in modern times, of one who stood richly gifted both in natural and spiritual discernment – and we know not what most to admire in him, whether the deep philosophy that issued from his pen, or the humble and child-like piety that issued from his pulpit . . . As the philosopher he could discern, and discern truly, between the sterling and the counterfeit in Christianity – still it was as the humble and devoted pastor that Christianity was made, or Christianity was multiplied, in his hands.'

THOMAS CHALMERS, *Works*, Vol. 14, pp. 316–17

'Never was there a happier combination of great power with great piety.'

THOMAS CHALMERS, quoted by G. D. Henderson in
'Jonathan Edwards and Scotland',
The Evangelical Quarterly, January 1944

'We have in our annals no clearer, more transparent, more impressive illustration of an entire consecration of genius and greatness to the promotion of the Christian faith.'

EGBERT C. SMYTH, *The Congregationalist and Christian World*, 3 October 1903, p. 458

'He was distinctly a great man. He did not merely express the thought of his time, or meet it simply in the spirit of his tradition. He stemmed it and moulded it. . . . His time does not explain him.'

F. J. E. WOODBRIDGE, *The Philosophical Review*,
xiii, 1904, p. 405

'Jonathan Edwards changed what I may call the centre of thought in American theological thinking. . . . More than to any other man, to

Edwards is due the importance which, in American Christianity, is attributed to the conscious experience of the penitent sinner, as he passes into the membership of the Invisible Church.

'The man we so often call our greatest American Divine . . . was indeed inexpressibly great in his intellectual endowment, in his theological achievement, in his continuing influence. He was greatest in his attribute of regnant, permeating, irradiating spirituality. It is at once a present beatitude and an omen of future good that, in these days of pride in wealth and all that wealth means, of pride in the fashion of this world which passeth away, we still in our heart of hearts reserve the highest honor for the great American who lived and moved and had his being in the Universe which is unseen and eternal.'

JOHN DE WITT, 'Jonathan Edwards: A Study'
in *Biblical and Theological Studies* by
Members of the Faculty of Princeton Theological
Seminary, 1912, pp. 130 and 136

'Jonathan Edwards, saint and metaphysician, revivalist and theologian, stands out as the one figure of real greatness in the intellectual life of colonial America.'

BENJAMIN B. WARFIELD, Studies in Theology,
1932, p. 517

'No man is more relevant to the present condition of Christianity than Jonathan Edwards. . . . He was a mighty theologian and a great evangelist at the same time. . . . He was pre-eminently the theologian of revival. If you want to know anything about true revival, Edwards is the man to consult. Revivals have often started as the result of people reading volumes such as these two volumes of Edwards' Works.'

D. MARTYN LLOYD-JONES in *The Puritan
Experiment in the New World*, The Westminster
Conference Papers, 1976, p. 103 ff.

Reinterpretations of Edwards. The painting of 1751 attributed to Joseph Badger (see frontispiece) was the only likeness made during his lifetime. Of this portrait, and that of Sarah Edwards, Abiel Walley, a New England merchant, says, 'They are done to the life, have a very exact resemblance' (The Works of John MacLaurin, *1860, vol. 1, pp. lvi–lvii) – an opinion with which at least some members of the Edwards family seem to have disagreed. All subsequent drawings of Edwards have consequently been dependent upon the 1751 portrait. One of the earliest, by Thomas Trotter, appeared in* Biographia Evangelica, *Erasmus Middleton, London, 1779–86, vol. 4.*
In the above (left), published as a frontispiece in The Memorial Volume *of the Edwards Family Meeting, 1871, the artist moves the subject back to early manhood, while the above (right), published in* Jonathan Edwards: Bibliographical Synopses, *Nancy Manspeaker, 1981, brings the portrait into line with modern criticism of Edwards. The contrast between the two drawings well illustrates the world of difference between the ways in which Jonathan Edwards is understood.*

INTRODUCTION:

On Understanding Edwards

Whether or not a biographer of Jonathan Edwards reveals his personal standpoint at the outset makes little difference, for inevitably it will soon be apparent. Edwards divided men in his lifetime and to no less degree he continues to divide his biographers. Certainly in the many books of which he is the subject there is no consensus of opinion. Almost the only statement about him which will command general acceptance is that he was a great man who was born in 1703 and died at the age of fifty-four in 1758. The nature of his greatness, the significance of his life and thought, an assessment of his character and writings – on all these, and much else, judgments are divided.

One school of opinion has considered Edwards worthy of remembrance as America's first systematic philosopher and her 'greatest thinker' of the eighteenth century. Yale University Press reflected this viewpoint when they began their republication of Edwards' *Works* in 1957 with the most philosophical of all his writings, his *Enquiry into the Modern prevailing Notions of that Freedom of Will which is supposed to be essential to Moral Agency.*

There are strong reasons for rejecting this image of Edwards. Such an evaluation cannot be harmonized with the chief impression which Edwards made on his own contemporaries. 'The great philosopher' image does not belong to the eighteenth century, rather it came to prominence in the century after Edwards' own lifetime. Those who knew him best never put 'the philosopher' first. A fellow preacher, Gilbert Tennent, announcing Edwards' death in a Philadelphia newspaper of March 28, 1758, described him as 'a great divine, divinity was his favourite study and the ministry his most delightful employment'. Another friend of Edwards, probably Samuel Finley, writing anonymously in the same year, believed that he was pre-eminently a spokesman for 'practical and vital Christianity' (1.144). For Ezra Stiles, as for so many others, he was, in the first instance, 'a great Divine'. And this oft repeated opinion was not confined to the American colonies. John Newton of London (1725–1807), when faced on one occasion with the question, 'Who was the greatest divine of his era?' replied unhesitatingly, 'Edwards'.[1]

Many New Englanders of the next century, however, saw it differently. They were certain that if Edwards were to be appreciated at all it must *not* be in terms of his theology. For theology means 'creed' and Edwards' creed was – thankfully – a thing of the past. In the oft-cited words of William Ellery Channing, 'Calvinism has passed its meridian and is sinking to rise no more'. Of Edwards, Oliver Wendell Holmes was sure that, 'If he had lived a hundred years later and breathed the air of freedom, he could not have written with such old-world barbarism as we find in his volcanic sermons'.

In the later nineteenth century almost all who wrote sympathetically of Edwards felt it necessary to apologize for his beliefs. Only as a 'philosopher', it seemed, could he retain some respectability. But this re-interpretation was bound to fail when it came to be scrutinized again in the light of the historical facts. The present century brought renewed study and new conclusions. As early as 1904 – when most writers were still saying the opposite – F. J. E. Woodbridge concluded an article on Edwards in *The Philosophical Review* with the words, 'We remember him, not as the greatest of American philosophers, but as the greatest of American Calvinists'.[2] The plain fact is that Edwards' excursions into philosophy were only occasional and peripheral to his main thought; it was theology, or 'divinity', which belonged to the warp and woof of his life. Edwards' place in history is not alongside Locke, Berkeley or Kant. His life and impact were essentially religious.

This much is now commonly admitted and yet still without any general agreement. The most popular modern interpreters of Edwards hold that, as a religious figure, his is the greatness of religious 'tragedy' – the 'tragedy' being that even for 'the greatest intellect in the history of American Christianity', his inherited Calvinistic beliefs were too strong for him to over-

[1]Quoted in *Memoir of John Elias*, E. Morgan, 1845, p. 150.
[2]Quoted by B. B. Warfield in an article 'Edwards and the New England Theology', *Studies in Theology*, 1932, p. 516.

come. So argues Henry B. Parkes, the first of the modern biographers, in his *Jonathan Edwards, The Fiery Puritan*, 1930. With the exception of Arthur C. McGiffert, who is less inclined to criticize Edwards' doctrine, every other twentieth-century biographer of Edwards appears to agree with Parkes. For Ola Winslow, in her factually valuable *Jonathan Edwards*, he was a prisoner in an outworn, obsolete theological system – 'his bondage seems almost a tragic pity'. Perry Miller, the best-known twentieth-century writer on Edwards, puts it bluntly: 'The life of Edwards is a tragedy. . . . Because of his faith Edwards wrought incalculable harm'.[1]

A host of lesser-known writers repeat this same theme. 'Jonathan Edwards,' says Peter Gay, 'was the greatest tragic hero', intent upon 'rescuing the essence of the Puritan faith, on clarifying it, defending it, and preaching it to an age that did not wish to listen'.[2] Herbert W. Schneider laments: 'His philosophical insight was buried under the ruins of his religion. He failed to see the futility of insisting on the Puritan principles'.[3]

Most of these writers, it should be said, are generous enough to consider that Edwards remains praiseworthy, for to have achieved what he did despite the handicap of his beliefs is greatness indeed. We must not, however, expect them to want to re-introduce the *doctrine* which Edwards taught. In a parody in verse on 'The Theology of Jonathan Edwards', Phyllis McGinley wrote in 1961:

> And if they had been taught aright,
> Small children carried bedwards
> Would shudder lest they meet that night
> The God of Mr. Edwards,
>
> Abraham's God, the Wrathful One,
> Intolerant of error –
> Not God the Father or the Son
> But God the Holy Terror.[4]

---

[1] *Jonathan Edwards*, 1949, pp. 16, 148.

[2] See Gay's chapter, 'An American Tragedy' in *Jonathan Edwards, A Profile*, ed. D. Levin, 1969.

[3] *The Puritan Mind*, 1930, p. 177, quoted in Nancy Manspeaker's valuable *Jonathan Edwards: Bibliographical Synopses*, 1981. For similar references in Manspeaker, see pp. 132, 153, 204, etc.

[4] Manspeaker, *op. cit.*, p. 123.

If such a division exists over the initial general view that has been taken of Edwards, it is not surprising that further differences emerge as we proceed. His character, for example, has received portrayals which are irreconcilable. Gilbert Tennent, in the obituary of 1758 already quoted, writes that, along with fidelity to God, 'nothing appeared with greater lustre and more striking charm in his conduct than his candor to man', but Perry Miller asserts, 'the people found him a man of deception'. Or again, Miller says, 'He was proud and overbearing and rash',[1] whereas Samuel Finley in 1758 writes, 'He had a natural steadiness of temper . . . the humility, modesty, and serenity of his behaviour much endeared him to his acquaintance' (1.44).

Clearly there is a difference here between eighteenth and twentieth-century judgments. But it would be an oversimplification to explain the matter in this way. Perry Miller's opinions found some exponents two centuries ago. Edwards himself tells us, four years before his death, 'I was often charged with acting only from sinister views, with stiffness of spirit, and from pride, and an arbitrary and tyrannical spirit.'[2]

It is no wonder, then, if Edwards' books should equally give rise to strong differences of opinion. Possibly the best known, and most frequently reprinted, is his *Life of David Brainerd*. In his original Preface to this book of 1749, Edwards says of Brainerd, 'Here is indeed a remarkable instance of true and eminent Christian piety in heart and practice' (2.315). Many agreed. John Wesley writes of Brainerd's 'absolute self-devotion, total deadness to the world, and fervent love to God and man'. As late as 1904, in an Introduction to a new edition of the *Diary and Journal of David Brainerd*, Alexander Smellie wrote, 'David Brainerd's consecration soars to ethereal altitudes, and it strains our eyes to accompany him in his Godward flight'. But more recent interpreters of Edwards' account of Brainerd see it very differently. In the words of Ola Winslow, they are confident that 'Brainerd's story can hardly be read with composure, much less with admiration'.[3]

[1] *Jonathan Edwards*, 1949, pp. 210, 211.
[2] Letter to Joseph Hawley, Nov. 18, 1754, in *Jonathan Edwards*, Representative Selections, Clarence H. Faust and T. H. Johnson, 1966, p. 395.
[3] *Jonathan Edwards 1703–1758*, 1940, p. 242.

Or again, while William Cunningham speaks of Edwards' volume on *Original Sin* as entitled 'to be regarded as one of the most valuable, permanent possessions of the Christian church,'[1] the historian, W. E. H. Lecky, on the contrary, is sure that it is 'one of the most revolting books that have ever proceeded from the pen of man'.[2]

Given such differences as these, the reader will not be surprised to find that Edwards' own opinions are also the subject of contradiction. I do not refer now to his theological opinions but to his view of events and of people. His contemporary, Charles Chauncy, was pleased to say that he was 'a visionary enthusiast, and not to be minded in anything he says'. Whether for the same reason, or for others, later writers have not been slow to set aside Edwards' own evaluations. The character and work of George Whitefield is a case in point. Edwards and Whitefield were contemporaries and their lives converged in the pivotal year 1740. After days together, Edwards subsequently wrote of Whitefield's 'good spirit', his 'zeal and courage' and his practical love for others (1.421, 424). Edwards is not surprised at 'the remarkable blessing that God has given Mr. Whitefield and the great success with which he has crowned him' (1.429). But Professor Perry Miller sees fit to write of the same man, 'a more repulsive individual never influenced history'.[3]

To say that writers on Edwards are divided is an understatement. How, then, are such multiplied differences of opinion to be explained? Are these writers really talking about the same person, the same books, the same events?

Certainly the explanation cannot be that we suffer from an absence of information which makes accurate evaluation impossible. Edwards is not some obscure figure, scarcely to be understood on account of lack of dependable source material. On the contrary, his thought and life is among the best documented of all the Americans of the eighteenth century. For a start there are over 1100 sermons existing in their original manuscript form. There are the many books, some partly

---

[1] *The Reformers and the Theology of the Reformation*, 1862 (reprint 1967), p. 520.
[2] *History of the Rise and Influence of the Spirit of Nationalism in Europe*, 1871, vol. 1, p. 368n.
[3] *Jonathan Edwards*, p. 133.

historical, published by Edwards in his lifetime. We have some autobiographical material, a portion of diary and about two hundred of his letters. There is, further, the testimony of many eye-witnesses and other contemporaries, and finally, the more than half-a-dozen biographies published since his death. A lack of reliable information cannot be the explanation for the differences we have noted.

As all the writers on Edwards quoted above might be expected to have read him, it may seem strange to say that the key to all their disagreements is to be found in his writings. It has to do with the nature of Christianity. In the normally accepted standards of modern thought, religious experience is only subjective and not to be conceived as related to timeless, spiritual realities. Similarly, prayer is a psychological exercise and theology a matter of changing human opinion. If the infinite and the eternal exist at all, they cannot be known to exert any direct influence upon the affairs of our real world. God, and heaven, and immortality, are concepts not to be considered as belonging to the realm of the factual and the testimony of the Bible upon such issues does not possess any more authority than the testimony of any other book. The progress of education and enlightenment has inevitably done away with the kind of moral universe in which Edwards saw himself. So there is, according to this view, no choice but to assess Edwards' life and thought from a standpoint alien to his own.

There is, however, a matter of history which ought to have given pause to all the advocates of this thesis. The fact is that the non-biblical view of life and religion, instead of being the result of recent progress, was perfectly familiar to Edwards himself. He was only thirty-three when Bishop Joseph Butler wrote in 1736: 'It is come, I know not how, to be taken for granted by many persons that Christianity is not so much as a subject of inquiry; but that it is now at length discovered to be fictitious. And accordingly they treat it as if, in the present age, this were an agreed point among all people of discernment.' The supposedly 'modern' standpoint is not so modern after all. Our contemporary scepticism would not have surprised Edwards. Further, and strange to say (if the modern thesis were true), the twentieth-century depiction of Edwards as 'religious tragedy' was also well-known to him for it uses the very idiom employed by eighteenth-century unbelievers in their treatment of his Christian predecessors. 'The first reformers, and others that succeeded them,' he tells us, in 'their teaching and maintaining such doctrines as are commonly called Calvinistic', are represented 'by many late writers' as men with 'their minds shackled, living in the gloomy caves of superstition', and consequently teaching 'monstrous opinions', worthy to be held in contempt by 'gentlemen possessed of that noble and generous freedom of thought which happily prevails in this age of light and inquiry' (1.88–89). And, as though echoing the very things to be said of him two hundred years later, Edwards notes that these enlightened critics 'in an ostentation of a very generous charity' have allowed that 'these ancient and eminent divines . . . were honest, well-meaning men, as though it were in great condescension and compassion to them, that they did pretty well for the day in which they lived, and considering the great disadvantages they laboured under'.

The modern writers, in general, have passed over in silence what was at the front of Edwards' own thinking. First of all, he was a Christian and a teacher of the Christian Faith. The reigning power of the sin in his heart, on account of which he was 'unable to love God, believe in Christ, or do anything that is truly good and acceptable in God's sight', had been ended by 'the interposition of sovereign grace'. By his own testimony this was not true of him from birth; rather, God had intervened, bringing him into a living experience of a Saviour whom thereafter he lived to worship, to serve and to enjoy. Such a conversion to faith is exactly what the New Testament teaches and would lead us to expect.

According to the New Testament, and therefore to Edwards also, the difference between the regenerate Christian and the remainder of men constitutes the most radical of all divisions.[1]

---

[1] In a brief reference, Peter Gay at least recognizes that the absence of faith in the Bible puts men in a different position from that of Edwards. Without explaining how one can believe in Christ without believing the only book in which he is made known, he writes, 'For Locke, the only dogma a Christian need believe – the only dogma he can believe – is that Christ is the Messiah. But Edwards went right on accepting the testimony of Scripture as literally true' (*Jonathan Edwards, A Profile*, p. 248).

What is revealed to babes is hidden from the proud. The reason, he says, 'why the things of the gospel seem all so tasteless and insipid to natural men' is that 'they are a parcel of words to which they, in their own minds, have no correspondent ideas'. 'It is like a strange or a dead letter, that is, sounds and letters without any signification. This is the reason they commonly account religion such a foolish thing, and the saints fools. This is the reason the Scripture is not sweet to them, and why the godly are called by the name of fanatics, and the like.'[1]

Those who consider that modern enlightenment has superseded the possibility of the supernatural and displaced the Bible as a revelation from a living God, ought at least to have considered the alternative reason which Edwards proposes for disbelief. Instead, like those of whom Butler complains in 1736, they simply assume that Christianity is 'discovered to be fictitious'. And they proceed to write about Edwards as though this makes no difference to any genuine understanding of his life and thought. They never address themselves to the question, What would follow if Edwards' religion is in accord with Christ and the Bible and if it be true? Any references which they make to the Bible at all are commonly as superficial as that of Henry Churchill King who at the Edwards' Bicentenary regretted that Edwards lacked 'Christ's wonderful faith in men'.

In this volume we offer Edwards' own key to the reason why the world will always disagree over Christian experience and Christian truth. It is that in all centuries the saving knowledge of God inevitably brings division: it opens to some a world of reality which remains closed to others:

> And none can truly worship but who have
> The earnest of their glory from on high,
> God's nature in them . . .

Of those who received the faith of the gospel, Christ says to God the Father, 'I have given them thy word; and the world hath hated them, because they are not of the world, even as I am not of the world' (John 17.14).

Here is the fundamental reason why opinions on Edwards are so divided, and why his biographers should also differ so

[1] J E 'Miscellanies' (123) in *The Philosophy of Jonathan Edwards*, H. G. Townsend, 1955, p. 246.

widely. The division runs right back to the Bible, and, depending on where we stand in relation to Christ, we shall join ourselves to one side or the other in interpreting this man who was, first of all, a Christian.

*　　　*　　　*

The first three biographers of Edwards were all men, who like their subject, had pastoral experience in the Christian ministry. Only the first, Samuel Hopkins (1721–1803) whose *Life and Character of the Late Reverend Jonathan Edwards* was published in 1765, knew Edwards personally and could write as an eye-witness. While an essential source book it is much too short to be a definitive Life. The next biography, while far the most important to be published to date, tends to the opposite extreme. Sereno Edwards Dwight (1786–1850), great-grand-son of Edwards, gave 'many years'[1] to the preparation of his *Life of President Edwards*, 1829. All subsequent biographers are dependent upon it, and it is still in print,[2] but the ponderous size of Dwight's *Life*, with many long unabridged letters and documents, prevents it from ever being a popular introduction to Edwards.

Perhaps it was for this reason that Jared Sparks asked Samuel Miller of Princeton to produce a new *Life of Jonathan Edwards* in 1839. Miller's work, long out-of-print, is largely an abridgement of Dwight, with some useful observations by Miller himself.

Hopkins, Dwight and Miller all understood Edwards and shared his basic vision for the Christian church. All three men also were witnesses of true revivals, in fact it was S. E. Dwight's labours in a time of awakening in the 1820's which broke his health and necessitated his resignation from his pastoral charge in 1826. Without that event we might never have had his biography, for Dwight was essentially a preacher and had he not fallen into poor health the pulpit would have continued to

[1] See S. E. Dwight in *Annals of the American Pulpit*, W. B. Sprague, 1857, vol. 2, p. 629ff.

[2] With certain omissions, Dwight's *Life* was reprinted in the 1834 London edition of Edwards' *Works*, which is the edition currently published by the Banner of Truth Trust.

claim the greater part of his time.

In the mid-1850's, Alexander B. Grosart, a Scots minister, crossed the Atlantic on a visit and busied himself examining the large collection of Edwards' manuscripts, then in the hands of the Rev. Dr. Tryon Edwards of New London, Connecticut. In an Introduction to *Selections from the Unpublished Writings of Jonathan Edwards*, 1864, Grosart explained that he had not included letters of Edwards, 'reserving those obtained, and others expected, for his "Life", one day to be written; and than which few comparable have been lived. I possess already priceless and hitherto unknown materials for a worthy Biography'.

What Grosart actually possessed the world cannot know for his biography of Edwards was never published. Had he written he would have been the last biographer sympathetic to Edwards' theology for over a century. The next major biographer makes the transition to the modern school of interpreters. This was Alexander V. G. Allen, professor in the Episcopal Theological School in Cambridge, Massachusetts, whose *Life and Writings of Jonathan Edwards* was published in Edinburgh in 1889. 'Valuable as Dwight's work is,' says Allen, 'it does not constitute an adequate biography. Much that would throw light upon Edwards' history is withheld from publication.' Yet Allen adds comparatively little and the perspective is all from the human viewpoint. Edwards is seen as 'the originator, the director, the champion' of the Great Awakening. *The Congregationalist and the Christian World*, Boston, in a special issue of October 3, 1903, to mark Edwards' bicentenary, could say with some justification that Edwards 'awaits a biographer'.

When interest in the literature and history of colonial America revived in the present century it was inevitable that, given his place as an eighteenth-century figure of international importance, the study of Edwards would revive. Henry B. Parkes led the way with *Jonathan Edwards, The Fiery Puritan*, in 1930, followed two years later by Arthur C. McGiffert's *Jonathan Edwards*. Parkes is a very racy writer with a grasp of New England background. These authors however, were largely replaced in 1940 by the appearance of Ola E. Winslow's *Jonathan Edwards 1703–1758* which has become the standard modern biography. By careful use of Edwards' own unpublished manuscripts and other sources, Winslow took the study of his life, in its human aspects, a major step forward, which makes it all the more regrettable that she is so determined to reject his theology. Only in her Prologue, written when the book was finished, does Winslow touch upon the truth about which her biography is so little concerned. Edwards, she says, could write of delighting in God and mean it. 'If he had a secret, it somehow concerned his own capacity for such delight, while he still had his feet on New England earth'. Secret it must remain to all who treat the faith which he preached as 'doomed'.

With Professor Perry Miller's *Jonathan Edwards*, 1949, the anti-supernatural animus comes to its fullest expression. In a review of Miller's book by William Young in the November 1950 issue of *The Westminster Theological Journal*, the opinion is stated that 'the arguments and conclusions of the author are open to severe criticism'. But this view went literally unheard as Miller's many students, and others, praised the 'perception' of the Harvard Professor's treatment of his theme. Patricia J. Tracy (*Jonathan Edwards, Pastor*, 1980) speaks of Miller's biography as the 'most challenging of all'. Ralph J. Coffman echoes the judgment of the University world in referring to Miller as 'a master of Puritan thought' (*Solomon Stoddard*, 1978, p. 218), and S. S. Webb, writing in 1962, says that Miller's biography of Edwards' mind is perhaps the outstanding single volume in the renaissance of Edwards' scholarship which had begun some twenty-five years earlier. Webb does add, however, that 'Miller's work has been criticized for slighting Edwards' relationship to the Bible and to Christianity in general'.

The above words from Webb are taken from his 'Selected Biography' in the Revised Edition (1962) of *Jonathan Edwards, Representative Selections*, with Introduction, Bibliography, and Notes, Clarence H. Faust and Thomas H. Johnson, 1935. The work of Faust and Johnson is of great value. Webb's bibliography, added to the Revised Edition, also carries forward to 1962 complete bibliographical data for works of Edwards published after 1940. All Edwards' writings published prior to 1940 are listed in *The Printed Writings of Jonathan Edwards, 1703–1758: A Bibliography*, T. H. Johnson, 1940. These two works show modern scholarship at its best. This present biography offers a popular account of Edwards. One day, we trust, a definitive and theologically dependable Life of Edwards will yet be written. Because of the location of the most important source material such a work will probably have to appear from the American side of the Atlantic. But in the meantime, given the contemporary state of the Christian church, there is urgent need of a new generation who will take up and read Edwards. Our hope is to achieve something towards that end, for Edwards ought not to be the preserve of academics and University students. While he has special value to all preparing for the Christian ministry or for other branches of Christian service, many of his writings are of permanent importance for the whole Christian church. Almost all his working life he was a pastor, speaking to the rank and file membership of churches, first in a country town, then in a frontier outpost. And because of the gifts which God gave him in the exposition of Scripture, Edwards remains today one of the foremost teachers of the church.

'The student of 18th-century New England', said Bancroft, 'must give his days and nights to the study of Jonathan Edwards'. The case of this biography is that there are yet higher reasons why Edwards must be read today.

* * *

For two days in September 1870, some 200 descendants of Edwards assembled for a Family Meeting at Stockbridge, Massachusetts. Various pleasant addresses were given, tea was taken on the lawns, sites were visited and Victorian charm and politeness prevailed. But amidst it all, one visitor grew somewhat impatient. S. Irenaeus Prime had not been expected to speak. Only when it was learned that a representative from Princeton, who was to have given the closing speech on the first day, could not be there, was Prime asked at 'very brief' notice to fill the gap. His short address was to be the most memorable of the whole assembly. He startled his hearers by declaring that to remember Edwards meant far more than a mere bow to history, for, he continued, the message he preached is relevant to every age:

'It has the life of Christ in it; it subordinates the reason to divine authority, and adores the Holy Ghost. . . . His *theology* had revivals and repentance, and salvation from hell, in it; and this made it, and makes it, and will keep it divine theology till Christ is all in all.'

A student coming to Princeton, Prime declared, hears that same theology and as he visits the graves of Edwards and his fellow-labourers of an earlier age, 'something of their fire kindles in his soul'.

We fail to understand Edwards aright until the record of his life begins to make the same impression upon us.

I

THE SON OF EAST WINDSOR

Thomas Hooker's Hartford house

In books, or work, or healthful play,
  Let my first years be past,
That I may give for every day
  Some good account at last.

ISAAC WATTS, 1715

Divine and Moral Songs For The Use of Children

.

I

n November 1620 when 'The Mayflower' landed a band of forty-one men and their families on Cape Cod it is not surprising that they, and those who followed them to 'New England', felt themselves to be like the patriarchs in Canaan, 'very few and strangers in it'. Within twenty years the population of the infant settlements clustered around the shores of Massachusetts Bay had swelled to more than twenty thousand, but the great hinterland[1] was virtually unknown territory when the eminent Puritan preacher, Thomas Hooker, struck out westwards from the Bay in the month of June, 1636. For about a fortnight Hooker's party of about a hundred people journeyed until they reached the Connecticut – 'the long river' as the Indians had aptly named it – and there at a site which they named Hartford, fifty miles inland from the mouth of the river, they settled. Just a few miles north, at Windsor, an English trader had built the first house in Connecticut in 1633 and fortified it against possible attack either from the native Indians or from the Dutch trade rivals.

For Hooker, with the years of his fellowship at Emmanuel, Cambridge, and his lectureship at Chelmsford, Essex – the Galilee of Puritan England – behind him, the change of aspect was immense. As Benjamin Trumbull writes of Connecticut,

[1]The boundaries of New England eventually included an area of about seventy thousand square miles – its greatest length, from North to South, being about 490 miles, and its breadth varying between 130 to 250 miles.

'When the English became first acquainted with that tract it was a vast wilderness. There were no pleasant fields, nor gardens, no public roads, nor cleared plots.' The whole was forest, water, or ground burned and wasted by the Indians in their pursuit of deer and other game.

Among those who travelled with Hooker was Ann Coles, who, with her husband, had exchanged the crowded streets of England's capital for this remote frontier colony. In the early 1620's she had lived in London as the wife of Richard Edwards, a clergyman- schoolmaster and a native of Wales, whose work at the Ratcliffe Free School ended with his sudden death in 1625. Thereafter Ann Edwards had married James Coles, and with her eighteen-year-old son, William Edwards, they had joined the company of those 'upon the wing for a wilderness in America, where they hoped for an opportunity to enjoy and practise the pure worship of the Lord Jesus Christ.'

William Edwards was the first generation of the Edwards' line in New England. He followed the trade of a cooper, married, and his son Richard, born in 1647, was the grand-father of the subject of these pages. In his seventy-one years Richard Edwards, a moderately prosperous merchant, came to share amply in the change which saw Hartford transformed from a struggling frontier settlement to an established trading town. At his death he was to leave an estate which showed his success as 'a man of business'. Yet Richard Edwards had no easy life. As Hooker, who died in the year of his birth, once said: 'They who had been lively Christians in the fire of persecution, would soon become cold in the midst of universal peace, except some few, whom God by sharp trials would keep in a faithful, watchful, humble, and praying frame.' Richard Edwards was one of these few. The reader of the account which his son, Timothy, wrote after his death – 'for my own use and comfort, concerning the life and death of my very dear and honoured father, Mr. Richard Edwards, late of Hartford' (1.ccxi) – will notice a total silence concerning the mother of the home. The truth is that Elizabeth Tuttle whom Richard Edwards married in 1667 was his sharpest trial. They were scarce married before she bore a child by another man and when this infidelity recurred repeatedly in later years it was combined with evidence of insanity.

[4]

Timothy Edwards had an abounding admiration for the character of his father. 'He was naturally cheerful, sprightly, and sweet tempered, of a ready wit, had a mind well stored with knowledge, particularly the knowledge of history and theology, and in conversation was uncommonly pleasant and entertaining.' But it was as a Christian that Timothy came to love his father most: 'In the presence of God, he appeared not only to believe but to delight . . . in prayer he seemed to draw very near to God . . . His feelings on religious subjects were at once strong and tender . . . From my own observation of other religious families, with which I have been familiarly acquainted, I have reason to believe that few children, even of Christian parents, have been better instructed.'

When Timothy first left home for Harvard College in 1687 his father gave him every encouragement. 'You may expect to meet with difficulties,' he wrote to him on one occasion, 'but still God is all-sufficient – the same God in all places and in all conditions'. Timothy certainly needed encouragement. Probably related to the fact that 'most of the country' knew of his family troubles, his early days at Harvard were so unsettled and unsatisfactory that he was sent down from the College early in 1688, with his name being marked in the College records for 'punishment' on account of an unspecified offence. In March of the same year, he and his sister, Abigail, made an official deposition against their mother and the matter finally came to its sad conclusion in 1691 with her divorce.

According to Dwight (1.ccviii), Timothy Edwards graduated with the Harvard Class of 1691, receiving the two degrees of Bachelor and Master of Arts on the same day, 'July 4, 1691'. This is a mistake. He ought to have graduated with the class of 1690, but in fact did not do so until 1694 when he was awarded both degrees with the first marked 'as of 1691'. That his two degrees were awarded simultaneously was not due, as Dwight supposed, 'to his extraordinary proficiency in learning', it was rather a consequence of his chequered College career. How long Timothy Edwards actually spent at Harvard between 1687 and 1694 is unclear. It is known that for a time during this period he was a student under the care of the minister of Springfield, and early in 1694 there is record of his teaching school in Northampton where his salary was paid in April of that year.

At some point during these student years Timothy Edwards met his future wife, Esther Stoddard, the mother of Jonathan Edwards. Perhaps their paths first crossed while he was at Springfield, or it could have been at Boston (close to Harvard) where Esther finished her education an hundred miles away from her home in Northampton. If this was so, then Timothy's school-mastering period in her home-town involved considerations above his financial needs. It was an uncommon thing for country girls to finish their schooling in Boston, but then Esther Stoddard belonged to no common family. Jonathan Edwards' parentage on his father's side bore no special distinction, save that of godliness. His father's Harvard graduation bore its own witness to that fact, for, in the usual tradition, the graduates' names were ranked according to the social standing of their parents: Timothy Edwards' name stood last among the eight names listed in his class. Esther Stoddard, on the other hand, while united to her future husband in their common spiritual inheritance, possessed one of the best-known surnames in New England. Stoddards were leaders in the land even before her father, Solomon Stoddard, had begun his eminent ministry in Northampton in 1669. Since then the town had become the largest in inland Massachusetts and its pulpit one of the most influential in the whole colony. Twenty-three items were in the course of being published from Stoddard's pen, and as late as 1740, when George Whitefield visited New England, the fame of his preaching was still a matter of common conversation. Esther was the second daughter in the Northampton parsonage, and her home was filled with five sisters and four brothers by the time that she finished her school days in Boston. Like herself, one of her brothers and four of her sisters were to spend their lives in various New England parsonages. Both the size and the distinction of her parents' family were to have particular relevance in the life of her son.[1]

Esther Stoddard was named after her mother who was the daughter of the Rev. John Warham. Warham had been minister of one of Connecticut's oldest churches,[2] the extensive

[1] For Solomon Stoddard's children see p. 74.

[2] As a congregation it was certainly the oldest, being formed in Plymouth, England, in 1630 on the eve of embarkation. It was made up of people from the counties of Devon, Dorset, and Somerset.

parish of Windsor, which lay on both sides of the Connecticut
river and adjoining Hartford to the south. Of this first minister
of Windsor, Cotton Mather writes, 'Though our Warham were –
as pious a man as most that were out of heaven, yet Satan often
threw him into those deadly pangs of melancholy, that made
him despair of ever getting thither'.[1]

It was to a part of the original Windsor parish that Timothy
Edwards was called in 1694. On November 6th he married –
Esther Stoddard at Northampton and eight days later they
came to East Windsor. Timothy Edwards was twenty-five, and
his bride twenty-three. In the words of Increase Tarbox, she
'brought to the humble East Windsor parsonage a culture and
refinement rare in those days'. Initially called for a trial period,
Timothy Edwards' flock soon confirmed their call. He was
ordained in March, 1695, and settled for life.

East Windsor was a new congregation in a district that had
changed considerably since Esther Edwards' mother had first
known it. Then the one parish had covered an area some ten
miles from north to south, and twelve from east to west, with a
large Indian population, including an estimated 2,000 'bow-
men'. In the 1660's it was supposed that there were nineteen
Indians to one Englishman. Thirty years later that era was
gone. The great Indian uprising of 1675–76 had passed into
history. The Pequots and their fellows who survived had
removed inland and Windsor's settlers, no longer requiring the
shelter of their original fortifications, had spread out into the
potentially rich farm land which surrounded them. To secure
some of the best of this land new homesteads had sprung up on
the eastern side of the river called 'the Farms'. By 1691, there
were more than fifty families, and 'near three hundred persons
capable of hearing the Word of God to profit', who had to cross
the unbridged Connecticut every Sunday to reach the church
which was located on the western side. This was manageable
enough by boat in summer, but in the higher water or ice of
winter, and in the floods of spring, the crossing was hazardous.
Only after a number of unsuccessful appeals to the General

---

[1] *The Great Works of Christ in America* (*Magnalia Christi Americana*), 1979
reprint, Banner of Truth Trust, vol. 1, 442. Mather's work, first published in
1702, remains indispensable in any thorough study of the New England
Puritans.

Court were the people of 'the Farms' permitted to organize their separate parish in 1694.

In this way East Windsor became one of the one hundred and twenty-nine parishes 'worshipping our Lord Jesus Christ in the several colonies of New England'. The river determined the location of most of its homes. Above the eastern bank of the Connecticut were half a mile or more of rich meadows, the 'bottom-lands', which were often overflowed by the spring floods. These meadows terminate with a further bank, with higher ground lying beyond. It was above the flood-level, along the irregular line of this second bank, and for several miles up and down river, that the houses were built. Inevitably, in a community where the Bible was enthroned in the minds of men, it was the new meeting-house, built just over the brow of the second bank, which was the centre of life. As a building nothing could have been plainer, it was merely a covered wood frame, initially without floor or seating except for the sills and projecting timbers. But the manuscript sermons of Timothy Edwards which survive show that such surroundings made no difference to the thoroughness of his preparation for each Lord's Day.[1] His view of the ministry of the Word was the same as that of his wife's father, Solomon Stoddard, who said, 'We are not sent into the pulpit to shew our wit and eloquence but to set the consciences of men on fire'.

A track ran beside the East Windsor meeting-house and less than a quarter of a mile to the north, on the east of this track, a home was built for the new minister. The cost for brick and hewn timber was met by Richard Edwards who, happily remarried, lived less than eight miles away in Hartford. The labour was given freely in the course of a year by the parishioners. Evidently the work was not stinted, for the parsonage was to

[1] In 1869, in an article on 'Jonathan Edwards' in *Bibliotheca Sacra*, pp. 243–68, I. N. Tarbox speaks of the existence until 'a few years since' of several of Timothy Edwards' manuscript sermons, the earliest which he saw bearing the note, 'On a Fast-day at Suffield, Oct. 19th, '95', being the first year of his ministry. Of these MSS he says, 'They have been given away as most interesting relics, until we fear the stock is about gone.' Four are published in J. A. Stoughton, *'Windsor Farmes': A Glimpse of an Old Parish*, 1883. Timothy Edwards wrote his sermons in full but, it seems, preached in the pulpit from a much shorter outline. Only one was published in his lifetime, *All the Living Must Surely Die and Go to Judgment*, 1732.

stand stoutly against all weathers and men still admired its strength when the day for demolition finally came in 1812. S. E. Dwight, who saw the house, says it was 'a solid substantial house of moderate dimensions' and regarded, 'at the time of its erection, as a handsome residence.' It stood, two storeys high, looking westwards towards the roof-tops of Windsor, and surrounded by farm land which Richard Edwards had also purchased for his son. A good farm was then regarded as 'a natural accompaniment to a New England parsonage'.[1] Behind the house the ground sloped down to a stream beyond which lay the woodland preserve of birds and wild-life.

It was here on October 5, 1703, that Jonathan Edwards was born. Four sisters, Esther, Elizabeth, Anne and Mary, had arrived before him, and six more were to follow after, but he was to be the only son. In later years, when the ten girls had grown to six feet in height, people spoke of Timothy Edwards' 'sixty feet of daughters'. The gentleness of Jonathan's bearing in later life, was no doubt in part the consequence of an upbringing with such companions.[2] Yet, if the East Windsor parsonage was decidedly feminine in its composition, it was not a place of delicate breeding. Esther Edwards, who was to live in that same home until she was ninety-eight, had the Stoddard strength of character and of constitution. Later generations recalled her as tall, affable, gentle, and 'surpassing her husband in native vigour of understanding' (1.ccx). She was married for twenty years before she openly professed faith in Christ and became a communicant. It cannot, on that account, be assumed that Jonathan's mother inherited a measure of her grandfather Warham's liability to depression. There is nothing known of her later life to support such a supposition. The truth is that Esther Edwards belonged to a tradition which dreaded a superficial and premature 'conversion'. In all probability she was godly before she herself had any strength of assurance

[1]A later generation was to be critical of this arrangement but an older observer of New England commented, respecting ministers, in 1851, that by spending more time in their studies 'the moderns gain in learning, but at the expense of their health'. W. B. Sprague, *Annals*, 2, p. 33.

[2]Hollister, in his *History of Connecticut*, says of Edwards: 'He enjoyed the rare advantage, never understood and felt, except by those who have been fortunate enough to experience it, of all the softening and hallowed influences which refined female society sheds.'

about her own salvation. Such outwardly slow beginnings tended to a deeper spirituality in the end. A later generation was to speak of the attractiveness of her spirituality and to recall how, in her widowhood, women both old and young would make a practice of gathering in her home to hear her speak and pray. One who remembered these meetings commented, 'Mrs. Edwards was always fond of books, and discovered a very extensive acquaintance with them in her conversation, particularly with the best theological writers'.

There is little material upon which to form any accurate portrait of Jonathan's father and certainly nothing to justify Ola Winslow's opinion that he was uninspiring and pedestrian. On the contrary, Timothy Edwards seems to have had something of his father's liveliness of temperament. His hearers certainly thought so when they later came to compare him with 'Mr. Jonathan' (1.ccx). Although of fair complexion and strong build, and evidently (as his letters reveal) fully cognisant of the affairs of their land, he could scarcely have passed for a Connecticut farmer. In bearing he was remembered as 'a man of polished manners, and particularly attentive to his external appearance'. Certainly his world was primarily the world of thought. Next to his Bible, the Greek and Latin classics were foremost, but his interests also included poetry and the study of nature. Given the absence of any school in the neighbourhood, it was inevitable that the parlour of the East Windsor parsonage came to fulfil that purpose. Timothy Edwards prepared several boys for College and at length established such a reputation as a teacher that when applicants for College admission came from East Windsor it used to be said by tutors 'that there was no need of examining Mr. Edwards' scholars'.

Jonathan's earliest memories would have included the many winter's nights when he sat beside some of his sisters at the great fire-place in the middle of their home – a fire-place which could burn logs up to six feet long and still leave room for seats on either side. When the fire became too hot for the occupants of these seats, the Edwards' black servant, Tim, would hurry to fetch green wood to dampen it. Then there were the long summer days, with much to watch on the farm and when, lying on his back in the meadows, Jonathan drank in the beauty of nature. The abundance of flying insects, including butterflies and moths, which he saw in late August and early September, particularly fascinated him: 'I remember that, when I was a boy, I have at the same time of year lien on the ground upon my back and beheld abundance of them, all flying south-east, which I then thought were going to a warm country'.[1]

Edwards' admiration of creation certainly began in his infancy at East Windsor. Of this local scenery, which so early impressed him, another New Englander has written:

From his father's door, and from all the region around, the eye had a grand and comprehensive sweep to the west. The sudden depression of the meadows gave the eye liberty in that direction to range at will up and down the river, and far off to the barrier of hills ten or twelve miles away. Every one who has watched the aspects of nature along this valley in winter and summer, in sunshine and in storm, will confess that, though it may seem tame compared with our mountain lands, there is much to charm and fascinate. On a clear, still afternoon of summer, when a passing shower has refreshed the earth, or in winter, when the world is covered with snow and the sun is going down behind these distant hills, a magic beauty rests over the landscape.[2]

The first major disturbance in Edwards' childhood home came when he was approaching eight years of age. In 1711 the conflict of interests between British and French in North America had a further half-century to run before it was resolved, and it was a comparatively minor event in that conflict when Connecticut troops were despatched upon an attempted invasion of part of French Canada in the summer of that year. But 'Queen Anne's War' was of great consequence to the East Windsor parsonage when Timothy Edwards was conscripted to serve as a chaplain. Once away from home he was pressed by the remembrance of many matters both small and great for which he could no longer be responsible, and in a correspondence with his wife which survives from this period we have a glimpse both of his own feelings and of the life at East Windsor which he had left behind. A letter of August 7, 1711, contains guidance for his wife on many practical matters: the old rope for the well required replacing by a new one; an injured

[1] J E (Yale) 6, p. 161.
[2] I. N. Tarbox, 'Jonathan Edwards', *Bibliotheca Sacra*, 1869, pp. 253–4.

horse needed special care; the cattle must be kept out of the orchard; and manure needed laying before winter. But the children were chiefly on his mind and his thoughts turned first to Jonathan:

I desire thee to take care that Jonathan don't lose what he hath learned but that as he hath got the Accidence, and above two sides of *propria quae moribus* by heart so that he keep what he hath got, I would therefore have him say [recite] pretty often to the girls. . . .

His son's progress in Latin was not, however, his only or his chief concern:

If any of the children should at any time go over the river to meeting I would have them be exceeding careful how they sit or stand in the boat lest they should fall into the river. . . . I hope thou wilt take special care of Jonathan that he don't learn to be rude and naughty, etc., of which thee and I have lately discoursed. I wouldn't have thee venture him to ride out into the woods with Tim.

The letter concludes:

The Lord Jesus Christ be with thy spirit, my Dear, and encourage thee to hope and trust in him, and discover his love to thy soul to whom I commit thee and all thine and mine, to whom remember my love, and also to Mercy Brooks and Tim Demming[1] and tell him that I shall much rejoice if I live to come home to know that he hath been a good boy, and tell my children that I would have them to pray daily for their Father, and for their own souls, and above all things to remember their Creator and seek after the Lord Jesus Christ now in the days of their youth. God be with and bless you all.

I am, my Dear, ever thine in the dearest love and affection,
Timo: Edwards

A fast 160-miles march in August, 1711, took the Connecticut troops in seven days to Albany from where Timothy wrote:

I have still strong hopes of seeing thee and our dear children again. I cannot but hope that I have had the gracious presence of God with me since I left home, encouraging and strengthening my soul, as well as preserving my life. I have been much cheered and refreshed respecting this great undertaking, in which I verily expect to proceed, and that I shall, before many weeks are at an end, see Canada; but I

[1]The household servants. Mercy Brooks died in 1734 (see I. N. Tarbox, 'Timothy Edwards and His Parishioners', *The Congregational Quarterly*, 1871, pp. 256–74.

trust in the Lord that he will have mercy on me, and thee, my dear, and all our dear children, and that God has more work for me to do in the place where I have dwelt for many years, and that you and I shall yet live together on earth, as well as dwell together for ever in heaven with the Lord Jesus Christ, and all his saints, with whom to be is best of all. . . . Remember my love to each of the children, to Esther, Elizabeth, Anne, Mary, Jonathan, Eunice, and Abigail. The Lord have mercy on and eternally save them all, with our dear little Jerusha! The Lord bind up their souls with thine and mine in the bundle of life (1.ccix).

So far Timothy Edwards had suffered no more than a cold and cough. But when the march resumed from Albany, fatigue and exposure brought on a severe illness, and after fifty miles he had to be left behind to be taken back to Albany by boat and wagon along with another invalid officer. By the evening of September 10, 1711, the night when his sick companion died, he was able tô sit up to write home. The same letter carried news of his discharge and of his hopes that neighbours would come soon from Windsor with horses and additional blankets to convey him home.

One sentence in Timothy Edwards' letters from the frontier is indicative of two of his concerns, 'I would have you very careful of my books,' he wrote to Esther, 'and account of rates'. The first of these items was a necessity for his work and the second a necessity for the maintenance of his large family. 'Rates' were the income paid to him as minister of the parish, paid generally not in money but in kind – in farm produce, or merchandise or in work done for him by shoe-makers, tailors or blacksmiths. These rates – or the insufficiency of them – were too frequently a source of problems between ministers and their people. Timothy Edwards augmented his income by the fees paid by various families for the education of their children. An account book which survives from a later period of his life records his receipt of rates and also the payments of various individuals. An entry beside the name of John Rockwell reads: 'To teaching his son one year and eight months – viz., his eldest son – in all, £10 17s 6d.' Or again: 'Reckoned with John Diggins by his father's order, and due to me for teaching him the tongues – viz., Latin and Greek – forty-seven weeks in all, £9 8s.'

Edwards' parents clearly did not find it easy to bring up their large family on a comparatively slender income. They eked it out, sometimes by renting their negro servant to work elsewhere by day. Esther Edwards also distilled cider brandy, or applejack, and Jonathan would no doubt have helped her to measure it out by the quart to the neighbours' children who came to buy. There were not many could afford to purchase it by the barrel. On the special occasions when Timothy Edwards went to Boston his girls were known to cut their long hair so that he could exchange it for fans and girdles. But despite this need for thrift there is no evidence that the head of the household was tight-fisted. On the contrary his Account Books contain such entries as the following: 'June 3 d Richard Skinner mowed my orchard, for which he asked 2s, but I thought it was too little and gave him 0.2.6d.'

Timothy Edwards had the largest influence upon his son's education. In most respects his educational methods were those common to his day – a day which saw no harm in children facing the memorizing of Latin at the age of seven. But there is reason to think that such regimentation in the East Windsor parsonage was balanced by encouragement to self-effort and to individual initiative. In particular, Edwards' father stressed the need for all work to be done with pen in hand and he regarded accuracy in writing as essential. In a letter to Esther during his chaplaincy in 1711 he advised her concerning Jonathan and his sisters, '[I] would have both him and them keep their writing, and therefore write much oftener than they did when I was at home'. The habit of writing was ingrained into Jonathan from his early years and was to remain with him all his days.

From his father, the son of East Windsor also learned high views of the Christian ministry. At the same time Jonathan saw that such work had its inevitable problems. When he was between the ages of seven and eleven there was considerable conflict in the parish over the location of a new meeting-house. The original building of 1694 had seen some improvements but it was now too small for the growing congregation. Long before it was determined where the new building would be placed the voters had decided that it should be 'forty feet square'. The clamour for a change in location was strong and one protagonist for a different site even considered his views worthy of publication in verse – an effort which included the stanza:

> It is almost four miles
>   Which some of us do go,
> Upon God's holy Sabbath-day
>   In times of frost and snow.

Not all the remarks which reached the East Windsor parsonage were as placid as those of the rustic poet. But, at length, in 1714, the new meeting-house was finished, and, after all, it was close beside the original building.

In the course of his ministry Timothy Edwards had a number of parish difficulties, and one of these was related to the inadequacy of his income. More disturbing, and not unrelated, was the element of complaint now being heard in the land against the authority of ministers. It was a sign of a growing unease over the government of the churches. The original settlement of all the New England churches was strictly Congregational, a full liberty and independency being possessed by each congregation, with decisive power vested in the church meeting. But the early congregations commonly possessed ministers of such personal authority and prestige that their role of leadership was rarely challenged by 'the power of the fraternity'. After all, their preachers were former clergy in the Church of England who had given up much to serve and suffer with their people. For a period pastoral authority was thus happily combined with that of the church meeting and a proof that the ministry desired no autocratic rule lay in the stipulated requirement of the Cambridge Synod's 'Platform' of 1648 that elders should share with pastors in the ruling of the church.

By the time, however, of Timothy Edwards' settlement at East Windsor a transition to a different era was already well advanced and ministers were being forced to emphasize their prerogative to lead. While some viewed this emphasis as a new clerical authoritarianism, the pastors themselves generally saw it as a necessity arising out of circumstances which had not been foreseen fifty years earlier.

Parishes were no longer the small and tightly-knit groups of Christians who had suffered together for their faith in the 1630's. At that date Connecticut had only four towns and some 800 people. By the end of the century Connecticut's towns had grown to thirty and the people to some 30,000. In the following thirty years, the years of Jonathan Edwards' youth, the further population growth was remarkably rapid. Few among these increasing numbers of people were without church connection, church and community being still virtually co-extensive, but the number of committed Christians had by no means kept pace with the rise in population. Standards of church membership had fallen but, in the words of one writer, 'The unregenerate were in nothing improved by becoming communicants, while the condition of the churches was, in many respects, much worse by it'.[1] Unspiritual church members had a different attitude to the authority of pastors and, consequently, the idea of 'popular control versus rule by an élite' was already beginning to find some support in the churches. Instead of the shared spiritual vision of pastor and people, there was now a tendency for both parties to view the scene differently. Ministerial leaders believed that they faced a serious decline in spiritual conditions and it was this decline which led to an increasing doubt among them over the competency of local congregations to govern their own affairs.

This doubt was strengthened by another factor, namely, the gradual disappearance of ruling elders. A New England writer in 1715 speaks of the ruling elder as being as rare as 'a black swan in the meadow'. The ministers themselves do not appear to have been chiefly responsible for this change. On the contrary, they gave warning in the 'Reforming Synod' of 1679 that, 'Unless a church have divers elders, the church-government must needs become either prelatic or popular'.[2] Between these two alternatives the pastors were now being caught. They desired neither a 'popular democracy', nor to be themselves independent 'prelates', and consequently – despite the danger of being charged with 'Presbyterianism' – they began to turn to the need for regular 'associations' where ministers could exercise some oversight both over one another and the churches as a whole.

[1]'New England Theology Historically Considered', *The British and Foreign Evangelical Review*, 1860, p. 863.

[2]Quoted in *The Congregationalism of the last Three Hundred Years*, H. M. Dexter, 1879, p. 482. Dexter remains one of the safest guides to the intricacies of New England church government.

We can be sure that this subject was often aired in the East Windsor parsonage in the days of Edwards' youth and not least on those important occasions when his grandfather, Solomon Stoddard, came the fifty miles down-river from Northampton. As early as 1700, and probably earlier, Stoddard was convinced that the unity and health of the churches required such measures of ministerial co-operation as were traditionally more characteristic of Presbyterianism. Speaking of the absolute independency of every particular congregation, he wrote in 1700: 'This is too Lordly a principle, it is too ambitious a thing for every small congregation to arrogate such an uncontroulable power, and to be accountable to none on earth; this is neither a probable way for the peace of churches, nor for the safety of church members. . . . '

At Boston, proposals put forward for formal associations of ministers, meeting regularly, failed to pass the legislature in 1705. Stoddard's influence lay more in western Massachusetts and in the Connecticut Valley. In his own county of Hampshire he did succeed in establishing an Association in 1714, in spite of its being rejected by nearly half of the county's churches. Prior to that, in 1708, Connecticut ministers and messengers meeting at Saybrook formally adopted a plan for twice-yearly associations of 'teaching elders' 'to consult the duties of their office and the common interest of the churches'. The Saybrook decision had the support of Timothy Edwards but when he put it to his congregation it was rejected. This same reaction among the people of other parishes was sufficiently common for the Saybrook Platform never to be implemented effectively. In at least one congregation the pastor was forced to resign for his part in drawing it up. In another, where the minister had just cause to decline to administer the Lord's Supper, he was also required to leave.[1] Clearly there were places where feelings ran high over alleged ministerial 'authoritarianism'. Even in the comparative quiet of East Windsor there may have been some of the class who showed little deference to the pastoral office, neglecting, as Timothy Edwards once told his hearers, to 'remove their hats when they meet their betters upon the street'.

[1]These and other strained relationships between pastors and people are dealt with by Paul R. Lucas in *Valley of Discord: Church and Society Along The Connecticut River, 1636–1725*, 1976.

By the time that his grandson, Jonathan, was a teen-ager, Stoddard was ready to challenge what had once been foundational to Congregational church polity. In his work, *An Examination of the Power of the Fraternity*, he asserts that the rule by church meetings had been decided by the fathers 'before they had much time to weigh those things'. 'The mistakes of one generation,' he believed, 'many times become the calamity of succeeding generations.' The brethren were not fit judges of all things in the church any more than they would be of all things in society, 'If the multitude were to be judges in civil causes things would quickly be turned upside down'.

As Stoddard and his son-in-law discussed these things there was one conclusion upon which they were always unanimous: no changes in church government as such would meet the need of the age. In the words of their Boston colleague and contemporary, Increase Mather, 'The Congregational Church discipline is not suited for a worldly interest or for a formal generation of professors. It will stand or fall as *godliness in the power of it* does prevail or otherwise.' It was in the area of the 'power' of godliness that Stoddard and Timothy Edwards saw their own chief responsibility. 'Ministers,' urged Stoddard, 'had need have the Spirit of the Lord upon them in order to the reviving of religion among the people.'

The fundamental problems of New England's churches in the early eighteenth century were thus deeper than questions of church government, and too often ministers themselves were a part of the problem. In the words of Richard Webster: 'A vast change was visible in the churches of New England: the discipline was relaxed, the doctrine was diluted, and the preaching tame and spiritless. A written form of words superseded the notes which had served for "a brief" in the pulpit; the confinement of the eye and the finger to the line, and the absorption of the minister in the reading of the scroll, left the young unawed and the aged slumbering, while the others glided in reverie to the farm or the traffic, the fireside or the forest.'[1]

Yet this condition was certainly not universal. Jonathan

[1]Webster, p. 133. For contemporary testimony on the decline see John Gillies, *Historical Collections Relating to Remarkable Periods of the Success of the Gospel*, 1845 (and 1981 reprint), pp. 279–81.

Edwards' chief memories of his early years were not of parish conflicts nor of dull services. At East Windsor – in the church and in his home – he saw not a little of a genuine 'reviving of religion'. There were times when God's presence was especially evident in the community – when issues other than those of eternity faded in significance and when an unusual seriousness and spiritual concern pervaded the whole parish. Numbers, hitherto nominally Christian, passed from death unto life, while Christians rejoiced in attaining to a full assurance of faith. In later life, writing of great ingatherings of souls to Christ, Edwards says: 'My honoured father's parish has in times past been a place favoured with mercies of this nature, above any on this western side of New England, excepting Northampton; there having been four or five seasons of the pouring out of the Spirit to the general awakening of the people there since my father's settlement amongst them' (1.349).

Jonathan saw at least two such periods of revival in his childhood. Speaking of his personal experience, he writes:

I had a variety of concerns and exercises about my soul from my childhood; but I had two more remarkable seasons of awakening before I met with that change by which I was brought to those new dispositions, and that new sense of things, that I have since had. The first time was when I was a boy, some years before I went to College, at a time of remarkable awakening in my father's congregation. I was then very much affected for many months, and concerned about the things of religion, and my soul's salvation . . . I experienced I know not what kind of delight in religion. My mind was much engaged in it, and had much self-righteous pleasure, and it was my delight to abound in religious duties. I, with some of my school-mates, joined together and built a booth in a swamp, in a very retired spot, for a place of prayer. And besides, I had particular secret places of my own in the woods where I used to retire by myself, and was from time to time much affected . . . I am ready to think many are deceived with such affections, and such kind of delight as I then had in religion, and mistake it for grace (1.xii).

The next season of revival occurred in East Windsor in the years 1715–16 as Timothy Edwards continued his normal course of preaching. It was at this time that Esther Edwards and two of her daughters made profession of their faith in Christ. In his 'Personal Narrative', the document from which we have quoted above, Edwards makes no comment on his own experience in these years but this revival does figure in the first piece of writing which has survived from his pen. His sister Mary – to whom he was nearest in age – had recently left home to stay with her mother's relatives at Hadley, close to Northampton. She was then fourteen and Jonathan twelve:

To Miss Mary Edwards, at Hadley.
Windsor. May 10, 1716.
Dear Sister

Through the wonderful mercy and goodness of God there hath in this place been a very remarkable stirring and pouring out of the Spirit of God, and likewise now is, but I think I have reason to think it is in some measure diminished but I hope not much. About thirteen have been joined to the Church in an estate of full communion. These are those which by enquiry I find you have not heard of that have joined to the Church, viz, John Huntington, Sarah Loomas the daughter of Thomas Loomas, and Esther Elsworth. And there are five that are propounded which are not added to the Church, namely, John Loomas, John Rockwell's wife, Sergt. Thomas Elsworth's wife, Isaac Bissel's wife, and Mary Osband. I think there comes commonly a Mondays above thirty persons to speak with Father about the condition of their souls.

It is a time of general health here in this place. There has five persons died in this place since you have been gone, viz. old Goodwife Rockwell, old Goodwife Grant, and Benjamin Bancroft who was drowned in a boat many rods from shore wherein were four young women and many others of the other sex, which were very remarkably saved. And the two others which died I suppose you have heard of. Margaret Peck of the New Town, who was once Margaret Stiles, hath lost a sucking babe who died very suddenly and was buried in this place.

Abigail, Hannah and Lucy have had the chicken pox and are recovered but Jerusha has it now but is almost well. I myself sometimes am much troubled with the toothache but these two or three last days I have not been troubled with it but very little. So far as I know the whole family is well except Jerusha.

Sister, I am glad to hear of your welfare. So often as I do I should be glad to hear from you by a letter and therein how it is with you as to your crookedness.

Your loving brother Jonathan E.

Father and Mother remember their love to you. Likewise do all my sisters and Mercy and Tim.

[20]

Among the many visitors, relatives and others, who were in the East Windsor parsonage in the days of Jonathan's youth there is record of one of the most interesting coming at this time. Stephen Williams, who commenced serving the church at Longmeadow in 1714, came on at least one occasion to hear Timothy Edwards at the time of the awakening of 1715–16. At eleven years of age Williams had suffered twenty-one months' captivity at the hands of Indians in Canada and, it is said, 'never seemed to be weary of recalling and relating those youthful adventures'. He would have found in Jonathan a receptive listener and at a later date we shall note both men united by a common concern for the Indians. Stephen Williams' diary, however, reveals that at this date other concerns were uppermost in his mind. He heard, he notes, Timothy Edwards on 'an awakening subject . . . there was an extraordinary stir among the people at East Windsor – many that were crying what shall we do to be saved.' And, thinking of his own parish (which he was to serve for sixty-six years) he added, 'Lord grant that there may be such as these among us'.

As the summer of 1716 drew to its close Jonathan was preparing to leave home for college. His eldest sister, Esther, was twenty-one, and the same year the youngest and last in the household, Martha, was born. Thus far the influence of home had surrounded him. When he rode downriver in September 1716, one month short of his thirteenth birthday, the childhood chapter was coming to its conclusion.

'THAT NEW SENSE OF THINGS'

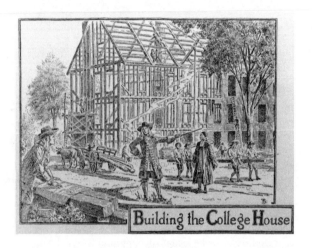

Building the College House

If there had anywhere appeared in space
    Another place of refuge, where to flee,
Our hearts had taken refuge in that place,
    And not with Thee.

For we against creation's bars had beat
Like prisoned eagles, through great worlds had sought
Though but a foot of ground to plant our feet,
    Where Thou wert not.

And only when we found in earth and air,
In heaven or hell, that such might nowhere be –
That we could not flee from Thee anywhere,
    We fled to Thee.

RICHARD C. TRENCH
Poems, 1885, vol. 2, p. 217

Conversion is the greatest change that men undergo in this world.

SOLOMON STODDARD

They who are truly converted are new men, new, creatures; new, not only within, but without; they are sanctified throughout, in spirit, soul and body; old things are passed away, all things are become new; they have new hearts, new eyes, new ears, new tongues, new hands, new feet; *i.e.*, a new conversation and practice; they walk in newness of life, and continue to do so to the end of life.

J E (1.316)

2

he Collegiate School of Connecticut, which Edwards joined in the autumn of 1716, had been a frequent subject of discussion in his home at East Windsor. Of that we may be sure, for since its origin in the second year of the eighteenth century the new college was a common matter for debate in the parsonages of New England. Prior to 1701, Harvard College, which the founding fathers had established at Cambridge, Massachusetts, was the only training ground for the students of the Colony. There, according to the vision of the founders, 'Everyone shall consider the main end of his life and studies to < know God in Jesus Christ.' But by the time Timothy Edwards had passed through Harvard the vision was growing dim for the generality of students. There was reason to fear that the distinctive witness of half a century would give way before the growing secularization of New England's intellectual life. Those who entertained this concern looked with confidence to Increase Mather, the head of the College, to uphold Puritan orthodoxy but in 1701 Mather, who maintained his congregation of fifteen hundred in Boston along with his headship at Harvard, was virtually compelled to resign his post. Thereafter it was to Connecticut's infant college that the old-school Puritan tradition looked with expectation. The founders of the new institution were not unmindful of their trust. According to the charter which they drew up in 1701 the rector of the college must take prayers twice daily, teach 'practical theology' on the

Sabbath, stand by the doctrine of the Westminster Confession, 'and in all other ways according to his best discretion, shall at all times studiously endeavour in the education of the students, *to promote the power and purity of religion, and the best edification of these New-England Churches.*' Timothy Edwards probably had few hesitations in transferring the family allegiance from Harvard to Connecticut's training school.

By the time Jonathan was ready to begin his college course the institution was vexed with problems peculiar to Connecticut. Not only did the college bear no name, it had no fixed location and was, in the words of one writer, 'wandering about the country like the tabernacle in the wilderness.' The explanation of this state of affairs lay in the part-time nature of the work of the Rector. As well as undertaking the instruction of students he had also to serve a congregation, and consequently, the students were first located in or around his home. When numbers grew, and the staff was enlarged to include tutors who also gave regular instruction, this meant that different classes began living in different places according to the location of the tutors. Besides militating against the best interests of the college this procedure raised the hopes of several successive parishes that they had the best claim to be chosen for the permanent site. Accordingly, Saybrook, New Haven, Wethersfield and Hartford all came to contend vigorously for the honour.

It was a controversy which proved exceedingly hard to settle. At the Commencement of the college term, on September 12, 1716, when Jonathan Edwards' name was entered among the freshmen at New Haven, the trustees met at Saybrook to determine the site of the institution. Once more no conclusion could be reached and Edwards, with nine other freshmen from Connecticut River towns, joined a group already established at Wethersfield. In what manner the division of the student body was made is not clear; it does not seem to have been dependent upon whether a student was in his first, second, third or fourth year. Parents as well as trustees were involved in this struggle over the permanent seat of the college and probably they told their sons to which teacher they should attach themselves. When, on October 17, 1716, the trustees at last settled on New Haven, the students who were at Wethersfield ignored the order to remove to that location. They could scarcely have done so if their parents had not been backing their tutor, the Rev. Elisha Williams.

Timothy Edwards obviously had reasons for being among the supporters of Elisha Williams. For one thing, there were family connections. Williams' father had married Christian Stoddard, a sister of Timothy's wife. This was his second marriage, Elisha being the son of a deceased wife and therefore only a half-cousin to Jonathan. More important, however, was the fact that although Elisha was only five years out of Harvard, and only nine years Jonathan's senior, he was already, it seems, the most competent and popular of the instructors who served the Collegiate School. So it was that when all the excitement and controversy surrounding the college Commencement in 1716 was over, Jonathan was to be found for the next two years with the Wethersfield group – only ten miles south of East Windsor – and probably boarding with cousin Elisha or with his uncle Stephen Mix, the minister of Wethersfield.

Although, geographically speaking, Edwards' horizons were little changed, he had entered upon a much larger world of thought. Elisha Williams followed the same curriculum which he had been through himself at Harvard and which was adopted by Connecticut's Collegiate School. This explains why Edwards had with him at Wethersfield the two volumes of hand-copied textbooks in logic and natural philosophy which his father had used at Harvard. Broadly speaking, this four-year course of training emphasized languages in the first year (Latin, Greek and Hebrew), logic in the second, natural science (including 'a system of geography') in the third, and arithmetic, geometry and some astronomy in the final senior year, when the whole course was also reviewed. At Harvard, Williams had the reputation for being particularly strong in classical learning, logic and geography. He was an able teacher, and supported by two other tutors, Samuel Smith and Samuel Hall, the Wethersfield students were better off than the under-staffed rival group at New Haven. According to Timothy Edwards' Account book, which survives from this period, most of the teaching received by Jonathan was given by Smith and Hall who were also young men and recently graduated from the Collegiate School.

In the absence of any resident rector, it was another young man, Samuel Johnson, a Collegiate School graduate of 1714, who was in charge of the student contingent at New Haven. Johnson's personality and views appear to have had a part in lengthening the dispute and in causing the minority of two trustees, 'men of considerable influence', to maintain their support for the Wethersfield branch. In his student days Johnson was an orthodox son of New England but he was to look back, in later years, upon his studies as 'nothing but the scholastic cobwebs of a few little English and Dutch systems'. He records of the year of his graduation that he and his fellow students heard rumours 'of a new philosophy that of late was all in vogue and of such names as Descartes, Boyle, Locke, and Newton, but they were cautioned against thinking of them because the new philosophy, it was said, would bring in a new divinity and corrupt the pure religion of the country'. This warning Johnson quickly came to regard as unwarranted: 'By next Thanksgiving, November 16, 1715, I was wholly changed to the New Learning'. The change in his ideas was with respect to philosophy and science, and in these departments he set out to modernize the college curriculum, but it was not without reason that some already feared that his divinity was also in a process of change.

The differences between the two branches of the Collegiate School reached a crisis in 1718. The Commencement, September 12, was, as usual, the high-day of the academic year, being the occasion when degrees were conferred upon the students who had successfully completed their course. But this year was to be historic as the College House facing the green was to be opened, and in 'solemn pomp' public testimony was to be paid by the trustees to their chief benefactor, Elihu Yale, by whose name the college would henceforth be known. Yet when the day came more than a third of the college was absent, for what was virtually a rival Commencement was simultaneously being held at Wethersfield 'in the presence of a large number of spectators'. Edwards, together with his parents, was to be found that day at Wethersfield, unperturbed at missing the celebrations in New Haven.

The General Assembly of Connecticut (the high court of the civil legislature) who were now involved in the dispute, took conciliatory measures when they met in October 1718 and, perhaps as a consequence of this, Edwards and others from Wethersfield joined the third-year classes in New Haven that same October. One month, however, under Samuel Johnson's tutorship proved enough! At the end of that time Elisha Williams' former students returned *en masse* to Wethersfield.

Mere fragments of information survive from this period of Edwards' life. A note from Timothy Edwards to one of his daughters on January 27th, 1718, reports: 'I have not heard but that your brother Jonathan is also well. He has a very good name at Wethersfield, both as to his carriage and his learning.' From March 26th, 1719, a letter survives from Jonathan himself to his sister Mary who was then at Northampton:

Dear Sister,

Of all the many sisters I have, I think I never had one so long out of my hearing as yourself; inasmuch as I cannot remember that I ever heard one tittle from you from the time you last went up the country until the last week, by Mr. B. who then came from Northampton. When he came in I truly rejoiced to see him, because I fully expected to receive a letter from you by him. But being disappointed, and that not a little, I was willing to make that, which I hoped would be an opportunity of receiving, the same of sending. For I thought it was a pity that there should not be the least correspondence between us, or communication from one to another, when at no farther distance. I hope also that this may be a means of exciting the same in yourself; and so, having more charity for you than to believe that I am quite out of your mind, or that you are not at all concerned for me, I think it fit that I should give you some account of my condition relative to the school. I suppose you are fully acquainted with our coming away from New Haven and the circumstances of it. Since then we have been in a more prosperous condition, as I think, than ever. But the council and trustees, having lately had a meeting at New Haven concerning it, have removed that which was the cause of our coming away, *viz.* Mr. Johnson, from the place of a tutor, and have put in Mr. Cutler, pastor of Canterbury, president; who, as we hear, intends very speedily to be resident at Yale college, so that all the scholars belonging to our school expect to return there as soon as our vacancy after the election is over.

I am your loving brother in good health,

Jonathan Edwards

The expectation of this letter was fulfilled and all the

Wethersfield students removed finally to New Haven early in the summer of 1719, under the charge of the thirty-five-year-old Timothy Cutler. Cutler's position was far from easy and receiving good wishes from Timothy Edwards he was quick to show appreciation. Writing to the pastor of East Windsor on June 30, 1719, he says:

Your letter came to my hands by your son. I congratulate you upon his promising abilities and advances in knowledge . . . I can assure you, Rev. Sir, that your good affection to me in this affair, and that of the ministers around you, is no small inducement to me: and if I am prevailed on thereby, it shall be a strong motive to me to improve my poor abilities in the service of such hopeful youths as are with us . . . I am no party man, but shall carry it, with an equal hand and affection, to the whole college; and I doubt not, but the difficulty and importance of the business will secure me your prayers.

There is no comment from Jonathan on how he enjoyed living in the New Haven College House, which had cost a thousand pounds to build, but he clearly thought there were advantages for learning in the new situation. In the course of a letter written to his father on July 21, 1719, he says:

I received, with two books, a letter from yourself bearing the date of July 7th; and therein I received, with the greatest gratitude, your wholesome advice and counsel; and I hope I shall, God helping of me, use my utmost endeavours to put the same in practice. I am sensible of the preciousness of my time, and am resolved it shall not be through any neglect of mine, if it slips without the greatest advantage. I take very great content under my present tuition, as all the rest of the scholars seem to do under theirs. Mr. Cutler is extraordinarily courteous to us, has a very good spirit of government, keeps the school in excellent order, seems to increase in learning, is loved and respected by all who are under him; and when he is spoken of in the school or town he generally has the title of President. The scholars all live in very good peace with the people of the town, and there is not a word said about our former carryings on, except now and then by aunt Mather. . . .

I have inquired of Mr. Cutler what books we shall have need of the next year. He answered, he would have me to get against that time, Alstead's Geometry and Gassendus's Astronomy; with which I would entreat you to get a pair of dividers, or mathematician's compasses, and a scale, which are absolutely necessary in order to learning mathematics; and also the Art of Thinking, which, I am persuaded,

would be no less profitable than the other necessary, to me who am,
        Your most dutiful son,
                        Jonathan Edwards
P.S. What we give a week for our board is £0 5s. od.

It is difficult for us at this point in time to grasp the extent to
which the religious element was pervasive in Edwards' early
life. This was true not only of his own home, and those of his
grandparents (at Hartford and Northampton), but of the whole
social and intellectual life of that era. At the Collegiate School,
as at Harvard, instruction in Christian doctrine was a constant
addition to the weekly curriculum. Key authors were John
Wollebius and William Ames, and the Westminster Assembly's
Shorter Catechism was recited every Saturday night. 'Orders
and Appointments' for the students, which each had to copy
out in full upon entering the College, included the following:

Every student shall exercise himself in reading Holy Scriptures by
himself every day that the word of Christ may dwell in him richly. . . .
All students shall avoid the profanation of God's holy name,
attributes, Word and ordinances and the Holy Sabbath, and shall
carefully attend all public assemblies for divine worship. . . . All
undergraduates shall publicly repeat sermons in the hall in their
course, and also bachelors, and be constantly examined on Sabbaths
at evening prayer. . . .[1]

That the extent of the religious duties required of young men
sometimes led to a mere formal Christianity cannot be doubted
and, as further letters of Edwards will show, there were not
lacking students for whom 'a godly sober life' meant nothing.
Edwards himself makes no comment on the religious instruction which he received at the Collegiate School. It seems that it
was the personal religion of his family circle which made the
deepest impression upon him as a youth. He must have listened
to many spiritual conversations, as well as prayers, in the home
of his childhood, for parsonages were always frequented by
visitors from near and far. In the company of his grandfather,
Richard Edwards, in nearby Hartford, he heard such things as:
'Make the glory of God your main end'; 'Depend on him by a

[1] *Biographical Sketches of the Graduates of Yale College*, Oct. 1701–May 1745, F.
B. Dexter, 1885, p. 347. It was a Puritan custom for young people to 'repeat'
sermons as evidence that they had listened with care.

lively faith in his promises'; and his frequent testimony, 'I carry my life in my hand every day, I am daily looking and waiting until my change come'. Jonathan was in his second year at the Collegiate School when Richard Edwards died in the confidence that he had 'laid hold on the rock of ages'. 'I trust in the Lord Jesus Christ,' he whispered at the last, 'and I desire to do so more and more'. The date was April 20, 1718, and it was the first death which Jonathan had known among his nearer relatives.[1]

At this time it is clear that the grandson had no inner experience which was akin to his grandfather's. The 'convictions and affections' which he had known at the time of revival 'some years' before he went to College had 'worn off' and with their absence he 'left off secret prayer'. If there was such a thing as personal knowledge of God in Christ he knew that he did not possess it:

I was at times very uneasy, especially towards the latter part of my time at College, when it pleased God to seize me with a pleurisy in which he brought me nigh to the grave and shook me over the pit of hell. And yet it was not long after my recovery before I fell again into my old ways of sin. But God would not suffer me to go on with any quietness; I had great and violent inward struggles . . . (1.xii).

By 'repeated resolutions' and vows, he goes on to say, he sought to 'wholly break off' from his former ways and from 'all ways of known outward sin and seriously to practise many religious duties'. These resolutions, however, proved ineffective and his 'inward struggle and conflicts' continued. Edwards does not speak of the specific temptations with which he was now struggling but we may find a hint as to their nature in a sheet of paper which has survived among his early manuscripts. It is a memorandum, without any heading, relating to his ambition to be an author. On this sheet he wrote a number of rules for himself including the following:

[What is] prefatorial, not to write in a distinct preface or introduction, but in the body of the treatise. Then I shall be sure to have it read by everyone.

---

[1]Richard Edwards left an estate of £1107 but, presumably due to the number of his dependents, Timothy Edwards only received £60.

'That New Sense of Things'

The world will expect more modesty because of my circumstances – America, young etc. Let there then be a superabundance of modesty, and though perhaps 'twill otherwise be needless, it will wonderfully make way for its reception in the world. . . .

Before I venture to publish in London, to make some experiment in my own country; to play small games first. . . .[1]

These words, written some time in the early years of the 1720's, indicate marked consciousness of his own abilities and a desire for their recognition in the world. There were good reasons for him to entertain such an opinion of himself. When only sixteen, in his senior year in 1719, he had been appointed college butler, apparently an unusual honour for an undergraduate. In the various weekly 'recitations' in the College Hall his powers were obvious and as the highest ranking student among those receiving the Bachelor of Arts degree he was called upon to give the Farewell oration at the College Commencement in September, 1720. Thereafter he had continued at New Haven for the further years of study required before he could receive the higher distinction of Master of Arts.

When Edwards later spoke of pride as *the* sin of the human heart he was speaking from experience as well as from Scripture. It was the 'gratification of vanity', or what the Scriptures call 'the desires of the mind' (Ephesians 2.3), rather than any temptations to unworthy conduct which were almost certainly involved in the prolonged spiritual struggle of which he speaks above. In his final year as an undergraduate at New Haven, and in his first year as a graduate, the awareness grew upon him that he needed a change *within* and such a deliverance from himself as could in no way be achieved by his own 'resolutions'. Speaking of this period he writes:

I was indeed brought to seek salvation in a manner that I never was before; I felt a spirit to part with all things in the world for an interest in Christ. My concern continued, and prevailed, with many exercising thoughts and inward struggles. . . .

The last surviving letter of Edwards written before he came to 'that new sense of things' was to his father, from Yale, on March

[1] *JE* (Yale) 6, 193–4. Words in italics were originally written in shorthand. For discussion of the dating of this MS see also p. 177 of the same volume.

[33]

1, 1721. He can no longer write of the College in the glowing terms which he employed two years earlier. The news of the student body is wholly bad. He has to report an 'insurrection' among the scholars over the food provided in the College Commons and the consequent displeasure of President Cutler; he regrets to tell his father that a former East Windsor pupil had been involved in the uproar and then made 'sorry that he did not take my advice in the matter'. Worse news was to follow:

Although these disturbances were so speedily quashed, yet they are succeeded by much worse and greater, and I believe greater than ever were in the College before. They are occasioned by the discovery of some monstrous impieties and acts of immorality lately committed in the College, particularly, stealing of hens, geese, turk pigs, meat, wood &c – unseasonable nightwalking, breaking people's windows, playing at cards, cursing, swearing and damning, and using all manner of ill language, which never were at such a pitch in the College as they now are. The Rector has called a meeting of the Trustees on this occasion, they are expected here today. It is thought the upshot will be the expulsion of some and the public admonition of others. Through the goodness of God I am perfectly free of all their janglings. My condition at the College at present is every way comfortable: I live in very good amity and agreement with my chambermate,[1] there has no new quarrels broke out betwixt me and any of the scholars, though they still persist in their former combination, but I am not without hopes that it will be abolished by this meeting of the Trustees. . . . I am at present in perfect health, and it is a time of health throughout the College and town. I am about taking the remainder of my *lignum vitae*.[2] I am much reformed with respect of visiting of friends, and intend to do more at it for the future than in time past. I think I shall not have occasion for the coat you mentioned in your letter till I come home. I received a letter from my sister Mary the week before last and have heard of her welfare this week by a man that came directly from thence. I pray you in your next letter to send me your advice whether or no I had best come home in May, or tarry till June. Please to give my humble duty to my Mother, hearty love to sisters, and Mercy, and still to be mindful before the throne of grace for me, who am, Honoured Sir, your most dutiful son, Jonathan E.

[1]His cousin, Elisha Mix of Wethersfield.
[2]The wood of a tropical American tree, once believed to have medicinal properties.

Although there is nothing of his present personal experience in this letter, Edwards is revealing something about himself. There is not simply the abiding problem of his retiring temperament which did not make it easy for him to reform 'with respect to visiting', but surely something positive is missing. He stands too far aloof in his moral judgments; he would 'advise' his wayward contemporaries but he could not walk among them as an exemplar of Christian happiness. As his parents read that letter in the East Windsor parsonage they would sense that the one thing needful was still absent.

Edwards' own words enable us to date his conversion with some accuracy. His 'sense of divine things', he tells us, began 'about a year and a half' before August, 1722 (1.xiii-iv). As we have already seen, there is no suggestion of such an experience in his letter of March 1st, 1721, so there is reason to conclude that 'that change by which I was brought to those new dispositions, and that new sense of things' occurred soon after that date, and that when he returned home, in the May or the June of 1721, he was a Christian in the full joy of his first love to Christ. Edwards' account of what took place in 1721, as given in his 'Personal Narrative', is the most important statement he ever wrote about himself:

The first instance that I remember of that sort of inward, sweet delight in God and divine things that I have lived much in since, was on reading those words [1 Tim. 1.17] 'Now unto the King eternal, immortal, invisible, the only wise God, be honour and glory for ever and ever, Amen.' As I read the words, there came into my soul, and was as it were diffused through it, a sense of the glory of the Divine Being; a new sense, quite different from any thing I ever experienced before. Never any words of scripture seemed to me as these words did. I thought with myself, how excellent a Being that was, and how happy I should be, if I might enjoy that God, and be rapt up in him in heaven, and be as it were swallowed up in him for ever! I kept saying, and as it were singing over these words of scripture to myself; and went to pray to God that I might enjoy him, and prayed in a manner quite different from what I used to do; with a new sort of affection. But it never came into my thought, that there was any thing spiritual, or of a saving nature in this.

From about that time, I began to have a new kind of apprehensions and ideas of Christ, and the work of redemption, and the glorious way of salvation by him. An inward, sweet sense of these things, at times, came into my heart; and my soul was led away in pleasant views and contemplations of them. And my mind was greatly engaged to spend my time in reading and meditating on Christ, on the beauty and excellency of his person, and the lovely way of salvation by free grace in him. I found no books so delightful to me, as those that treated of these subjects. Those words *Cant* 2.1, used to be abundantly with me, 'I am the Rose of Sharon, and the Lily of the valleys'. The words seemed to me, sweetly to represent the loveliness and beauty of Jesus Christ. The whole book of Canticles used to be pleasant to me, and I used to be much in reading it, about that time; and found, from time to time, an inward sweetness that would carry me away, in my contemplations. . . . The sense I had of divine things, would often of a sudden kindle up, as it were, a sweet burning in my heart; an ardor of soul, that I know not how to express.

Of his joyful homecoming that summer he speaks as follows:

Not long after I first began to experience these things, I gave an account to my father of some things that had passed in my mind. I was pretty much affected by the discourse we had together; and when the discourse was ended, I walked abroad alone, in a solitary place in my father's pasture, for contemplation. And as I was walking there, and looking up on the sky and clouds, there came into my mind so sweet a sense of the glorious *majesty* and *grace* of God, that I know not how to express – I seemed to see them both in a sweet conjunction; majesty and meekness joined together: it was a sweet, and gentle, and holy majesty; and also a majestic meekness; an awful sweetness; a high, and great, and holy gentleness.

We conclude this chapter with the remainder of Edwards' words about the beginning of his new life as a Christian:

After this my sense of divine things gradually increased, and became more and more lively, and had more of that inward sweetness. The appearance of every thing was altered; there seemed to be, as it were, a calm, sweet cast, or appearance of divine glory, in almost every thing. God's excellency, his wisdom, his purity and love, seemed to appear in every thing; in the sun, moon, and stars; in the clouds, and blue sky; in the grass, flowers, trees; in the water, and all nature; which used greatly to fix my mind. I often used to sit and view the moon for continuance; and in the day, spent much time in viewing the clouds and sky, to behold the sweet glory of God in these things; in the mean time, singing forth, with a low voice my contemplations of the Creator and Redeemer. And scarce any thing, among all the works of nature, was so sweet to me as thunder and lightning; formerly, nothing had been so terrible to me. Before, I used to be uncommonly terrified with thunder, and to be struck with terror when I saw a thunder storm rising; but now, on the contrary, it rejoiced me. I felt God, so to speak, at the first appearance of a thunder storm; and used to take the opportunity, at such times, to fix myself in order to view the clouds, and see the lightnings play, and hear the majestic and awful voice of God's thunder, which oftentimes was exceedingly entertaining, leading me to sweet contemplations of my great and glorious God. While thus engaged, it always seemed natural to me to sing, or chant for my meditations; or, to speak my thoughts in soliloquies with a singing voice.

I felt then great satisfaction, as to my good state; but that did not content me. I had vehement longings of soul after God and Christ, and after more holiness, wherewith my heart seemed to be full, and ready to break; which often brought to my mind the words of the Psalmist [*Psa.* 119.20] 'My soul breaketh for the longing it hath'. I often felt a mourning and lamenting in my heart, that I had not turned to God sooner, that I might have had more time to grow in grace. My mind was greatly fixed on divine things; almost perpetually – in the contemplation of them. I spent most of my time in thinking of divine things, year after year; often walking alone in the woods, and solitary places, for meditation, soliloquy, and prayer, and converse with God; and it was always my manner, at such times, to sing forth my contemplations. I was almost constantly in ejaculatory prayer, wherever I was. Prayer seemed to be natural to me, as the breath by which the inward burnings of my heart had vent. The delights which I now felt in those things of religion, were of an exceeding different kind from those before mentioned, that I had when a boy; and what I then had no more notion of than one born blind has of pleasant and beautiful colours. They were of a more inward, pure, soul-animating and refreshing nature. Those former delights never reached the heart; and did not arise from any sight of the divine excellency of the things of God; or any taste of the soul-satisfying and life-giving good there is in them (1.xiii).

NEW YORK : THE PURSUIT OF HOLINESS

A Yale Undergraduate of 1720

Thy testimonies have I taken as an heritage for ever: for they are the rejoicing of my heart.

Psalm 119.111

Resolved, To study the Scriptures so steadily, constantly, and frequently, as that I may find and plainly perceive myself to grow in the knowledge of the same.

J E (1.xxi), 1722

I do not spend time enough endeavouring to affect myself with the glories of Christianity.

J E (1.xxvi), Diary entry for January 21, 1723

3

here is much to bear out the great change of interests which occurred in Edwards at the time of his conversion. For one thing, instead of waiting until the normal three years of graduate study for his Master's degree had been completed (a period which would have taken him to the summer of 1723), he was licensed for the work of the ministry in 1722 and terminated his residence at Yale. This was in his nineteenth year. There was evidently a general belief that he should not be detained further from preaching. Accordingly, when a request came to New England from Presbyterians in New York for a supply preacher for a new congregation, it was Edwards' name which was recommended. A subsequent invitation was accepted by him and thus he began a regular preaching ministry in New York at the beginning of August, 1722. All his personal papers from this period indicate that a new master-interest possessed him: it was to enjoy the Word of God. 'I had then,' he later wrote, 'and at other times, the greatest delight in the holy Scriptures, of any book whatsoever. Oftentimes in reading it every word seemed to touch my heart. I felt a harmony between something in my heart, and those sweet and powerful words. I seemed often to see so much light exhibited by every sentence, and such a refreshing food communicated, that I could not get along in reading; often dwelling long on one sentence to see the wonders contained in it, and yet almost every sentence seemed to be full of wonders' (1.xiv).

This new priority is equally evident in his various manuscripts which survive from the same period, written in a very small, round hand similar to his father's. The earliest of these manuscripts represent some of his College work. The title, 'Of Insects', probably dates from his senior years as a student, 1719–20. It is followed by pieces headed, 'Of the Rainbow', 'Of Light Rays', and by the beginnings of a much larger collection of papers on scientific subjects (known to Edwards as 'Natural Philosophy'). These appear to have been written or commenced in 1720–21, that is to say, in his first graduate year. The first entry in the folder of material on Natural Philosophy, which covers a wide variety of subjects, was headed 'Of Atoms'. Another set of papers, with a heading, 'Things To Be Considered and Written Fully About', was also begun at approximately the same date, and is wholly concerned with such matters of science as the refraction of light, optics, blood circulation, atmospherics, etc. It is clear that to all these, and kindred themes, Edwards was giving very close attention.[1]

In the first twelve months of his Christian life, however, the emphasis begins to change. He still thought and studied, pen in hand, as his father had early trained him, but a new and very different series of manuscripts were now commenced. In 1722 he is writing his first sermons, his 'Resolutions', and his theological 'Miscellanies', the last-named consisting of papers and folders to which he was to be constantly adding throughout his life. His manuscripts on scientific themes (the themes upon which he was tempted to make a name for himself in Europe) became left behind in Connecticut when he went to New York – and only temporarily resumed later – while his biblical writings became, for the first time, the all-absorbing interest of his life.

Nothing shows more clearly the new prevailing bent of Edwards' mind and heart than his seventy 'Resolutions'. Of these, the first twenty-one were all written at one sitting (probably while he was still at New Haven in 1722); others followed, and a total of thirty-four was reached before December 18, 1722. Thereafter further additions were made until the

[1]There has been a major advance in the correct understanding of the date of Edwards' 'Scientific and Philosophical Writings' since their publication, with excellent editorial material by Wallace E. Anderson, as vol. 6 of J E (Yale) in 1980.

last resolution, the seventieth, was written on August 17, 1723, two months before his twentieth birthday. The following extracts may be taken as representative of the spirit of the whole:

Being sensible that I am unable to do anything without God's help, I do humbly entreat him, by his grace, to enable me to keep these Resolutions, so far as they are agreeable to his will, for Christ's sake. . . .

Resolved, Never to do any manner of thing, whether in soul or body, less or more, but what tends to the glory of God, nor be, nor suffer it, if I can possibly avoid it.

Resolved, Never to lose one moment of time, but to improve it in the most profitable way I possibly can.

Resolved, To live with all my might, while I do live.

Resolved, To strive every week to be brought higher in religion, and to a higher exercise of grace, than I was the week before.

Resolved, Never to say anything at all against any body, but when it is perfectly agreeable to the highest degree of Christian honour, and of love to mankind, agreeable to the lowest humility, and sense of my own faults and failings, and agreeable to the golden rule.

Resolved, To inquire every night, as I am going to bed, wherein I have been negligent – what sin I have committed – and wherein I have denied myself; also, at the end of every week, month and year.

I frequently hear persons in old age say how they would live, if they were to live their lives over again: Resolved, That I will live just so as I can think I shall wish I had done, supposing I live to old age.

Resolved, To endeavour, to my utmost, so to act, as I can think I should do, if I had already seen the happiness of heaven and hell torments.

Resolved, Never to give over, nor in the least to slacken, my fight with my corruptions, however unsuccessful I may be.

Resolved, Never to do anything, which I should be afraid to do, if I expected it would not be above an hour before I should hear the last trump.

Let there be something of benevolence in all that I speak (1:xx–xxii).

The same ardency of commitment and desire displayed in these 'Resolutions' is to be seen still more fully in the surviving records of Edwards' Diary which begins abruptly on December 18, 1722, when he had been in New York for some six months.[1]

---

[1] The Diary, as given by Dwight, runs from 1722 to 1735 (with only six entries after 1725). Probably it began at an earlier date but nothing has survived apart from what Dwight printed. The original Diary which Dwight had is now lost.

Biographers and other writers on Edwards have expressed their regret that the Diary – the most important biographical source dating from the New York period – is so filled up with the spiritual and the intangible. Ola Winslow registers her disappointment over all that is missing. The Diary, she says, contains no observations on 'New York as a place of ships, a new speech, and more crowded ways of life. . . . The foreground was to him totally unimportant, he had no zest for exploration and no curiosity about men and their doings.'[1] Clarence H. Faust and Thomas H. Johnson pursue the same theme in describing Edwards' Diary as 'a colourless document, largely a supplement of his *Resolutions*, introspective and self-condemnatory. He does not record his readings, interest in affairs or people, or his doings from day to day'.[2]

These comments miss the magnitude of what had happened to Edwards in becoming a Christian. It was not that he now disdained the external world of affairs and the subjects which had once filled his letters written home from College. No doubt letters from New York which have not survived still went back to East Windsor with news of such matters. But, for importance, these things no longer compared with the realities of the kingdom of God. New standards and new affections had broken into his experience and in the 'Resolutions' and Diary, coupled with his 'Personal Narrative', there is the key to the understanding of his whole life and future ministry. He no longer 'resolves', as once he did, dependent upon his own efforts. His endeavours after holiness are no more the self-conscious strivings of a moralist: rather they are the response of love to the God who had made him a new creature in Jesus Christ. Sanctification he saw now as a personal experience flowing from communion with God and fellowship with Christ. In his Diary he can write: 'I think I find in my heart to be glad from the hopes I have that my eternity is to be spent in spiritual and holy joys, arising from the manifestation of God's love, and the exercise of holiness and burning love to him'.

New though this was to Edwards, it was not new in the least to the Christian tradition of New England. In this same decade,

[1] *Jonathan Edwards*, p. 87.
[2] *Jonathan Edwards, Representative Selections*, with Introduction, Bibliography, and Notes, Revised Edition, 1966, p. 418.

for example, Dr. Cotton Mather (who died in 1728 at the age of sixty-five) was preparing one of his last books for the press, *Manuductio ad Ministerium,* Directions for a Candidate of the Ministry, or The Angels Preparing to Sound the Trumpets. No man can live unto God, says Mather, until he is converted. There must be 'the experience of a principle infused from above into you, that shall be indeed Christ formed in you and Christ living in you. . . . A principle of piety, even the love of God, thus produced in you shall be the root of the righteous in you, perpetually bringing forth fruits of righteousness, which are by Jesus Christ unto the glory of God'. Without this principle, adds Mather, 'all the ornaments on which the great men of the earth value themselves are but gilded vanities'.

The meaning of such words had become as clear as noon-day to Edwards by 1722. This is not to say that his first writing as a young Christian reflects a fully balanced delineation of Christian experience. His feelings at this date were not always guided by sufficient scriptural knowledge; nevertheless, his 'Resolutions' and Diary, which he wrote for no eye but his own, are one of the most stirring examples in evangelical literature of the fervent spirituality which a Christian can enjoy even upon his entrance into the kingdom of God. As Samuel Miller notes: 'The character of his piety, from its very commencement, bears the stamp of unusual depth, fervour, clearness, and governing power. . . . To some readers a portion of this language may appear to indicate an excited imagination, and a state of feeling bordering on enthusiasm. . . . The truth is, he entered more heartily and thoroughly into the character of the great objects of pious emotion than most Christians do, and no wonder that he spoke a corresponding language.'[1]

While Edwards says nothing directly personal about himself in his sermons of this date, it would be clear enough to his hearers that his heart overflowed with the subjects about which he spoke. He had prepared some eight or ten sermons while still in Connecticut and what was probably his first, on Isaiah 3.10, may have been preached at the time of his licensing. The emphasis of that sermon was the happiness of the Christian ('a good man is a happy man, whatever his outward circum-

---

[1] *Life of Jonathan Edwards,* 1839, p. 20–21.

stances') and his New York hearers heard much more on similar themes: 'When a man is enlightened savingly by Christ, he is, as it were, brought into a new world . . . the excellency of religion and the glorious misteries of the gospel seemed as a strange thing to him before, but now . . . he sees with his own eyes and admires and is astonished.' 'What a sweet calmness, what a calm ecstasy doth it [holiness] bring to the soul!' 'A life of love, if it be upon rational principles, is the most pleasant life in the world . . . there is no such near or intimate conversation between any other lovers as between Christ and the Christian.' 'The pleasures of religion raise one clear above laughter, and rather tend to make the face shine than screw it into a grimace.'[1]

While Edwards worked with the usual type of sermon structure, proceeding from 'text' to 'doctrine' to 'application', Wilson Kimnach notes that 'an internal or spiritual energy constantly threatens to demolish conventional decorum'. Speaking of the impressive range of subjects dealt with in the twenty-four manuscript sermons which survive from the New York pastorate, it is Kimnach's opinion that the nineteen-year-old preacher 'manages to touch upon most of the issues and themes of his later writings'.

From other surviving manuscripts, as well as from his sermons, we can gain an impression of particular subjects which were foremost in Edwards' personal studies during his New York ministry. What the Puritans knew as 'practical divinity', particularly the doctrine of a saving conversion and the evidences of genuine godliness, were much in his thoughts. 'It is a subject,' he could write in the 1740's, 'on which my mind has been peculiarly intent, ever since I first entered on the study of divinity' (1.234). He was early aware that the means of determining whether a professed devotion to God is genuine are by no means simple and it was probably at this time that he had a powerful illustration that zeal in 'the

---

[1]Wilson H. Kimnach, 'Jonathan Edwards' Early Sermons' in the *Journal of Presbyterian History*, 1977, pp. 255–266. None of these sermons is yet published, in fact, in the words of Thomas A. Schafer, 'Of the more than 250 sermons spanning the first decade of Edwards' ministry only nine have ever been printed'. Comment by Kimnach on Edwards' sermons is currently in preparation. It will appear in the Yale edition of his Works.

external exercises of religion' proves nothing: 'I once lived for
many months next door to a Jew (the houses adjoining one to
another) and had much opportunity daily to observe him, who
appeared to me the devoutest person that ever I saw in my life;
a great part of his time being spent in acts of devotion, at his
eastern window, which opened next to mine, seeming to be
most earnestly engaged, not only in the daytime, but sometimes
whole nights' (1.255).

A notebook which Edwards began keeping at this time,
marked as his 'Catalogue', indicates something of his reading
priorities, and it is significant that the first two titles listed were
books relating to a 'saving conversion' by Solomon Stoddard.
His grandfather was the best-known living author on the
conversion pattern which, in at least some New England
churches, had become too traditional and stereotyped.
Edwards' diary from 1722–23 indicates that he had some
difficulties with regard to this 'pattern':

Dec 18 [1722] The reason why I in the least question my interest in
God's love and favour is: 1. Because I cannot speak so fully to my
experience of that preparatory work of which divines speak; 2. I do
not remember that I experienced regeneration exactly in those steps
in which divines say it is generally wrought . . . (1.xxiv)

Monday morning, Aug 12 [1723]. The chief thing, that now makes
me in any measure to question my good estate, is my not having
experienced conversion in those particular steps wherein the people of
New England, and anciently the dissenters of Old England, used to
experience it, wherefore, now resolved, never to leave searching till I
have satisfyingly found out the very bottom and foundation, the real
reason, why they used to be converted in those steps.

Edwards probably had principally in mind the fact that he
had not experienced what some described as 'terror' while
under conviction of sin prior to his conversion (1.xii). It is
interesting to note that as his subsequent thought on this
subject matured he reflects a high esteem for the writings of
Thomas Shepard who has been principally blamed (along with
Thomas Hooker) for supposedly imposing a standard pattern
of conversion upon New England. Edwards found that, taking
the Puritan writings as a whole, they do not reflect an
unbiblical stereotyped understanding of conversion. Certainly
his own problems over this subject as a young Christian

convinced him that there is no rigid, set pattern within which the Holy Spirit always works.[1]

Another biblical subject to which Edwards now began to give more serious thought was that of unfulfilled prophecy. This new interest sprang directly from his eager longings to see the gospel which he himself enjoyed received by all mankind. In part of his 'Personal Narrative', dealing with the time of his pastorate in New York, he writes:

I had then, abundance of sweet, religious conversation, in the family where I lived, with Mr John Smith, and his pious mother. My heart was knit in affection to those in whom were appearances of true piety; and I could bear the thoughts of no other companions, but such as were holy, and the disciples of the blessed Jesus. I had great longings for the advancement of Christ's kingdom in the world; and my secret prayer used to be, in great part, taken up in praying for it. If I heard the least hint of any thing that happened in any part of the world, that appeared, in some respect or other, to have a favourable aspect on the interests of Christ's kingdom, my soul eagerly catched at it; and it would much animate and refresh me. I used to be eager to read public news-letters, mainly for that end; to see if I could not find some news favourable to the interest of religion in the world.

I very frequently used to retire into a solitary place, on the banks of Hudson's River, at some distance from the city, for contemplation on divine things and secret converse with God, and had many sweet hours there. Sometimes Mr Smith and I walked there together, to converse on the things of God; and our conversation used to turn much on the advancement of Christ's kingdom in the world, and the glorious things that God would accomplish for his church in the latter days (1.xiv).

The extent of his early interest in unfulfilled prophecy is also to be seen in his several entries bearing upon the subject in his 'Miscellanies' written at this period, under such headings as Antichrist, Apocalypse and Millennium. It was about the spring or early summer of 1723 that he decided to have a separate notebook on these themes and in this, a quarto of two hundred and eight pages, he immediately began to write Notes on the Apocalypse. These notes reveal that, in its main outline,

[1]His New York sermons already show him exercising care in stating the truth, i.e., 'the effect of godly contrition is not always to the same degree, but it is always of the same nature'.

his view of unfulfilled prophecy was already largely formed and that it corresponded with beliefs which had been general among the Puritans.[1] When 'the fulness of the Gentiles' is brought in, then ethnic Israel will also be largely saved and, while restored to their own land, they will be united with all the church of Christ and 'look upon all the world to be their brethren, as much as the Christians in Boston and the Christians in other parts of New England look on each other as brethren'.[2] But before this can happen Antichrist – the great barrier to the success of the gospel – must fall. And this Antichrist is not some dread secular power to arise in history, rather he 'does all under the shew of sanctity and holiness, and being the spouse of Jesus Christ . . . He is Antichrist inasmuch as he usurps Christ's offices in opposition to him.'[3] Thus, they saw Antichrist as 'his holiness' the primate of the Roman Church, the pretended vicar and successor to Christ upon earth: 'Popery is the deepest contrivance that ever Satan was the author of to uphold his kingdom'.[4] The overthrow of this great evil, prior to the millennium, will be gradual and by means of the power of the truth.

From this early period in his Christian life Edwards sought to correlate these beliefs with the teaching of the Book of the Revelation. The symbolic character of the language of the Apocalypse he clearly recognized. He saw, also, that the symbols could have more than one fulfilment and that different parts of the prophecy could refer to the same events. But he never seems to have doubted whether the Apocalypse is chronological in its presentation, that is to say, whether it is intended to provide a chronology with which the successive centuries of history can approximately be correlated prior to the 'millennium' of Revelation chapter 20. Consequently it was of great moment for him to judge where the church of his day stood in relation to the unfolding narrative of history symbolically portrayed in the Apocalypse. To this same subject we must

[1] I have documented this subject in *The Puritan Hope*, Revival and the Interpretation of Prophecy, 1971.
[2] J E (Yale) 5, p. 135. In this volume, edited by Stephen J. Stein, Edwards' 'Notes on the Apocalypse' are printed for the first time.
[3] *Ibid*, p. 138.
[4] *Ibid*, p. 119.

later return. What must here be emphasized is that Edwards' interest in prophecy was not some theoretical idiosyncrasy, unrelated to the knowledge of God and the gospel; rather it stemmed from concerns which patently lie at the heart of Christian prayer and endeavour. It is misleading, therefore, to isolate 'the millennium' in his thinking and to speak of it in the words of Stephen J. Stein, as 'a matter of consuming private interest for him',[1] and incredibly wrong for another writer to assert, 'This ideal of the millennial kingdom was more important to him than his Puritan or Calvinist heritage'.[2] Edwards' interest in unfulfilled prophecy is not centred upon the millennium, indeed he was to write far more on heaven itself than on 'the latter day glory', but what he viewed as the millennium came into his larger concept of the providential rule of God. Stein revised his earlier statement in the right direction when he later wrote:

In the Reformed tradition the doctrine of providence was a rich theological construct – richer perhaps than the idea of the millennium. . . . Millennialism features the future eschatological moment of triumph on earth. By contrast, providence expands the scope of eschatology, bringing past, present, and future into focus within the divine economy and balancing both earthly and heavenly dimensions. This fuller providential perspective is evident in Edwards' lifelong preoccupation with the fortunes of the church militant through the ages and in the present, as well as in his concern with the glories of the church triumphant, anticipated on earth and fulfilled ultimately in heaven.[3]

But we must proceed to another subject which outweighs all others among Edwards' interests at this early date. It stands *first* in his 'Miscellanies', and much of the explanation of his later life lies in the fact that it never ceased to be first in his concerns. The title to the initial entry in his 'Miscellanies' reads 'Of Holiness'. And it is of holiness that he speaks most fully at a later period when, in his 'Personal Narrative', he recalls his

[1] In Editor's Introduction to J E (Yale) 5, p. 18.

[2] R. G. Clouse, reviewing *Jonathan Edwards and the Visibility of God* in *Christianity Today*, April 26, 1968, p. 750.

[3] 'Providence and the Apocalypse in the Early Writings of Jonathan Edwards', in *Early American Literature*, vol. xiii, 1978/9, p. 263.

time in New York. Speaking of the year 1722 he writes:

My sense of divine things seemed gradually to increase, until I went to preach at New York, which was about a year and a half after they began; and while I was there, I felt them, very sensibly, in a much higher degree than I had done before. My longings after God and holiness, were much increased. Pure and humble, holy and heavenly, Christianity appeared exceeding amiable to me. I felt a burning desire to be in every thing a complete Christian; and conformed to the blessed image of Christ; and that I might live, in all things, according to the pure, sweet and blessed rules of the gospel. I had an eager thirsting after progress in these things; which put me upon pursuing and pressing after them. It was my continual strife day and night, and constant inquiry, how I should *be* more holy, and *live* more holily, and more becoming a child of God and a disciple of Christ. I now sought an increase of grace and holiness, and a holy life, with much more earnestness than ever I sought grace before I had it. I used to be continually examining myself, and studying and contriving for likely ways and means how I should live holily, with far greater diligence and earnestness than ever I pursued any thing in my life. . . .

The heaven I desired was a heaven of holiness; to be with God, and to spend my eternity in divine love, and holy communion with Christ. My mind was very much taken up with contemplations on heaven, and the enjoyments there; and living there in perfect holiness, humility and love: and it used at that time to appear a great part of the happiness of heaven, that there the saints could express their love to Christ. It appeared to me a great clog and burden, that what I felt within I could not express as I desired. The inward ardor of my soul seemed to be hindered and pent up, and could not freely flame out as it would. I used often to think, how in heaven this principle should freely and fully vent and express itself. Heaven appeared exceedingly delightful, as a world of love; and that all happiness consisted in living in pure, humble, heavenly, divine love. . . .

Holiness, as I then wrote down some of my contemplations on it, appeared to me to be of a sweet, pleasant, charming, serene, calm nature; which brought an inexpressible purity, brightness, peacefulness and ravishment to the soul. In other words, that it made the soul like a field or garden of God, with all manner of pleasant flowers; all pleasant, delightful, and undisturbed; enjoying a sweet calm, and the gently vivifying beams of the sun. The soul of a true Christian, as I then wrote my meditations, appeared like such a little white flower as we see in the spring of the year; low and humble on the ground, opening its bosom to receive the pleasant beams of the sun's glory; rejoicing as it were in a calm rapture; diffusing around a sweet fragrancy; standing peacefully and lovingly, in the midst of other flowers round about; all in like manner opening their bosoms to drink in the light of the sun. There was no part of creature holiness, that I had so great a sense of its loveliness, as humility, brokenness of heart and poverty of spirit; and there was nothing that I so earnestly longed for. My heart panted after this – to lie low before God, as in the dust; that I might be nothing, and that God might be ALL, that I might become as a little child (1.xiii–xiv).

*   *   *

Despite Edwards' evident personal enjoyment of his time in New York he was not without difficulties. His Diary speaks of days when he felt cold and downcast as well as of those of spiritual sunshine. There were evidently difficulties also in the congregation which he served – difficulties not made easier either by his youth or his unofficial status as the 'supply' preacher. The people of his charge had only recently seceded from the Presbyterian congregation which had been formed in New York in 1716. Under its first pastor, the Rev. James Anderson, the Presbyterian church had grown and built what a later writer calls, 'a commodious edifice' on Wall Street, near Broadway, in 1719. It is evident, however, that numbers remained small, for we read of the unfinished state of the building in the 1720's, 'a house without galleries, six out of its eight windows being closed with boards, poverty preventing their being glazed, and the fraction of light being enough for the handful of people'.[1] Anderson, a determined Scot, was not supported by all his people. The trouble lay, in part, in the difference between the religious inheritance of the Scots-Irish settlers and the outlook of New-Englanders with their English background. Both, certainly, had enough in common to enjoy the same preaching but in the week-by-week practices of the church there were variations between the two traditions. Speaking of some of Anderson's people, Samuel Miller writes: 'A number of them, having been accustomed to the less regular and rigid habits of the Congregational Churches of South Britain and of New England, were not pleased with the strict Presbyterianism, according to the Scottish model, which Mr.

[1]Webster, p. 120.

Anderson endeavoured to support. They charged him with ecclesiastical domination, and also with an interference in the temporal concerns of the church.[1] The outcome of this was that a dissatisfied minority withdrew and commenced meeting on their own in a building on William Street in proximity to the docks. It was among this group that Edwards had settled in August, 1722.

Apparently some of Edwards' congregation soon came to question whether they had been over-hasty in their secession and to believe that they were too weak to support a separate work. Their size may be judged from the fact that they were a minority from a church which was itself small while still united. By the beginning of 1723 the termination of their independent existence was being discussed by the church and one argument used against that step was that it could 'issue in our deprivation of the much Respected Mr. Edwards'. It seems that Edwards himself came to believe that a re-union was in the best interests of the people and that he should therefore leave. In a letter of January 16, 1723, he wrote from New York: 'Considering the circumstances of the Society, and my Father's inclination to the contrary, it seems most probable I shall not settle here, but am ready to think I shall leave them in the spring.' A call which he received at this same time from the newly settled town of Bolton, in Tolland County and just sixteen miles from East Windsor, may also have influenced his final decision. Yet it was far from easy to leave New York as he later recalled in his 'Personal Narrative':

I came away from New York in the month of April, 1723 and had a most bitter parting with Madam Smith and her son. My heart seemed to sink within me, at leaving the family and city where I had enjoyed so many sweet and pleasant days. I went from New York to Wethersfield by water; and as I sailed away, I kept sight of the city as long as I could. However, that night, after this sorrowful parting, I was greatly comforted in God at Westchester, where we went ashore to lodge: and had a pleasant time of it all the voyage to Saybrook. It was sweet to me to think of meeting dear christians in heaven, where we should never part more. At Saybrook we went ashore to lodge on Saturday, and there kept the Sabbath; where I had a sweet and refreshing season, walking alone in the fields.

[1] *Life of Jonathan Edwards*, 1839, p. 24.

After I came home to Windsor, I remained much in a like frame of mind, as when at New York; only sometimes I felt my heart ready to sink, with the thoughts of my friends at New York. My support was in contemplations on the heavenly state; as I find in my Diary of May 1, 1723. It was a comfort to think of that state, where there is fulness of joy; where reigns heavenly, calm, and delightful love, without alloy; where there are continually the dearest expressions of this love; where is the enjoyment of the persons loved, without ever parting; where those persons who appear so lovely in this world, will really be inexpressibly more lovely, and full of love to us. And how sweetly will the mutual lovers join together, to sing the praises of God and the Lamb! (1.xiii-xv).

From the last day of April, 1723, when Edwards was once more back in East Windsor, there is much difficulty in interpreting the slender information which exists on the months which followed. In mid-May, his Diary reveals that he spent a week 'in journeying to Norwich, and the towns thereabouts'. Early in June he is in Boston. The variety of homes which he visited contributed to the concern expressed in his Diary that he should be more careful in his conversations, and the number of days which he was giving to travelling gives rise to his query, 'How shall I make advantage of all the time I spend in journeys?' Part of his answer to that latter question was the commencement of a practice which he was to continue. He decided to have with him some means of writing notes when he travelled. 'Remember,' he wrote on August 28, 1723, 'as soon as I can to get a piece of slate, or something, whereon I can make short memorandums while travelling' (1.xxvi).

The strong probability is that these various journeys in the summer of 1723 were the result of invitations to preach as a candidate in various churches which were looking for a minister. Dwight says, 'About this time, several congregations invited him to become their minister'. As already mentioned, one of these congregations was that of Bolton. It would appear that their first call to him, while he was in New York, was not accepted but that it was later renewed. At length, on November 11, 1723, Edwards was to write in the town book of Bolton,

Upon the terms that are here recorded I do consent to be the settled Pastor of the town of Bolton.

The terms to which he refers had to do with the salary and provisions – home, wood and pasture land – which he was to receive as pastor. But from this point, the name of Bolton again vanishes from the record of Edwards' life. For reasons unknown his settlement at Bolton was never carried into effect.

The explanation would appear to lie in another field of interest and endeavour which Edwards was also prosecuting in 1723 – an interest of sufficient importance even to interfere, finally, with his planned pastorate at Bolton. Basing his words on Edwards' manuscripts which survive from this date, Wallace E. Anderson writes: 'Upon returning to East Windsor in the early summer of 1723 Edwards entered a period of intense study and intellectual growth. He worked upon his M.A. thesis during the summer, regularly added entries in his "Miscellanies", and took up writing in "Natural Philosophy" again.'[1]

Edwards received his M.A. degree in September, 1723, at which time, says Dwight, 'He was elected a tutor in the college. . . . As there was no immediate vacancy in the office of tutor, he passed the ensuing winter and spring at New Haven, in study and in the occasional discharge of the active duties of his profession' (1.xxxii). This statement may well not be wholly accurate. Yale records give May 21, 1724 as the date when he was elected a tutor, and at the end of October, 1723, we know that Edwards was at East Windsor, not New Haven. But given the need at Yale (of which we shall speak in the next chapter), and given Edwards' availability, it is highly probable that efforts to place him in Connecticut's only college were under active consideration in 1723. It may well also have been the case that Timothy Edwards regarded a further period of study as a tutor at Yale as being in Jonathan's best long-term interests. He knew well that more than warm piety is needed for the right discharge of the work of the ministry. Confronted by these perplexing alternatives and not yet twenty years of age, Edwards is likely to have depended upon his father's counsel. We have already noted that Timothy Edwards' advice had played a part in his not continuing in New York and in the summer of 1723 parents and son were closer than they had ever

[1] J E (Yale) 6, p. 29.

been. A Diary entry for May 18, 1723, reads: 'I now plainly perceive what great obligation I am under to love and honour my parents. I have great reason to believe that their counsel and education have been my making'.

The choice, then, before Edwards in 1723 was between taking up a pastorate and the spiritual work which he had so greatly enjoyed in New York, or responding to the need at Yale with the prospect of wider studies which a Yale tutorship would provide. The fact that he went as far as formally to accept the call to Bolton, only to withdraw from it, is proof enough that the decision was not an easy one. As we shall see, the three years now before him were not among those which he regarded as his happiest, yet the additional discipline involved was to contribute largely to his future usefulness. The comment of Samuel Miller on Edwards' decision to return to Yale is worthy of repetition:

Many a young man since, as well as before his time, of narrow views and crude knowledge, has rushed into the pastoral office with scarcely any of that furniture which enables the shepherd of souls 'rightly to divide the word of truth'; but Jonathan Edwards, with a mind of superior grasp and penetration, and with attainments already greater than common, did not think three full years of diligent professional study enough to prepare *him* for this arduous charge, until, after his collegiate graduation, he had devoted *six years* to close and appropriate study.

4

TUTOR AT YALE

The First Yale College House

Edwards might have been a naturalist or a great literary figure, but he chose theology because he believed that an exploration of the relation between man and God was infinitely more important. He would have considered our modern efforts to explore outer space as of minor importance, since their objects are merely to extend human knowledge. He looked beyond all stellar systems and galaxies, to save men's souls for eternal life.

SAMUEL ELIOT MORISON
The Oxford History of the American People, 1965, p. 151

4

here is nothing in Edwards' Diary to suggest that he returned to take up residence again at Yale in June, 1724, with any spirit of enthusiasm. For one thing, the ungainly three-storey wooden structure which had been dedicated to Elihu Yale in 1718 was a poor substitute for the home-life which he had enjoyed, both at East Windsor and New York, in the previous two years. The fact that the building was to stand only to the mid-eighteenth century suggests that the fifty occupants it could house were not well shielded from New Haven's sea air and southerly winds. More important, however, were the reservations which Edwards must have felt over the change of occupation which the tutorship would demand. If he had been slow to respond to those who wanted him at Yale it was not because he lacked an eagerness to pursue such studies in natural science and philosophy as could be combined with an appointment to the College. But a tutorship would represent a loss of freedom to plan his days in his own way, and in addition to the study and teaching required of him, he knew that there would necessarily be many time-consuming commitments in the administration of the student body. The first entry in his Diary after his settlement at Yale reads:

Saturday night, June 6 [1724]. This week has been a very remarkable week with me with respect to despondencies, fears, perplexities, multitudes of cares, and distraction of mind: it being the week I came

[59]

hither to New Haven, in order to entrance upon the office of tutor in the college. I have now abundant reason to be convinced of the troublesomeness and vexation of the world, and that it will never be another kind of world.

The month of September brought the usual College Commencement, an event in New England which a Harvard historian described as the 'puritan mid-summer's holiday'. It was hardly to be described in that way in the eighteenth century. The formal academic exercises, characteristic of the Commencement, were often followed by student festivities and disorders, which were not infrequently intensified by the presence of a rabble from the town. Liquor ran freely, bonfires were lit and firecrackers set off. 'For an entire week, a carnival air prevailed in New Haven', writes Louis T. Tucker, describing the scene as it was in the mid-eighteenth century. This was certainly not Edwards' idea of pleasure, and the responsibilities of his new situation weighed upon him:

Saturday night, September 12. Crosses of the nature of that which I met with this week, thrust me quite below all comforts in religion.

Wednesday, September 30. . . . The hurries of commencement and diversion of the vacancy, has been the occasion of my sinking so exceedingly, as in the last three weeks.

The 'vacancy' to which Edwards refers presented the most serious of all Yale's problems at this date and it requires some explanation. In an earlier chapter we noted how the termination of Samuel Johnson's tutorship in 1719 and the appointment of Timothy Cutler as rector had unified the College. Even so, disciplinary problems persisted as revealed in Edwards' letter of March 1st, 1721, to his father. It was not, however, until Edwards had left Yale in June, 1722, that an issue of discipline occurred which rocked the whole colony. Until this time in all parts of New England the Congregational form of church order had been followed. The re-establishment of Episcopacy in England in 1660, which shortly turned the English Puritans into a dissenting minority, had had no such effect across the Atlantic and as late as 1720 there was no Episcopalian clergyman in the whole colony. The New England churches could accommodate their convictions to some extent with Presbyterianism – as they did in the Saybrook

Confession of 1708 – but the claims of the Church of England made any compromise in that direction impossible. The possibility that any New England minister, nurtured in 'the Congregational way', should endorse Episcopal claims seemed as remote as the possibility that Boston might surrender to the French. Yet in 1722 rumours were circulating in New Haven that just such a change of belief was taking place, not indeed among Yale's students but among their teachers as well as among some local ministers. Accordingly, following the Commencement in September, the trustees required Rector Cutler and others to state their views. The result was that from both Cutler and Daniel Brown, a tutor, as well as from two neighbouring ministers – one of whom was Samuel Johnson – they heard to their astonishment that it was the Church of England and not New England Dissent which could claim conformity to the Apostolic pattern. Following the argument of the Caroline divines, Cutler and his friends urged that no form of church government could be determined from Scripture and that therefore an appeal to tradition is the surest course: in which case it was episcopacy (or prelacy, as it was generally called by the Puritans) which had the best claim to a lineal descent from the early Church.

The following month the trustees proceeded to 'excuse the Rev Mr Cutler from all further services as rector of Yale College' and to accept the resignation of Mr Brown. While these two men, and Johnson, proceeded to England to obtain, in their view, valid ordination, the trustees enacted that all who would thereafter be elected to office in the College must assent to the Saybrook Confession of Faith 'and shall particularly give satisfaction to them of the soundness of their faith, in opposition to Arminian and prelatical corruptions'.[1]

This defection to Anglicanism had placed the trustees in acute difficulty; as one of them wrote to Cotton Mather, 'We need pity, prayer and counsel.' At one point the whole teaching staff had been reduced to one tutor, William Smith, a young graduate of the class of 1719 who had been appointed in 1722. In 1724 Robert Treat was Edwards' senior colleague, to be replaced the following year by Edwards' cousin, Daniel

[1] Benjamin Trumbull, *A Complete History of Connecticut*, vol. 2, 1898 reprint, p. 16. This rule held at Yale, it seems, until 1823.

Edwards, with whom he had been a room-mate in his student days. But in 1724 the rectorship was still vacant and the trustees were attempting to supply the deficiency by each of them residing for a month in turn in the College. It is questionable if the practice was effective and it appears that for the five years, from 1722 to 1726, the College was virtually without a head.

Accustomed to orderly habits and early trained in personal
— discipline, Edwards was not troubled by his return to the daily routine at Yale. As each day the college bell summoned the students from their beds the same pattern followed. In the words of the 'Orders and Appointments to be Observed', which each student had to write out for himself:

No undergraduate shall . . . be absent from his study or appointed exercises in the school except half an hour at breakfast, an hour and half at noon after dinner, and after the evening prayer till nine of the clock. . . .

No student . . . shall be absent from his chamber after nine a clock nor have light in his chamber after eleven nor before four in the morning except some extraordinary occasion.

Every student shall be called by his sirname except he be the son of a nobleman or a knight's eldest son.

Every student shall be present morning and evening at public prayer in the Hall at the accustomed [hour] which is usually at six a clock in the morning from the tenth of March to the tenth of September, and from thence again to the tenth of March at sun rising and between four and five of the clock at night all the year.

No scholar shall use the English tongue in the College with his fellow scholars unless he be called to public exercise proper to be attended in the English tongue but scholars in their chambers and when they are together shall talk Latin. . . .

Probably, as many students saw it, they were,

> In the same round condemn'd each day,
> To study, read, recite and pray.

Not surprisingly the bounds of legitimate recreation were often exceeded. With a tutor's permission, such things as hunting ('gunning'), fowling and fishing were allowable, as were such other innocent amusements as walking and snow-balling. But tutors frequently found themselves in collision with students about other 'pastimes', including tavern-visiting, chicken-stealing, food-throwing in the College Hall, ringing the College bell at the wrong hours, plundering the provisions of other students and so on. Sometimes, indeed, the tutors themselves became the victims of the students' amusement and might find themselves locked in their rooms, or smoked out, or kept awake at night by disturbances outside their windows – to mention just a few student 'frolics'.

How Edwards and his colleagues dealt with such matters we have no means of knowing. Probably the ill-effects of the vacancy continued to trouble him until the end of his tutorship in 1726. It is possible that he was not strong in handling problems posed by personal relationships and it is not difficult to conceive that the young tutors had oftentimes an unenviable task dealing with the forty students of 1724 and the sixty of 1725. The vacancy was at last filled by the appointment of Elisha Williams (the popular tutor at Wethersfield in Edwards' student days) who took up the rectorship in September, 1726. 'No sooner was Mr Williams established in his office', says Trumbull, 'than he began effectually to suppress vice and disorder among the students.' This suggests that the tutors had not been able to achieve much with respect to discipline. Ezra Stiles, however, a later rector of Yale, described them as: 'pillar tutors, and the glory of the college, at the critical period between Rector Cutler and Rector Williams. Their tutorial renown was great and excellent. They filled and sustained their offices with great ability, dignity, and honour.'

From Edwards' manuscripts, some of which have been only recently published, a clear impression can be gained of his studies at this period. In 1723, as already mentioned, he gave renewed attention to natural science. At this date his father was in touch with Judge Paul Dudley, a justice of the Supreme Court of Massachusetts and a member of the Royal Society of London. In at least one of Dudley's frequent contributions to the *Philosophical Transactions* of the Royal Society, which dealt with 'remarkable instances of the nature and power of vegetation', he acknowledges the help of Timothy Edwards ('worthy divine') who had given him information on 'a prolific pumpkin vine'. Assured of Dudley's willingness to receive further items from him, Timothy Edwards encouraged Jonathan to send an account on 'Spiders' with a view to its possible publication. This the latter did in a letter to Dudley of October 31, 1723, in which he says in his first paragraph, 'Although everything pertaining to this insect is admirable, yet there are some phenomena relating to them more particularly wonderful'. The letter – perhaps the most attractive and interesting of Edwards' early writings – concludes; 'Pardon me if I thought it might at least give you occasion to make better observations on these wondrous animals, that should be worthy of communicating to the learned world, from whose glistening webs so much of the wisdom of the Creator shines.'[1]

It appears that it was also towards the end of 1723 that Edwards began a new notebook, headed 'The Mind'. The occasion of its origin has been pin-pointed by Thomas Schafer who noted that Edwards, having written an item on 'Excellency' in his 'Miscellanies' then crossed it out and made the same item a first entry in this new notebook, the contents of which were to be more philosophical than theological. Work on this notebook was pursued during his tutorship, with such entries as, 'Place of Minds', 'Space', 'Thought', 'Existence'. It is in this manuscript that Edwards' first references to the English philosopher John Locke occur. Edwards was using at this date the second edition of Locke's *Essay Concerning Human Understanding*, first published in 1690. His own thinking was stimulated by Locke and years later Samuel Hopkins was to quote Edwards as saying that he derived more pleasure from Locke's pages 'than the most greedy miser finds when gathering up handfuls of silver and gold'. Nonetheless, the attempt of Perry Miller to reconstruct the whole of Edwards' outlook in terms of Lockean philosophy has long since been abandoned as untenable.

Edwards' most noteworthy work during his Yale tutorship lay in natural science, the subject in which his interest – stimulated by the works of Isaac Newton and William Whiston – had been stimulated in his graduate years. Wallace Anderson has judged Edwards to be 'nearly unique' among the early

[1] J E (Yale) 6, pp. 163–169. No part of Edwards' letter, nor reference to it, appeared in subsequent publications of the Royal Society. Although the account of spiders bears the date 1723, its substance was evidently prepared some time earlier (see p. 414 of vol. 6 above).

eighteenth-century colonial scientists in his concentration upon problems in physics. He writes: 'In his early essays and throughout "Natural Philosophy" he attempts to formulate and apply explanatory hypotheses to account for such phenomena as the appearance of the rainbow and other meteors, the evaporation of water, combustion, respiration, the circulation of blood, the freezing of ice, elasticity, and the reflection, refraction, and diffraction or "incurvation" of light. His "Spider" papers might appear to be an exception; they have been widely praised, not only by students of Edwards' thought but by professional scientists as well, for their contributions to the natural history of the spider. . . . But a careful study of "Of Insects", the earliest of the papers and the foundation of the others, shows that Edwards' primary and original concern was to discover the physical principles that would account for the flight of this wingless insect.'[1]

Anderson, with the aid of Thomas Schafer's research into the dating of Edwards' early manuscripts, has shown that Dwight gave dates to several manuscripts which were as much as seven or eight years too early. Items credited to Edwards' pen when he was supposedly aged twelve were actually written when he was twenty. This revision corrects an earlier view that Edwards, in childhood, was displaying scientific abilities akin to genius. Even so, high admiration is warranted for what Edwards actually achieved in his studies at Yale. His theory of the nature of the physical world, says Anderson, 'belongs decidedly to the modern rather than the medieval age', and he concludes, 'In the light of Edwards' background, education, and circumstances, it is in fact remarkable enough that he accomplished what he did in his notes and essays'.

The actual form of Edwards' manuscript notebooks deserves comment as they indicate a method of study which he was to pursue all his life. Some of Edwards' earliest writing was done on loose folio sheets which he folded into quarto. Recognizing the difficulty of handling and preserving such sheets he early began a method of sewing folded sheets of paper together. A Diary entry of Jan. 14, 1723, tells us that this is what he did with the sheets of his Diary, 'About 10 o'clock in the morning made

[1] J E (Yale) 6, pp. 39–40.

this book, and put these papers in it'. He had not observed his sisters' needle-work in vain. In these gathered folders of papers – his 'notebooks' – remarks were placed as they occurred to him, each entry having no necessary connection with what precedes or follows. By a careful index system he had a ready method for finding every entry. His largest work of this kind, the 'Miscellanies', was to run to nine notebooks, of which the first is a folio of forty-four sheets of foolscap, stitched together. In the end the 'Miscellanies' were to contain no less than fourteen hundred entries in 1700 pages. As Dwight says, 'When he began the work, he had obviously no suspicion of the size to which it was to grow' (1.xix). Another notebook entitled 'Notes on the Scriptures' was begun probably in 1723 and was also to be continued throughout his life. By the time of his death it contained more than five hundred entries.

Besides the general duties of his tutorship, Edwards (in conjunction with his senior colleague, Robert Treat) was given an additional duty with respect to the College library which stood in urgent need of sorting and cataloguing. The library was already a far cry from the first books of old standard divinity, only sufficient in number, it is said, to fill a five-foot shelf and, in the opinion of Ola Winslow, 'already outmoded and therefore doomed'. A major enlargement had occurred in 1715, with the arrival from London of a collection of books assembled by Jeremiah Dummer, the free-thinking London agent for Massachusetts Colony. It was to this collection that Samuel Johnson and his friends were much indebted, for not only did they find 'the new learning' in a number of the Dummer volumes, but there were also up-to-date Anglican replies to Puritanism, as, for instance, the treatise by Benjamin Hoadly, the Bishop of Winchester, on *A Defence of the Reasonableness of Conformity to the Church of England* (1707). It was these latter books which silently led the way to the defection of Cutler, Brown and Johnson in 1722. It seemed to be true, as Johnson had been warned in 1715, that 'the new philosophy would bring in a new divinity.' Whether Edwards and his colleagues were given any instructions to remove certain volumes from the Library in 1725 we do not know; certainly Thomas Clap, president of Yale after Elisha Williams, was to resort to that expedient on occasions. It is not likely that it was done in the 1720's.

Of one thing we can be sure, when Edwards surveyed the Library's shelves his mind was by no means hostile to new authors. He did not consider himself necessarily bound to the defence of the intellectual traditions of a past generation. Ola Winslow's claim that he had been 'well schooled in conformity', and that 'Tutorship in those years meant strict maintenance of the *status quo*,' does not do justice to what we know of Edwards. In his college years he consciously set himself against adopting ideas simply because of the example of others: 'Men follow one another like a flock of sheep', and the 'prejudices and customs' are so strong, he observed, that even great men are insensible of the influence which these things have upon their opinions. In another rough note he jotted down, 'How difficult it is to get a people out of their old customs. In husbandry, how difficult to persuade that a new way is better!' Similarly, on September 23, 1723, he wrote in his Diary: 'I observe that old men seldom have any advantage of new discoveries because they are beside the way of thinking to which they have been so long used.' Edwards' thinking in physics and philosophy, as we have seen above, shows that he was no mere follower of traditional opinions. He was also in touch with 'the new learning.' 'He read all the books from which he might hope to derive any aid in his pursuit of knowledge', writes Samuel Hopkins, his first biographer, and M. C. Tyler, in *A History of American Literature*, speaks of him as 'The most original and acute thinker yet produced in America.'

Yet despite this, the fact is that as Edwards worked in the College Library he was forming convictions respecting theology which were poles apart from those of Samuel Johnson and his friends. The volumes which the defecters of 1722, and Ola Winslow after them, considered to be 'outmoded' were the very ones which were to be his life-long companions. As B. B. Warfield writes, 'He fed himself on the great Puritan divines, and formed not merely his thought but his life upon them'.[1]

More evidence on his assessment of the respective merits of different schools of religious literature is found in his 'Catalogue' already mentioned. This is a notebook of forty-three

---

[1] *Studies in Theology*, 1932, p. 529.

pages, measuring eight by six inches, in which he listed either what he had read or volumes which he wished to read. Many of the 690 entries in the Catalogue belong to a later period in his life but they follow the lines upon which he was already settled by 1725. There are 452 entries in all on religious books and these have been divided as follows: Church History, 62; Bible, 33; devotional, 24; Works, 17; Sermons, 37; and Theology, 279.[1]

While it is apparent that Edwards read theological writers who were his contemporaries, including promoters of 'new divinity', the names which predominate in the catalogue are those of the old authors of Reformed and Puritan persuasion: Calvin, Perkins, Van Mastricht, Sibbes, Manton, Flavel, Owen, Charnock and so on. Against an early reference to John Owen he notes the view of Thomas Halyburton, 'recommended by Mr Halyburton to the young students of Divinity at St Andrews above all human writings for a true view of the Mystery of the Gospel.' Although the Catalogue is not an exhaustive guide to all his reading, at least it proves beyond dispute that in his tastes and preferences he was a thorough Puritan. The questions, then, deserve to be asked – Why was it that Edwards, modern though he was in many respects, took so different a path from that of Johnson and Cutler in the 1720's? Why was he to take opposite sides to them in later life? Why did he choose to preach just the same theology as was heard in Boston a century before? The answer to each of these questions is one and the same, and it has to do with a wholly different interpretation of history. By the early eighteenth century New England Puritanism seemed to have lost its way: clearly it had lost its vigour. Boston pulpits had long been giving warning that a change had come for the worse – 'You that are aged', Increase Mather said to his hearers in 1702, 'and can remember what New England was fifty years ago, that saw

---

[1] The entries on non-religious authors in the Catalogue number 238 and have been divided as follows: Education, 8; Geography, 16; History, 43; Household and Etiquette, 6; Languages, 43; Dictionaries, 18; Literature, 28; Lives, 11; Mathematics, 12; Natural History, 23; Philosophy, 19; Unclassified, 11. [See Ralph G. Turnbull, *Jonathan Edwards The Preacher*, 1958]. The Catalogue, however, does not cover all his reading for it is obvious from his Works that he had read titles not listed here.

these churches in their first glory, is there not a sad decay and diminution of that glory! How is the gold become dim!'

Across the Atlantic the decay in the Dissenting churches was equally marked. In England, within fifty years, Calvinistic theology had fallen from a position of immense influence into comparative insignificance. This situation was fully reflected in the literature of the day. The cause which the Puritans had represented was depicted as worn out, and such journals as the *Spectator*, which also circulated in New England, were not averse to holding up the old Puritan divines as a theme for jest. The day of 'bigotry' was over and it was the common opinion that if Christianity was to hold any place in the new age it would have to be of a far more liberal kind.

In these religious conditions the Church of England was not without particular attractions: its old traditions offered stability, its status in society contrasted with an impotent Dissent, and its ethos permitted a latitude of opinion not to be found elsewhere in the English-speaking world. So even in far-off New Haven young intellectuals could be won to its fold.

But Edwards' viewpoint was wholly different from that promoted by London's publishing houses. In his case, beliefs were not to be judged by their apparent success or failure; they, and history, must be judged by Scripture. While this may well have been his opinion before his conversion in 1721, without question it was thereafter the dominating conviction in his intellectual life. His fundamental criticism of the learning of the eighteenth century was that it failed to recognize the native darkness of the human mind in spiritual things and therefore it placed itself above the revelation of God in Scripture:

When Christ came into the world learning greatly prevailed; and yet wickedness never prevailed more than then. . . . So now, learning is at a great height in the world, far beyond what it was in the age when Christ appeared; and now the world, by their learning and wisdom, do not know God; and they seem to wander in darkness, are miserably deluded, stumble and fall in matters of religion, as in mid-night darkness. Trusting to their learning, they grope in the day-time as in the night. Learned men are exceedingly divided in their opinions concerning the matters of religion, running into all manner of corrupt opinions, pernicious and foolish errors. They scorn to submit their reason to divine revelation, to believe any thing that is above their comprehension; and so being wise in their own eyes they become fools (1.601).

The reason why Edwards put a high value upon the Puritans and their writings is that he judged their theology to be, in its essentials, biblical theology. On matters of science and philosophy which could not be authoritatively settled by Scripture his ·mind was open: on issues of doctrine, which the Reformed churches had settled by exposition of Scripture, it was fixed. This is not to say that he considered all problems of religious belief capable of immediate solution by reference to Scripture. At the age of twenty-two he was already too mature to be so dogmatic. In a Diary entry on Friday, May 21, 1725 he writes:

If ever I am inclined to turn to the opinion of any other sect: *Resolved* beside the most deliberate consideration, earnest prayer, etc, privately to desire all the help that can possibly be afforded me from some of the most judicious men in the country, together with the prayers of wise and holy men, however strongly persuaded I may seem to be that I am in the right.

In other words, he recognized that there might be some issues relating to denomination and church practice respecting which his views might yet change. But the fundamental beliefs, those which had to do with Calvinistic and experimental Christianity, were for him firmly settled and the future course of his life was determined accordingly. The claim that these beliefs were worn-out made no more impression upon him than a fire-cracker thrown into the Connecticut. In God's time, he believed, they would be revived.

Before 1725 was to end, however, Edwards may well have wondered if he would live to see that day. On September 29, when the trustees voted that he and his colleagues should have five pounds added to their salaries 'for the extraordinary services of the year past, and their trouble and pains in sorting the books and fixing Catalogues to the boxes', he lay critically ill in the home of Isaac Stiles, the minister of North Haven [North Village]. Falling sick immediately after the Commencement in that month, he had set out for home only to get as far as the Stiles parsonage where he lay between life and death, nursed by his mother, for the greater part of three months. Edwards has recorded something of this experience in his

'Personal Narrative':

In September, 1725, I was taken ill at New Haven, and while endeavouring to go home to Windsor, was so ill at the North Village, that I could go no further; where I lay sick for about a quarter of a year. In this sickness God was pleased to visit me again with the sweet influences of his Spirit. My mind was greatly engaged there, on divine and pleasant contemplations, and longings of soul. I observed, that those who watched with me, would often be looking out wishfully for the morning; which brought to my mind those words of the Psalmist, and which my soul with delight made its own language, *My soul* waiteth for the Lord, more than they that watch for the morning; I say, more than they that watch for the morning. And when the light of the day came in at the window, it refreshed my soul, from one morning to another. It seemed to be some image of the light of God's glory.

As already noted, Edwards' years as a tutor were not, in his judgment, among the happiest of his life and the cause of this he attributes to his spiritual declension. In retrospect his time in New York seemed to be a near Elysium compared with the years which followed. In his 'Personal Narrative', after writing of his joy in New York (in the passage already quoted), he proceeds: 'I continued much in the same frame, in general, as when in New York, till I went to New Haven as tutor of the college. . . . After I went to New Haven, I sunk in religion, my mind being diverted from my eager pursuits after holiness, by some affairs that greatly perplexed and distracted my thoughts.' After the time of his illness at North Haven he says, 'I was again greatly diverted with some temporal concerns, that exceedingly took up my thoughts, greatly to the wounding of my soul. . .' (1.xxxiii). His Diary, while much briefer for the years 1724–26, conveys the same impression.

Any evaluation of this judgment of Edwards upon himself has to be cautious. Certainly the difference between the comparative leisure of New York and the sheer busyness of New Haven is part of the explanation. It may be, also, that his courtship of a young lady in New Haven – a subject to which we have yet to turn – contributed to his unsettlement in his tutorship years. More probably the lack of satisfaction which he expresses was connected with the amount of attention which he was having to give to disciplines in which, at heart, he had now only a secondary interest. In his Diary for May 23, 1724, he notes, 'Those times when I have read the Scriptures most, I have evermore been most lively and in the best frame'. It was at this point that his tutorship brought an inevitable change in his habits and current of thought. While he continued with personal Bible reading and some theological studies (as his notebooks of 'Miscellanies' and of 'Notes on Scripture' show), the priority had changed and he felt the loss. Thus, while recovering from his illness in the home of Isaac Stiles, he determined, 'as near as I can in my studies, to observe this rule: To let half a day's, or at most a day's, study in other things, be succeeded by half a day's or a day's study in divinity'. It is doubtful if he succeeded while at Yale.

This tension in Edwards' interests should not be exaggerated. His view of truth was such that he would have accepted no distinction between 'spiritual' and 'secular'. He saw no conflict between his Christian convictions and his interests in science and philosophy. All true knowledge leads to divinity. Thus, in the midst of his studies at Yale, he can write in his Diary on February 12, 1725: 'The very thing I now want, to give me a clearer and more immediate view of the divine perfections and glory of God, is as clear a knowledge of the manner of God's exerting himself, with respect to spirits and mind, as I have of his operations concerning matter and bodies'. Edwards found no cause for humiliation in the fact that his attraction to philosophy and science did not end with his conversion.[1] Yet there was a difference in importance between these different departments of knowledge. When he lay so seriously ill at North Haven in the autumn of 1725 we can be sure that it mattered nothing to him whether or not any of his writings should be honoured in the *Philosophical Transactions of the Royal Society*. He believed that the gospel and the Word of God were of incomparably greater significance. The fact is that at Yale in the years 1724–26 Edwards was not where he most wanted to be.

[1]His notebooks reveal that at one time he contemplated writing a book 'to show how all the arts and sciences, the more they are perfected, the more they issue in divinity and coincide with it, and appear to be parts of it'. J E (Yale) 6, 397. The quotation from S. E. Morison at the beginning of this chapter therefore requires qualification.

In this situation, and during a long convalescence at East Windsor in 1726, Edwards waited upon God for guidance. In the early summer of that year he resumed full duties at Yale. These, however, were short-lived. The guidance he awaited came on August 29, 1726, when the church of his grandfather, Solomon Stoddard, at Northampton, invited him to come with a view to his appointment as assistant minister. Edwards at once accepted and in September, as he laid down his tutorship, his spirits brightened. Looking back three years, to the Commencement of 1723, he reviewed what had been 'for the most part' his 'low sunk estate', and wrote in his Diary for September 26, 1726, 'Just about the same time this year, I began to be somewhat as I used to be'.

Preaching was to be his life-work and gladly did he take the road from Windsor to his mother's old home in Massachusetts. For the next twenty-three years he was to be 'Mr. Edwards of Northampton'.

SOLOMON STODDARD'S FAMILY

Solomon Stoddard = Esther (Warham) Mather

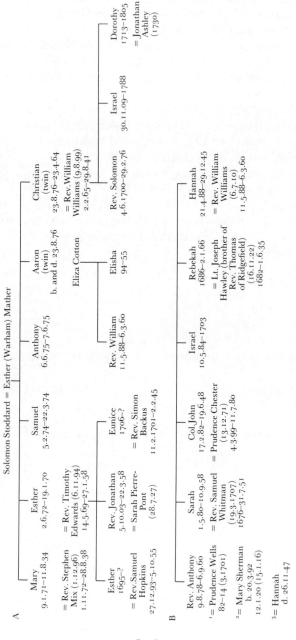

Key: Lines A and B list the twelve children of Stoddard, with their respective marriages (marriage dates in brackets). Eliza Cotton was the first wife of William Williams Sr. His second wife, Christian, was thus the sister of Hannah who later married a son of his first marriage. Details of Jonathan Edwards' other eight sisters will be found in his *Works* 1.ccxiv.

STODDARD AND NORTHAMPTON

*Simeon Stoddard, Boston councillor
and brother of Edwards'
grandfather, Solomon Stoddard.*

The town of Northampton is of about 82 years standing, and has now about 200 families, which mostly dwell more compactly together than any town of such a size in these parts of the country. . . . The people of the county, in general, I suppose, are as sober, orderly, and good sort of people, as in any part of New England; and I believe they have been preserved the freest by far of any part of the country from error, and variety of sects and opinions. Our being so far within the land, at a distance from sea-ports, and in a corner of the country, has doubtless been one reason why we have not been so much corrupted with vice as most other parts. But without question, the religion and good order of the county, and purity of doctrine, has, under God, been very much owing to the great abilities and eminent piety of my venerable and honoured grandfather Stoddard.

J E in 1737 (1.346)

5

outh and age were now combined for the first
time in Northampton's pulpit. It is not sur-
prising that the church had experienced
difficulty in finding a colleague for Solomon
Stoddard. For more than half a century he had
served the one congregation until he was the
oldest minister in the province. Yet even in
1726, at the age of eighty-three, Stoddard had not grown feeble.
He hated dull preaching as much as he had ever done and until
the winter of 1728 would still preach with vigour. Stoddard's
last published sermon, in 1723, had been entitled *The Defects of
Preachers Reproved*. In it he blamed the ministry for the low
spiritual conditions. There was, Stoddard believed, 'a great
want of good preaching; whence it comes to pass, that among
professors a spirit of piety runs exceeding low'.

Perhaps it was not easy for the townsmen of Northampton to
recognize that their renowned pastor's powers were failing in
the 1720's. Such was the veneration which they had for him,
Edwards recalled many years later, 'that many looked on him
almost as a sort of deity' (1.cxxxiii). But an inner circle of
leaders in the church certainly saw the need for a helper and in
April 1725 they resolved to 'get some meet person to assist him
in the work'. Stoddard's occasional indisposition had already
occasioned the presence of more visitors in the Northampton
pulpit than had been common in earlier years, one of the most
frequent being his son, Anthony, pastor of Woodbury, Connecticut. Of Stoddard's two sons who grew to manhood, only

[77]

Anthony had entered the ministry, but with five daughters (including Esther) all married to ministers – and some of them with sons who were already ministers – there was no lack of help near to hand.

The family of Williams was the most prominent among those with which the Stoddards had inter-married. Christian Stoddard, four years younger than Jonathan's mother, had married the Rev. William Williams of nearby Hatfield who was one of the best-known pastors of western Massachusetts. It was Williams' son, by a previous marriage, Elisha whom we have already noted as teaching Edwards at Yale. Two sons of Christian and William Williams were also to be public figures: Solomon (1700–1776), who followed his father into the ministry and Israel (1709–1788), who, as a merchant, judge and soldier was later to be 'the monarch of Hampshire'. It was Solomon Williams who was first approached as a possible successor to his grandfather. Nothing came of this, but the more determined efforts decided upon and pursued in 1725 led to the settlement of Israel Chauncy, a young Harvard graduate and member of another prominent ministerial family. Chauncy was appointed as 'colleague' to Stoddard, but troubled by a mental depression, which was not helped by the demands of his situation, he was to remain less than a year.

Understandably, after these difficulties, the Northampton church was more cautious in its approach to Jonathan Edwards. He was only asked to 'assist' and apparently a trial period was stipulated. Aged not quite twenty-three when he first sat beside the man who had been 'favoured with a more than ordinary presence of God in his work', Edwards certainly felt the weight of his responsibility.

Stoddard's own entrance into the ministry had been unusual. In 1669 the young Eleazer Mather (first minister of Northampton) died, and a parish committee which applied to Boston for advice was urged to obtain Stoddard. When the committee's invitation reached the twenty-six-year-old Harvard graduate his possessions were on board ship and he ready to sail for London the next day. Instead Stoddard went to Northampton in November 1669. In March 1670, the same month that he married Esther Mather (the widow of Eleazer), he was called to settle. Yet, while continuing to preach, he waited two whole years before accepting. Only in April 1672 did he become a member of the Northampton church and he was formally ordained the following September. The reason for this delay lay in a deficiency in his spiritual condition of which Stoddard himself was apparently conscious. Although his hearers found him to be orthodox and eloquent they perhaps missed what his wife is reported to have been the first to see. When they married it is said that even 'with his graces of character and manner, he had really no experimental acquaintance with the Gospel.' Possibly Stoddard's problem had more to do with *assurance* than with conversion itself. Between 1670 and April 1672 the question of whether or not he was a Christian was finally resolved for him and it happened when he was in the very act of ministering to others:

One Sabbath as he was at the table administering the Lord's supper, he had a new and wonderful revelation of the Gospel scheme. He caught such a full and glorious view of Christ and his great love for men as shown in his redemptive work, that he was almost overpowered with emotion, and with difficulty went forward with the communion service. By reason of this peculiar experience of his he was led to think, that the place where the soul was likely to receive spiritual light and understanding was at the Lord's table – that there, in a special manner, Christ would be present to reveal himself, in all his fulness of love to the souls of men.[1]

Probably the Northampton congregation was first attracted to Stoddard on account of his exceptional natural abilities, some of which at least were inherited from his father, Anthony Stoddard, Recorder of Boston, and for nineteen years consecutively chosen a representative.[2] Edwards says, 'My grandfather was a very great man, of strong powers of mind, of great grace and authority, of a masterly countenance, speech, and be-

[1] I. N. Tarbox, 'Jonathan Edwards as a Man and the Ministers of the Last Century', *The New Englander*, xxxiii (1884), pp. 625–26, quoted by Ralph J. Coffman, *Solomon Stoddard*, 1978, p. 60. A dependable biography of Stoddard is greatly to be desired. A helpful introduction to some aspects of his thought will be found in an article by Thomas A. Schafer, 'Solomon Stoddard and the Theology of Revival', *A Miscellany of American Christianity*, ed. S. C. Henry, 1963.

[2] Admitted a freeman in 1639, Anthony Stoddard owned two houses and gardens in Boston.

haviour' (1.cxxi). There are two recorded instances of his life being preserved from Indian attack and on at least one of these occasions his deliverance was due to his reputation. Once he was spared by marauding Indians who watched him meditating in an orchard behind the church in Deerfield prior to a service, and, another time, he was allowed to pass through an ambush at Dewey's hole, a point on the road between Northampton and Hatfield. On the latter occasion a Frenchman was taking aim at Stoddard when an Indian beside him, who had previously been among the English, intervened, warning him not to fire because 'that man was Englishman's *God*'.[1]

Stoddard never forgot the lesson of his own premature entrance into the ministry. For him, *experience* of the grace of God was the first necessity in a minister, 'Every learned and moral man,' he would say, 'is not a sincere convert, and so not able to speak exactly and experimentally to such things as souls want to be instructed in. . . . Experience fits men to teach others. . . . ' Certainly he valued his grandson's attainments at Yale but it was a weightier consideration which led him to believe that God had raised Jonathan up to continue the work in Northampton. The church agreed and within three months of Edwards' arrival they secured his permanent settlement. The event is noted in the records of the Town Book under the date, November 21, 1726:

The Town taking into Consideration a vote passed by the Town August 29th last past for the Invitation of the reverend Mr Jonathan Edwards to Assist our Reverend Pastor Mr Stoddard in the work of the Ministry, in order to a Settlement & from what Experience we have had of him by his preaching & conversation as also from his Character from other places.

The Question was put whether it was the mind of the Town that the Committee Should invite the reverend Mr Jonathan Edwards to Settle amongst them in the work of the Ministry and in Convenient Time to take office Amongst them, & it passed in the Affirmative by a very great Majority.

Attest Ebenezer Pomeroy, Moderator.

The succession to Stoddard's eminent pulpit was an event of

[1]T. Dwight, *Travels*, Vol. 1, p. 331.

significance throughout New England and the town and meetinghouse were crowded with ministers and other visitors for Edwards' ordination as 'a Pastour of the Church at Northampton' on February 22, 1727. Perhaps sensing that history was in the making, the Rev. John Williams of Deerfield laid by his copy of the invitation he received from Stoddard

> Northampton, Jan 26, 17^{26}/$_7$
>
> Rev, Sir, – Our Church do desire your presence and attendance at the ordination of Mr Jonathan Edwards this day three weeks.
> Your servant,
> Solomon Stoddard.

In some respects, the fifty-seven years of Stoddard's work in Northampton had seen no great changes in the town. The everyday life of the people remained much as it had been in the previous century. The potential of good soil had been the first attraction when the fortified village had first sprung up on the hill between the forest and the Connecticut river in the 1650's. Sheltered to the South and South-West by the slopes of Mounts Tom and Holyoke and, in its natural situation 'uncommonly pleasant', its farm land and its agriculture made it one of the most important of all the inland towns of New England. Life remained firmly bound to the soil, for, apart from a small circle of trades and professional people, every family still worked on the land in 1727. The original 'town' (about a mile by a mile-and-a-half in 1700) had been divided into 'home lots', frequently of four acres each, with the best alluvial soil, east of the town centre towards the river, reserved as 'common land' and divided by such names as Bark Wigwam, Walnut Trees and Old Rainbow. Rising at dawn, to a breakfast of bread and corn-meal pudding, eaten off pewter or wooden dishes, Northampton men went to work in harmony with the procession of the seasons as their fathers had done. Corn and wheat were sown in spring, calves and lambs were born and cared for, then came hay-making and harvest, and before winter, apples were stored, animals slaughtered, and fields ploughed. Timber felling and wood cutting were constant necessities for building, for furniture and, not least, for heating because there was to be no coal used in New England until after 1830. Such duties as the milking of cows and the feeding of horses were as constant as a household's own mealtimes.

At twelve noon, each day, the meeting house bell brought men back to their homes for dinner, when there was more corn-meal pudding, followed by meat and vegetables. Not until the mid-century did tea and coffee come into general use. Milk, beer and cider were still the traditional drinks. More work followed until nightfall when there was a supper of cold meat, bread and milk. Then prayer and Bible reading, before clay pipes and the drawing of chairs around the fireside on winter's evenings.

Feminine industry was no less regular. In addition to the usual work of a small farm-house, including the making of butter and cheese, New England housewives were able to supply a range of products for family use from homespun, woven on a spinning-wheel, to beds made of wool, corn-husks, or occasionally of feathers. Apart from one general store, and Ebenezer Hunt's hat shop, there seems to have been little else that could be called shops in Northampton. Then the care of children (families had an average of five in the town's second generation) took more time than is commonly given to it today.

In 1727, as in 1670, there was no mail service, and no stage coach, nor would there be any such services for a long time to come. Country life was thus marked by an 'immobility and sameness'. From week to week, and year to year, life went on as usual. Yet it should not be supposed that Northampton was typical of such agricultural communities as were to grow up in many parts of North America beyond the borders of New England. Although the people's 'home-lots' were scattered and 'the town' (in terms of the ground thus allocated) over a mile in diameter, the actual homes – around 180 in number – were built in comparatively close proximity on streets which ran outwards from Round Hill – an elevation in the centre. These streets, being far from straight, resembled in Timothy Dwight's mind 'the claws of a crab', and he reports, 'It has been said that they were laid out by the cows, and that, wherever these animals when going to feed in the forests made their paths, the inhabitants located their streets.' Dwight himself took the view that the origin of Northampton's streets was not quite so haphazard; rather he believed that the driest ground had been selected for houses and that this determined the direction of the paths which were finally to be roads. What is certain is that the settlers, instead of building amidst the scattered fields where they intended to work, determined instead to live close together. Mutual defence against Indian attack was not the principal reason. For the first twenty years of the town's settlement there was indeed no strong threat from Indians. The local tribe, the 'Nonotuc', from whom the land was bought, were always friendly and 'were always considered as having a right to dwell, and to hunt, within the lands which they had sold'. In 1664 they had even been given permission to build a fort within the town. Speaking of the people of Northampton and the Nonotuc, Timothy Dwight further says, 'These Indians they defended, and were defended by them in their turn'. Real Indian danger came from further-afield and in 1704 the town was temporarily overrun though not destroyed.

The close-grouping of the Northampton community was rather the result of a principle carried over from English village life and followed throughout New England. Dependent upon the soil for their livelihood as they were, there were higher considerations which influenced them. For social friendships, for the education of their children in a common school, and, above all, for united public worship, a people had to live together. Timothy Dwight visited other parts of the United States before the end of the eighteenth century and noted the different outlook of farmers where their homes were not close together. He found such scattered settlers to be better acquainted with oxen and horses than with human society, and easily deterred by 'foul weather' or the 'ill state of roads' from hearing such itinerant preachers as might visit their district.

A New-Englander, passing through such settlements, is irresistibly struck with a wide difference between their inhabitants and those of his own country. The scene is changed at once. That intelligence and sociality, that softness and refinement, which prevail among even the plain people of New England, disappear – intelligence bounded by the farm; conversation confined to the price of a horse or the sale of a load of wheat; ignorance at fifty years of age of what is familiarly known by every New-England school-boy . . . all spread over a great proportion of the inhabitants. . . .

New-England presents a direct contrast to this picture. Almost the whole country is covered with villages: and every village has its

[83]

church, and its suit of schools. Nearly every child, even of beggars and blacks, in considerable numbers, can read, write, and keep accounts. Every child is carried to the church from the cradle; nor leaves the church but for the grave. All the people are neighbours: social beings; converse; feel; sympathize; mingle minds; cherish sentiments; and are subjects of at least a degree of refinement. In almost every village are found literary men and social libraries. A great number of men also, addict themselves to reading and acquire extensive information. Of all these advantages the mode of settlement has been one, and, it is believed, a powerful cause.[1]

Although the population of New England lived close to nature, it was the events of redemption which fixed the weekly calendar. On Saturday evenings the Sabbath began at six o'clock according to the New England understanding that the duty required by the Fourth Commandment commenced at nightfall. Almost the whole population would be at the one meeting house on Sunday mornings and again at 2 pm in the afternoon, at which times, it is said, sermons might last for two hours. And not content to wait for weekend, the church also expected a 'lecture' on Thursday afternoons at 2 pm. Communal life indeed revolved around the church and even the town-meetings were held in the meeting house at Northampton until the late 1730's when a separate building was erected for that purpose.

At a later date, writers were to marvel at the colonial New Englander as 'a meeting-going animal' and to deplore the views of the Christian Sabbath which then prevailed. Responding to such criticism, when still in its early stages, Timothy Dwight wrote to a correspondent in England: 'The Sabbath is observed in New England with a greater degree of sobriety and strictness than in any other part of the world. . . . By many Christians of this country the strict observation of the Sabbath is esteemed a privilege and not a burden.' To be released from the obligation to keep one day holy, he argued, would be 'a diminution, not an increase of the blessings given to the Jewish Church'.[2]

But a form of religion, alien to the views of a later age, was so ingrained into the life of eighteenth-century New England that no words of Dwight could relieve later writers of their

[1] *Travels*, 1, pp. 336–38.
[2] *Travels*, 4, pp. 361–2.

impressions of gloom. In his *Three Episodes of Massachusetts History*, Charles Francis Adams, writing in 1892 of such places as Northampton in earlier times, says

The stern conventionalities and narrow modes of thought, the coarse, hard, monotonous existence of the old country town would, to one accustomed to the world of to-day, not only seem intolerable, but actually be so. He would find no newspapers, no mails, no travellers, few books, and those to him wholly unreadable, Sunday the sole holiday, and the church, the tavern and the village store the only places of resort or amusement.[1]

Among the varied interests of earlier New-Englanders which the above quotation omits was the universal training then necessary in military skill and discipline. Every man was – required to possess a musket[2] and the whole population was involved in militia duties. Northampton, like other towns, had its 'training days', when men were mustered and drilled under the eye of the veteran defender of the frontiers, Colonel John Stoddard, son of the pastor and younger brother of Anthony. Commissions in the militia were eagerly sought and such titles as captain, lieutenant and ensign were proudly used by their holders in everyday life.

Probably the business of living had changed little from the time of Stoddard's ordination to that of his grandson in 1727, yet things certainly were not precisely the same, either in the community or in the church.

Between 1670 and 1700 Stoddard had seen Northampton's population grow from 500 to about 1000. Thereafter there was a much smaller addition as land became increasingly scarce and expensive. Between 1700 and 1729 only nine new families moved into the town. The result was that the enlarged population had become a largely closed community by the 1720's. Prospective settlers who supposed that they might earn a living by trade were told that the town was many miles above the head of navigation on the Connecticut River, and warned of 'the charge and trouble in transporting by land near 50 miles'.

[1] *Three Episodes*, 2, pp. 802–3.
[2] Yet Timothy Dwight says, 'I know not a single instance in which arms have been the instruments of carrying on a private quarrel. . . . On a country more peaceful and quiet, it is presumed, the sun never shone'.

Stoddard had also seen a changing mood in Northampton. The people were almost homogeneous English stock – drawn from Essex, Lancashire and other parts of their native land. The hardship and peril of early years had established a strong community spirit. Work and effort were combined in defence, in tillage, in road-making and in much else. Yet, as in the villages of their homeland, upon which much was still patterned, this co-operation did not work on a basis of full equality. Free-holders though New Englanders were, patterns of social status still remained. Thus while the town-meeting could discuss and decide a variety of issues, the 'town-land' which was originally given to the settlement was the responsibility of a group of 'proprietors' – men of stature, related to the town's founders and within whose families the leadership of the town was tenaciously held. Their wealth did not grow at an equal rate with that of others, for often they possessed many acres of the best soil and, with profit proportionate to the surplus which could be sold, it was these same families which grew affluent. Trade was the basis of the town's improved prosperity. Cattle were fattened for the Boston market, grain was sold, and timber could provide tar, turpentine, and potash which became an ingredient for soap.

With the more peaceful years of the eighteenth century, and the corresponding weakening of any danger to their corporate survival, townsmen became more likely to be motivated by individual interests and ambitions. The upkeep of roads ceased to be a common labour (it was now paid for by the town taxes) and even the common lands became of less importance as men struggled to improve and, when they could, to multiply their own acres. Inevitably the gap widened between those at the top and those beneath in the town hierarchy. Northampton records show that while the poorest ten per cent of the population held only two per cent of the land, the richest ten per cent held about one quarter of all the land. Not only as the hereditary proprietors of town land but in much else these chief families in the community exercised their power. Theoretically any townsman might be elected a representative of the General Court of Massachusetts, be chosen a 'selectman', a treasurer, constable or town clerk in local affairs, or a committee-man in the meetinghouse, but during Northampton's first hundred years

[86]

all these offices were shared among only fifty-eight surnames. And only twenty-four surnames served as 'selectmen' for more than two one-year terms.[1] This situation clearly contributed to a weakening of unity long before 1727, and, given the provincial, semi-closed nature of the community it is little wonder that Stoddard had lived to see less harmony than in his early days. Edwards (who writes of this many years later), gives this account of a basic division in the town:

It has been a very great wound to the church of Northampton, that there has been for forty or fifty years, a sort of settled division of the people into two parties, somewhat like the *Court* and *Country party*, in England (if I may compare small things with great). There have been some of the chief men in the town, of chief authority and wealth, that have been great proprietors of their lands, who have had one party with them. And the other party, which has commonly been the greatest, have been of those, who have been jealous of them, apt to envy them, and afraid of their having too much power and influence in town and church (1.cxxxii).

It seems generally to have been the case that prominent men in the community were also leaders in the church. The Strong family, for example, held a monopoly of the tanning trade, and father and son, John and Ebenezer Strong, were two of the three elders which served the church during Stoddard's ministry. Ebenezer Pomeroy, recorder in the Town Book at the time of Edwards' arrival, was one of the richest men in the town, being the blacksmith and gunsmith, as his father, Medad, was before him. Medad Pomeroy had been a deacon of the church from 1675 to his death in 1720 and we shall subsequently note his grandson, Ebenezer Pomeroy Jr., following him in the same office.

With church and community so overlapping, the problems and the benefits of both tended to be common. Contention in the church was far from unknown. Edwards writes:

There were some mighty contests and controversies among them, in Mr Stoddard's day; which were managed with great heat and violence: some great quarrels in the church, wherein Mr Stoddard, great as his authority was, knew not what to do with them. In one

[1]See Patricia Tracy, *Jonathan Edwards, Pastor*, 1980, p. 252.

ecclesiastical controversy in Mr Stoddard's day, wherein the church was divided into two parties, the heat of spirit was raised to such a degree, that it came to hard blows. A member of one party met the head of the opposite party, and assaulted him, and beat him unmercifully (1.cxxxii).

Taken on their own the above quotations would give a very misleading impression of church life under Stoddard. The other side – as Edwards makes clear – is that Christianity had a deep and powerful influence in the community. Much that we take for granted today – such as the existence of a criminal class in society – was unknown in rural New England. One fight was the sensation of a generation. Everyone in Northampton knew that Joseph Hawley, the town lawyer, could never find enough work to live on in that occupation; he was also town merchant, besides, no doubt, his own measure of farming. Hawley, we should also note, was Edwards' uncle. He had married Rebekah, the one Stoddard girl who did not spend all her days in a parsonage.

Writing ten years after his arrival in Northampton, Edwards was to attribute the high moral and religious tone of the community to Stoddard's ministry and he referred to five periods of special spiritual awakening – 'five harvests' was his grandfather's phrase – which saw 'the conversion of many souls'. In each of these times, writes Edwards, 'I have heard my grandfather say, the greater part of the *young* people in the town seemed to be mainly concerned for their eternal salvation' (1.347). In part, as a consequence of these revivals, the percentage of communicant members in Northampton was very different in 1727 from what it had been in the town fifty years earlier.

In 1677 only 35 men and 41 women were communicants. In this respect there was a wide difference between the spiritual strength of the congregation at the time of Stoddard's ordination and that of his grandson. In the 1720's there must have been upwards of four or five hundred communicants. This latter figure, however, requires some qualification. In 1706, despite the earlier revivals, it is said that there were only 46 men and 50 women who were communicant members. Clearly there was an evident slowness among many whom Stoddard considered to be true Christians to make public profession at the

Lord's Table. Troubled at this state of affairs, Stoddard modified his view of what was required to become a communicant. Previously it had been commonly understood that to profess faith in Christ included professing one's experience of Christ; a communicant professed not simply objective truths but also the godliness which those truths entail. Stoddard, no doubt influenced by what had happened to him at the Lord's Table, now came to believe that, provided people possessed Christian knowledge, and lived upright lives, they need not be required to profess anything about *themselves* before becoming communicants. For whatever they might lack could be supplied by Christ himself at the Table. It was better for the church and for the community, Stoddard came to argue, that the qualifications required for communion should be as broad as possible. This change led to a temporary controversy in New England but it soon became widely accepted in the churches and had been long established in Northampton by 1727. The number of communicants in Northampton at the time of Edwards' arrival should not therefore be understood as the equivalent of those who professed to be converted. Edwards may have been struck by the proportion of communicants to the total congregation compared with his father's parish where the old practice still prevailed. But at the age of twenty-three, and with great respect for his grandfather and his church, to accommodate himself to this change was not a problem.

It must, of course, be remembered that a large part of the entire population attended the one church. Given Edwards' figure of two hundred families in Northampton in the 1730's, if the average number of people per family were still seven or if it were six and a quarter (the statistical figure for Hampshire County later in the century), this would give a population of between 1,250 and 1,400. (In 1764 it is known that Northampton had 203 families, in 186 houses, and a total population of close to 1,300).[1] Excluding the sick and aged, and mothers with babies or infants too young to be quiet in church, it is nevertheless surprising how the 42-feet square, boxlike meetinghouse, with its three galleries, could have accommodated

[1] In 1743 the district of Southampton, originally part of Northampton, was formed into a separate town with a population of 76 families (437 people) by 1764.

the numbers which attended. Timothy Dwight (who was a child in the town in the 1750's) says that until the 1780's 'probably no people were ever more punctual in their attendance on public worship'.

Edwards has left no comment on the degree to which his move from Connecticut to Northampton meant a different environment and even some difference in weather. In the opinion of his grandson, Timothy Dwight, the winter here was more uniform than nearer the coast. Snow usually commenced to fall from the middle to the end of December and was to be expected until the 10th to the 20th of March. A snowfall of six feet was recorded at Northampton in 1740. By way of compensation, the same grandson adds, 'A pleasanter spring is not found anywhere in this country, nor a more serene and beautiful autumn'.

For Edwards' first ten months in Northampton he almost certainly lived in the home of his grandparents, Solomon and Esther Stoddard, beside the church on Round (or 'Meetinghouse') Hill. He pays tribute to the benefit he received from his grandfather's public ministry – 'I have reason to bless God for the advantage I had by it' (1.347) – and much help would be gained privately within the household from his friendship and counsel. His grandfather was a born conversationalist and could speak as freely and authoritatively beside his fireside as in the pulpit. Already accustomed himself to be more reserved and of slower speech, Edwards no doubt at this time admired an element in his grandfather upon which he was, many years later, to express a mild criticism: 'Mr Stoddard, though an eminently holy man, was naturally of a dogmatical temper'. Another member of the family, who was often in the Northampton parsonage, records that Stoddard's conversation was 'grave but delightful and very profitable, accompanied with a very sweet affability and a freedom from moroseness.'

Beside the Stoddard parsonage lived Colonel John Stoddard, forty-five years of age in 1727. From the outset he built a friendship with the nephew who was more than twenty years his junior. A man of action and born to lead, John Stoddard was foremost in influence in Northampton even before his father's death. He was Colonel in the militia by 1721 and commander-in-chief of the western Massachusetts frontier by 1744. But, a

Harvard graduate, Colonel Stoddard was much more than the 'Indian fighter' he has sometimes been called. Edwards came to appreciate him as 'one of the first rank' in strength of reason, and 'probably one of the ablest politicians that ever New England bred' (2.38–39). He was a county judge, a representative to the General Court and seven times selectman. 'No man,' writes Timothy Dwight, 'possessed the same weight of character during the last twenty years of his life: and it may be said, almost literally, that "after him men spake not again."' It was in church affairs, however, that John Stoddard became of most personal help to Edwards who writes: 'He was no inconsiderable divine. He was a wise casuist, as I know by the great help I have found from time to time by his judgment and advice in cases of conscience, wherein I have consulted him. And indeed I scarce knew the divine that I ever found more able to help and enlighten the mind in such cases than he.'

*   *   *

Less than a year after his arrival in Northampton Edwards exchanged his grandparents' company for the presence of one who had attracted both his attention, and probably his affections, several years earlier. Such help as he had from others during his life and ministry was limited and impermanent but his marriage to Sarah Pierrepont in New Haven on July 28, 1727, brought a strength and sweetness to his side which was to abide through the next thirty years. As Samuel Miller observes, 'Perhaps no event of Mr Edwards' life had a more close connexion with his subsequent comfort and usefulness than this marriage.' Edwards' first sight of his future wife had probably been in the meetinghouse of the First Church of New Haven (which he attended in the latter part of his student days at Yale) sitting beside her widowed mother, Mary Pierrepont. Pierrepont was a distinguished name. James Pierrepont, the father, had been minister of the New Haven congregation from 1685 until his death in 1714 and was one of the leading men of Connecticut where his services included a prominent part in the foundation of Yale College. A later generation remembered him as 'clear, lively and impressive' in the pulpit, and 'eminent in the gift of prayer.' When it is added that Mary Pierrepont was herself a grand-daughter of Thomas Hooker, it can be seen that the home into which Sarah had been born on January 9, 1710, was rich in spiritual privileges. She was four when her father died and only eight when the tall, pale student from East Windsor first came to reside beside the Green at New Haven. Yet even at that age she had known 'the life and power of religion', being, as Dwight says, 'a rare example of early piety.' Edwards' first reference to her is a paragraph, which he wrote for his own satisfaction in 1723 on a leaf in one of his student books. He was then twenty and she but thirteen:

They say there is a young lady in New Haven who is beloved of that Great Being who made and rules the world, and that there are certain seasons in which this Great Being, in some way or other invisible, comes to her and fills her mind with exceeding sweet delight, and that she hardly cares for any thing, except to meditate on him – that she expects after a while to be received up where he is, to be raised up out of the world and caught up into heaven; being assured that he loves her too well to let her remain at a distance from him always. There she is to dwell with him, and to be ravished with his love and delight for ever. Therefore, if you present all the world before her, with the richest of its treasures, she disregards it and cares not for it, and is unmindful of any pain or affliction. She has a strange sweetness in her mind, and singular purity in her affections; is most just and conscientious in all her conduct; and you could not persuade her to do anything wrong or sinful, if you would give her all the world, lest she should offend this Great Being. She is of a wonderful sweetness, calmness and universal benevolence of mind; specially after this great God has manifested himself to her mind. She will sometimes go about from place to place, singing sweetly; and seems to be always full of joy and pleasure; and no one knows for what. She loves to be alone, walking in the fields and groves, and seems to have some one invisible always conversing with her.

Not a fragment remains to tell us how their friendship ripened to the wedding day of four years later. Possibly, if certain short-hand entries made in his Diary had been deciphered before that document was lost, we should have known more, and, as already suggested, it may be that awakened affection had something to do with the occasions when diverting thoughts 'violently beset' him in 1723 and later. Be this as it may, there is no question about the joy in Northampton on the summer day in 1727 when Edwards returned there with his seventeen-year-old bride. When the congregation had settled his salary at one hundred pounds[1] a year they had also allocated him three hundred pounds for the purchase of a homestead, ten acres of pasture land 'against Slowbridge', and forty more acres five miles up the river. With this provision Edwards bought the home which was to be the scene of so many of the happiest years of their lives.

The financial arrangements made for Edwards' settlement reflected the prevailing view of the importance of the Christian ministry. The church had stipulated, as noted in the Town Record, that Edwards' support should be 'Suitable and well adapted to that honourable office.' No one therefore questioned the standing apart of the Edwards' home in its own ground on a track which ran eastwards from the church. In later years it was to be named 'King Street' but in the 1730's it was only a rural lane on the edge of the community.

Here Sarah Edwards welcomed for the first time her husband's many relations with a hospitality for which the Edwards' parsonage was to become proverbial. Uncles and aunts, cousins, sisters and brothers-in-law, came from near and far.

In 1728 there came the first entry of a new generation in the Family Bible. Beneath the record of their wedding, and his wife's date of birth, Edwards wrote:

My daughter Sarah was born on a Sabbath Day, between 2 and 3 o'clock in the afternoon. Aug. 25, 1728.

The following February Solomon Stoddard died and was mourned throughout New England. In Boston Benjamin Colman reminded his hearers that Stoddard was 'a Prophet and a Father not only to the neighbouring churches, and pastors of his own country, but also to those of the whole land. . . . He was a Peter among the disciples and ministers of our Lord Jesus; very much our Primate and Prince among us,

---

[1]It is not surprising that the monetary system in 'old tenour' currency should be so difficult for us to follow when even Edwards' grandson, Timothy Dwight, writes, 'The exact value of the currency at this time I am unable to ascertain'.

in an evangelical and truly apostolic sense'.

The funeral sermon was preached at Northampton by William Williams, senior minister of the Hampshire Association. Several months before that event the full preaching and pastoral responsibilities had fallen on Edwards, and experience confirmed what he already believed, that it was no light thing to prepare three sermons a week for a people 'well instructed, having had a name, for a long time, for a very knowing people.' Significantly, perhaps, his sole diary entry in 1728 reads: 'I think Christ has recommended rising early in the morning by his rising from the grave very early.' Edwards needed every hour he could find. Like many other ministers, he probably experienced more difficulties in sermon preparation in his early years than later on. Dwight reports that in the spring of 1729 his health, 'in consequence of too close application, so far failed him that he was obliged to be absent from his people several months.' Time was spent with his wife and the baby at New Haven and then at East Windsor before they were welcomed back enthusiastically in the late summer, finding that in their absence, 'a good large barn' had been built for them. Timothy Edwards wrote to one of Jonathan's sisters on September 12, 'The people of Northampton seem to have a great love and respect for him', and a month later he reported hearing a 'Very comfortable account of your brother, who now hath for a considerable [time] preached both parts of the day, and done the whole work of the ministry.'

Edwards' summer visit to East Windsor in 1729 was to be his last meeting with Jerusha, the nineteen-year-old sister with whom he had always felt the closest friendship. In temperament there was some difference between them; she 'was sprightly and active, and had an uncommon share of native wit and humour', yet in spiritual things they were one. Jerusha, we are told, looked upon such duties as prayer and reading the Bible not as 'a prescribed task, but a coveted enjoyment . . . to her no society was so delightful as solitude with God. She read theology with the deepest interest. . . . Her observance of the sabbath was exemplary and in the solemn and entire devotion of her mind to the duties of the sanctuary, she appeared, habitually, to feel with David, "Holiness becometh thine house for ever".' There were occasions in her Christian life when her experience could be best described in a line from Isaac Watts,

And sudden, from the cleaving skies, a gleam of glory broke,

and so it was to be at the end. A day or two before her death in December 1729, as her mind wandered heavenwards, contemplating God's grace in Christ, she exclaimed to herself, 'It is wonderful, it surprises me.'

On April 26 of the following year, Edwards hurried home from the Sabbath afternoon service to find that a second daughter had been safely born ['towards the conclusion of the afternoon exercise', he noted in the Family Bible]. She was named 'Jerusha' after her aunt, and in both life and death the two resembled each other.

No contemporary accounts exist of the first impression which Edwards made at Northampton. He was quieter than his grandfather both in the pulpit and elsewhere. If he read his sermons, as he seems to have done at this date, there were no complaints. The people noticed that, unlike many ministers, he did not intend to be a part-time farmer, yet even so he seemed to have no time on his hands. From the outset it was not his custom to pull up his horse and pass the time of day with his many parishioners. The world of crops and cattle was clearly not his principal interest. He lived somewhat apart and socially he was clearly related to the men who wore white shirts rather than the common chequered ones. Yet, judging by Timothy Edwards' letter of September 1729 already quoted, the people were well-pleased three years after Edwards' settlement. Sarah's brother, Benjamin, was often in Northampton at that time and it was he who supplied the news to the family at East Windsor that the people of Northampton 'take great content in his ministry.'

The beginnings of Northampton's new ministry were full of hope.

6

THE GREEN VALLEY OF HUMILIATION

Edwards' Parsonage at Northampton, reproduced from
The Sunday at Home *No. 1165, August 26 1876.*

It was that we might know ourselves to be wholly in the hands of this God of perfect righteousness and goodness – not in those of men, whether ourselves or some other men – that he was so earnest for the doctrine of predestination: which is nothing more than the declaration of the supreme dominion of God. It was that our eternal felicity might hang wholly on God's mighty love – and not on our sinful weakness – that he was so zealous for the doctrine of election: which is nothing more than the ascription of our entire salvation to God. As he contemplated the majesty of this Sovereign Father of men, his whole being bowed in reverence before Him, and his whole heart burned with zeal for His glory. As he remembered that this great God has become in His own Son the Redeemer of sinners, he passionately gave himself to the proclamation of the glory of His grace. Into His hands he committed himself without reserve: his whole spirit panted to be in all its movement subjected to His government – or, to be more specific, to the 'leading of His Spirit.' All that was good in him, all the good he hoped might be formed in him, he ascribed to the almighty working of this Divine Spirit.

BENJAMIN B. WARFIELD
Calvin and Calvinism, 1931, p. 23

He looked upon those who called themselves Calvinists, that were for palliating the matter by, as it were, trimming off the knots of Calvinism, that they might conform it more to the taste of those who are most disposed to object against it, [as men who] were really giving up and betraying the cause they pretended to espouse.

SAMUEL HOPKINS
Life of Jonathan Edwards, p. 52

6

dwards opened a sermon in the 1730's with the words, 'It is the manner of God before he bestows any signal mercy on the people, first to prepare them for it' (2.57). In the exposition which followed, as in a number of other discourses of that period, he went on to indicate the nature of the change required if the gospel was to prosper among the many who were as yet 'unresolved in religion.'

At the same time he was himself being prepared. Convictions were being confirmed and feelings deepened which were to exercise a controlling influence in subsequent years. For light on this subject we are again dependent upon his 'Personal Narrative.' While telling us almost nothing of his outward life, the document gives us the key to his mind and, as Cromwell once told the English Parliament, 'The mind is the man.'

The 1730's are the last decade covered in the 'Personal Narrative' for it breaks off finally in 1739. Throughout the pages of his autobiographical record the personal knowledge of God is the main theme and this remains the case after his settlement in Northampton:

Since I came to this town, I have often had sweet complacency in God, in views of his glorious perfections and the excellency of Jesus Christ. God has appeared to me a glorious and lovely Being, chiefly on account of his holiness. The holiness of God has always appeared to me the most lovely of all his attributes. . . . I have loved the doctrines of the gospel; they have been to my soul like green pastures.

The gospel has seemed to me the richest treasure; the treasure that I have most desired, and longed that it might dwell richly in me. The way of salvation by Christ has appeared, in a general way, glorious and excellent, most pleasant and most beautiful. It has often seemed to me that it would in a great measure spoil heaven to receive it in any other way. . . .

Sometimes, only mentioning a single word caused my heart to burn within me; or only seeing the name of Christ, or the name of some attribute of God. And God has appeared glorious to me on account of the Trinity. It has made me have exalting thoughts of God, that he subsists in three persons; the Father, Son and Holy Ghost. The sweetest joys and delights I have experienced, have not been those that have arisen from a hope of my own good estate, but in a direct view of the glorious things of the gospel.

Once, as I rode out into the woods for my health, in 1737, having alighted from my horse in a retired place, as my manner commonly has been, to walk for divine contemplation and prayer, I had a view that for me was extraordinary, of the glory of the Son of God, as Mediator between God and man, and his wonderful, great, full, pure and sweet grace and love, and meek and gentle condescension. This grace that appeared so calm and sweet, appeared also great above the heavens. The person of Christ appeared ineffably excellent with an excellency great enough to swallow up all thought and conception – which continued, as near as I can judge, about an hour; which kept me the greater part of the time in a flood of tears and weeping aloud. I felt an ardency of soul to be, what I know not otherwise how to express, emptied and annihilated; to lie in the dust, and to be full of Christ alone; to love Him with a holy and pure love; to trust in Him; to live upon Him; to serve and follow Him; and to be perfectly sanctified and made pure, with a divine and heavenly purity. I have, several other times, had views very much of the same nature, and which have had the same effects (1.xlvi–xlvii).

Such experiences of holy joy are reminiscent of Edwards at the beginning of his Christian life, but at this stage of his life there also appears a depth of conscious unworthiness and spiritual need which he had not known in those early years. Certainly, at the outset, he had felt conviction of sin: 'While at New York, I was sometimes much affected with reflections of my past life, considering how late it was before I began to be truly religious, and how wickedly I had lived till then.' The conviction, however, was incomplete. It related almost entirely to his past, while in the present he had anticipated constant

progress in holiness and was 'continually studying and contriving for likely ways and means' to achieve this goal. Later,
while he was far from repudiating the earnestness of those
first-days, he came to see more about himself than he had been
aware of at the time he penned his resolutions. He had pursued
holiness, he subsequently reflected: 'with far greater diligence
and earnestness than ever I pursued anything in my life, but yet
with too great a dependence on my own strength, which
afterwards proved a great damage to me. My experience had
not then taught me, as it has done since, my extreme feebleness
and impotence, every manner of way; and the bottomless
depths of secret corruption and deceit there was in my heart.'

The year before he settled in Northampton he had resolved
in his Diary, 'To set apart days of meditation on particular
subjects; as, sometimes, to set apart a day for the consideration
of the greatness of my sins.' The lesson, however, became the
subject not for days but years. In *Pilgrim's Progress*, John
Bunyan relates how Christiana and her children were led
'down the hill into the Valley of Humiliation.' Edwards was
now taken by the same path:

Often, since I lived in this town, I have had very affecting views of my
own sinfulness and vileness; very frequently to such a degree as to
hold me in a kind of loud weeping, sometimes for a considerable time
together; so that I have often been forced to shut myself up. I have had
a vastly greater sense of my own wickedness, and the badness of my
heart, than ever I had before my conversion. It has often appeared to
me that if God should mark iniquity against me I should appear the
very worst of all mankind – of all that have been, since the beginning
of the world to this time, and that I should have by far the lowest place
in hell.

My wickedness, as I am in myself, has long appeared to me
perfectly ineffable, and swallowing up all thought and imagination;
like an infinite deluge or mountains over my head. I know not how to
express better what my sins appear to me to be than by heaping
infinite upon infinite, and multiplying infinite by infinite. Very often,
for these many years, these expressions are in my mind, and in my
mouth, 'Infinite upon infinite . . . Infinite upon infinite!'[1] When I

[1]Other evangelical leaders, subsequent to Edwards, have found his
language appropriate for themselves. In a letter in 1771 Henry Venn writes:
'I sympathize with you in the feeling of a heart desperately wicked. Once I
thought some humiliating expressions of the saints of God too low for me –

look into my heart, and take a view of my wickedness, it looks like an abyss infinitely deeper than hell.

I have greatly longed of late for a broken heart, and to lie low before God; and, when I ask for humility, I cannot bear the thoughts of being no more humble than other Christians. It seems to me, that though their degrees of humility may be suitable for them, yet it would be a vile self-exaltation in me, not to be the lowest in humility of all mankind. Others speak of their longing to be 'humbled to the dust'; that may be a proper expression for them, but I always think of myself, that I ought, and it is an expression that has long been natural for me to use in prayer, 'to lie infinitely low before God.' And it is affecting to think, how ignorant I was, when a young Christian, of the bottomless, infinite depths of wickedness, pride, hypocrisy and deceit, left in my heart.

Sixty years before Edwards wrote these words, Bunyan had described the Valley of Humiliation as rich and green: 'I have known many labouring men that have got good estates in this Valley of Humiliation (for "God resisteth the proud, but giveth grace to the humble"); for indeed it is a very fruitful soil, and doth bring forth by handfuls.' One who prospered there, says the Puritan allegorist, was Mr. Fearing: 'I never saw him better in all his pilgrimage than he was in that valley. Here he would lie down, embrace the ground, and kiss the very flowers that grew in this valley.'

So it was also with Edwards, and of the benefits which came to him in this condition none was greater than his deepening awareness that only sovereign, divine grace can achieve and guarantee salvation. He learned by experience, as others had done before him, that while those who have little awareness of the real nature of sin may assert man's ability to repent and believe, to hate sin and love God, those who know the true

---

proud, blind wretch as I was! Now I can say, with Edwards, "Infinite upon infinite only reaches to my sinfulness".' Horatius Bonar, an ardent reader of Edwards in his early ministry, employed the same phrase in his well-known hymn, 'No, not despairingly, Come I to thee':

> Ah, mine iniquity
>   Crimson has been;
> Infinite, infinite,
>   Sin upon sin . . .

The words have a biblical basis in the A.V. rendering of Job 22.5.

condition of human nature can find comfort only in the knowledge that God saves by his sovereign good pleasure and for the praise of the glory of his grace. Spiritual experience and sound theology go together. Accordingly, the Reformers, and the Puritans after them, had attributed opposition to the doctrines of grace as evidence of spiritual ignorance. 'The Papist', wrote William Perkins, 'ascribes his conversion not wholly to grace, but partly to grace, and partly to nature, or the strength of man's will helped by grace.'[1] He did so because he lacked a true knowledge of sin.

This explanation of the reason why the 'Calvinistic' aspect of biblical theology is so commonly unwelcome to men harmonizes with the evidence of Edwards' own personal history. In his youth, he tells us, he had no sympathy at all with the idea that God appoints men to salvation: 'From my childhood up, my mind had been full of objections against the doctrine of God's sovereignty in choosing whom he would to eternal life, and rejecting whom he pleased; leaving them eternally to perish, and be everlastingly tormented in hell. It used to appear like a horrible doctrine to me.' Following his conversion he found his objections silenced, and he came to a new conviction upon the subject: 'But I have often, since that first conviction, had quite another kind of sense of God's sovereignty than I had then. I have often since had not only a conviction, but a delightful conviction. The doctrine has very often appeared exceeding pleasant, bright and sweet. Absolute sovereignty is what I love to ascribe to God. But my first conviction was not so.'

As we have already indicated, the development of his convictions came with his heart-felt awareness of the power and desert of sin. Men must be saved by sovereign mercy or not at all, and the more he saw of *this* way of salvation – God giving grace to those who had no claim or right – the more he saw his own dependence upon it:

It appears to me that were it not for free grace, exalted and raised up to the infinite height of all the fulness and glory of the great Jehovah, and the arm of his power and grace stretched forth in all the majesty of his power, and in all the glory of his sovereignty, I should appear sunk

[1] *A Commentarie Upon the first five Chapters of the Epistle to the Galatians*, 1617, p. 308.

down in my sins below hell itself – far beyond the sight of every thing but the eye of sovereign grace that can pierce even down to such a depth. And yet it seems to me, that my conviction of sin is exceeding small, and faint; it is enough to amaze me, that I have no more sense of my sin. . . .

I have a much greater sense of my universal, exceeding dependence on God's grace and strength, and mere good pleasure, of late, than I used formerly to have; and have experienced more of an abhorrence of my own righteousness. The very thought of any joy arising in me, on any consideration of my own amiableness, performances, or experiences, or any goodness of heart or life, is nauseous and detestable to me. And yet I am greatly afflicted with a proud and self-righteous spirit, much more sensibly than I used to be formerly. I see that serpent rising and putting forth its head continually, everywhere, all around me.

Though it seems to me, that, in some respects, I was a far better Christian, for two or three years after my first conversion, than I am now; and lived in a more constant delight and pleasure; yet, of late years, I have had a more full and constant sense of the absolute sovereignty of God, and a delight in that sovereignty; and have had more of a sense of the glory of Christ, as a Mediator revealed in the gospel (I.xlviii).[1]

Edwards' spiritual life was deeply affected by his belief that God owes salvation to no one and that he may justly withhold pardon from any. The doctrines of election and preterition teach that pardon is not a divine duty and, as W. G. T. Shedd writes, wherever this truth is rightly received it must have a practical effect: 'Without it, some of the indispensable characteristics of a genuine Christian experience are impossible. Hence it is that St. Paul continually employs it in producing true repentance for sin, deep humility before God, utter self-distrust, sole reliance on Christ's sacrifice, and a cheering hope and confidence of salvation, founded not on the sinner's ability and what God owes him, but on God's gracious and unobliged purpose and covenant. This is the doctrine which elicits from him the rapturous exclamation, "O the depth of the riches both of the wisdom and knowledge of God. For who hath first given to him, and it shall be recompensed unto him again? For of him, and through him, and to him are all things: to whom be glory

---

[1]This kind of experience was commonly commented on in Puritan theology. 'After conversion we need bruising,' wrote Richard Sibbes, 'to let us see that we live by mercy'. *Works*, I, p. 44.

for ever. Amen." This is the doctrine which instructs the believer to ascribe all his holy acts, even the act of faith itself, to the unmerited and sovereign grace of his redeeming God.'[1]

The high degree of importance which Edwards came to attach to Calvinistic belief was to have far-reaching consequences for his whole ministry.

In the first place, it affected his over-all assessment of the need of the Church in the eighteenth century. A hundred years earlier, the Puritans had argued that Arminianism – that is to say the belief that God loves all men equally, and that the reception of the benefits of Christ's redemption depends upon the right use of man's free-will – was a serious distortion of the gospel and that it would necessarily lead to a superficial, worldly Christianity. But before the end of the seventeenth century a noticeable change of attitude over this controversy had occurred in England. It was not so much that the descendants of the Puritans wished to sanction the distinctive tenets of Arminianism; they simply doubted whether the whole subject was worthy of continued attention. Reflecting on the new mood John Owen had said in a fast-day sermon in London in 1676:

Little did I think I should ever have lived in this world to find the minds of professors grown altogether indifferent as to the doctrine of God's eternal election, the sovereign efficacy of grace in the conversion of sinners, justification by the imputation of the righteousness of Christ; but many are, as to all these things, grown to an indifferency: they know not whether they are so or not. I bless God I know something of the former generation, when professors would not hear of these things without the highest detestation; and now high professors begin to be leaders in it: and it is too much among the best of us. We are not so much concerned for the truth as our forefathers; I wish I could say we were as holy.[2]

Notwithstanding such warnings, indefiniteness with respect to strict Calvinism became the new order. By Edwards' day the profession of orthodoxy was still general in New England – as late as 1726 Cotton Mather believed there was no Arminian minister in Boston – but the attitude which Owen reprobated had taken firm hold, and open opposition to the old theology

[1] *Calvinism: Pure and Mixed*, W. G. T. Shedd, 1986 reprint (Banner of Truth), p. 55.
[2] *Works of John Owen*, 9, p. 327.

was not far away. There were too many ministers of the spirit of Benjamin Wadsworth, the ultra-conciliatory president of Harvard, and of Edward Wigglesworth, who was in 'no ways rigid in his attachment to any scheme.' Another New England representative of moderation was Edward Holyoke who had this fashionable compliment expressed about him by a friend: 'I think Mr Holyoke as orthodox a Calvinist as any man; though I look upon him as too much of a gentleman, and of too catholic a temper, to cram his principles down another man's throat.'[1]

By the 1730's Edwards was in open disagreement with the judgment of such temperate brethren. 'There is very little appearance of zeal for the mysterious and spiritual doctrines of Christianity', he wrote in 1739, and this he took to be a sure sign of the low state of religion. Moreover, he saw, as Owen before him, that Christianity itself could not long be upheld if concessions were made to accommodate objections to Calvinism. The danger from Arminianism lay not simply in a few particular errors but in its whole tendency. While it claimed to be based upon Scripture the popular strength of its arguments depended on the contention that Calvinistic belief is not reconcilable with human reason: How, its exponents asked, can a sovereign election be reconciled with God's universal compassion? or the unchangeable purpose of God in salvation with man's free agency? This mode of argument by-passed two facts; first, that reason is 'impaired, depraved and corrupted', and second, that 'the gospel requires men to believe things above reason merely on the authority of divine revelation.' If all the doctrines 'which have anything of spiritual mystery in them and so not absolutely reconcilable unto reason as corrupt and carnal' were judged as Arminianism judges the doctrine of sovereign grace, how much Christianity would remain?[2] By the very same procedure Arianism would displace the mystery of

---

[1] Quoted by Perry Miller, *Jonathan Edwards*, 1959, p. 24.

[2] The argument, as here stated, is John Owen's in his *Nature and Causes of Apostasy from the Gospel*, 1676 [*Works*, vol. 7]. Cotton Mather in his *Magnalia Christi Americana*, sharing Owen's viewpoint, says: 'The last words of the most renowned prebend of Canterbury, Dr Peter du Moulin, who died a very old man, about eleven years ago, were, "Since Calvinism is cried down, Christianity is in danger to be lost in the English nation".' *Magnalia*, vol. 1, 1852 edition, p. 251.

the twofold nature of Christ in one Person, and Socinianism would empty the atonement of its glory.

The first indication that Edwards' convictions on this issue were going to be heard far beyond Northampton came in 1731. In that year, at the age of twenty-eight, he had the distinction of being invited to give the Public Lecture in Boston on July 8. We may be sure that he preached to a packed congregation and in the presence of not a few of the leading ministers of Massachusetts. The text he chose was 1 Corinthians 1.29–31, 'That no flesh should glory in his presence . . .' and the doctrine to be expounded was set out in the words, 'God is glorified in the work of redemption in this, that there appears in it so absolute and universal a dependence of the redeemed on God for all their good.' It was the full-orbed old theology, spiritually presented, powerfully urged and, at the close, applied against 'those doctrines and schemes of divinity that are in any respect opposite to such an absolute and universal dependence on God.' We are dependent upon God, he argued, not only for redemption itself but for our *faith* in the Redeemer,[1] not only for the gift of his Son but for the Holy Ghost for our conversion:

Man is naturally exceeding prone to exalt himself and depend on his own power or goodness, as though from himself he must expect happiness.

He is prone to have respect to enjoyments alien from God and his Spirit, as those in which happiness is to be found. But this doctrine should teach us to exalt God *alone*; as by trust and reliance, so by praise. *Let him that glorieth, glory in the Lord.* Hath any man hope that he is converted, and sanctified, and that his mind is endowed with true excellency and spiritual beauty? that his sins are forgiven, and he received into God's favour, and exalted to the honour and blessedness of being his child, and an heir of eternal life? let him give God all the glory who alone makes him to differ from the worst of men in this world, or the most miserable of the damned in hell.

No doubt some who heard the youthful Edwards on that summer's day in 1731 regarded him as a mere echo of the past. But the two Boston ministers who had the sermon published,

[1] This point always lies at the heart of controversy between Arminianism and biblical theology. As Perkins writes, 'We are not elected (as some teach) either for our faith, or according to our faith, but to our faith, that is, elected that we might believe'. *Commentarie on Galatians*, p. 271.

Thomas Prince and William Cooper, recognized the significance of the event and prayerfully anticipated the possibility
that 'by the blessing of Heaven' the colleges of New England
might yet be 'a fruitful mother of many such sons as the author'
(2.2). *God Glorified in Man's Dependence* was the first of Edwards'
published works.

*　　*　　*

By the mid-1730's those who feared that Harvard was con-
tributing to a doctrinal weakening had more definite evidence
for their opinion. In October 1733, Benjamin Kent, a Harvard
graduate, was ordained at Marlborough, Massachusetts.
Almost immediately he was charged with being a 'profest
Arminian' and these charges were sustained by the Marlborough association of ministers in February 1735. The
Council advised that Kent be suspended. Much nearer to
Northampton a similar controversy began in 1734. As mentioned earlier, ministers of Hampshire County had been
organized into an Association by Solomon Stoddard in 1714.
By the 1730's various such Associations were a regular part of
the church life of New England, providing a bond of fellowship
for ministers and a means of more corporate oversight over the
churches. It was by no means unknown for senior ministers in
Associations to hinder the settlement of a pastor when they
deemed it justified. In 1730 Benjamin Pierrepont, Edwards'
brother-in-law who was then living at the Northampton
parsonage, had been invited to the pastorate at Deerfield in the
same county. Edwards' uncle, the Rev. William Williams of
Hatfield, disapproved and he was a powerful figure whose
abilities, in the opinion of some, even exceeded those of
Stoddard. Pierrepont, Williams believed, was 'vain, apish, and
jovial, particularly among females'. The invitation to Sarah's
brother was revoked and he had to return to New Haven.

In 1734, also in Hampshire County, a far more controversial
case arose. Robert Breck, a Harvard graduate and not yet
twenty-one, was asked to preach in the First Parish in
Springfield with a view to his settlement. Concerned at Breck's
apparently weak doctrinal stance, the Hampshire Association
intervened in an attempt to stop a call. It was perhaps their
action and the opposition which it aroused which revealed that

even in Hampshire County there was a readiness for theological change on the part of some. Details to give us a complete picture are lacking but clearly what Edwards calls the 'lamentable Springfield contention' began about the same time as controversy over the error which Breck was alleged to favour: 'About this time,' Edwards writes, 'began the great noise, in this part of the country, about Arminianism, which seemed to appear with a very threatening aspect upon the interest of religion here' (1.347). Towards the end of 1734, to counter any doubts among his own people, Edwards began to preach directly on doctrines involved in the dispute with Arminianism. We shall have occasion to notice this again but for the moment our subject is the Breck case. After protracted debate and, finally, the intervention of the Massachusetts General Assembly, the Hampshire Association was overruled in its opposition to Breck's settlement and he was duly installed at Springfield. Edwards, it must be said, did not lead the opposition to Breck – once more, it was his uncle, William Williams of Hatfield who acted as chief guardian for the Association. He took, however, the principal hand in writing in justification of the Association, *A Narrative and Defence of the Proceedings of the Ministers of the County of Hampshire* (1736). The book became a reminder of differences now established within Hampshire County and thereafter there would always be an unsympathetic attitude to Edwards in Springfield's First Parish where Breck remained until his death in 1784.

In the mid' 1730's there was also another difference emerging in the county which, in the long term, was to prove of major personal significance for Edwards. This concerned an estrangement between him and the family of his uncle, William Williams. Information is lacking on the nature and origins of this family division. Some have surmised that it went back to Mrs. Williams' (Christian Stoddard's) childhood at Northampton when, it is supposed, she and her sister, Esther (Edwards' mother) were not close to one another. As noted above, Edwards worked publicly with William Williams, who was seventy in 1735, and there is no evidence to support the allegation that the older man regarded him, in the words of C. C. Goen, as 'his upstart nephew'.[1] In personal correspondence

[1] J E (Yale) 4, p. 37.

Edwards refers to the minister of Hatfield as 'honored Uncle Williams', and when he preached his funeral sermon in 1741 he spoke in words of high esteem (2.967–8). In a footnote to that sermon, when published, Edwards added a message of his uncle's after Williams had attended his last Association meeting: 'I do not expect to be with you another Association meeting: but I give you this advice, Love your master, love your work, and love one another'. Upon this Edwards comments, 'How very expressive of his own spirit! Like John the beloved disciple'.

It may be that it was some of the children of William and Christian Williams who were chiefly involved in the breach with their cousin at Northampton. They were certainly responsible for continuing it, and, notably Israel Williams, and his sister, Dorothy, who married the Rev. Jonathan Ashley, minister at Deerfield. Although only twenty-six in 1735, Israel Williams was already an influential figure in the community. A graduate of Harvard in 1727, he seems to have been imperious from his youth. As early as 1733 he was a selectman in Hatfield and to this position he was annually re-elected until 1763. S. E. Dwight believed that it was Israel Williams, particularly, to whom Edwards was referring when, speaking of his preaching against Arminianism in 1734, he said, 'Great fault was found with "meddling" with the controversy in the pulpit' (1.347). Dwight may have had some information which he suppressed when he wrote his biography of Edwards in the 1820's. He avoids naming the family about whose criticisms of Edwards he tells us a good deal, but it is the Williamses of whom he writes when he says of the years 1734–35

Among those who opposed Mr Edwards on this occasion, were several members of a family, in a neighbouring town, nearly connected with his own, and possessing, from its numbers, wealth, and respectability, a considerable share of influence. Their religious sentiments differed widely from his,[1] and their opposition to him, in the course which he now pursued, became direct and violent. As his defence of his own opinions was regarded as triumphant, they appear to have felt, in some degree, the shame and mortification of a defeat; and their opposition to Mr Edwards, though he resorted to every honourable method of conciliation, became on their part, a settled personal hostility. It is probable that their advice to Mr Edwards to

[1]This cannot have been true of William Williams, senior.

[110]

refrain from the controversy, and particularly, not to publish his sentiments with regard to it, was given somewhat categorically, and with a full expectation that he, young as he was, would comply with it. His refusal so to do, was an offence not to be forgiven (1.xliii fn).

In the fourteen years following 1735, although always passing the Edwards' home on his frequent visits to Northampton, Israel Williams 'refused except in three instances to enter his door, though Mr. Edwards regularly called on him and his family'.[1] The domineering Israel Williams, who was to spend his life as a successful merchant at Hatfield, was scarcely an exponent of the brotherly love which Edwards saw in his father. After old William Williams was laid to rest, the estrangement, as we shall see, only deepened.

[1]Dwight, p. 434.

A Faithful

NARRATIVE

OF THE

Surprizing Work of GOD

IN THE

CONVERSION

OF

Many HUNDRED SOULS in *Northampton*, and the Neighbouring Towns and Villages of ~~New~~-*Hampſhire* in *New-England.*

In a LETTER to the Rev^d. Dr. BENJAMIN COLMAN of *Boſton.*

Written by the Rev^d. Mr. EDWARD^s, Miniſter of *Northampton,* on *Nov.* 6. 1736

And Publiſhed,

With a Large PREFACE,

By Dr. WATTS and Dr. GUYSE.

LONDON:
Printed for JOHN OSWALD, at the *Roſe and Crown*, in the *Poultry,* near *Stocks-Market.* M.DCC.XXXVII.

Price ſtitch'd 1 s. Bound in Calf-Leather, 1 s. 6 d.

Title page of A Faithful Narrative, *1737*

THE BREAKING OF THE SPIRIT OF SLUMBER

The Tennent Church at Neshaminy Creek, Pennsylvania, in the Presbytery of Philadelphia North. The 'Log College' established by William Tennent Sr. was about a mile from the Church.

Wheresoever God works with power for salvation upon the minds of men, there will be some discoveries of a sense of sin, of the danger of the wrath of God, and the all-sufficiency of his Son Jesus to relieve us under all our spiritual wants and distresses.

ISAAC WATTS and JOHN GUYSE in their Preface
to <i>A Faithful Narrative of the Surprising Work of God</i>,
1737, J E (1.345)

The most successful method of preaching is that which aims at thorough and radical *convictions* of sin. The law must be applied with power to the conscience, or the preciousness of grace will be very inadequately known.

JAMES HENLEY THORNWELL,
Collected Writings, 2, p. 100

7

ixteen years after the last local revival in Northampton of 1718, and in the eighth year after his settlement in the town, Edwards witnessed the first period of uncommon spiritual power and success under his own ministry. 'Then it was', he wrote in his *Faithful Narrative of the Surprising Work of God*, 'in the latter part of December [1734], that the Spirit of God began extraordinarily to set in, and wonderfully to work amongst us: and there were, very suddenly, one after another, five or six persons, who were to all appearances savingly converted.'

In the opening weeks of 1735, he continues, 'A great and earnest concern about the great things of religion, and the eternal world, became universal in all parts of the town and among persons of all degrees and all ages. All other talk but about spiritual and eternal things was soon thrown by; all the conversation, in all companies and upon all occasions, was upon these things only, unless so much as was necessary for people carrying on their ordinary secular business. . . . The minds of people were wonderfully taken off from the world, it was treated amongst us as a thing of very little consequence.' Such a change in conviction speedily produced a visible difference in the life of the town:

When once the Spirit of God began to be so wonderfully poured out in a general way through the town, people had soon done with their old quarrels, backbitings, and intermeddling with other men's matters. The tavern was soon left empty and persons kept very much at home;

none went abroad unless on necessary business, or on some religious account, and every day seemed in many respects like a Sabbath-day. The place of resort was now altered, it was no longer the tavern, but the minister's house that was thronged far more than ever the tavern had been wont to be. (1.351)

The greatest change of all appeared in the meetinghouse itself:

Our public assemblies were then beautiful: the congregation was alive in God's service, everyone earnestly intent on the public worship, every hearer eager to drink in the words of the minister as they came from his mouth; the assembly in general were, from time to time, in tears while the Word was preached; some weeping with sorrow and distress, others with joy and love, others with pity and concern for the souls of their neighbours.

Our public praises were then greatly enlivened; God was then served in our psalmody, in some measure, in the beauty of holiness. It has been observable that there has been scarce any part of divine worship wherein good men amongst us have had grace so drawn forth, and their hearts so lifted up in the ways of God, as in singing his praises. . . .

Persons after their conversion often speak of religious things as seeming new to them: that preaching is a new thing: that it seems to them they never heard preaching before; that the Bible is a new book: they find there new chapters, new psalms, new histories, because they see them in a new light. Here was a remarkable instance of an aged woman, of above seventy years, who had spent most of her days under Mr Stoddard's powerful ministry. Reading in the New Testament concerning Christ's suffering for sinners, she seemed astonished at what she read, as what was real and very wonderful, but quite new to her. At first, before she had time to turn her thoughts, she wondered within herself, that she had never heard of it before; but then immediately recollected herself, and thought she had often heard of it, and read it, but never till now saw it as real. She then cast in her mind how wonderful this was that the Son of God should undergo such things for sinners and how she had spent her time in ungratefully sinning against so good a God and such a Saviour – though she was a person, apparently, of a very blameless and inoffensive life. And she was so overcome by those considerations that her nature was ready to fail under them: those who were about her, and knew not what was the matter, were surprised and thought she was a dying. (1.348, 356)

The revival was at its height in March and April of 1735, at which time, Edwards believed, the work of conversion 'appears to have been at the rate, at least, of four persons in a day, or near thirty in a week, take one with another, for five or six weeks together.' The Lord's Supper, he tells us, was customarily administered every eight weeks: 'I received into our communion about a hundred before our sacrament . . . I took in near sixty before the next sacrament day, whose appearance, when they presented themselves together to make an open explicit profession of Christianity was affecting to the congregation.' (1.350). Another sixty were added between that occasion and the next communion. His conclusion on the numbers savingly influenced was as follows:

I am far from pretending to be able to determine how many have lately been the subjects of such mercy, but if I may be allowed to declare anything that appears to be probable in a thing of this nature, I hope that more than 300 souls were savingly brought home to Christ in this town in the space of half a year, and about the same number of males as females. . . . I hope that by far the greater part of persons in this town, above sixteen years of age, are such as have the saving knowledge of Jesus Christ. . . . There are very few houses in the whole town into which salvation has not lately come, in one or more instances. (1.350)

The origin of Edwards' first book, *A Faithful Narrative of the Surprising Work of God*, from which we have quoted above, requires some explanation. A widespread revival was so unknown at this date that news of it did not meet with immediate belief and approval in other parts of New England. Concerned to know the truth, Benjamin Colman, one of Boston's senior ministers, wrote to enquire of Edwards, who replied on May 30, 1735 in a comparatively short letter. After describing the revival Edwards says: 'The extraordinariness of the thing has been, I believe, one principal cause that people abroad have suspected it . . . I have given you a particular account of this affair which Satan has so much misrepresented in the country.'[1]

Perhaps Colman retained some reservations but he was impressed enough to pass on part of Edwards' reply in a letter to the two English Nonconformist leaders, Doctors John Guyse and Isaac Watts, with whom he regularly corresponded. When

[1] J E (Yale) 4, pp. 107–9.

Watts shared this with his London congregation there was an immediate request to have the news of the revival in print and with more details. Accordingly Guyse wrote to Colman who, this time, wrote not directly to Edwards but to his uncle, William Williams at Hatfield. In view of the international interest in what had occurred in Hampshire County, Colman doubtless wanted the endorsement of the County's senior minister. Williams' confirmation was forthcoming and he passed on the request from London for more information to his nephew at Northampton. This resulted in a much fuller letter from Edwards to Colman (November 6, 1736) in which, in eight large and tightly-packed sheets, he elaborated upon his earlier report of May, 1735. In this second letter he gives the numbers of probable converts (the figures quoted above) and instances two case-histories, those of Abigail Hutchinson and Phebe Bartlet, at some length.

Receiving this enlarged narrative, Colman took advantage of the full liberty which Edwards had given him as to its possible use (1.364). What was later to be a 132-page book, Colman, by careful abridgement and omissions (including both case histories), greatly reduced and had printed as an 18-page appendix to a book of sermons by William Williams, which he was then supervising through a Boston press on Williams' behalf. This book, *The Duty and Interest of a People*, came out in mid-December, 1736. The Edwards' appendix was apparently the first printed news of the revival and at its conclusion Colman added the announcement: 'If the taste here given of Mr. Edwards his excellent letter excite in persons of piety a desire to have the whole of it published, it is hereby notified that subscriptions for that end will be taken.'[1]

Watts and Guyse received Colman's abridgement of Edwards in February, 1737 and were immediately among those who wanted to see 'the whole' in print: 'So strange and surprising work of God that we have not heard anything like it since the Reformation . . . should be published and left upon record.'[2] The two London leaders sent five pounds to aid printing the whole in Boston.

[1] J E (Yale) 4, p. 127.
[2] Fuller information on this Boston-London correspondence will be found in C. C. Goen's Editor's Introduction to vol. 4 of the Yale edition of J E.

Despite this support, Colman did not proceed. The cause of his hesitancy can only be conjectured. One of Edwards' modern editors suggests that Colman, having evidently added the Edwards' material to Williams' book without Williams' permission, was subsequently caught in the 'cross-fire' of the Williamses' differences with Edwards. Perhaps Colman was even asked by Williams not to publish his nephew's full narrative. This surmise is improbable, yet it seems that Colman heard at least something to suggest a lack of harmony between Hatfield and Northampton. Depending on word from an unnamed source, Colman wrote to Watts in December, 1736 that 'Mr. Edwards is not altogether pleased with the liberty we have taken of so general an extract'. But when Colman then wrote to Edwards to express regret for any offence given, the latter replied:

You mention, Sir, my being displeased at the liberty taken in the extract at the end of my Uncle Williams's sermons: certainly somebody has misrepresented the matter to you. I always looked upon it as an honor too great for me, for you to be at the trouble to draw an extract of my letter to publish to the world, and that it should be annexed to my honored Uncle Williams's sermons; and my main objection against it was that my Uncle Williams himself never approved of its being put into his book.[1]

Clearly Colman's addition of the Edwards' material in Williams' book, without the prior knowledge of either of them, was an embarrassment. It is not difficult to identify one reason. The title page of Williams' sermons indicated that they were 'Preached at a Time of General Awakenings', and the extra Edwards' material which the book contained was noted as 'a Letter Giving an Account of the late wonderful Work of God in Those Parts'. Yet although the sermons were preached in Hatfield, only one brief sentence of the Edwards' letter describing the revival refers to that town and simply reports that 'many have been added to the church'. It is clear from various sources that the Awakening was general in Hampshire County and in many towns of the Connecticut Valley in 1735. Other ministers refer to this and make no special reference to

[1]May 19, 1737. Original with the Colman Papers at the Massachusetts Hist. Soc., Boston.

Northampton. Elisha Williams of Yale, for instance, wrote to Watts on May 24, 1736, that 'there has been a remarkable revival of religion in several parts of this country, in ten parishes in the county of Hampshire, in the Massachusetts province, where it first began a little more than a year since, and in near twenty parishes of this colony [Connecticut]'.[1] Edwards' account certainly makes clear that the revival at Northampton was by no means local and yet events at Northampton constitute by far the major part of his report.

In addition, although Edwards speaks of revivals occurring in some places where there was no knowledge of what was happening at Northampton, a general impression is given that it was from his own congregation that revival spread elsewhere: 'At length the same work began evidently to appear and prevail in several other towns in the county' (1.349). He clearly believed this but it was a sensitive point in a county where churches had long felt they were under the shadow of Northampton's large congregation and famous pulpit and the more so when it was Williams' sermons preached during the awakening at Hatfield which became the means of drawing further public attention to the better-known church across the river.

For spiritual reasons, also, the experienced William Williams may have doubted the wisdom of throwing the spot-light so much on Northampton. If Williams did entertain this doubt it was one with which Edwards himself, in later years, could concur. The unexpected appendix to his uncle's book cannot have helped the measure of estrangement already existing between the two families.[2]

Colman, however, may have sensed little of this in 1737. The probability is that he delayed printing Edwards' full letter of November 6, 1736, partly to await more subscriptions and partly because he was too busy to transcribe and edit the whole

[1]Quoted in J E (Yale) 4, p. 23.

[2]When Edwards' letter was published in London the sentence respecting 'many added to the church' at Hatfield was changed to read, 'the work of God has been great there' (1.349). It should also be remembered that if, as S. E. Dwight believed, Israel Williams was the person whose 'advice' to Edwards on not 'meddling' with Arminianism in his pulpit was rejected, he cannot have been pleased to have seen this fact (without his name) published in a book of his father's!

for a printer. Then, in the light of the enthusiasm in London, he decided to send the Edwards' original letter to Watts and Guyse. After all, they could publish for a wider readership than New England could ever offer. In this way it came about that Edwards' long letter to Colman was published as a book in London in the autumn of 1737. Watts and Guyse supplied a lengthy Preface (1.344–46) and the title, *A Faithful Narrative of the Surprising Work of God in the Conversion of Many Hundred Souls in Northampton, and the Neighbouring Towns and Villages of New Hampshire, in New England.*

In some ways these two elder statesmen of English nonconformity were risking their reputations in identifying themselves with the testimony of an unknown, thirty-four-year-old New England pastor. Even the location of Northampton was so obscure to Londoners that an error in geography was built in to the title of the *Faithful Narrative*, Hampshire being confused with New Hampshire, and in the text the 'county' of which Edwards wrote became the 'country'.[1] Watts and Guyse were conscious of their need to safeguard themselves to some degree. This they did both by securing evidence from Colman that the 1735 revival had the support of senior ministers,[2] and by submitting Edwards' narrative of the revival to some revision before its publication. Watts was later to say that he 'omitted many things' from the Edwards' material and further he wrote to Colman: 'It was necessary to make some alterations of the language, lest we together with the book should have been exposed to much more contempt and ridicule on this account, though I may tell my friend that it is not a little of that kind we have both met with'.[3]

---

[1]Strangely these mistakes, for which Watts apologized to Colman, persisted in the current two-volume edition of Edwards' *Works*. Watts had an excuse not available to later publishers: 'Mr. Edwards's Narrative was written in so small a hand and so hard to be read, that if a word or two was mistaken by the printer or by us, I do not wonder at it'.

[2]Six Hampshire ministers, headed by William Williams, wrote an Attestation dated October 11, 1738. To Colman they say, 'We take this opportunity to assure you that the account Mr. Edwards has given in his narrative of our several towns or parishes is true; and that much more of the like nature might have been added with respect to some of them'. This attestation was printed in the 1738 Boston edition of the *Faithful Narrative*.

[3]Letter of May 31, 1738 quoted in J E (Yale) 4, p. 45. It is impossible to

The chief reason for a measure of caution in Watts and Guyse was that so much had happened in England since the age when conversions of the kind described by Edwards had been more common. The prevailing mood, even in many churches, was against the need or expectation of any emotion in those professing to be Christians. Watts and Guyse mourned that fact and believed that things would change in any God-given revival. This was clearly their main concern in promoting the publication of Edwards: 'May a plentiful effusion of the blessed Spirit also descend on the British isles, and all their American plantations, to renew the face of religion there!'

Edwards' *Faithful Narrative* was possibly the most significant book to precede the great evangelical awakening on both sides of the Atlantic. Between 1737 and 1739 it went through three editions and twenty printings. In Britain it gained the attention of the younger generation of men whose voices were soon to startle both the church and nation. John Wesley's *Journal*, for instance, contains an entry for October 9, 1738:

I set out for Oxford. In walking I read the truly surprising narrative of the conversions lately wrought in and about the town of Northampton, in New England. Surely 'this is the Lord's doing, and it is marvellous in our eyes'.[1]

*   *   *

---

determine the extent of the Watts-Guyse revision as neither the original of Edwards' narrative, nor any copy of it, survives. Edwards noted on the flyleaf of a presentation copy of the first edition of the *Faithful Narrative* at Yale that 'the Rev. publishers' had indulged in 'much abridging'. Edwards probably had no copy of his original and when the *Faithful Narrative* was printed in Boston in 1738 it was the Watts-Guyse edition with the only changes being a few corrections which Edwards presumably had supplied. The older men clearly saw some weakness in the *Narrative* of which Edwards was still unconscious. The Watts-Guyse Preface refers to 'whatever defects any reader may find or imagine in this narrative' – a sentence which was removed from the Preface in the Boston printing of 1738.

[1] *The Journal of John Wesley*, Ed. N. Curnock, 2, pp. 83–4. As well as reaching Oxford, Edwards' book penetrated to rural corners of England. At Waltham Abbey Baptist Church (Essex), in the Accounts for 1737, there is listed, 'Nov. 12, For 2 Hists. of remark Convers. in N. England £00–02–00'. So the Edwards' *Narrative* was selling at a shilling per copy, equal, as the same Accounts show, to the cost of '2 bushels of coals' or of 'cleaning chimney'.

Although there were as yet no reports of revival in Britain there were in another part of North America, in New Jersey where Edwards already had some contacts through his student-pastorate in New York in 1722–23. Exhausted and unwell by the autumn of the revival year, 1735, and believing in the health-giving properties of horse-riding, he had taken the 'long journey' down to New York and the Jerseys at that time. This visit renewed contacts and made new ones which were to remain an important part of his life. In New York he found the re-united Presbyterian congregation much stronger under the leadership of another New-Englander, Ebenezer Pemberton (1704–1777), who, after the dismission of Anderson in 1726, had begun a twenty-six-year pastorate on Wall Street in 1727. Speaking of the change in the church building since its impoverished early years, Webster says, 'Now the pews on the ground-floor were filled, three galleries were constructed, and the sun blazed unobstructed through the whole line of windows'.

The Presbyterian Church at this time in the Middle Colonies was only in its early years. A Presbytery had been established in Philadelphia in 1705 and, with other Presbyteries added, a 'full Synod' was meeting by the 1720's. Immigration was a primary cause of growth. 'The influx from abroad, from 1718 to 1740, was wholly Protestant and largely Presbyterian.'[1] In one year alone (1736) a thousand families sailed from Belfast for the Middle Colonies.

The arrival of Presbyterian ministers from Britain could not keep pace with this growth and the role of men from New England was becoming increasingly important. Senior among these was Jonathan Dickinson (1688–1747), a Yale graduate, who had settled at Elizabethtown, south of New York, in 1708, and become one of the Presbyterian leaders.[2] Almost certainly Edwards would have renewed contact with him during his visit in 1735, and with another Yale graduate, John Pierson, who had been settled near Dickinson in the parish of Woodbridge since 1717.

[1] Webster, pp. 119–20.
[2] If we except Edwards, says Sprague, 'It may be doubted whether Calvinism has ever found an abler or more efficient champion in this country, than Jonathan Dickinson.' *Annals*, 3, p. 17.

But there were also important new contacts for Edwards among the Presbyterians on this return to the Jerseys in 1735. It was at this date that he became consciously engaged in a common cause with the Tennent brothers, of whom some notice must be introduced at this point. The Tennent name was just being heard in New England, for that same year Gilbert Tennent's *A Solemn Warning to the Secure World* and John Tennent's *The Nature of Regeneration Opened* were both published in Boston.

William Tennent, Senior, had joined the many Scots-Irish already settled in Pennsylvania in 1718. As a Presbyterian pastor and – after 1726 – as a teacher in his 'log college' on Neshaminy Creek (twenty miles north of Philadelphia), he became a strong spokesman for a revitalized Christianity. But it was in Tennent's four sons, Gilbert, William, John and Charles, as well as in some of his pupils, that his influence multiplied. Gilbert Tennent began a sixteen-year pastorate in New Brunswick, New Jersey, in 1726, and John Tennent, called to the pastorate at Freehold, in 1730, followed him into the same work. When John died suddenly in 1732 he was succeeded by his elder brother William Tennent, Jr. William Tennent was thirty years of age when Edwards met him in 1735 and it was no doubt from him that Edwards first heard of 'divine blessing' in 'no small degree of it' being manifested beyond New England (1.349). The three Tennent brothers had all witnessed awakenings in local congregations a few years previous to the work at Northampton though it was not until the 1740's that notice of these revivals appeared in print.[1]

*　　　*　　　*

In all the revivals of the 1730's there were many striking similarities and perhaps foremost in significance among these common features was the oneness of conviction evident in the ministers involved with respect to the nature of the preaching needed by their age. Prior to the 1730's, the state of professing Christians in most parts of the English-speaking world ap-

[1] See Archibald Alexander's outstanding book, *The Log College*, Biographical sketches of William Tennent and his students, 1851 (Banner of Truth Trust reprint 1968).

peared reminiscent of the wise and foolish virgins, 'they all slumbered and slept'. There was small difference between the church and the world. Almost any degree of religious interest, or of adherence to the forms of religion, was considered enough to justify a person's Christian profession, and all who grew up in the church were commonly treated as belonging to Christ, irrespective of evidence to the contrary. Commenting on the state of affairs among the Presbyterian churches of the Middle Colonies, Archibald Alexander writes that there was soundness in the faith 'but as to the vital power of godliness, there is reason to believe that it was little known or spoken of. . . . The habit of the preachers was to address their people as though they were all pious and only needed instruction and confirmation. It was not a common thing to proclaim the terrors of a violated law and to insist on the absolute necessity of regeneration.'

This assessment would have been accepted by all the preachers of whom we are now speaking. They judged that the fundamental need of their contemporaries was to understand the meaning of being a true Christian and, further, they were convinced that the absence of this understanding was to be attributed chiefly to a defective view of sin. It had become assumed that men could be savingly related to Christ without any prior conviction about the sin which made their salvation necessary. Men were treated as saved who never knew they were lost. In New England spiritual conditions were probably better than in other parts, yet even there Solomon Stoddard could write: 'Multitudes of souls perish through the ignorance of those that should guide them in the way to heaven: men are nourished up with vain hopes of being in a state of salvation before they have got half the way to Christ.'[1]

It has sometimes been assumed that the preaching of the eighteenth-century leaders in the revivals in North America was simply continuing a well-established tradition. That, however, is not the case. The commonly-accepted preaching was not calculated to break through the prevailing formalism and indifference, and the preaching which did bring men to a sense of need and humiliation before God was of a very different order.

---

[1]*A Guide to Christ,* 1714 [1763 reprint, p. xix].

Edwards reflects on this difference in his first book of published sermons, *Discourses on Various Important Subjects, Nearly Concerning the Great Affair of the Soul's Eternal Salvation*, published 'at the desire and expense of the town' of Northampton in 1738. Addressing the reader in a Preface, he writes, These sermons were chiefly preached in 1735 in 'a very plain unfashionable way':

Yet, if in these sermons he shall find the most important truths exhibited and pressed home on the conscience with that pungency which tends to awaken, convince, humble, and edify; if he shall find that serious strain of piety which, in spite of himself, forces upon him a serious frame of mind; if in the perusal, he cannot but be ashamed and alarmed at himself, and in some measure feel the reality and weight of eternal things; if, at least he, like Agrippa, shall be almost persuaded to be a Christian; I presume he will not grudge the time required to peruse what is now offered him. These, if I mistake not, are the great ends to be aimed at in all sermons, whether preached or printed, and are ends which can never be accomplished by those modern fashionable discourses which are delivered under the name of sermons.

Again, a few years later, he returned to the same theme:

I know it has long been fashionable to despise a very earnest and pathetical way of preaching, and they only have been valued as preachers who have shown the greatest extent of learning, strength of reason, and correctness of method and language.[1] But I humbly conceive it has been for want of understanding or duly considering human nature that such preaching has been thought to have the greatest tendency to answer the ends of preaching, and the experience of the present and past ages abundantly confirms the same. An

---

[1] It is against precisely this error that Isaac Watts complained: 'There are too many persons who have imbibed and propagate this notion, that it is almost the only business of a preacher to teach the necessary doctrines and duties of our holy religion by a mere explication of the Word of God, without enforcing these things on the conscience by a pathetic address to the heart' *Discourses of the Love of God*, 2nd edit., 1734, p. vii. Thomas Hooker gives a fine summary of the Puritan and biblical view of preaching when he says that the pastor is 'to work upon the will and the affections and by savoury, powerful and affectionate application of the truth delivered, to chase it into the heart, to woo and win the soul to the love and liking, the approbation and practice of the doctrine which is according to godliness'. *A Survey of the Summe of Church-Discipline*, 1648, Part II, p. 19.

increase in speculative knowledge in divinity is not what is so much needed by our people as something else. Men may abound in this sort of light, and have no heat. How much has there been of this sort of knowledge, in the Christian world, in this age! Was there ever an age wherein strength and penetration of reason, extent of learning, exactness of distinction, correctness of style, and clearness of expression, did so abound? And yet, was there ever an age, wherein there has been so little sense of the evil of sin, so little love to God, heavenly-mindedness, and holiness of life, among the professors of the true religion? Our people do not so much need to have their heads stored as to have their hearts touched, and they stand in the greatest need of that sort of preaching which has the greatest tendency to do this.

Those texts, Isaiah 58.1, 'Cry aloud, spare not, lift up thy voice like a trumpet, and show my people their transgression, and the house of Jacob their sins', and Ezekiel 6.11, 'Thus saith the Lord God, Smite with thine hand, and stamp with thy foot, and say, Alas, for all the evil abominations of the house of Israel!' I say, these texts (however the use that some have made of them has been laughed at) will fully justify a great degree of pathos, and manifestation of zeal and fervency in preaching the word of God. (1.391).

In the preaching which Edwards, the Tennents, and others were recovering in the 1730's there was much more than a new degree of earnestness. Their *understanding* of what was required of a preacher was different. As Reformed pastors they knew that the purpose of preaching was not to induce the regeneration of their hearers. The giving of new life to the spiritually dead is solely the act of the Spirit of God. None can *enter* the Kingdom of God without first being born from above.[1] But they also believed that it was God's usual way and manner, in bestowing grace, to work in sinners *prior* to their regeneration in order to reveal their false security and to bring them to conscious emptiness and need. While they did not deny that faith may be given to infants, or even to some in older years, without any prior period of conviction, they understood the Bible to teach that, as a general rule, conviction precedes

[1] It is also important to note that this doctrinal conviction governed their theology of revival. As the regeneration of a single individual is the act of God, so the multiplied conversions witnessed in revivals are no less his sovereign work. Any idea that a revival could be planned or 'got-up' was entirely foreign to Edwards' whole theology.

conversion. Such conviction, in their view, is not a qualification which entitles a sinner to believe, nor can it savingly separate a man from sin, but it brings those who are destined for salvation to the acknowledgment of their need of mercy.[1]

Edwards and his brethren consequently denied that 'Believe on the Lord Jesus Christ' was the one message to be addressed to the unconverted. Certainly that command presents the one *term* of salvation, and as such it is to be made known to all, but something else is first needed to make the command relevant. In the words of Robert Bolton:

> A man must feel himself in misery, before he will go about to find a remedy; be sick before he will seek a physician; be in prison before he will seek for a pardon. A sinner must be weary of his former wicked ways before he will have recourse to Jesus Christ for refreshing. He must be sensible of his spiritual poverty, beggary, and slavery under the devil, before he thirst kindly for heavenly righteousness, and willingly take up Christ's sweet and easy yoke. He must be cast down, confounded, condemned, a cast away, and lost in himself, before he will look about for a Saviour.[2]

How then are men to be brought into this condition? To that question Edwards had clear answers. First, they will not come to it of themselves for they are by nature 'secure': 'They do not realize that God sees them when they commit sin and will call them to an account for it. They are stupidly senseless to the importance of eternal things' (2.818). There is, therefore, secondly, a necessity that by the Holy Spirit truth is applied to the consciences of men in order to their 'awakening'. A rightly

---

[1] In their view of the 'preparatory work' the Calvinistic leaders of the eighteenth-century revivals consciously recovered the teaching of the Puritans on that subject. It is a teaching which has not infrequently been misunderstood, even by the young C. H. Spurgeon [see *Metropolitan Tabernacle Pulpit*, 1863, p. 531]. They did not teach that preparation by conviction provided a fitness which subsequently qualified sinners to believe the gospel. Among the best-known Puritan works were Thomas Shepard's *The Sound Believer*, 1649, and Thomas Hooker's *The Application of Redemption*, 1659. Shepard and Hooker were rightly criticized on one point by Giles Firmin, *The Real Christian*, 1670, but their over-all correctness and value remained. For a wise and excellent epitome of the Scriptures on the preparatory work see William Guthrie's *The Christian's Great Interest*, 1658 [reprinted 1969, Banner of Truth].

[2] *Instructions for a Right comforting Afflicted Consciences*, 1640, p. 175.

instructed conscience will convince a man that his heart is bad and in this work preachers have a God-given role. 'It is the duty of ministers to preach such things to sinners as are proper to work this preparation', writes Stoddard in his *Guide to Christ*. David Dickson, in an earlier, well-known Puritan volume, elaborates on this duty by distinguishing between a 'voluntary examination' of the conscience – such as Christians are frequently engaged in – and 'a forced examination and wakening up of the conscience, whether the sinner wills or not.' This is where the preacher's work comes in: thoughtless, worldly hearers have to be addressed as Paul addressed Felix (Acts 24.25): 'The pastor's part here is, not only to exhort men to a voluntary examination of themselves, but also by the sword of the Spirit, he must labour to open the apostums[1] of proud sinners, discovering unto them as occasion serves, their wickedness, and denouncing the wrath of God against them, if possibly the Lord shall give them repentance, as he did to the hearers of Peter, Acts 2.37'.[2]

This was precisely Edwards' view. Fallen, and by nature indifferent, as men are, they still have a conscience: 'Conscience', he says, 'is a *principle natural* to men: and the work it doth naturally, or of itself, is to give an apprehension of *right* and *wrong*, and to suggest to the mind the relation that there is between right and wrong and a retribution'. Men have to be so dealt with that 'their conscience stares them in the face and they begin to see their need of a priest and sacrifice'. Or, to state the same principle in the words of Robert Bolton: 'Pressing upon men's consciences with a jealous, discreet powerfulness, their special, principal, fresh-bleeding sins, is a notable means to break their hearts and bring them to remorse.'

The primary means of so dealing with the conscience is the law of God, 'for by the law is the knowledge of sin' (Rom. 3.20). The law, rightly preached, does not simply bring sin into focus by the proclamation of broken commandments, it places man before the divine holiness of which those commandments are an expression. It faces men with the majesty of God and it shows them why they have reason to fear God. Its function is 'that

---

[1] 'apostums', festering sores or abscesses.
[2] *Therapeutica Sacra: Shewing briefly the Method of Healing the Diseases of the Conscience concerning Regeneration*, 1695, p. 231.

every mouth may be stopped, and all the world may become guilty *before God*' (Rom. 3.19).

The characteristic of a revival is that a profound conscious-ness of sin and need is produced in many persons at the same time by an awareness of God. Thus in Northampton in 1735 attention to the gospel was suddenly made supremely urgent to many who had hitherto given it only minimal regard:

The only thing in their view was to get the kingdom of heaven and every one appeared pressing into it. The engagedness of their hearts in this great concern could not be hid, it appeared in their very countenances. It then was a dreadful thing amongst us to lie out of Christ, in danger every day of dropping into hell; and what persons' minds were intent upon was *to escape for their lives*, and to *fly from wrath to come*. . . . The town seemed to be full of the presence of God; it never was so full of love, nor of joy, and yet so full of distress, as it was then (1.348).

This change came from God himself and yet God worked through his own Word. The sense of fear which Edwards describes was not an irrational hysteria, it was the effect of truth brought home powerfully to the conscience. In this connection, a perusal of the sermons which Edwards was preaching prior to, and during the revival, is illuminating. The titles of many of them are sufficient to show how he aimed to awaken concern. For example: 'The warnings of Scripture are in the best manner adapted to the Awakening and Conversion of Sinners' (Luke 16.31); 'The Unreasonableness of Indetermination in Religion' (Kings 18.21); 'The Precious-ness of Time' (Eph. 5.16); 'The Folly of Looking back in fleeing out of Sodom' (Luke 17.32); 'When the wicked shall have filled up the measure of their sin, wrath will come upon them to the uttermost' (1 Thess. 2.16); 'Pressing into the Kingdom of God' (Luke 16.6); and 'The justice of God in the damnation of sinners' (Rom. 3.19).

The distress which men felt under such sermons was just the response which natural men must experience when the Holy Spirit convinces them of the truth. Possibly the greatest practical lesson from the 1735 revival for the pulpit of our day is that when ministers have to deal with indifference and unconcern they will simply beat the air unless they begin where the Holy Spirit begins, 'When he is come he will convict

the world of sin, and of righteousness, and of judgment' <
(John 16.8). Thomas Prince of Boston, speaking of how
multitudes on another occasion were brought into a condition
of great spiritual concern, asserted that 'searching preaching
was both the suitable and principal means of their conviction'.
Precisely the same could be said of all the revivals of the
1730's.

It would be interesting if we knew more of the influences
which impressed the importance of this manner of preaching
upon Edwards. There was undoubtedly some influence from
his grandfather. Stoddard's *A Guide to Christ, or the way of
directing souls that are under the Work of Conversion, Compiled for the
help of young ministers*, which we have already quoted, had been
published in 1714. In essence it was an earnest re-statement of
the older Puritan teaching on the need for men first to be <
humbled if they are to be soundly converted. Stoddard at that
date was aware of a declining sympathy for this kind of
preaching:

Some there be that do deny any necessity of the preparatory work of
the Spirit of God in order to a closing with Christ. If this opinion
should prevail in the land, it would give a deadly wound to religion, it
would expose men to think themselves converted when they are not.

A man that knows there must be work of preparation will be careful
how he encourages others [to believe] that they are in Christ; he will
enquire how God has made a way for their receiving of Christ; but
another that is a stranger to it, will be ready to take all for gold that
glitters and if he sees men religiously disposed will be speaking peace
to them; he will be like the false prophets, saying, *Peace, Peace, where
there is no peace*. So men will be hardened. It is a dismal thing to give
men sleepy potions and make them sleep the sleep of death.

There are many echoes of Stoddard in his grandson's
writings and yet we can be sure that this was not the main
influence in the development of Edwards' thoughts respecting
preaching. In a previous chapter we considered something of
his inner, personal experience, and saw how an increasing
knowledge of God led him to humbling discoveries of his own
sinfulness. This is highly relevant to our present subject. It was
what he learned of his own heart that made it impossible for
him to deal superficially with others. And, similarly, it was his
own dealings with God in secret which enabled him to reach

into the lives of others in public. It was this latter truth which, at a later date, he referred to by quoting another preacher: 'When ministers were under the special influences of the Spirit of God, it assisted them to come at the consciences of men, and as it were to handle them with hands: whereas, without the Spirit of God, said he, whatever reason and oratory we make use of, we do but make use of stumps, instead of hands' (2.35-6).

In other words, true heart-searching, humbling and convicting preaching requires an experimental acquaintance with the Spirit of God on the part of the preacher.

In the case of Gilbert Tennent we do know explicitly how he came to adopt the method of preaching we have been discussing. Not long after his settlement at New Brunswick he was seriously ill and in the course of this illness he reflected with grief on the fact that any effects of his preaching upon the unconverted had only been transitory. He began also to believe that his absence of success, compared with the comparative fruitfulness of the searching ministry of Jacobus Frelinghuysen, who ministered to Dutch settlers in the same place, was connected with a deficiency in his preaching – orthodox though it had been. 'I therefore prayed to God', he later testified, 'that he would be pleased to give me one half year more and I was determined to promote his kingdom with all my might and at all adventures'. Tennent was enabled to keep the resolution which the Holy Spirit had formed in his heart:

After I was raised to health, I examined many about the grounds of their hope of salvation, which I found in most to be nothing but as the sand. With such I was enabled to deal faithfully and earnestly in warning them of their danger and urging them to seek converting grace. By this method many were awakened out of their security, and of those, divers were to all appearances effectually converted. . . . I did then preach much on original sin, repentance, the nature and necessity of conversion, in a close, examinatory and distinguishing way; labouring in the meantime to sound the trumpet of God's judgements and alarm the secure by the terrors of the Lord as well as to affect them with other topics of persuasion, which methods was sealed by the Holy Spirit. . . . [1]

[1] *The Log College*, 1968 reprint, p. 64.

One of the most forceful of all denunciations of unfaithful preaching was later to be published by Tennent. 'Cold and sapless' sermons, he asserted, such as 'freeze' between the lips of preachers, indicate the absence of true love to Christ and the souls of men. Preachers of such sermons lack 'that divine authority with which the faithful ambassadors of Christ are clothed, who herein resemble their blessed Master, of whom it is said, that "He taught as one having authority, and not as the scribes" (Matt. 7.29)'. Their sermons were the very opposite of what was required:

The application of their discourses is either short, or indistinct and general. They difference not the precious from the vile, and divide not to every man his portion, according to the apostolic direction to Timothy. No! they carelessly offer a common mess to their people, and leave it to them to divide it among themselves, as they see fit. This is indeed their general practice, which is bad enough. But sometimes they do worse, by misapplying the Word, through ignorance or anger. They often strengthen the hands of the wicked by promising him life. They comfort people before they convince them; sow before they plow; and are busy in raising a fabric before they lay a foundation. These foolish builders do but strengthen men's carnal security by their soft, selfish, cowardly discourses. They have not the courage, or honesty, to thrust the nail of terror into sleeping souls![1]

The preaching through which the spirit of slumber was broken in the 1730's was searching and convincing. A band of men was being raised up for whom the gravity of sin, the possibility of an unsound profession of Christ, and the carelessness of a lost world were pressing burdens. Behind their public utterances was their vision of God and of eternity. Their valleys of personal humiliation had been made valleys of vision and, in the words of one who followed in Edwards' steps a century later, 'When ministers get a sight of the valley of vision, and of the bottomless gulf into which bone after bone is sinking, they *do* feel that it is of importance that they should warn and alarm sinners; and then alone do they preach for death, preach for eternity, preach for the judgement seat, preach for heaven and preach, too, for hell'.[2]

[1] *The Danger of an Unconverted Ministry*, A sermon on Mark 6.34, 1740, pp. 9–10.

[2] *Notes of Addresses by the late William C. Burns*, 1869, p. 178.

8

Northampton Church, opened 1737

Some are greatly affected when in company but have nothing that bears any manner of proportion to it in secret, in close meditation, secret prayer, and conversing with God, when alone and separated from all the world. A true Christian doubtless delights in religious fellowship and Christian conversation, and finds much to affect his heart in it, but he also delights at times to retire from all mankind to converse with God. . . . True religion disposes persons to be much alone in solitary places for holy meditation and prayer. So it wrought in Isaac, Gen. 24.63. And which is much more, so it wrought in Jesus Christ. . . . The most eminent divine favours that the saints obtained, that we read of in Scripture, were in their retirement. . . . True grace delights in secret converse with God.

J E (1.311–12)

The true Christian, who delights in communion with the Holy Spirit, and meditates upon his law, daily acquires a stronger vision and gains a clearer and more distinct appreciation of heavenly realities. They begin to assume for him a distinctness almost equal to that of the objects of natural sense around him; and eventually he is impressed with the unsubstantial, fleeting character of terrestrial things, and the greater permanency and reality of the heavenly world.

G. M. GIGER on 'Religious Retirement' in
The Princeton Pulpit, Ed. John T. Duffield, 1852, p. 279

8

I f there is any one sentence in Hopkins' *Life of Edwards* which requires special comment it is the oft-quoted words, 'He commonly spent thirteen hours, every day, in his study'. The reasons which he found to be there were various but they are basic to an understanding of his life and they all have to do with what he regarded as his foremost work as a minister of the gospel.

In the first instance, it must be remembered that the main routine of each week was related to preparation for the Lord's Day. As Henry T. Rose said, 'His Sundays were his great days, and those among his own people were his best'.[1] This alone entailed long hours in the writing of sermons. The Sunday sermons were generally, it seems, one subject divided into two parts for morning and afternoon. With some justification, Edwards has been accused of indifference to style, yet his manuscript sermons show that he could take care over words, striking out one and substituting another for added force or clarity. From the time of his early sermons, which were sometimes overloaded with divisions and lacking in unity of theme, he made progress in sermon construction but not without much hard work. His hearers had little conception what both the Sunday sermons and the mid-week lecture cost him in terms of time.

Away from Northampton, the same sermons would often be

[1] In an address 'Edwards in Northampton', *Jonathan Edwards, A Retrospect*, Ed. H. Norman Gardiner, p. 190.

preached again, sometimes with changes and revision, or even entire recasting. Thus a sermon on Canticles 1.3 (Northampton, 1728) was re-written for preaching in Boston in 1733. His first published sermon, the Boston lecture on 'God Glorified in Man's Dependence', was first preached in two parts at Northampton. Wilson Kimnach, who draws attention to this, has noted the care with which Edwards gave fresh thought to every preaching opportunity, 'the immediate occasion of each sermon is indelibly stamped upon it by shadings of diction, choice of metaphors, and allusions'.[1] But even with the long hours which Edwards gave to preparation for the pulpit there are occasional indications that he was not always able to command the amount of time which he required. In the manuscript of one sermon, for example, having written on 'the text' and 'the doctrine', for the 'application' he simply detached some pages which had been part of an earlier sermon. This expedient of removing pages of notes from one sermon to another seems to have been employed at various times.

A great deal was also written by Edwards in his study which had no direct bearing on his pulpit preparations and the large number of these other manuscripts is another clear indication of how much of his time was employed. He always read with pen in hand, his notebooks open to record extracts or references, or, more often, to put down his own thoughts. So habitually committed was he to writing, observes a great-grandson, that 'he not only often stopped, in his daily rides, by the way-side, but frequently rose even at midnight, to commit to paper any important thoughts that had occurred to him'.[2]

Most of these private writings remain today. A considerable part is made up of thoughts on the Scriptures themselves. In addition to continuing his 'Notes on the Scriptures' (commenced, as already noted about 1723 as a series of numbered exegetical notes) he also now began a parallel work. His brother-in-law, Benjamin Pierrepont, had given him a Bible with more than 900 blank interleaved pages, possibly at the time of his return from Northampton to New Haven in 1730. This 'Blank Bible', as it has been called, was gradually filled

[1]'Jonathan Edwards' Sermon Mill' in *Early American Literature*, X, 1975, p. 170.
[2]Tryon Edwards, *Charity and Its Fruits*, 1852 and 1969, p. iii.

with an extended commentary on many parts of the Word of God, and it constitutes, in the opinion of A. B. Grosart, some of the most important of Edwards' writings which are still unpublished.

For more general subjects, largely of a doctrinal nature, Edwards kept his general notebooks going, his 'Miscellanies'. These notebooks were finally to contain fourteen hundred entries, and some of the entries, if printed, long enough to make small books in themselves. The nine notebooks of 'Miscellanies', writes Harvey G. Townsend, are, 'in effect, a commonplace book. The author drew upon it in preparing sermons and publications, often lifting from it phrases, illustrations, and whole passages. But as it stands it is a private notebook and must be thought of as a mere record of miscellaneous observations put down from time to time as they occurred to him.'[1]

As the 'Miscellanies' were clearly not written for publication, it is all the more remarkable that they contain so many passages which are strikingly or beautifully written. Entry '800', for example, is one of a number of entries on the 'Being of a God'. In the course of this long entry Edwards argues that design in the nature of the world – 'so wonderfully fitted for man's habitation and use, with such a variety of substances, earth, water, air, light . . . excellently ensuring all ends' – makes the idea of existence by 'mere chance' impossibly irrational. And, he proceeds, even to suppose that all this came to pass in 'an infinite length of time' would in no way reduce the proof of a supervising intelligence and wisdom:

An infinite length of time has no tendency to alter the case. If we should suppose people travelling in the snow, one after another, thousands in a day for thousands of years together, and all should tread exactly without the least variation in one another's steps so as, in all this time, to make no beaten path but only steps with the snow not broken between, this is a demonstration of intention, design, and care. Of if we suppose that, in the showers of rain that fall out of the clouds on all the face of the earth for a whole year, the drops should universally fall in order on the ground so as to describe such figures that would be Roman letters in such exact order as to be Virgil's

[1] *The Philosophy of Jonathan Edwards, From His Private Notebooks*, Ed. H. G. Townsend, 1955. The title of Townsend's book is unfortunate for it is largely a collection on various spiritual subjects taken from the 'Miscellanies'.

Aeneid written on every acre of ground all over the world, or so as exactly to write the history of the world and all nations and families in it through all ages without departing from truth in one fact or minutest circumstance – that would distinctly demonstrate a designing cause. Length of time has no tendency at all to produce such an effect of itself. If we multiply years never so much to give large opportunity, it helps not the case without a designing cause.[1]

An extract from entry '990', which was perhaps a winter's day meditation in his study, is typical of the vividness of his conceptions. The theme of the entry is 'That the world will come to an end' and in the world of nature outside his window he sees a parallel with the life of man:

As it is with the body of man – its meat and its clothing perishes and is continually renewed . . . there is a constant succession of new food and its garments are worn out and new garments are put on, one after another; at last the body itself, that is thus fed and clothed, wears out – so there is all reason to think it will be with the world, it that needs nourishment. The face of the earth continually needs a new supply of rain, and also of nitrous parts by the snow and frost or by other means gradually drawn in from the atmosphere that it is encompassed with, and of nourishment by falling leaves or rotting plants or otherwise to feed it. The sea is constantly fed by rain and rivers to maintain it. The earth, in all parts, has constant new supplies of water to maintain its fountains and streams that are, as it were, its arteries and veins. . . . And so the world is continually changing its garments, as it were. The face of the earth is annually clothed, as it were, with new garments and is stripped naked in the winter. The successive generations of inhabitants and successive kingdoms and empires and new states of things in the world are, as it were, new garments; and as these wear out, one after another, so there is reason to think the world itself, whose meat and clothing thus perishes, will itself perish at last. The body of man often lies down and sleeps and rises up again, but at last will lie down and rise no more. So the world every year, as it were, perishes in the winter or sinks into an image of death, as sleep is in the body of man, but it is renewed again in the spring. But at last it will perish and rise no more.[2]

In such language it was customary for Edwards to put down his personal thoughts. He also used the 'Miscellanies' to think

[1]Townsend, p. 102.
[2]Townsend, p. 265.

over and clarify doctrinal issues. There are, for instance, copious notes on the subject of how men are prepared to receive the gospel. The Holy Spirit does not normally immediately renew men but he first works upon their natural conscience in 'common grace'[1] and brings them to 'conviction': 'This conviction that causes men to think it worth the while to seek salvation is hardly ever a conviction of the worth of the reward but of the dreadfulness of the punishment.'[2]

Some writers on Edwards have suggested that in his pulpit practice of calling his hearers to obedience and to faith he was an inconsistent Calvinist. He lapsed, they suppose, from his belief that God has decreed whatever comes to pass by summoning his hearers to undertake action and duty themselves. No such dichotomy, however, existed in Edwards' mind between divine action and human endeavour. God does decree all things, *including* all the actions of men, and yet all falls harmoniously within his sovereign purpose. Thus, in an early entry (29) in the 'Miscellanies' he notes

When He decrees diligence and industry, He decrees riches and prosperity; when He decrees prudence, He often decrees success; when He decrees striving, then often He decrees the obtaining of the Kingdom of Heaven; when He decrees the preaching of the Gospel, then He decrees the bringing home of souls to Christ; when He decrees good natural faculties, diligence, and good advantage of them, He decrees learning; when He decrees summer, then He decrees the growing of plants; when He decrees conformity to His Son, He decrees calling; and when He decrees will, He decrees justification; and when He decrees justification, He decrees everlasting glory. Thus all the decrees of God are harmonious.[3]

Edwards' extensive work in his 'Miscellanies' was not a kind of hobby, pursued as an aside from the regular labours of the ministry. Townsend suggests that Edwards was compelled to muse with his thoughts alone because his ideas were so

[1]'Common grace', he notes, 'is only the assistance of natural principles; special is the infusing and exciting supernatural principles . . . common grace only assists the faculties of the soul to do that more fully which they do by nature.'
[2]See Townsend, pp. 109–126.
[3]Townsend, p. 154.

unrelated to the everyday world about him: 'He must have found scant occasion to share his abstruse philosophical doctrines with the good neighbours of his parish; and even his colleagues . . . would usually have found his mind beyond their depth. He had to commit his thoughts to paper and turn them over in his own mind.'

This viewpoint is certainly not that of Edwards. While not *directly* related to sermon preparation, he saw the entries in his 'Miscellanies' as an integral part of his life and thought both as a Christian and as a minister of the Word of God. He was not an academic recluse who would have preferred to spend his life in the libraries of Harvard and Yale without the distraction of public engagements. Study and writing were not ends in themselves. They were for the service of the gospel.

This brings us to what is most important of all in any understanding of Edwards' private hours. His view of his public work as a calling to speak to men in the name of God was inseparable from his conviction that the first demand in such a calling was that his own knowledge of God should be personal and first-hand. He knew that the command of Christ that men should be evangelized could not be fulfilled without obedience to another command, 'When thou prayest, enter into thy closet, and when thou hast shut thy door pray to thy Father which is in secret'. For any effective ministry God himself must be immediately involved. In the words of J. S. Stewart, 'It is one thing to learn the technique and mechanics of preaching: it is quite another to preach a sermon which will draw back the veil and make the barriers fall that hide the face of God'.[1] Edwards' whole ministry, as that of the Puritans, was based upon the conviction that the usefulness of a preacher's work is invariably related to the nature of his inner life. Personal communion with God must come first. Speaking of this characteristic of the Puritans, Macaulay has written of how their minds 'derived a peculiar character' from the nature of their daily contemplation: 'To know God, to serve him, to enjoy him, was with them

---

[1] *Heralds of God*, 1946, p. 101. Stewart speaks for the true tradition of Protestant preaching when he writes that its first essential is that the preacher 'get closer to God'. 'Nothing so transforms the spirit of a man as communion with God doth,' says John Flavel. 'Those are most like unto God that converse most frequently with him' (*Works*, 4, p. 250).

the great end of existence. . . . Instead of catching occasional glimpses of the Deity through an obscuring veil, they aspired to gaze full on the intolerable brightness, and to commune with him face to face.'

Edwards was speaking the language of reality when he told his people:

The enjoyment of God is the only happiness with which our souls can be satisfied. To go to heaven, fully to enjoy God, is infinitely better than the most pleasant accommodations here. Fathers and mothers, husbands, wives, or children, or the company of earthly friends, are but shadows; but God is the substance. These are but scattered beams, but God is the sun. These are but streams, but God is the ocean (2.244).

Edwards maintained daily set times for prayer, when it was probably his custom to speak aloud. He also had, as already noted, particular days which he set aside for solitude, meditation and fasting. But prayer was not a compartment in his daily routine, an exercise which possessed little connection with the remainder of his hours alone. Rather he sought to make his study itself a sanctuary, and whether wrestling with Scripture, preparing sermons or writing in his notebooks, he worked as a worshipper. Thought, prayer and writing were all woven together.

Many entries in his 'Miscellanies' illustrate this point. Prayer is not a mystical reaching after the Unknown; it is response to the God who speaks in Scripture, the God who personally acts in the lives of his people. 'God is a communicating being,' Edwards writes. He saw that truth as lying behind the very meaning of creation: 'Creation is the disposition of God to communicate himself, to diffuse his own fullness.' Though fellowship with God has been lost for men in general through sin, it is renewed in Christians who receive 'the communications of his Spirit'. For such the highest joy is not to be found in reflection upon their salvation, it is rather in knowing and loving God himself. 'What,' he asks in his 'Miscellanies', 'is man made for? Surely men are not made for beasts. . . . Man was undoubtedly made to glorify the Creator. Without doubt there is an immediate communication between the Creator and this highest of creatures. . . . As the intelligent being is exercised immediately about God the Creator, so the Creator immediately influences the intelligent being, immediately influences the soul – for it is but an immediate step from the soul to God. Those that call this enthusiasm talk very unphilosophically.'[1]

For Edwards, the reality of communion with God belongs to the very nature of redemptive Christianity. All Christians, therefore, are to be people of prayer. 'Seeing we have such a prayer-hearing God as we have,' he tells his hearers, 'let us all be much employed in the duty of prayer, let us live prayerful lives, continuing instant in prayer' (2.118). For ministers this is a yet greater privilege and obligation. To serve God aright the priorities of Christ's ministry must also be their own. Preaching on 'Christ the Example of ministers' he says:

Christ himself, though the eternal Son of God, obtained the Holy Spirit for himself in a way of prayer. Luke 3.21, 22, 'Jesus being baptized, and praying, the heaven was opened, and the Holy Ghost descended like a dove upon him'. If we have the Spirit of God dwelling in us, we shall have Christ himself thereby living in us. . . . If that fountain of light dwells richly in us, we shall shine like him (2.964).

In another sermon on 'He was a burning and a shining light' (John 5.35), he writes:

In order to this, ministers should be diligent in their studies, and in the work of the ministry; giving themselves wholly to it. . . . And particularly, ministers should be very conversant with the Holy Scriptures, they are the light by which ministers should be enlightened and they are the fire whence their hearts and the hearts of their hearers must be kindled.

They should earnestly seek after much of the spiritual knowledge of Christ, and that they may live in the clear views of his glory. For by this means they will be changed into the image of the same glory and brightness, and will come to their people, as Moses came down to the congregation of Israel after he had seen God's back parts in the mount, with his face shining. If the light of Christ's glory shines upon them, it will be the way for them to shine with the same kind of light on their hearers, and to reflect the same beams, which have heat, as well as brightness. . . . Ministers should be much in seeking God, and conversing with him by prayer, who is the fountain of light and love . . . (2.959–60).

In a sermon on Paul as an example (Phil. 3.17) Edwards argues that it is through intimacy with heaven that men are

[1]Townsend, pp. 127–28.

made 'great blessings in the world'. 'Moses enjoyed a great intimacy with God, but the apostle Paul in some respects a greater. . . . And though we cannot expect to be honoured with intimacy with heaven in just the same way, yet if we in good earnest apply ourselves, we may have greater intimacy, so that we may come with boldness, and converse with God as a friend' (2.865).

It was such convictions which kept Edwards from believing that study and learning in themselves can succeed in advancing the kingdom of God. Only as men are in a vital relationship to God, and endued with the Holy Spirit, will the world come to the truth. Referring to the promise, 'The knowledge of God shall fill the earth, as the waters the sea,' he asserts: 'Whenever this is accomplished, it will not be effected by human learning, or by the skill or wisdom of great men. "Not by might, nor by power, but by my Spirit, saith the Lord of hosts". It will not be by the enticing words of man's wisdom, but by the demonstration of the Spirit and of power' (2.254). Accordingly, throughout Edwards' writings there is this emphasis upon the need 'to be much in seeking the influences of his Spirit'. He underlines the lesson in his later *Life of Brainerd* (2.456), a book which shows so clearly the conviction he shared with Brainerd about the Spirit-anointed preaching which alone can revive the church and awaken the world: 'I longed for a Spirit of preaching to descend and rest on ministers, that they might address the consciences of men with closeness and power. I saw God "had the residue of the Spirit", and my soul longed it should be "poured from on high"' (2.383). Elsewhere Edwards says: 'We who are ministers, not only have need of some true experience of the saving influence of the Spirit of God upon our heart, but we need a double portion at such a time as this. We need to be as full of light as a glass that is held out in the sun. . . . The state of the times extremely requires a fulness of the divine Spirit in ministers, and we ought to give ourselves no rest till we have obtained it' (1.424).

Edwards' long hours in private were thus occupied with much more than study. He sought closer fellowship with God himself and every experience he had of God's nearness only encouraged him to seek him more. His notebooks are indirectly suggestive of this life of prayer and realization of God's presence but it is in his 'Personal Narrative' that the curtain

[145]

upon his privacy is drawn back somewhat further and we have glimpses of experiences which he never intended for publication. Writing in that document of some of the most memorable hours which he knew in his study, he says:

I have, many times, had a sense of the glory of the Third Person in the Trinity, and his office as Sanctifier; in his holy operations, communicating divine light and life to the soul. God, in the communications of his Holy Spirit, has appeared as an infinite fountain of divine glory and sweetness; being full, and sufficient to fill and satisfy the soul; pouring forth itself in sweet communications; like the sun in its glory, sweetly and pleasantly diffusing light and life. And I have sometimes an affecting sense of the excellency of the word of God as a word of life; as the light of life; a sweet, excellent, life-giving word; accompanied with a thirsting after that word, that it might dwell richly in my heart.

It is a further reminder that Edwards' time in his study was not spent in self-centred interests that the evenings alone before the public duties of the Lord's Day are mentioned particularly at the conclusion of his 'Personal Narrative'. All the hard work of another week was done, his sermons were prepared, and as he prayed them over – in the light of the needs of his people – a fire was kindled which made him impatient for the hour when the church bell would summon Northampton to join in the praise of God:

On one Saturday night, in particular, I had such a discovery of the excellency of the gospel above all other doctrines, that I could not but say to myself, 'This is my chosen light, my chosen doctrine;' and of Christ, 'This is my chosen Prophet.' It appeared sweet, beyond all expression, to follow Christ, and to be taught, and enlightened, and instructed by him; to learn of him, and live to him. Another Saturday night (*Jan.* 1739) I had such a sense, how sweet and blessed a thing it was to walk in the way of duty; to do that which was right and meet to be done, and agreeable to the holy mind of God; that it caused me to break forth into a kind of loud weeping, which held me some time, so that I was forced to shut myself up, and fasten the doors. I could not but, as it were, cry out, 'How happy are they, who do that which is right in the sight of God! They are blessed indeed, *they* are the happy ones!' I had, at the same time, a very affecting sense, how meet and suitable it was that God should govern the world, and order all things according to his own pleasure; and I rejoiced in it, that God reigned, and that his will was done (1.xlviii).

It should be noted that for Edwards profound humiliation before God *and* spiritual joy belong together. A sense of sin and real praise are not opposites: 'The saints in glory are so much employed in praise because they are perfect in *humility*, and have so great a sense of the infinite distance between God and them' (2.917).

We shall return again, in another chapter, to the subject of Edwards' 'thirteen hours, every day,' commonly spent in his study and note how the statement needs to be qualified. In terms of the understanding of the ministerial office then existing, and the practice of other men, the duration was by no means extraordinary. If it was excessive in one direction there can be no doubt that the routine of our contemporary Christian ministry is excessive in another, and that the basic reason why so much church busyness accomplishes so little at the present time is that private spiritual priorities have been neglected. In the words of A. W. Tozer, 'Our religious activities should be so ordered in such a way as to have plenty of time for the cultivation of the fruits of solitude and silence'.

Edwards would certainly have agreed with James Stalker who, when speaking of the efficacy of a minister, writes, 'Unless he has spent the week with God and received Divine communications, it would be better not to enter the pulpit or open his mouth on Sunday at all. . . . A ministry of growing power must be one of growing experience. . . . Power for work like ours is only to be acquired in secret. . . . The hearers may not know why their minister, with all his gifts, does not make a religious impression on them; but it is because he is not himself a spiritual power.'[1]

*　　*　　*

[1] *The Preacher and His Models*, 1892, pp. 52–55. Emphasizing the same point which is so prominent in Edwards, Stalker quotes Dean Church's words to clergy, 'You must have time to be alone with yourselves, alone with your own thoughts, alone with eternal realities which are behind the rush and confusion of mortal things, alone with God'. Archibald Alexander, speaking of the discriminating, searching preaching of the Puritans 'and the most distinguished preachers of our own country – the Mathers, Shepards, Stoddards, Edwardses . . . ' writes: 'This requires more than a ready utterance – more than the learning of the schools, or profound critical acumen. It requires that the preacher study much upon his knees . . . ' *The Princeton Pulpit*, Ed. J. T. Duffield, 1852, p. 41.

Before we leave Edwards in the 1730's there are some scattered facts which need to be set down. By 1738 the family had grown to six children. Sarah and Jerusha were followed by the birth of Esther in 1732, then at two-yearly intervals, more daughters, Mary and Lucy, until – at last – the sex changes in the list which Edwards wrote in the Family Bible: 'My son Timothy was born on Tuesday, July 25, 1738, between 6 and 7 o'clock in the morning.' There were also bereavements. His grandmother, Esther Stoddard, died in February 1736, and he preached her funeral sermon from the words, 'And their works do follow them'. At the age of ninety-six and long crippled by sciatica she was ready to go. It was otherwise with Joseph Hawley, Edwards' uncle, who brought his own life to an end one Sunday morning the preceding year. 'This extraordinarily affected the minds of people here,' writes Edwards, 'and struck them as it were with astonishment'. That Hawley's death occurred in the midst of the revival, when so many were entering into life and joy, compounded the tragedy. 'Religious in his behaviour, and a useful and honourable person in the town' he died in despair, but the real cause lay much further back. The 'disease of melancholy' was hereditary in his family, his mother having died the same way. A coroner's inquest judged him 'delirious' at the time of suicide (1.363). With his fatherless young sons, Joseph Jr. and Elisha, before them every Sunday in the meetinghouse, the sadness was not soon forgotten. Edwards himself helped in the education of at least one of these bereaved cousins.

On a Sunday in March 1737 an event occurred which might well have led to a multiple funeral in the 'burying place' on Bridge Street. The old meetinghouse in which the church met had stood since 1661, and it had not been easy in November 1735 to secure a vote in the church meeting for a new building. Summer was nearing its close in 1736 before real progress was made on a larger building, adjacent to the old. The main frame and belfry were finished by September when work seems to have stopped for what was to prove an extreme winter. When the thaw came in March, the ground heaved and for some of the timber beams on the warmer south-side of the old church the strain was too much. The same month, soon after Edwards had begun his sermon one Sunday morning in the old building, the beams holding the gallery above the door, and facing the pulpit, snapped like a thunder-crack, throwing people on to the pews and floor below. 'The house,' says the preacher, 'was filled with dolorous shrieking and crying, and nothing else was expected than to find many people dead and dashed to pieces' (1.345). General amazement and thankfulness followed the discovery that there was not a single fatality. Certainly the new building was to be available none too soon. By June 1737 the spire was raised high above the surrounding countryside although it was not until December 25 that the congregation finally took possession.

It is probable that the delay in opening the new meeting-house was due to a common problem in New England. Except for children (who commonly moved down from the gallery to join their parents), people sat in the same seat in the meetinghouse for many years, sometimes for a lifetime, and the — location of that seat was no accident. 'Seating the meeting-house' had to be done according to an order of precedence related to the age and station of every individual or head of household. A committee of five was appointed to settle these arrangements, with a general direction to place males to the — left, facing the pulpit, and females to the right. This was traditional but now there were new considerations – not least the large size of the new building. Measuring about 70 feet long by 46 to 48 feet in width, it was more oblong than square. The pulpit was in the middle of the wall which faced the main entrance and so arranged as to bring the preacher close to a large number of people.

Doubting at least part of the traditional scheme for sittings, the Committee came back to the Town meeting with the question, 'Should wives and husbands sit together?' The answer was 'No', but with the proviso that they should not be forbidden if they 'incline to sit together'. By December 22 the Committee's plan was at last finished and the following Sunday, December 25, it was put into operation. Christmas Day was unobserved and virtually unknown in New England and in so far as there might be distractions in some minds that first day in the new meetinghouse Edwards knew what they were. His sermon from John 14.2, 'In my Father's house are many mansions,' included this application, 'You that are pleased with your seats in this house because you are seated high in a place that is looked upon hungrily by those that sit round about . . . consider it is but a very little while before it will [be] all one to you whether you have sat high or low here'.

A faded piece of paper still recalls the ground-floor seating which was decided upon. In the box pews to Edwards' immediate left (along the same wall as the pulpit) were first a pew of aged widows, second, Mrs. Edwards: third, Colonel Stoddard with his wife and his bereaved sister, Rebecca Hawley; while to his right were first, eminent widowers, then other major families, led by pews for the Pomeroys and the Strongs.

Edwards regretted that affairs connected with the building of the new meetinghouse were indeed a distraction from the serious concerns which previously had been occupying so many of the people. It seems that Northampton did not escape a measure of contention over the reorganization of the meeting-house. Reproving the people for their proneness to 'contention and party spirit', Edwards said in May 1737: 'I suppose for these thirty years people have not known how to manage scarcely any public business without dividing into parties . . . of late, time after time that old party spirit has appeared again, and particularly this spring. Some persons may be ready to think that I make too much of things . . . [but] I do not know but I have trusted too much in men, and put too much confidence in the goodness and piety of the town'.[1]

Despite the converts of the recent revival, Edwards thus expresses a fear of which we shall hear again later. Even in the year that his *Narrative of Surprising Conversions* was going out to the world he questioned whether Northampton religion was as deep as it was reputed to be. In the light of this it may well be that he adjusted the emphasis of his preaching in the later 1730's, with more attention now placed on growth in holiness of life. Certainly the two best-known of his early series in the new meetinghouse, *Charity and its Fruits* (in 1738) and *A History of the Work of Redemption* (in 1739), were designed principally for Christian growth. In the first series – lectures on 1 Corinthians 13 – Edwards develops the theme prominent throughout his

---

[1] MS sermon on 2 Samuel 20.19 (Andover MSS).

later ministry: holiness is love to God, and that love is the source of perseverance in Christian practice, 'He that truly loves God, constantly seeks after God in the course of his life: seeks his grace, and acceptance, and glory'. Conversion is not an end in itself:

God is seeking your love, and you are under unspeakable obligation to render it. The Spirit of God has been poured out wonderfully here. Multitudes have been converted. Scarcely a family has been passed by. In almost every household some have been made nobles, kings and priests unto God, sons and daughters of the Lord Almighty! What manner of persons, then, ought all of us to be! how holy, serious, just, humble, charitable, devoted in God's service, and faithful to our fellow-men!

In addition to his preaching, Edwards took another step in 1739 which was designed to strengthen the life of the church. In that year, when one of his deacons died, only two were left in office. They were Ebenezer Wright, ordained deacon in 1704, and John Clark, ordained in 1730. In a further election of deacons three men were now added, Ebenezer Pomeroy Jr., Noah Cook and Stephen Wright. Some of these names there will be occasion to note at a later and less happy period in Edwards' ministry.

THE GREAT AWAKENING

*A nineteenth-century drawing of The Old South Church,
Boston, built (1729) during the ministry of Thomas
Prince whose pulpit was frequently used by Edwards
and Whitefield.*

Now, God is pleased again to pour out his Spirit upon us; and he is doing great things amongst us. . . . You have had your life spared through these six years past, to this very time, to another outpouring of the Spirit.

J E in December, 1740 (2.205)

It was no "superstitious panic", but a plentiful effusion of the Holy Ghost.

GEORGE WHITEFIELD,
'A Vindication and Confirmation of the Remarkable Work
of God in New England.' *Works*, 4, p. 80.

The apostolical times seem to have returned upon us: such a display has there been of the power and grace of the divine Spirit in the assemblies of his people, and such testimonies has he given to the word of the gospel.

WILLIAM COOPER
November, 1741 (2.258)

9

‘I mmediately preceded by a long season of < coldness and indifference, the Great Awakening’, wrote one New England minister, ‘broke upon the slumbering churches like a thunderbolt rushing out of a clear sky’.[1] Even so, with the hindsight of the year 1740, we may see in 1739 the signs that America was on the threshold of a great revival. Preachers had been prepared. A spirit of prayer was present in various churches and in some places men were already showing the concern for the salvation of their souls which was to become so general.

When George Whitefield reached Philadelphia from England, at the beginning of November 1739, it was his intention to stop only briefly before continuing to the Orphanage at Savannah, Georgia, where he intended to be ‘above six months’. Events were to change these plans as he now made his first acquaintance with the Middle Colonies, meeting the Tennents and witnessing, at times, the same power present with the preaching of the Word as he had already seen in England. On November 13, 1739, while at New Brunswick with Gilbert Tennent, Whitefield wrote of their conversation in his *Journal*, ‘He recounted to me many remarkable effusions of the blessed Spirit, which have been sent down among them’. The next day the two men journeyed to New York and there in the home of Thomas Noble, a wealthy merchant known to Edwards,

[1]J. F. Stearns in W. B. Sprague’s *Annals of the American Pulpit*, 1, p. 339.

Whitefield wrote his first letter to the parsonage at Northampton:

New York, Nov. 16, 1739

√ Rev Sir,

Mr Noble, and the report of your sincere love for our dear Lord Jesus, embolden me to write this. I rejoice for the great things God has done for many souls in Northampton. I hope, God willing, to come and see them in a few months. The journal sent with this, will shew you what the Lord is about to do in Europe. Now is the gathering time. A winnowing time will shortly succeed. Persecution and the power of religion will always keep pace. Our Lord's word begins to be glorified in America. Many hearts gladly receive it. Oh Rev Sir, it grieves me to see people, everywhere ready to perish for lack of knowledge. I care not what I suffer, so that some may be brought home to Christ. . . . May the God of all grace give you all peace and joy in believing! May he increase you more and more, both you and your children! May you every day be feasted, and built up with fresh anointings of his blessed Spirit! And by your fervent prayers, may you be enabled to hold up the hands of, reverend Sir,

> Your unworthy brother, fellow labourer and
> servant in our dear Lord,

G.W.

'What the Lord is about to do' was a sentiment which had also been much with Edwards through the year 1739. His sermons on *A History of The Work of Redemption* included his expectation that 'The Spirit of God shall be gloriously poured out for the wonderful revival and propagation of religion. . . . The Gospel shall begin to be preached with abundantly greater clearness and power than heretofore' (1.605). And in this grand redemptive purpose Edwards saw all the details of providence and history working together:

God's providence may not unfitly be compared to a large and long river, having innumerable branches, beginning in different regions, and at a great distance one from another, and all conspiring to one common issue (1.617).

The friendship of Whitefield and Edwards, which dates from this period, was certainly the joining of two hitherto separate 'branches' of this 'river'. Perhaps Whitefield's letter was delayed somewhere in transit for when Edwards wrote what appears to have been his first letter to the English preacher he makes no mention of it:

Northampton in New-England, Feb 12, 1739, 40

Rev. Sir,

My request to you is that in your intended journey through New-England the next summer you would be pleased to visit Northampton. I hope it is not wholly from curiosity that I desire to see and hear you in this place, but I apprehend, from what I have heard, that you are one that has the blessing of heaven attending you wherever you go, and I have a great desire, if it be the will of God, that such blessing as attends your person and labours may descend on this town. Indeed I am fearful whether you will not be disappointed in New England, and will have less success here than in other places. We who have dwelt in a land that has been distinguished with light, and have long enjoyed the Gospel, and have been glutted with it, and have despised it, are I fear more hardened than most of those places where you have preached hitherto. But yet I hope in that power and mercy of God that has appeared so triumphant in the success of your labours in other places, that he will send a blessing with you even to us, tho' we are unworthy of it. I hope, if God spares my life, to see something of that salvation of God in New England which he has now begun in a benighted, wicked and miserable world and age and in the most guilty of all nations.

It has been with refreshment of soul that I have heard of one raised up in the Church of England to revive the mysterious, spiritual, despised and exploded doctrines of the Gospel, and full of a spirit of zeal for the promotion of real, vital piety, whose labours have been attended with such success. Blessed be God that hath done it! who is with you, and helps you, and makes the weapons of your warfare mighty. We see that God is faithful and never will forget the promises that he has made to his church, and that he will not suffer the smoking flax to be quenched, even when the floods seem to be overwhelming it, but will revive the flame again, even in the darkest times. I hope this is the dawning of a day of God's mighty power and glorious grace to the world of mankind . . . and may God send forth more labourers into his harvest of a like spirit, until the kingdom of Satan shall shake and his proud Empire fall throughout the earth and the kingdom of Christ, that glorious kingdom of light, holiness, peace and love, shall be established from one end of the earth unto the other!

. . . I believe I may venture to say that what has been heard of your labours and success has not been taken notice of more more [*sic*] in any place in New-England than here, or received with fuller credit. I hope therefore if we have opportunity, we shall hear you with greater attention. The way from New York to Boston through Northampton

[157]

is but little further than the nearest that is and I think leads through as populous a part of the country as any. I desire that you and Mr Seward would come directly to my house. I shall account it a great favour and smile of providence to have opportunity to entertain such guests under my roof. . . .

    I am Rev. Sir

unworthy to be called your
fellow labourer,
Jonathan Edwards

To the Rev. Mr George Whitefield[1]

No part of Edwards' life makes more exacting demands upon a biographer than the Great Awakening. In the narratives of not a few writers the whole story is reduced to a record of eminent personalities, of unusual preaching and of much emotion. Perry Miller gives this interpretation in its baldest form when he speaks of New England, as 'a powder keg': 'Jonathan Edwards had already put a match to the fuse, and Whitefield blew it into flame'. It was, he believes, simply 'revivalism' carried out in circumstances particularly conducive to success.

    Those who offer this view seem to be oblivious of the fact that Edwards has already commented upon such thinking. The human instruments in the Awakening, he wrote in 1742, were not the reason why it had commenced:

They have greatly erred in the way in which they have gone about to try this work . . . in judging of it . . . from the way that it began, the instruments that have been employed, the means that have been used, and the methods that have been taken and succeeded in carrying it on. . . . We are to observe the effect wrought and if, upon examination of that, it be found to be agreeable to the word of God, we are bound to rest in it as God's work; and we shall be like to be rebuked for our arrogance if we refuse so to do till God shall explain to us how he has brought this effect to pass, or why he has made use of such and such means in doing it. . . . It appears to me that the great God has wrought like himself in the manner of his carrying on this work; so as very much to show his own glory, exalt his own sovereignty, power and all-sufficiency (1.366).

Far from being the mere language of theology, these words

[1]Methodist Archive and Research Centre, London; first printed in *The William and Mary Quarterly*, 1974, pp. 488–89.

point to the only accurate explanation of the events to which we now turn. The American colonies in 1740 were *not* in a condition favourable to a sudden transformation. On the contrary, as Samuel Blair of New Londonderry in the Middle Colonies wrote of the situation in the Spring of that year, 'Religion lay as it were a-dying and ready to expire its last breath of life in this part of the visible church'. In New England also the formalism of half-a-century continued to prevail, unchecked by the local revivals of 1734–35. Nor can the impact of personalities, in itself, account for the change. It is evident that the results of the Great Awakening were not in invariable proportion to the presence or absence of certain of the best-known figures. The leading preachers did not have consistent success: sermons, repeated with the same earnestness as before, could differ markedly in result. And the days which were longest to be remembered were not the outcome of carefully made arrangements. Those who stood closest to the centre of events were also those who were most deeply persuaded that success was not in the hands of man to bestow. Unitedly they felt with new force the words of Christ: 'The wind bloweth where it listeth, and thou hearest the sound thereof, but canst not tell whence it cometh and whither it goeth' [John 3.8]. In short, the Great Awakening is one of the many confirmations of the statement: 'The history of religious revival proves that all real, spiritual awakenings of the national mind have been those in which God and not man, has been the prime mover.'[1]

* * *

In the event, more than 'a few months' were to elapse between Whitefield's letter to Edwards from New York in November 1739 and his visit to Northampton. When at length he arrived through the forest horse-trails on October 17, 1740, a general revival in the country had already begun. The Middle Colonies felt its strength first in the Spring and Summer. Ministers spoke in a new way of what they saw: 'God is present in our assemblies'; 'God's Spirit came upon the preacher and the people'. In places where it was not customary for anyone to be

[1] Octavius Winslow, *A Plea for a National Baptism of the Holy Ghost*, 1858, p. 84.

disturbed by preaching, 'Men saw hell opening before them and themselves ready to fall into it'. Before the end of May, 1740, it was being said that 'there was never such a general awakening and concern for the things of God known in America before'. When Whitefield reached Boston in New England in September, where he preached for ten days, there followed indications of awakening in the town, but signs were already present in the colony before that date. At Natick, a growing conviction had appeared among the people and elsewhere more than one minister was later to note that God was dealing personally with him at this period in an unusual way. For example, David Hall, a friend of Edwards and minister at Sutton, Massachusetts, says how in April 1740, God humbled him with the conviction that religion 'was sunk down to a very low and melancholy ebb', but his feelings did not end there:

Now I was again at this time filled with an encouraging persuasion that I should behold the power of religion reviving among us in the conversion of souls to the Lord Jesus Christ. Together with this persuasion, a most ardent thirst came upon me, that I might gain souls for whom Christ died: to which end I longed for the sanctuary. And from this time I had more knowledge than ever before, what it means to preach with the Spirit and with the understanding also: although still attended with great weakness. . . . [1]

Edwards' fullest account of Northampton's participation in the Great Awakening is contained in a letter he wrote to one of the ministers of Boston. In this letter he commences by speaking of the 'great and abiding alteration' in the town since 'the great work of God' in 1735. The youth of the community were more free of 'revelry, frolicking, profane and licentious conversation, and lewd songs' than they had been in sixty years. He continues:

And though after that great work nine years ago, there has been a very lamentable decay of religious affections, and the engagedness of people's spirit in religion; yet many societies for prayer and social worship were all along kept up, and there were some few instances of awakening, and deep concern about the things of another world, even in the most dead time.

[1]Gillies, *Historical Collections*, p. 395.

Statue of George Whitefield at the University of Pennsylvania.

The Housatonic River, about half-a-mile from the site of Edward's home at Stockbridge.

In the year 1740, in the spring before Mr Whitefield came to this town, there was a visible alteration: there was more seriousness and religious conversation, especially among young people; those things that were of ill tendency among them, were forborne; and it was a very frequent thing for persons to consult their minister upon the salvation of their souls; and in some particular persons there appeared a great attention, about that time. And thus it continued, until Mr Whitefield came to town, which was about the middle of October following (1.lvii).

A page and-a-half in Whitefield's Journal describes this memorable visit which lasted from a Friday afternoon until Sunday evening. Writing of Friday, October 17, 1740 Whitefield says:

We crossed the ferry to Northampton where no less than three hundred souls were saved about five years ago. . . .

Mr Edwards is a solid, excellent Christian, but, at present, weak in body. I think I have not seen his fellow in all New England. When I came into his pulpit, I found my heart drawn out to talk of scarce anything beside the consolations and privileges of saints, and the plentiful effusion of the Spirit upon believers. . . . In the evening, I gave a word of exhortation to several who came to Mr Edwards' house.[1]

The next morning Edwards had a programme arranged for his twenty-five-year-old visitor to the Parsonage. First, the guest spoke to the Edwards children (and perhaps to others invited in), then a five-mile ride to Hatfield for a sermon at the meetinghouse of the aged William Williams and finally a service at Northampton at four in the afternoon of which Whitefield writes: 'I began with fear and trembling, but God assisted me. Few eyes were dry in the assembly. I had an affecting prospect of the glories of the upper world and was

---

[1] *George Whitefield's Journals*, 1960 reprint, p. 476. In a revision of his Journals Whitefield later inserted the words 'as was supposed' before the number of converts. While it is absurd to say that Whitefield at this time 'caught the tone and imbibed the opinions of Edwards' (L. Tyerman, *Life of Whitefield*, 1876, 1, p. 274) there can be no doubt that his first visit to the Middle Colonies and New England did strengthen his adherence to Puritan convictions. He wrote to John Wesley in May 1740, 'The work of God is carried on here (and that in a most glorious manner) by doctrines quite opposite to those you hold' (*Works* 1, p. 182).

enabled to speak with some degree of pathos.'

Two sermons on the Sunday brought the visit to a conclusion: 'Preached this morning and good Mr Edwards wept
during the whole time of exercise. The people were equally
affected; and, in the afternoon, the power increased yet more. I
have not seen four such gracious meetings together since my
arrival'. Without referring to himself, Edwards confirms that
'the congregation was extraordinarily melted by every sermon;
almost the whole assembly being in tears for a great part of
sermon time'. And he adds, 'Mr Whitefield's sermons were
suitable to the circumstances of the town.'

With that memorable Lord's Day over, Whitefield, accompanied by Edwards, set off south by horse the same
evening. On Tuesday afternoon they reached East Windsor,
where Whitefield preached 'to a thronged congregation' before
supper in the old family home. On Wednesday morning they
parted, Whitefield headed for New Haven and Edwards back
up the Connecticut. The same week Sarah Edwards wrote to
her brother in New Haven, the Rev. James Pierrepont, to tell
him of Whitefield's visit and to encourage him to welcome the
preacher:

It is wonderful to see what a spell he casts over an audience by
proclaiming the simplest truths of the Bible. I have seen upwards of a
thousand people hang on his words with breathless silence, broken
only by an occasional half-suppressed sob. He impresses the ignorant,
and not less the educated and refined. It is reported that while the
miners of England listened to him, the tears made white furrows down
their smutty cheeks. So here, our mechanics shut up their shops, and
the day-labourers throw down their tools, to go and hear him preach,
and few return unaffected. . . . He speaks from a heart all aglow with
love, and pours out a torrent of eloquence which is almost irresistible.
Many, very many persons in Northampton date the beginning of new
thoughts, new desires, new purposes, and a new life, from the day on
which they heard him preach of Christ and this salvation. Perhaps I
ought to tell you that Mr Edwards and some others think him in error
on a few practical points; but his influence on the whole is so good we
ought to bear with little mistakes.[1]

[1]Quoted from *Hours at Home*, August, 1867, p. 295, by J. B. Wakeley in
Anecdotes of George Whitefield, 1879, p. 278.

Sarah Edwards' words were confirmed again many times even before her brother read the letter. Whitefield's sermon at East Windsor on the Tuesday night had been the sixth since he left Northampton forty-eight hours before. On Wednesday he preached at Hartford and Wethersfield. On Thursday the record of a farmer, Nathan Cole, gives some idea both of the interest now kindled in spiritual things and of the way great congregations could be gathered at brief notice:

Now it pleased God to send Mr. Whitefield into this land and my hearing of his preaching at Philadelphia, like one of the old apostles, and many thousands flocking after him to hear the gospel and great numbers converted to Christ, I felt the Spirit of God drawing me by conviction. . . . Next I heard he was on Long Island and next at Boston and next at Northampton and then, one morning, all on a sudden, about 8 or 9 o'clock there came a messenger and said, 'Mr. Whitefield preached at Hartford and Wethersfield yesterday and is to preach at Middletown this morning at 10 o'clock'. I was in my field, at work, I dropped my tool that I had in my hand and ran home and ran through my house and bade my wife get ready quick to go and hear Mr. Whitefield preach at Middletown and ran to my pasture for my horse with all my might, fearing I should be too late to hear him. I brought my horse home and soon mounted and took my wife up and went forward as fast as I thought the horse could bear, and when my horse began to be out of breath I would get down and put my wife in the saddle and bid her ride as fast as she could and not stop or slack for me except I bade her, and so I would run until I was almost out of breath and then mount my horse again, and so I did several times to favour my horse . . . for we had twelve miles to ride double in little more than an hour.

On high ground I saw before me a cloud or fog rising, I first thought off from the great river but as I came nearer the road I heard a noise something like a low rumbling of horses feet coming down the road and this cloud was a cloud of dust made by the running of horses feet. It arose some rods in the air, over the tops of the hills and trees, and when I came within about twenty rods of the road I could see men and horses slipping along in the cloud like shadows and when I came nearer it was like a steady stream of horses and their riders, scarcely a horse more than his length behind another, all of a lather and some with sweat. . . .

We went down with the stream, I heard no man speak a word all the way, three miles, but everyone pressing forward in great haste, and when we got down to the old meetinghouse there was a great multitude – it was said to be 3 or 4000 people assembled together. We got off from our horses and shook off the dust, and the ministers were then coming to the meetinghouse. I turned and looked towards the great river and saw ferry boats running swift, forward and backward, bringing over loads of people, the oars rowed nimble and quick. Everything, men, horses and boats, all seemed to be struggling for life, the land and the banks over the river looked black with people and horses. All along the 12 miles I saw no man at work in his field but all seemed to be gone.[1]

Despite such scenes as this it is clear that the revival in New England was only beginning at this date. When Whitefield returned to New York the following week, spiritual concern, far from diminishing, was steadily to increase. Speaking of Northampton, Edwards writes:

Immediately after this, the minds of the people in general appeared more engaged in religion, showing a greater forwardness to make religion the subject of their conversation, and to meet frequently for religious purposes, and to embrace all opportunities to hear the word preached. The revival at first appeared chiefly among professors, and those that had entertained hope that they were in a state of salvation, to whom Mr Whitefield chiefly addressed himself; but in a very short time there appeared an awakening and deep concern among some young persons, that looked upon themselves in a Christless state; and there were some hopeful appearances of conversion, and some professors were greatly revived. In about a month or six weeks, there was a great attention in the town, both as to the revival of professors and the awakening of others. By the middle of December a considerable work of God appeared among those that were very young; and the revival of religion continued to increase, so that in the Spring an engagedness of spirit about the things of religion was become very general amongst young people and children, and religious subjects almost wholly took up their conversation when they were together (1.lvii-lviii).

The revival at Northampton was to continue throughout the year 1741. At a sermon preached by Edwards in a private house in May 'one or two persons, that were professors, were so greatly affected with a sense of the greatness and glory of divine

[1] From Coles' manuscript entitled 'Spiritual Travels', part of which is printed in *Some Aspects of the Religious Life of New England*, G. L. Walker, 1897, pp. 89–91, and elsewhere.

things' that it overcame their strength, 'having a very visible effect upon their bodies'. Such scenes were to become common. No meetings were held at night but sometimes, after services, people were 'so overcome that they could not go home, but were obliged to stay all night where they were'. The work was at its height in August and September, summarized by Edwards in the sentence, 'There was an appearance of a glorious progress of the work of God upon the hearts of sinners, in conviction and conversion, this summer and autumn, and great numbers, I think we have reason to hope, were brought savingly home to Christ'.

Nothing was more encouraging to Edwards than the apparent influence of the gospel upon the children and the youth of the town. On one occasion, after public worship, young people under seventeen were gathered separately and as Edwards gave them 'some counsels proper for their age' the whole number were 'greatly affected'. Pressure for an immediate profession of Christ would have brought a universal response but their counsellor made no such appeal and a number were still crying as they made their way home. 'The like appearances', Edwards comments, 'attended several such meetings of children that were appointed. But', he continues, 'their affections appeared by what followed to be of a very different nature: in many they appeared indeed but childish affections, and in a day or two would leave them as they were before. Others were deeply impressed; their convictions took fast hold of them and abode by them'. Other meetings were held for young people between the ages of sixteen and twenty-six. The younger members of this age group, together with the children, were to provide the largest number of hopeful converts. Those who were already grown-up at the time of the work of the Spirit in 1735, and who had witnessed that revival without coming to the obedience of faith, 'seemed now to be almost wholly passed over and let alone'. It was a new generation, principally, says Edwards, which was now brought in: 'Now we had the most wonderful work among children that ever was in Northampton. . . . Many, of all ages, partook of it; but yet, in this respect, it was more general on those that were of the younger sort.'

Besides there being more demand for preaching in Northampton than Edwards could well supply, calls for his help were multiplied through the summer of 1741 as, across New England, pastors witnessed what most of them had never seen before. In the words of Benjamin Trumbull: 'There began a very great and general concern among the people for the salvation of their souls. The awakening was more general and extraordinary than any ever before known'. In April of 1741, after three remarkable months in New England, Gilbert Tennent informed Whitefield of more than twenty places known to him to which the revival extended, including Boston itself where there were 'many hundreds, if not thousands, as some have judged, under soul concern'. Thomas Prince, was soon to write of the town's unparalleled harvest:

The more we prayed and preached, the more enlarged were our hearts, and the more delightful the employment. And O how many, how serious and attentive were our hearers. . . . Now was such a time as we never knew. The Rev Mr Cooper was wont to say, that more came to him in one week in deep concern about their souls, than in the whole twenty-four years of his preceding ministry. I can also say the same as to the numbers who repaired to me. By Mr Cooper's letter to his friend in Scotland, it appears he has had about six hundred different persons in three months' time: and Mr Webb informed me, he has had in the same space about a thousand.[1]

As spring passed into summer in 1741 no one could well keep track of the number of places which were also witnessing the revival. Churches which in some cases had been cold and dry at the beginning of the year were transformed before the end. 'It is astonishing,' wrote Edwards, 'to see the alteration that there is in some towns, where before was but little appearance of religion.' Across New England there were great increases in church membership. In the parish of Suffield, also in Hampshire County, where the pastor died in April, 1741, Edwards appears to have given regular help and to have admitted ninety-five new members in the following months. At Hartford twenty-seven were added to the church in 1741; at North Stonington one hundred and four; sixty in six months at the Old South Church in Boston and one hundred and two in twelve months at the New North Church in the same town. Hingham had forty-five admissions in 1741–42, Plymouth

---

[1] *Historical Collections*, John Gillies, p. 352.

eighty-four and Middleborough one hundred and seventy-four.

In some instances interest and concern seem to have appeared gradually in congregations, but in others the change was so sudden that particular days were never to be forgotten. Jonathan Parsons was a man who had studied theology for a time under Edwards in the early 1730's. Under a sermon at Lyme on May 14th, 1741, 'Many had their countenances changed. . . . Great numbers cried out aloud in the anguish of their souls: several stout men fell as though a cannon had been discharged and a ball had made its way through their hearts.' At Middleborough, on November 23rd, 'Seventy-six that day struck and brought first to enquire what they should do to escape condemnation'. November 27th at Portsmouth was 'The most remarkable day that was ever known among us', and so on.

Speaking of conditions in general at this date Benjamin Trumbull writes:

There was in the minds of people, a general fear of sin, and of the wrath of God denounced against it. There seemed to be a general conviction, that all the ways of man were before the eyes of the Lord. It was the opinion of men of discernment and sound judgment, who had the best opportunities of knowing the feelings and general state of the people at that period, that bags of gold and silver, and other precious things, might, with safety, have been laid in the streets, and that no man would have converted them to his own use. Theft, wantonness, intemperance, profaneness, sabbath-breaking, and other gross sins, appeared to be put away. The intermissions on the Lord's day, instead of being spent in worldly conversation and vanity, as had been too usual before, were now spent in religious conversation, in reading and singing the praises of God.[1]

It is no wonder that at such a time Edwards speaks of his physical exhaustion and of 'prodigious fullness of business'. While trying to assist in other churches he himself needed help, as he told Eleazer Wheelock in a letter on June 9, 1741. Wheelock, one of the leading preachers in the Awakening, had graduated from Yale in 1733, and was now minister of the Second Church at Lebanon. Edwards first appealed to him and Benjamin Pomeroy to go and preach at a settlement in the

[1] *History of Connecticut*, 1898, 2, pp. 111–2.

remote northern part of his father's parish where the people, spiritually, were in 'wretched circumstances'. 'If ever they are healed', he urged upon Wheelock, 'I believe it must be by a reviving and prevailing of true religion among them. By all that I can understand, they are wholly dead in their extraordinary day of God's gracious visitation.'

'Old Mr Edwards' (as Whitefield called Timothy Edwards) was evidently beyond the journey and labour which was required, whereas it was said of Wheelock that 'he preached a hundred more sermons than there are days in the year'. The Edwards' letter continued:

Another thing that I desire of you is, that you would come up hither and help us, both you and Mr Pomeroy. There has been a reviving of religion among us of late; but your labours have been much more remarkably blessed than mine. Other ministers, I have heard, have shut up their pulpits against you; but here I engage you shall find one open. May God send you hither, with the like blessing as he has sent you to some other places. . . . (1.lii)

It would seem that following Edwards' June letter to Wheelock the latter agreed to visit Northampton. Certainly a month later the two men were together at Enfield, Connecticut. According to one tradition it was not intended that Edwards should preach at the Enfield meetinghouse on July 8 but he stood in as a substitute for another man. The district, apparently, was as yet untouched by the Awakening and indeed so unconcerned whether it should be, that neighbouring Christians had given a considerable part of the previous night to prayer lest 'while the divine showers were falling around them' Enfield would be passed by. Edwards took as his text Deuteronomy 32.35, 'Their foot shall slide in due time', repeating a sermon which he had given in his own church shortly before on the subject, 'Sinners in the Hands of an Angry God'. Wheelock reported to Trumbull how the people, whom he characterized as 'thoughtless and vain', were so changed before the sermon was ended that they were 'bowed down with an awful conviction of their sin and danger'.[1] Stephen Williams, another eye-witness wrote the story the same day more

[1]*Ibid*, 2, p. 112.

graphically in his diary:

We went over to Enfl- where we met dear Mr E- of N-H- who preach^d a most awakening sermon from these words – Deut. 32–35 and before sermon was done – there was a great moaning and crying out through ye whole House – What Shall I do to be sav^d – oh I am going to Hell – Oh what shall I do for Christ &c. So y^t ye minister was obliged to desist – ye shrieks & cry^s were piercing & Amazing – after Some time of waiting the Congregation were Still so y^t a prayer was made by Mr. W. & after that we descen^d from the pulpitt and discours^d with the people – Some in one place and Some in another – and Amazing and Astonishing ye power God was seen – & Several Souls were hopefully wrought upon yt night, & oh ye cheerfulness and pleasantness of their countenances yt receiv^d comfort – oh yt God wd strengthen and confirm – we sung an hymn & pray^d & dismiss^d ye Assembly.[1]

Edwards himself says nothing of the Enfield sermon although it proved, says Trumbull, 'the beginning of the same great and prevailing concern in that place with which the colony in general was visited'. There were, after all, many similar days in the year 1741. Writing, for example, of what happened at Wethersfield at the end of the same year, Wheelock reported to a friend, 'The whole town seems to be shaken. . . . Last Monday night the Lord bowed the heavens and came down upon a large assembly in one of the parishes of the town, the whole assembly seemed alive with distress, the groans and outcries of the wounded were such that my voice could not be heard'.[2]

The strong, sometimes even agonizingly overwhelming, conviction of sin so widespread at this date was nothing more than is common to all true revivals. Men suddenly, and in large numbers, are made to feel the real nature and danger of sin. In the words of W. G. T. Shedd, a later New Englander: 'All great religious awakenings begin in the dawning of the august and terrible aspects of the Deity upon the popular mind, and they reach their height and happy consummation in that love and faith for which the antecedent fear has been the preparation'.[3]

---

[1]The Diary is printed in Oliver Means, *A Sketch of the Strict Congregational Church of Enfield, Conn.* (Hartford, 1899). Quoted by Ola Winslow, p. 192.

[2]Letter to Daniel Rogers, Jan 18, 1742, quoted by E. S. Gaustad, *The Great Awakening*, p. 46.

[3]*Sermons to the Natural Man*, 1876 (1977 reprint), p. 331.

Yet such emotion, far from being the mere general movement of a crowd, is strikingly personal and individual. In the words of another writer: 'One of the prominent features of the great awakening was that the gospel was armed by the Holy Ghost with a tremendous and irresistible *individualizing* power. Man was made to come forth into the light and take his appropriate place before God as guilty and accountable'.[1] The same author quotes the words of Isaac Taylor:

Instead of that interchange of smiles which lately had pervaded the congregation while the orator was doing his part, now every man feels himself alone in that crowd. Even the preacher himself is almost forgotten; for an immortal guilty spirit has come into the presence of Eternal Justice.

The nature of the preaching in the Great Awakening was often alarming, and intentionally so.[2] The preachers knew, in Shedd's words, that 'it is the lack of a bold and distinct impression from the solemn objects of another world, and the utter absence of fear, that is ruining man from generation to generation'. But they also believed that neither they, nor even the truth itself, could induce the fear which leads to life. Only a *consciousness* of the presence of God can make the truth preached startlingly real to preachers and hearers alike. Then the fact of final judgment can be no more doubted than if it were already present. What a youth said of Edwards' preaching in 1739 was equally true of the speech of others at this date: 'He fully supposed that as soon as Mr. Edwards should close his discourse, the Judge would descend and the final separation take place' (1.clxxxix).

*   *   *

[1] 'Evangelism of the Eighteenth Century' in *The British and Foreign Evangelical Review*, Jan. 1862.

[2] Of Aaron Burr, representative of the younger circle of men who were now foremost in preaching, it was said: 'He was none of those downy doctors who soothe their hearers into delusive hopes of the divine acceptance, or substitute external morality for vital godliness. He scorned to proclaim the peace of God till the rebel had laid down his arms and returned to his allegiance. He searched the conscience with the terrors of the law, before he assuaged its anguish with the sweet emollients of a bleeding Deity.' Webster, p. 451.

Edwards' experiences at Suffield, Enfield and elsewhere in 1741 must have confirmed him in his belief that it was his duty to preach away from home whenever it was possible to accept invitations. In September we read of him at the Yale Commencement at New Haven and towards the end of the year he was away on a 'missionary tour'. In Northampton itself the scene was quieter in the later months of 1741, but of the country as a whole Edwards could write to Joseph Bellamy on January 21, 1742:

Neither earth nor hell can hinder God's work that is going on in the country. Christ gloriously triumphs at this day. . . . By what I can understand, the work of God is greater at this day in the land than it has been at any time. O what cause have we, with exulting hearts, to agree to give glory to him who thus rides forth in the chariot of his salvation, conquering and to conquer. . . .

It is not probable that I shall be able to attend your meeting at Guilford. I have lately been so much gone from my people, and don't know but I must be obliged to leave 'em again next week about a fortnight, being called to Leicester, a town about half way to Boston, where a great work of grace has lately commenced; and probably soon after that to another place; and having at this time some extraordinary affairs to attend to at home (1.lvi).

On Monday, January 25th, 1742, Edwards left for Leicester. On his return home in February, he says, 'I found the town in very extraordinary circumstances, such as, in some respects, I never saw before'. Such indeed had been the events since his departure that before his homecoming some had feared Mrs Edwards was going to die out of sheer joy. For knowledge of what had followed Edwards' departure on January 25th we have Sarah Edwards' own personal record written at the time and later printed by Dwight. Two days after her husband left, his place was taken by the young Samuel Buell who had been licensed to preach by the New Haven association in the preceding September. 'I had left to him', wrote Edwards, 'the free use of my pulpit, having heard of his designed visit before I went from home'. From Wednesday, January 27th, Buell was to preach in the meeting house almost every day, and from the first service there was a distinct quickening of the people. 'At 3 o'clock in the afternoon', writes Sarah Edwards, 'a lecture was preached by Mr Buell. . . . To my mind there was the clearest evidence that God was present in the congregation on the work of redeeming love; and in the clear view of this, I was at once filled with such intense admiration of the wonderful condescension and grace of God, in returning again to Northampton, as overwhelmed my soul and immediately took away my bodily strength'. For three hours, filled with joy and thankfulness at 'the great goodness of God', she was to remain with others in the meetinghouse after the service was over.

We shall return to Sarah Edwards' experience at this time in the next chapter.

*   *   *

Some impression of Edwards' labours away from home at the beginning of 1742 can be gained from the diary of Ebenezer Parkman, minister at Westborough, a place between Northampton and Boston. As recorded below, Parkman heard Edwards preach at Leicester and succeeded in getting him to extend his time away from home:

January 28, 1742. There being at Leicester very considerable awakenings among some of the people, they set apart this day for fasting and prayer, for obtaining a plentiful effusion of the Holy Spirit upon them; and they having sent for me to assist on that occasion, I went up. Mr Edwards, of Northampton, was there, and preached a very awakening sermon on Rom. 9.22 – 'Vessels of wrath.'

29. Mr Edwards preached on John 12.23, a peculiarly moving and useful sermon. May God bless it to me to draw my heart effectually to Jesus Christ, by his love, by his bitter and ignominious sufferings on the cross for me! I prevailed on Mr Edwards, before we went out of the pulpit, to come by divine leave next week to Westborough.

31. I cannot help remarking what a wonderful time was now appearing: for there are great movings upon the hearts of the people of the country, in one part thereof and another. O! that I and mine might be stirred up earnestly and seasonably to put in for a share! The Lord grant us this mercy, and let us not be left behind!

February 1. It was a rainy day, but I rode to Grafton and Sutton. Mr Edwards was come from Leicester. Mr Edwards preached to a large assembly on Ps. 18.25. At evening, in a very rainy, stormy time, I preached to a considerable assembly on Ps. 68.8. Religion has of late been very much revived in Sutton, and there is a general concern about their souls.

2. A rainy morning. Mr Edwards put on resolution and came with me to Westborough. Mr Edwards preached to a great congregation

on John 12.32, and at eve at my house on Gen. 19.17. N.B. Mr James
Fay was greatly wrought on by the sermon on John 12.32. so were
Samuel Allen and Ezekiel Dodge, who manifested it to me; and
doubtless multitudes besides were so. *Deo Opt. Max. Gloria.*[1]

The year 1742 was to prove the last year of the great revival
both in Northampton and in most parts of New England.
Speaking of his own congregation, Edwards says, 'In the
beginning of the summer of 1742 there seemed to be an
abatement of the liveliness of people's affections in religion'
though in the fall and winter following there were still, at times,
'extraordinary appearances'. 'To this day', he wrote in his
letter to Boston on December 12, 1743, 'there are a considerable number in town that seem to be near to God, and maintain
much of the life of religion, and enjoy many of the sensible
tokens and fruits of his gracious presence.'

The ebb-tide of the revival brought issues to the forefront
which have still to be considered. In the light of the above records
how impossible it ought to be to regard the Great Awakening as a
record of human achievement. The judgment of Alexander V. G.
Allen, that Edwards 'stands forth as the originator, the director,
the champion of the movement',[2] is lamentable. Those who have
looked for uniform causes on the human level to explain the
similarity of results have singularly failed to deal with the known
information. 'The overwhelming effects', say some, 'were
produced by fear and by the preaching of terror'. But 'terror' was
by no means the one message by which the multitudes were
moved – witness Whitefield's preaching at Northampton – and
Sarah Edwards, who was herself so much a subject of the Spirit's
work in the revival, gives testimony to feelings which are the very
opposite of fear. It was not any one doctrine which characterized
the revival. Nor were the effects confined to any one group of
people. Men and women of all ages and descriptions felt
themselves to be in the presence of God. Unbelievers felt it with
profound conviction, but so also did Christians with no less
although different, effect. Some Christians rejoiced in full
assurance, others, writes Edwards, 'passed under a very

[1] 'To God, best and greatest, be glory'. Printed in *The Great Awakening*,
Joseph Tracy, p. 204.
[2] *Life and Writings of Jonathan Edwards*, 1889, p. 162.

remarkable new work of the Spirit of God, as if they had been the subjects of a second conversion' (1.lix).

This influence of the revival upon Christians is one which no modern critic has attempted to explain and yet it is clear that the experience which Sarah Edwards depicts was by no means uncommon. Jonathan Parsons of Lyme, for instance, speaks of October 11th, 1741, as 'our Pentecost' when 'a considerable number trembled in the anguish of their souls', yet, simultaneously:

> Many more began to put on immortality, almost, in the look of their faces. . . . Their looks were all love, adoration, wonder, delight, admiration, humility. In short, it looked to me a resemblance of heaven. . . . Many old Christians told me they had never seen so much of the glory of the Lord, and the riches of his grace, nor felt so much of the power of the gospel before . . . never been so sensible of the love of God to them . . . they could not support themselves, many of them, under the weight of it, they were so deeply affected with it. Had not Christ put underneath his everlasting arms for their support, I know not but many would have expired under the weight of divine benefits.[1]

Nor does the diversity in the revival stop at the differing experiences of those who were its subjects. The preachers themselves, and the circumstances in which they were used, show no common pattern on the human level. Whitefield's visit to Boston and New England was well-publicized beforehand and therein, it has been suggested, lay a good part of his success. But Gilbert Tennent was yet more used in Boston and he arrived unheralded and comparatively unknown in December 1740 when the town was experiencing the heaviest snow-falls in living memory. In style Whitefield and Tennent had little in common. Whitefield had 'too much action', thought one Boston minister, whereas Tennent 'seemed to have no regard to please the eyes of his hearers with agreeable gesture, nor their ears with delivery'.[2]

---

[1]Gillies, *op. cit.*, p. 389.

[2]Thomas Prince, who has written the fullest account of Tennent in Boston (reprinted in Gillies, p. 349 ff). Tennent, says Prince, 'did not indeed at first come up to my expectation, but afterwards exceeded it'. After speaking of the great effects of Tennent's ministry, Prince reveals his biblical understanding when he adds, 'If Mr Tennent was to come here again, and preach more rousingly than ever, it may be not one soul would come under conviction by him'.

The contrast between Whitefield and Edwards is still more marked. Whitefield, says Ola Winslow, had 'oratorical talents nothing short of amazing' and he employed them so effectively that 'those who followed him lost all sense of rational discrimination'.[1] If this is the explanation of Whitefield's usefulness how are we to account for the same spiritual results attending 'the ministry of the Rev Mr Edwards of Northampton: a preacher of low and moderate voice, a natural way of delivery, and without any agitation of body, or anything else in the manner to excite attention, except his habitual and great solemnity, looking and speaking as in the presence of God'?[2]

The common factor among the preachers of the Great Awakening did not consist in their possession of the same natural gifts. Their dissimilarity on the human level is plain to see and we are brought back to the same explanation: 'It is just as the Holy Spirit pleases', observed Thomas Prince, 'who hides occasions of pride from man.'

The conviction that the Great Awakening was a glorious work of God had one very practical consequence upon the mind of Edwards and his brethren. It left them unconcerned to proclaim 'success' in terms of numerical results and, because they knew they could neither induce saving conversion nor infallibly register its existence in others, they made no claim even to know the results with any exactness. Edwards did give a figure in his *Narrative of Surprising Conversions* of 1736 but the mistake was not repeated in his maturer writings of the 1740's. He does not even state the number of new communicants although the figure was probably around 200. As C. H. Maxson says, 'It was not the custom of Whitefield or of the various pastors who published detailed reports of the course of the revival in their congregations to state the number of conversions. Any estimate, therefore, of the number of conversions in the Great Awakening is a mere guess'.[3] Trumbull gives an

[1] *Jonathan Edwards*, p. 176.
[2] Gillies, p. 352.
[3] *The Great Awakening in the Middle Colonies*, 1920, p. 33 fn. Speaking of his weeks in the Middle Colonies in November and December 1739, Whitefield writes, 'I have great reason to think many are brought home to God.' But he adds, 'When I return it will then be seen who has received the word into an honest and good heart' *Works*, 1, p. 135.

estimate for the figure in New England as between 'thirty or forty thousand' – others have gone to 'fifty thousand' but, as Maxson says, it is mere conjecture and the latter figure is probably 'absurd'.[1] Certainly the increase in church membership was impressive but much more so was the religious and moral change which the Awakening brought to the colonies in general. Speaking of this period, the cautious Samuel Miller of Princeton had no hesitation in writing in 1837, 'A revival of religion more extensive and powerful then ever occurred before or since, was vouchsafed to the American churches.'[2]

A minister in the great Ulster revival of the last century wrote, 'It were worth living ten thousand of ages in obscurity and reproach to be permitted to creep forth at the expiration of that time and engage in the glorious work of the last six months of 1859'.[3] That was precisely how Edwards felt in 1740–42, for God 'appeared so wonderfully in this land.'

[1]G. L. Walker, *Religious Life of New England*, p. 102.
[2]*Life of Jonathan Edwards*, 1839, p. 75.
[3]*The Year of Grace: A History of the Ulster Revival of 1859*, William Gibson, 1860, p. 89.

10

PERSONAL PORTRAITS

Elm planted by Edwards, reproduced from The Sunday at Home *No. 1165, August 26 1876.*

On August 20, 1881 Andrew Bonar of Glasgow wrote home from Massachusetts: 'The day was beautiful, everything bathed in sunshine . . . We came to what was an old street where Jonathan Edwards' house stood. The two great elm trees in front of the house are remarkable in themselves. In those days the ground all round was a grove of pines where Jonathan Edwards used to walk and pray.'

Northampton, Sunday, October 19, [1740]. Felt great satisfaction in being at the house of Mr. Edwards. A sweeter couple I have not yet seen. Their children were not dressed in silks and satins, but plain, as become the children of those who, in all things, ought to be examples of Christian simplicity. Mrs. Edwards is adorned with a meek and quiet spirit; she talked solidly of the things of God, and seemed to be such a helpmeet for her husband, that she caused me to renew those prayers, which, for some months, I have put up to God, that He would be pleased to send me a daughter of Abraham to be my wife.

George Whitefield's Journals (1960 reprint, pp. 476–7)

What a blessed thing is the marriage of two believers, of one hope, one discipline, servants of the same Master! . . . Together they offer up their prayers – together they lie in the dust, and keep their fasts, teaching each other, exhorting each other, bearing up each other. They are together in God's Church, together at God's feast, together in straits, persecutions, consolations; freely the sick are visited and the indigent supported; there are alms without trouble; sacrifices without scruple; daily unimpeded diligence. Christ sees it and rejoices.

Tertullian, *Ad Ux*. lib.ii.c 9.

Every Christian family ought to be as it were a little church, consecrated to Christ, and wholly influenced and governed by his rules. And family education and order are some of the chief of the means of grace.

J E (1.ccvi)

IO

At the time there would have been nothing memorable about the arrival of a heavily-built twenty-year-old student for the ministry at the Edwards' parsonage one winter's day in December 1741. Samuel Hopkins came unannounced, having ridden eighty miles from his parents' home in Connecticut. Three months earlier he had taken his degree at Yale and it was at that time, at the College Commencement, that he had first heard Edwards preach. Prior to hearing Edwards, his purpose had been to complete his training by going to live with Gilbert Tennent ('the greatest and best man, and the best preacher'). Edwards' visit to New Haven changed his plans. He writes: 'Though I then did not obtain any personal acquaintance with him, any further than by hearing him preach . . . I altered my former determination with respect to Mr Tennent, and concluded to go and live with Mr Edwards as soon as I should have opportunity'.

It says much about the hospitality of New England parsonages that Hopkins had no apprehensions about arriving unexpectedly as 'an utter stranger' in mid-winter. Most parsonages were akin to inns, with almost constant visitors and guests and certainly this was the case in Northampton. Ever since Sarah Edwards' brother, Benjamin Pierrepont, had stayed with them soon after their marriage, ministerial students had often boarded at the house in King Street. John Sergeant, at this date a missionary to the Indians at Stockbridge, had been there, so also had Joseph Bellamy in 1738. There is no list of others who shared the same privilege.

'When I arrived there,' writes Hopkins of his first visit in 1741, 'Mr Edwards was not at home; but I was received with great kindness by Mrs Edwards and the family, and had encouragement that I might live there during the winter. Mr Edwards was absent on a preaching tour as people in general were greatly attentive to religion and preaching'.

What made Hopkins' stay with the Edwards so important for posterity is that the Connecticut student was later to supply the only biography by an eyewitness.[1] Without Hopkins' record we should know much less of the personal life of Edwards as it was observed by others. It is by his help that Jonathan and Sarah Edwards emerge as life-like figures.

When Hopkins arrived, Sarah was thirty and her husband thirty-eight. Of the children, Sarah, the eldest was now thirteen, Jerusha eleven, Esther nine, Mary seven, Lucy five, Timothy three and Susannah – the latest arrival – only eighteen months. On March 9, 1741, Edwards had written to Benjamin Colman that the past winter had been 'a time of the most remarkable and visible blessing of heaven upon my family that ever was . . . I hope that my four eldest children have been savingly wrought upon.' In all the work which such a household entailed Sarah Edwards was, of course, not single handed. Black household servants (bought as slaves, or belonging to households from birth) were comparatively common in New England and there were several connected with the Edwards' home at various times. 'Mercy' appears to have been one of the favourites among the children. The life of these blacks, who took their place at family worship and in the meetinghouse every Sunday, had little in common with the slaves depicted by a later New Englander, Harriet Beecher Stowe, in her *Uncle Tom's Cabin*.

With Edwards away for many days, Hopkins came to know

---

[1]He remained until late March 1742 when he returned home 'to obtain a license to preach'. In May, he says, 'I returned to Northampton, proposing to spend some time in pursuing my studies with Mr Edwards, where I lived during the summer, preaching sometimes in Mr Edwards's pulpit and to private meetings'. See the Memoir by Edward A. Park in *The Works of Samuel Hopkins*, 1854, vol. 1, pp. 23–24.

Mrs Edwards first. Her liveliness in managing the entire household, her kindness ('she knew the heart of a stranger') and her 'more than ordinary' beauty, were among his first impressions. On her part, Sarah Edwards was also forming impressions of this further candidate for the ministry, noting that, despite the welcome he had received, he was 'gloomy and dejected' and inclined to remain alone in his room. It was there, after a few days, that Hopkins and his hostess had their first extended conversation as her friendly enquiries broke through his reserve. His trouble, he told her, was concern arising out of his spiritual condition. 'I was,' he later wrote, 'in a Christless, graceless state, and had been under a degree of conviction and concern for myself for a number of months'. Mrs. Edwards' readiness to enter into 'a free conversation' revealed a deeper aspect of her character and her own evident confidence towards God arrested him. It was as though she could see things presently hidden from him. She told him that 'she trusted I should receive light and comfort, and doubted not that God intended yet to do great things by me' (1.lvii).

When Edwards arrived home, Hopkins may have doubted whether the cordiality and ready conversation of Mrs. Edwards was capable of being matched by her husband. Edwards' seriousness, both in appearance and in behaviour, was always to be foremost in Hopkins' memory. It was not an affected gravity, he recalled, but 'the natural genuine indications and expression of a deep, abiding sense of divine things on his mind and of his living constantly in the fear of God'. Possibly Edwards had little gift in putting the younger man at ease on their first meeting. 'He was not a man of many words and was somewhat reserved among strangers, and those on whose candour and friendship he did not know he could rely.' So Hopkins later wrote. Yet if his host was no ready socializer his capacity for friendship was much deeper than first impressions might suggest. As with other men who stayed at the parsonage, a bond was to develop between Edwards and Hopkins which endured for life. There were to be many other visits by Hopkins to Northampton following the six or seven months which he spent there in 1741–42. Of those later visits Hopkins' Journal records such entries as the following:

Northampton, May 30, 1743, Rode to-day from Westfield hither, – am kindly received by Mr. Edwards and his family. I have thoughts of staying here this summer. . . .

It would appear that he only stayed for a month at that date but he was soon back:

Northampton, July 23, 1743. Am kindly received by Mr. Edwards and his family. Made Miss Jerusha a present of a Bible. Mr. Edwards is desirous that I would preach for him part of the day to-morrow, but I cannot be willing.

Sunday, July 24, 1743. Heard Mr. Edwards preach all day. I have been very dull and senseless; much discouraged about preaching. Hearing Mr. Edwards makes me ashamed of myself. . . .

Brookfield, Thursday, May 24, 1744. Set out to-day from North-ampton for Boston, in company with Madam Edwards and her daughter, who rides behind me [on horseback]. We lodge at Colonel Dwight's,[1] at Brookfield.

Years later Hopkins had no hesitation in defending his deceased friend from the charge of being 'stiff and unsociable'. 'His known and tried friends,' writes Hopkins, 'always found him easy of access, kind and condescending; and though not talkative, yet affable and free. Among such whose candor and friendship he had experienced, he threw off the reserve, and was most open and free.'

Hopkins attributes Edwards' quietness to his physique: 'He possessed but a comparative small stock of animal life: his animal spirits were low, and he had not strength of lungs to spare, that would be necessary in order to make him what would be called, an affable, facetious gentleman in all com-panies.' It is more likely that the explanation lies in his temperament rather than in his 'lungs', although it is clear that his health was not robust. 'Weak in body', Whitefield had noted a year earlier. 'He was of a weakly, infirm constitution,' says Hopkins, but what he also tells us of Edwards' daily programme excludes the idea that he was comparable to a semi-invalid: 'He used himself to rise by four or between four and five in the morning . . . he was wont to have his family up in season in the morning; after which, before the family entered on

[1] Joseph Dwight, who plays a large part in Edwards' life at a later date.

the business of the day, he attended on family prayers, when a chapter in the Bible was read, commonly by candle-light in the winter, upon which he asked his children questions according to their age and capacity.' The most frequently quoted of Hopkins' descriptive paragraphs on Edwards proceeds:

Though he was of tender constitution, yet few students are capable of a closer or longer application, than he was. He commonly spent thirteen hours, every day, in his study. His usual recreation in summer, was riding on horseback and walking. He would commonly, unless prevented by company, ride two or three miles after dinner to some lonely grove, where he would dismount and walk a while. At such times he generally carried his pen and ink with him, to note any thought that might be suggested, and which promised some light on any important subject. In the winter, he was wont, almost daily, to take an axe, and chop wood, moderately, for the space of half an hour or more.

We have already given consideration to the words in the above quotation on the numbers of hours which Edwards 'commonly' spent daily in his study. Some further comment is now needed for the 'thirteen hours' have too often been understood as proof that he was a man absorbed in his own affairs and far removed from the ordinary events of home or parish. Other sentences from Hopkins are quoted to confirm this view:

He was less acquainted with most of his temporal affairs than many of his neighbours, and seldom knew when and by whom his forage for winter was gathered in, or how many milk kine he had, whence his table was furnished, etc.

He did not make it his custom to visit his people in their own houses, unless he was sent for by the sick, or he heard that they were under some special affliction. . . .

A century later a folklore on this subject existed among the people of Northampton. At the 'Edwards Family Meeting' convened in 1870 one speaker produced the following:

I have heard one of his grandsons say, that, on one occasion, Mr Edwards rode on horseback to his pasture for his cows; and, when he came near the bars of his pasture, a small boy ran to them, and let them down for him. As the minister was riding over the bars, he bowed to the boy, and asked, 'Whose boy are you?' – 'John Clark's

[183]

boy', was the answer. Mr Edwards soon came back, driving his cows before him. The boy stood ready to put up the bars, and took off his hat as the pastor drew near. 'Whose boy are you?' was the question asked the second time; and the answer came, 'The same man's boy that I was five minutes ago.' This incident shows how absorbed Mr Edwards was in his studies, and how abstracted from the world.

These references to Edwards' apparent abstractedness require closer attention for taken alone they certainly give a wrong impression.

First, Edwards' 'thirteen hours' in his study were by no means always spent *alone*. On the contrary, Hopkins makes it clear that Edwards was readily accessible, not only to his family (Sarah Edwards, he says, was 'frequently' there), but also to all in his large congregation who had any spiritual need. One reason why he did not visit from house to house, says Hopkins, was that 'he believed he could do more good conversing with persons under religious impressions in his study where they might be sure to be allowed easy access to him, and where they were treated with all desirable tenderness, kindness and familiarity'.

In times of revival, we read of the parsonage study being 'thronged with persons'. It was also Edwards' practice with people and children who might be nervous to approach him, to invite them to the parsonage, 'when he used to pray with them and treat with them in a manner suited to their years and circumstances'.

To be sure, Edwards coveted time alone in his study for the purposes already discussed. Hopkins was impressed by the fact that a man already twenty years in the ministry had still 'an uncommon thirst for knowledge . . . he read all the books, especially books of divinity, that he could come at'. But the way in which Edwards could suspend this normal daily routine in order to be away preaching in other places – as he was when Hopkins first arrived – is another reminder that study, as such, was not his first interest.

There is good reason to believe that Edwards was not the impractical, absent-minded figure which some have depicted. Hopkins does not say that it was any lack of ability or aptitude which kept Edwards from the temporal affairs of house and farm. If *necessary* he could attend to crops, to the purchase of cattle, or to shopping in Boston, as well as any. Letters to his friend Joseph Bellamy show that he was familiar with the price of sheep and well-able to make good arrangements for their purchase, and for shearing and wool deliveries. Bills which survive from visits to Boston also show how he concerned himself with the family's every-day happiness: among his shopping we hear of a gold locket and chain for Sarah, lute strings, silk handkerchiefs, children's toys, chocolate and so on. It was a matter of policy that he normally left so much of every-day matters to his wife. 'She took almost the entire charge of the temporal affairs of the family, without doors and within,' writes Hopkins. 'He gave himself wholly to the work of the ministry, and entangled not himself with the affairs of this life.' But on occasions when Sarah had to be away her husband could undertake the larger role as we shall later note.

There is a further reason for rejecting the image of Edwards as an absent-minded academic. It is that such an image cannot be harmonized with the impression which visitors received. Hopkins is far from alone in speaking of the warmth of the Edwards' hospitality. Clearly no one felt that their host grudged the time which they enjoyed in his company. George Whitefield was obviously at home during his three-day stay in 1740. Joseph Emerson, another minister, wrote after being in the Edwards' home: 'Very courteously treated here. The most agreeable family I was ever acquainted with. Much of the presence of God here. Mr Edwards was so kind as to accompany us over Connecticut River and bring us on our way.'

What Emerson perhaps did not know was that it was Edwards' custom to prolong his time with guests by riding out some distance with them as they left Northampton. With Whitefield he was to ride as far as East Windsor – certainly one of the many occasions when there was no 'thirteen hours' in the study!

Letters from Edwards to Bellamy show how eagerly he enjoyed and looked for such visits from friends. He begins one letter, 'I have been for some time in expectation of seeing you here and though you are not yet come, I hope it will not be long . . . '. Another letter presses the same point, 'We have so many affairs to confer upon, that concern us both, that I would propose you should come this way again in February or March. You haven't a great family to tie you at home as I have.'

Edwards' relationship with his children suggests that they also did not view their father as aloof and remote. As the girls grew older we know that it was his frequent custom to take one of them with him on horseback on journeys away from home. With one of his sons we find him engaged one day in the business of measuring Mount Tom, which they found to be sixty-three rods high (1,202 feet on our modern maps). The children were no doubt also in his company, and probably helping him, as he planted trees, including the two elms reputedly planted by him in front of the homestead. Dwight speaks of family gatherings in the parlour after tea when Edwards relaxed 'into cheerful and animated conversation' and entered 'truly into the feelings and concerns of his children'. The testimony of his daughter, Esther, on her father's enjoyment of those evening hours will occur later.

In the light of all this what is to be made of the nineteenth-century tale of Edwards and John Clark's boy? Even if the anecdote is apocryphal it probably reflects a feeling in Northampton that Edwards was not a familiar figure among his people. We shall return to this in a subsequent chapter when it will be seen that the town had a vested interest in the circulation of such stories.

*   *   *

We could wish that Hopkins had recorded more of his Sundays in Northampton. Edwards' high view of the Lord's day is clear enough in his writings and especially in his three early sermons on 'The Perpetuity and Change of the Sabbath' (2.93–103). 'The christian sabbath is one of the most precious enjoyments of the visible church . . . The Sabbath seems to have been appointed very much for this end, viz. to uphold the visibility of religion in public, or among professing societies of men. . . . The Lord Jesus Christ takes delight in his own day; he delights to honour it; he delights to meet with and manifest himself to his disciples on it. . . . ' All that Hopkins does tell us confirms what the Lord's day meant to Edwards personally: 'As he believed that the Sabbath or holy time began at sunset the evening before the Day, he ordered his family to finish all their secular business by that time or before, when they were all called together, and a psalm was sung and prayer attended, as an introduction to the sanctifying the Sabbath'.

There is no description from Hopkins' pen of a service at the meetinghouse. The form of the service would be uniform with the prevailing custom in New England. The praise was made up of psalmody – The Bay Psalm Book[1] – unaccompanied by musical instrument or choir. In their singing, says Edwards, 'our congregation excelled all that ever I knew . . . the men generally carrying regularly, and well, three parts of music, and the women a part by themselves' (1.348). It must have been an inspiring volume of song in a building which we can assume was generally densely packed. 'The duty of singing praises to God seems to be appointed wholly to excite and express religious affections,' Edwards believed. 'No other reason can be assigned why we shall express ourselves to God in verse rather than in prose' (1.242). As praise is commanded in public worship, therefore, he would often remind his people, everyone is to sing and 'parents ought to be careful that their children are instructed in singing' (2.917).

We have already noted that the total population would have been as high as 1,200, with a considerable percentage of that number being young people and children. Edwards at this date speaks of 620 communicants 'which include almost all our adult persons' (1.350). These he seems to identify, elsewhere, as people 'above fourteen years of age'. This could easily leave a few hundred children under fifteen who were old enough to attend church and so the congregation at this period must have numbered upwards of 700. The accommodation figure of 795 clearly referred to regular seating for we have noted Sarah Edwards speaking of 'upwards of a thousand people' hearing Whitefield in the Northampton church and Timothy Edwards refers to a later occasion when 'fourteen hundred and sixty persons were once counted in the Church on a Sabbath

[1]This was strictly a metrical version of the Psalms but although Edwards always retained his high regard for the Psalms 'by the direction of the Holy Ghost penned for the use of the church of God in its public worship' (1.240) he was to defend the introduction of other forms of praise (1.396) and Watts' paraphrases were introduced in his own congregation about 1743.

afternoon; amounting to five-sixths of the inhabitants'.[1] Some, and especially children, would simply be crowded in. Towards the end of the century it was ruled that children should not sit on the pulpit stairs. No one in those days doubted whether children should be attenders throughout public worship.[2]

Much more time was spent in public prayer than is common today, the people all standing as Edwards led them. The majority of the pews were high square 'boxes', with seats on three sides which could be turned up during prayer so that worshippers might lean on the top of the pew. Edwards' prayers were always extempore. Hopkins writes: 'He was the farthest from any appearance of a form, as to his words and manner of expression, as almost any man. He was quite singular in this, inimitable by any who have not a spirit of real and undissembled devotion. . . . He appeared to have much of the grace and spirit of prayer.'

It is to be regretted that Hopkins does not tell us more about the actual manner of Edwards' preaching for there is reason to believe that this subject also has been distorted by a later folklore. 'He *wrote* his sermons,' says Dwight in 1829, 'and in so fine and so illegible a hand that they could be read only by being brought near to the eye' (1.clxxxix). From this statement the inference has been drawn that Edwards was unmistakably and lamely dependent upon a manuscript which he had to lift up to his face while he preached. There is, however, a whole series of facts which militate against such a supposition.

First, as late as 1723, Solomon Stoddard had spoken forcefully in print against 'reading' preachers. Is it likely that three years later he would have approved of a colleague who could only read?

Second, allowing that Edwards' convictions about preaching underwent some development, even his early preaching of the 1730's, already considered, does not fit the above representation. He believed that preaching is *not* the equivalent to reading a book. 'God has ordained that his Word be opened, applied and set home upon men in preaching.' God has appointed 'a

---

[1] *Travels*, 1, p. 330.
[2] On the need for children to hear the *same* truths as adults see 1.393, 'I have seen the happy effects of dealing plainly and thoroughly with children in the concerns of their souls'.

particular and lively application of his Word' to affect men's hearts and affections (1.242).

Third, when Edwards came to Northampton in 1726 he changed the size of the paper on which he wrote his sermons from octavo to the much smaller duodecimo, that is to say, his sermon 'booklet' became about 3–7/8 inches by 4–1/8 inches, a size which could be 'palmed', almost unseen, in his hand. The obvious explanation for this is that he did not mean to parade his use of notes. Such an exercise would have been pointless had the people seen him reading word for word from an uplifted manuscript.

Fourth, from around 1741, Edwards gave up the practice of the previous twenty years and ceased to write his sermons in full. Thereafter, he generally appears to have written only an outline of notes. By the time of his death over a third of his surviving sermon manuscripts were outlines rather than the fully written work of earlier years. From 1741, then, with few exceptions no manuscripts existed which could have been read word for word as a sermon! Apparently looking at the post-1741 manuscripts of Edwards' sermons, A. B. Grosart wrote, 'His MSS. shew, beyong all gainsaying, that his rule – in the proportion of 95 to 100 – was to jot down the leading thoughts and illustrations, and trust to the suggestions of the moment for the recall of previous study, and meditation and prayer, and for the language'.[1] If Edwards had laboriously read every word of his sermons before 1741, and then suddenly changed, it is surprising that no one seems to have commented upon it at the time.

Fifth, there are no eye-witness accounts of Edwards reading a sermon. It was to be said, *later*, that his famous Enfield sermon of June, 1741 was read but the nature of the surviving notes for that occasion appear to deny it. One Northampton

[1] *Selections from the Unpublished Writings of Jonathan Edwards*, 1865, p. 14. Grosart's percentage is clearly wrong. Possibly his mistake arose from seeing only the sermon MSS. in the Andover Collection, of which 50 are outlines and only 5 complete. But the Yale Collection of 1,102 MSS. is said to be made up of 702 full manuscripts (including about 400 marked with the occasions when preached) and '177 outlines, 52 fragments and 171 brief outlines', R. G. Turnbull, *Jonathan Edwards, The Preacher*, p. 159. Manuscripts of some of Edwards' sermons (including many of those subsequently published) do not survive.

hearer says: 'Mr. Edwards in preaching used no gestures, but looked straight forward; Gideon Clark said, "he looked on the bell rope until he looked it off".'

Samuel Hopkins, writing nearly twenty years after his frequent visits to Northampton, says something on Edwards' manner of preaching that falls somewhere between the words of Gideon Clark and the wrong inference drawn from Dwight's nineteenth-century statement given above. Somewhat loosely his words do approximate with the facts given above. He corroborates the manuscript evidence that Edwards stopped writing sermons in full about 1741. Edwards followed the practice, Hopkins writes, 'nearly twenty years after he first began to preach' (*i.e*, 1722). It must have been with respect to these full notes that he also says, 'He read most that he wrote: still he was not confined to them; and if some thoughts were suggested to him while he was preaching, which did not occur to him when writing, and appeared pertinent, he would deliver them with as great propriety and fluency, and often with greater pathos, and attended with a more sensibly good effect on his hearers, than what he had written'.

What probably happened was that Edwards for some twenty years took his full manuscript into the pulpit. He never read it word for word and he gradually became less dependent upon it. Then, for an intermediate period, he continued to write at some length but took only a brief skeleton – 'thumb papers' as the East Windsor people called them – into the pulpit with him.[1] Finally he ceased to write in full and prepared only an extended outline. That the Great Awakening period coincided with this change is not without interest. It is not that he simply became too busy to write his sermons fully. Rather he was now more fully convinced, as Grandfather Stoddard had been long before, that freedom from dependence on a manuscript was in best accord with the true nature of preaching. His former attachment to notes, says Hopkins, he came to regard as 'a defect and infirmity . . . he was inclined to think it had been better if he had never accustomed

---

[1] The Enfield sermon, for example, is an approximately duodecimo booklet with 22 written sides but for the *same* sermon there is a 4-page outline as small as 3 inches –1/8 by 3–6/8. The same is true of other sermons of this date. Such skeleton outlines would appear to be pointless unless they were meant for pulpit use.

himself to use his notes at all'. Thus, in his later ministry at least, Edwards would have agreed with Grosart who asserts that the practice of reading sermons, '*except in rare instances,* quenches all real eloquence' and 'breaks the spell of influence which ought to bind a speaker and his audience'.

Further examination of Edwards' manuscripts may throw more light on this subject, although the point may be of technical interest to preachers rather than to the general reader. What is clear is that the impression made by Edwards as a preacher owed little to the actual manner of his delivery. His voice was low and calm. He aimed to avoid 'a sad tone' and the 'very ridiculous whining tone' which he heard from some men.[1] 'He made but little motion with his head or hands,' observes Hopkins. What was striking was the distinctness and clarity of his thought ('he handled concepts,' in McGiffert's phrase, 'as scrupulously and precisely as a banker handles currency') together with a seriousness arising from 'a solemn consciousness of the presence of God'. This seriousness, says Dwight, 'was visible in his looks and general demeanor. It obviously had a controlling influence over all his preparations for the pulpit.' On the same point he quotes Hopkins: 'He appeared with such gravity and solemnity, and his words were so full of ideas, that few speakers have been able to command the attention of an audience as he did.'

It would be true to say that Edwards was not as 'popular' a preacher as some of his contemporaries, but his manner of ministry is an important reminder that Spirit-anointed preaching is not to be identified with any one type of delivery.[2]

*　　　*　　　*

Perhaps the most attractive part of Hopkins' portrait of the Edwards family is in the relation of husband and wife to each other and to the children. Edwards preached against husbands

[1] Townsend, p. 235.
[2] Hopkins says that Edwards 'had the most universal character of a *good* preacher of almost any minister in America' and he assigns three reasons for his excellence: (1) The great care he took in composing his sermons; (2) His great acquaintance with divinity, and knowledge of the Bible; (3) His spiritual experience, 'He well knew what was in man, both the saint and the sinner'.

who 'treated their wives like servants' and who failed to 'study to suit' their partner. No one could suppose that Sarah's heavy share of labour in directing the home was due to any thoughtlessness on his part. Their respective work was happily agreed. 'No person of discernment could be conversant in the family,' writes Hopkins, 'without observing and admiring the great harmony and mutual love and esteem that subsisted between them'.

The Edwards' views on the care of their children obviously coincided. Apart from moral duties, the only rule strictly required concerned the regular pattern of daily life. Family life was unified by adherence to the same time-table. No one was to be out after nine in the evening or to have friends in beyond that hour. 'The hour for retirement was firmly kept'. Even when the daughters were old enough to have admirers and suitors, and left free to be on their own with 'a room and fire', the same hours were kept and nothing allowed which would 'intrude on the religion and order of the family'.

As for the discipline exercised upon the Edwards' children, Hopkins observed the rarity of any corporal punishment. Edwards corrected 'with the greatest calmness and commonly without striking a blow'. Similarly, he writes: Sarah Edwards 'knew how to make them regard and obey her cheerfully, without loud, angry words, much less heavy blows. She seldom struck her children, and in speaking to them adopted mild, gentle, and pleasant terms'.

It must be granted that Hopkins' view of the success of this family government is somewhat idealized. 'Quarrelling and contention, which too frequently take place among children were not known among them'. We can be sure that there was plenty to harass the parents on occasion even in their large and happy household. Not all the children were as mild as Jerusha or as obedient as Esther. The quick-temper of Sarah, the eldest daughter, so persisted that, according to tradition, when her hand was asked in marriage by Elihu Parsons ten years later, Edwards 'plainly disclosed to him the unpleasant temper of his daughter'. 'But she has grace, I trust?' asked Parsons, to which Edwards replied, 'I hope she has, but grace can live where you cannot'. Here was the usual Edwardean seriousness lightened with a touch of humour.

*Sarah Edwards at the age of 41, a painting attributed to Joseph Badger.
Reproduced by courtesy of Yale University Art Gallery, bequest of Eugene
Phelps Edwards.*

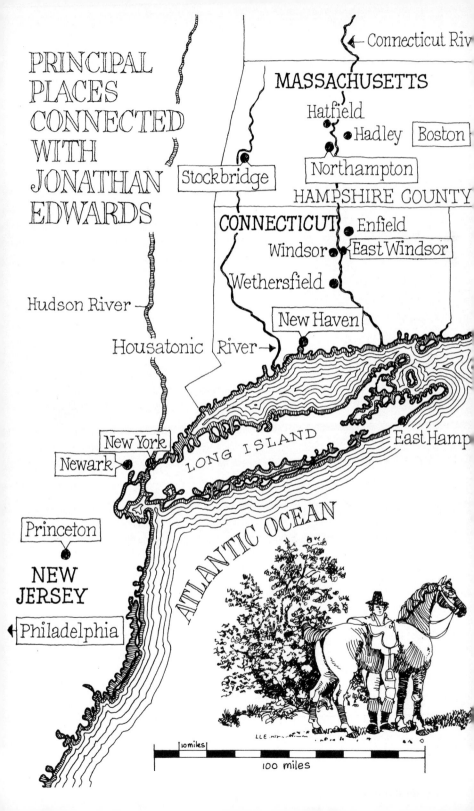

PRINCIPAL PLACES CONNECTED WITH JONATHAN EDWARDS

← Connecticut Riv

MASSACHUSETTS

Hatfield

Hadley

Boston

Northampton

HAMPSHIRE COUNTY

Stockbridge

CONNECTICUT

Enfield

Windsor

East Windsor

Wethersfield

Hudson River –

New Haven

Housatonic River →

New York

Newark

LONG ISLAND

East Hamp

Princeton

NEW JERSEY

ATLANTIC OCEAN

Philadelphia

10 miles

100 miles

LLE

When we turn to Hopkins' admiration of Mrs Edwards there is so much to confirm his impression that we have no grounds for accusing him of exaggeration. But it is necessary to emphasize that it was more than natural gifts or temperament that made her what she was. At its deepest level, as Edwards himself brings out, her life had not always been what it was in 1742. His account of his wife's spiritual experience is one of the most striking passages in all he ever wrote, and Sarah's own narrative – recorded at Jonathan's request and to be found in Dwight's *Life of Edwards* – is an amazing testimony to how much of heaven can be enjoyed upon earth.

Edwards believed that his wife had been converted when she was a child[1] and we have already noticed what he wrote about her when she was only thirteen. Those words, however, written in 1723 and four years before their marriage, needed to be modified. Until the revival of 1735, says Edwards, Sarah 'had formerly, in lower degrees of grace, been subject to unsteadiness, and many ups and downs, in the frame of mind, being under great disadvantages through a vaporous habit of body, and often subject to melancholy, and at times almost overborne with it, it having been so even from early youth' (1.376). In 1735, when she was brought to a 'more entire devotion of heart to the service and glory of God, she experienced a degree of spiritual joy not previously known (1.xlvi). Not until the summer of 1740, however, did she experience such a degree of assurance that all her previous fears seemed 'to be overcome and crushed by the power of faith and trust in God, and resignation to him'. Thereafter, says Edwards, writing 'near three years' later (*i.e.* in 1742), she 'has remained in a constant, uninterrupted rest, humble joy in God, and assurance of his favour, without one hour's melancholy or darkness . . . vapours have had great effects on the body, such as they used to have before, but the soul has been always out of their reach.' This assurance, he continued, perhaps with reference to the birth of Susannah, remained even in 'times of the most extreme pain and apparent hazard of immediate death'. It was, says her husband, 'the greatest, fullest, longest continued, and most

[1]'Converted above twenty-seven years ago' (1.376) he wrote of his thirty-three-year-old wife in 1742.

constant assurance of the favour of God and of a title to future glory, that I ever saw any appearance of in any person'.

Thus Sarah Edwards was enjoying 'the riches of full assurance' when Hopkins arrived in December 1741. The following month, as already noted, when her husband was away from home, there was a further outpouring of the Spirit in Northampton, the pulpit being occupied by Samuel Buell, a candidate for the ministry. 'There were very extraordinary effects of Mr Buell's labours,' writes Edwards. 'The people were exceedingly moved, crying out in great numbers in the meeting house, and a great part of the congregation commonly staying in the house of God, for hours after the public service . . . almost the whole town seemed to be in a great and continual commotion, day and night, and there was indeed a very great revival of religion. But it was principally among professors; the appearances of a work of conversion were in no measure as great as they had been the summer before. When I came home, I found the town in very extraordinary circumstances, such as, in some respects, I never saw it in before (1.lix).

It was upon these weeks that Sarah Edwards' own testimony centres in the narrative she sets down and which needs to be read in full[1] (1.lxii-lxviii). Speaking of January 20, 1742, she writes:

While Mr. Reynolds was praying, these words, in Rom. 8.34, came into my mind, 'Who is he that condemneth; it is Christ that died, yea rather that is risen again, who is even at the right hand of God, who also maketh intercession for us . . . ' which occasioned great sweetness and delight in my soul. But when I was alone, the words came to my mind with far greater power and sweetness. They appeared to me with undoubted certainty as the words of God, and as words which God did pronounce concerning me. I had no more doubt of it, than I had of my being. . . . I cannot find language to express how *certain* this appeared – the everlasting mountains and hills were but shadows to it. My safety, and happiness, and eternal enjoyment of God's immutable love, seemed as durable and unchangeable as God himself. Melted and overcome by the sweetness of this assurance, I

---

[1]Only as this, and Edwards' own comments, are read in full will it be rightly seen that their interest is not in *experience* as such. It is the knowledge of God which is first.

fell into a great flow of tears. . . . The presence of God was so near, and
so real, that I seemed scarcely conscious of anything else. . . . The
peace and happiness, which I hereupon felt, was altogether inexpressible. I seemed to be lifted above earth and hell, out of the reach of
everything here below. The whole world, with all its enjoyments, and
all its troubles, seemed to be nothing: My God was my all, my only
portion. . . .

On Thursday, January 28, her mind and soul were 'drawn so
powerfully towards Christ and heaven' that she could write:

I felt more perfectly subdued and weaned from the world and more
fully resigned to God than I had ever been conscious of before. I felt
an entire indifference to the opinions, and representations, and
conduct of mankind respecting me; and a perfect willingness that God
should employ some other instrument than Mr Edwards in advancing the work of grace in Northampton. I was entirely swallowed up
in God, as my only portion, and his honour and glory was the object of
my supreme desire and delight. At the same time, I felt a far greater
love to the children of God than ever before. . . .

I continued in a sweet and lively sense of divine things, until I
retired to rest. That night, which was Thursday night, Jan. 28, was
the sweetest night I ever had in my life. I never before, for so long a
time together, enjoyed so much of the light, and rest, and sweetness of
heaven in my soul, but without the least agitation of body during the
whole time. The great part of the night I lay awake, sometimes asleep,
and sometimes between sleeping and waking. But all night I
continued in a constant, clear, and lively sense of the heavenly
sweetness of Christ's excellent and transcendent love, of his nearness
to me, and of my dearness to him; with an inexpressibly sweet
calmness of soul in an entire rest in him . . . there seemed to be a
constant flowing and reflowing of heavenly and divine love, from
Christ's heart to mine; and I appeared to myself to float or swim, in
these bright, sweet beams of the love of Christ, like the motes
swimming in the beams of the sun, or the streams of his light which
come in at the window. My soul remained in a kind of heavenly
elysium. So far as I am capable of making a comparison, I think that
what I felt each minute, during the continuance of the whole time,
was worth more than all the outward comfort and pleasure which I
had enjoyed in my whole life put together. It was a pure delight,
which fed and satisfied the soul. It was pleasure, without the least
sting, or any interruption. It was a sweetness, which my soul was lost
in. It seemed to be all that my feeble frame could sustain, of that
fulness of joy which is felt by those who behold the face of Christ, and

share his love in the heavenly world.

The next day a special afternoon service had been appointed when William Williams Jr.[1] of Hadley was the preacher. During a time of fellowship at the parsonage in the morning when these words of a hymn were read,

> My sighs at length are turn'd to songs;
> The Comforter is come,

Sarah Edwards was so conscious of 'the joyful presence of the Holy Spirit' that only with difficulty could she refrain from 'leaping with transports of joy'. Of the afternoon service at which Williams preached she writes:

He preached on the subject of the assurance of faith. The whole sermon was affecting to me, but especially when he came to show the way in which assurance was obtained, and to point out its happy fruits. When I heard him say, that *those who have assurance, have a foretaste of heavenly glory*, I knew the truth of it from what I then felt: I knew that I then tasted the clusters of the heavenly Canaan: my soul was filled and overwhelmed with light, and love, and joy in the Holy Ghost, and seemed just ready to go away from the body.

With such experiences her days were now so filled that, as she admits, 'It was with difficulty that I could pursue my ordinary avocations'. Yet her joy, it should be noted, was far from the exuberance of mere excitement. 'Towards night', she noted on the Monday following the above, 'I had a deep sense of the awful greatness of God, and felt with what humility and reverence we ought to behave ourselves before him. Just then Mr. W- came in, and spoke with a somewhat light, smiling air, of the flourishing state of religion in the town; which I could scarcely bear to see. It seemed to me, that we ought greatly to revere the presence of God, and to behave ourselves with the utmost solemnity and humility, when so great and holy a God was so remarkably present, and to rejoice before him with trembling.'

Modern writers have been nonplussed by Sarah Edwards' narrative. McGiffert speaks of her 'pathological traits' and

---

[1] A son of Williams of Hatfield by his first marriage and, like his father, married to a Stoddard. See p. 74.

Patricia Tracy – despite Edwards saying that his wife was 'converted above twenty-seven years' before 1742 (1.376) – speaks of that date as the time of Sarah's 'conversion'. Perry Miller, misusing Edwards' words, says that 'he came back in February to find the town "running wild"' (1.lix). In fact Edwards regarded the experience of his wife (as well as that of other Christians at the time) as a glorious evidence of New Testament Christianity. God had filled Sarah, he says, with 'joy unspeakable and full of glory'. Her longing was that her life might be 'one continued song of praise to God', and such were her views of Christ's person that she 'did as it were swim in the rays of Christ's love, like a little mote swimming in the beams of the sun that come in at a window' (1.376).[1]

Samuel Hopkins had indeed chosen a happy time in which to reside in the parsonage in King Street!

When Edwards put the above words into print in 1742 he took care not to reveal that it was his wife about whom he was writing. He does not even reveal the sex of the 'person of discretion' whose experience he reports. As we shall see when we come to consider the volume in question, it was not biography but the defence of an important biblical truth with which he was concerned. Perhaps, however, the anonymity served little purpose, for though Sarah Edwards lived in the comparative remoteness of Western Massachusetts the closeness of her walk with God was common knowledge in New England. The diary of Ebenezer Parkman is one source which gives us a glimpse of how Edwards' wife appeared to others. When she made an over-night stop *en route* to Boston in May, 1742, he wrote:

May 18, 1742. . . . Mrs Edwards from Northampton, and Searl, a Freshman of New Haven College,[2] here, and lodged here.

[1] It is evident that such experiences have not been regarded as strange among Christians in times of revival. Donald McQueen, for example, who passed through the great revival in Skye in the early nineteenth century, when shown Mrs Edwards' testimony of her experience in 1742, commented that 'instead of being surprised or thinking her experience uncommon, he had seen the day when Mrs Edwards' experience was a common experience with some who were turned to the Lord in Skye'. *Brief Sketch of D. McQueen*, James Ross, 1891, p. 6.

[2] Evidently Hopkins was not the only student to spend time at Northampton in 1742.

19. Sweet converse with Mrs Edwards, a very eminent Christian.

The next week Parkman was himself in Boston and, on a day when he and other ministers engaged in 'a very useful conversation' on the subject of assurance, he notes that he also 'sought Mrs Edwards fruitlessly'. But a few days later she was again a welcome guest at Parkman's Westborough parsonage:

May 29. Mrs Edwards, and young Searl with her, on her journey to Northampton.
30. On Song 2.16. N.B. Mrs Edwards' conversation very wonderful, – her sense of divine things.
31. I rode with Mrs Edwards to Shrewsbury. . . .

It was Sarah Edwards' reputation as a Christian which a few years later helped an embarrassed minister in Portsmouth, New Hampshire, to recover his composure after a memorable incident. The occasion was the ordination of Job Strong. Edwards had been invited to preach but due to the distance, another minister, Samuel Moody (1676–1747) of York, had agreed to be a substitute should the Northampton pastor not arrive. With a full church, and many eager to hear Edwards, the hour for the service arrived with no sign of the expected preacher. Reluctantly Moody – 'a gentleman of unquestioned talents and piety but perfectly unique in his manners,' says Dwight – took his place and proceeded with the service. In the prayer immediately preceding the sermon he took the liberty of expressing his own disappointment and that of the congregation in not having with them 'that eminent servant of God, the Rev. Mr Edwards of Northampton'. But having launched into this line of thought the substitute proceeded to thank God for Edwards, making reference to his 'uncommon piety', his 'great excellence as a preacher', his ministry and his writings. Unknown to him, Edwards had entered the church as he was beginning his prayer and was standing quietly at his side when he opened his eyes!

Recovering quickly from his surprise, Moody shook Edwards by the hand and greeted him with the words,

Brother Edwards, we are all of us much rejoiced to see you here today, and nobody, probably, as much so as myself; but I wish that you might have got in a little sooner, or a little later, or else that I might

[198]

have heard you when you came in, and known that you were here. I didn't intend to flatter you to your face; but there's one thing I'll tell you: They say that your wife is a-going to heaven by a shorter road than yourself (1.cix).

Edwards bowed in silent response before giving out the psalm — to be sung before his sermon based on John 13.15, 16. No doubt he smiled inwardly.

DIVISION AND DISORDER

The President's House, Yale. At the time of the
Great Awakening this was the home of Thomas
Clap (1703–1767), who succeeded Elisha Williams
as Rector of the College in 1739.

Revivals of religion were nowhere heard of, and an orthodox creed and a decent external conduct were the only points on which inquiry was made when persons were admitted to the communion of the church. The habit of the preachers was to address their people as though they were all pious, and only needed instruction and confirmation. . . . Under such a state of things, it is easy to conceive that in a short time vital piety may have almost deserted the church. And nothing is more certain, than that when people have sunk into this deplorable state they will be disposed to manifest strong opposition to faithful, pointed preaching; and will be apt to view every appearance of revival with an unfavourable eye. Accordingly, when God raised up preachers, animated with a burning zeal, who laboured faithfully to convince their hearers of their ruined condition, and of the necessity of a thorough conversion from sin, the opposition to them was violent. The gospel, among people in such a condition, is sure to produce strife and division between those who fall under its influence and those whose carnal minds urge them to oppose it.

The Log College, ARCHIBALD ALEXANDER, 1851
(reprinted, Banner of Truth Trust 1968), pp. 17–18

'I suppose', wrote Edwards in 1742, 'there is scarcely a minister in this land but from Sabbath to Sabbath is used to pray that God would pour out his Spirit and work a reformation and revival in religion in the country' (1.375). Accordingly, as he goes on to say, 'when so great and extensive a reformation is so sudden and wonderfully accomplished', was it not to be expected that New England's four hundred ministers would be united in their acknowledgment of answered prayer? But he already knew that it was not to be. The previous September, in a sermon at the Yale Commencement at New Haven, while upholding the revival as, in the main, a glorious work of God's Spirit, he had referred to the fact that 'in many places people see plainly that their ministers have an ill opinion of the work'. Such anti-revival opinion was not, indeed, openly expressed, rather it was the 'long-continued silence' of some, in the midst of the blessing, which showed their 'secret kind of opposition' (2.271–2).

This New Haven sermon of September 1741 was one of the first titles in print relating to the revival. With a lengthy preface by William Cooper of Boston, it was published in that city before the end of 1741 under the title, *The Distinguishing Marks of a work of the Spirit of God, Applied to that uncommon Operation that has lately appeared on the Minds of many of the People of New England.* . . .

It was, in part, Edwards' knowledge of the existence of opposition which led him during 1742 to give close attention both to a defence of the Awakening and to the kind of Christian experience which it had revived. The result was that even amidst so many engagements he wrote a book of 378 pages entitled, *Some Thoughts Concerning the Present Revival of Religion in New England, in 1742*, and began to lay the foundations of a second, yet larger work, *A Treatise Concerning Religious Affections*, in a series of sermons which he commenced that same year.

Long before *Some Thoughts Concerning the Present Revival* was published, opposition to the Awakening had ceased to be mute. What no one had cared to question at the beginning was to become a subject of strong debate in 1742. One of the first critical items in print was 'a Letter' (89 pages in printed form) written by an anonymous hand in New Haven, dated January 10, 1742, detailing 'to a Friend' in Boston the history both of the French Prophets (a Protestant group whose delusions had been much spoken of in Europe towards the end of the seventeenth century) and of other fanatics. The receiver of this letter added a fifteen-page Introduction, applying the history to 'the unusual Appearance among us', and published the whole under the title *The Wonderful Narrative: Or, A Faithful Account of the French Prophets, Their Agitations, Extasies, and Inspirations*. The writer of the Introduction, who signed himself 'Anti-Enthusiasticus', disavows any intention 'to oppose the good Work of God, going on among us': 'I am not against allowing that a good number of sinners have (probably) been converted into saints; and as great a number of saints enlivened in their Christian Work', but he clearly believed that 'Enthusiasm' – the eighteenth-century term for religious fanaticism – was the main feature in 'the unusual Appearance'. He refused to allow for the possibility of any connection between the Holy Spirit and the bodily effects accompanying the revival.

It is commonly believed that the writer of this Introduction to *The Wonderful Narrative* was Charles Chauncy, the thirty-seven-year-old junior pastor of Boston's First church. Another anonymous piece, dated August 4, 1742, is also attributed to Chauncy, *A Letter from a Gentleman in Boston to Mr George Wishart, one of the Ministers of Edinburgh*. If this assignation is correct, it confirms that by mid-1742 Chauncy had become more decided in his opposition – a fact which other sources substantiate.

Answering the opinion that Whitefield had been instrumental of 'great good' in New England, he writes:

You will doubtless be disposed to enquire, what was the *great good* this gentleman was the instrument of? In answer whereto, I freely acknowledge, wherever he went he generally moved the passions, especially of the younger people, and the females among them; the effect whereof was, a great Talk about religion, together with a disposition to be perpetually hearing sermons, to neglect of all other business, especially, as preached by those who were sticklers for the *new Way*, as it was called. And in these things *chiefly* consisted the *Goodness* so much spoken of. I deny not, but there might be here and there a person stopped from going on in a course of sin; and some might be made really better: But so far as I could judge upon the nicest observation, the town, in general, was not much mended in those things wherein a reformation was greatly needed. . . .

Various are the sentiments of persons about this *unusual Appearance* among us. Some think it is *a most wonderful Work of God's Grace*; others a *most wonderful Spirit of Enthusiasm*; some think there is *a great deal of Religion*, with some *small Mixture* of Extravagances; others, *a great deal of Extravagance* with some *small Mixture* of that which may be called *good*; some think the *Country* was never in such a *happy* state on a *religious* account, others that it was never in a worse.

For myself, I am among those who are clearly in the Opinion, that there never was such a *Spirit* of *Superstition* and *Enthusiasm* reigning in the Land before. . . .

A good Number, I hope, have settled into a truly *Christian* temper: Tho' I must add, at the same time, that I am far from thinking, that the Appearance, in general, is any other than the effect of *enthusiastick Heat*. The goodness that has been so much talked of, 'tis plain to me, is nothing more, in general, than a *Commotion in the Passions*.

Yet more hostile in tone was another Letter, dated May 24, 1742, entitled *The State of Religion in New England since the Rev. Mr George Whitefield's Arrival there, In a letter from a Gentleman in New England to his Friend in Glasgow*. This letter was also anonymous, merely bearing the letters 'A.M.' which were probably a camouflage for the author's true initials. According to this writer, the only persons (in May 1742) who continued to support the excitement raised in 1740–41 were 'men of narrow minds and great bigotry'. 'Almost everyone', he claimed, 'of but tolerable sense and understanding in religious matters, in great measure changed their opinions of the spirit that prevailed here.'[1]

Two things are at once apparent concerning this anti-revival literature. The first is the delay in its appearance which we have already noted. Speaking of this hesitancy among the critics, there is weight in the comment of Gilbert Tennent in 1743: 'A work of conviction and conversion spread not long since in many places of these provinces, with such power and progress as even silenced, for a time, the most malignant opposers: they were then either afraid or ashamed openly to contradict such astonishing displays of the Divine almightiness'. Secondly, it is notable that such was the strength of support for the revival that the first authors to write against it needed the cover of anonymity. If the major change of opinion in New England claimed by the writer 'to his Friend in Glasgow', in May 1742, had indeed taken place, it is strange that opponents of the work remained concerned not to reveal their identities. The truth is that they were still a decided minority. Referring to 'the grand question', namely, 'Whether it be a work of God, and how far it is so?' seven of the leading Boston ministers wrote in August

---

[1] *The State of Religion in New England*, Glasgow, 1742, 1–2. Whitefield was so astonished at this claim that he questioned whether the letter was a forgery and wrote a refutation (reprinted in his *Works*, vol. 4). The Glasgow publishers replied with a second edition, published the same year, rejecting the forgery charge and with an appendix of nearly 100 pages made up exclusively of a careful selection of quotations from New England which were critical of *any* features connected with the revival; by this means they dishonestly sought to add the weight of names such as Benjamin Colman's to the claim made in the letter itself. The great interest in Scotland over what was happening in New England was due to the fact that the revivals at Cambuslang and Kilsyth – which began early in 1742 – were closely similar to the Great Awakening and were viewed with disfavour by many 'Moderates' among the clergy. The opposition on both sides of the Atlantic thus supported the same publications. Conversely, the leaders among the revival in Scotland made use of New England material to defend what was happening in Scotland. Foremost among this material was Edwards' *Distinguishing Marks*, different editions of which appeared in both Edinburgh and Glasgow in 1742. The Glasgow edition carries an 'Advertisement', being an extract from a letter of Whitefield to the Reverend William M'Culloch of Cambuslang: 'There is a sermon published by Mr Edwards of Northampton in New England, and printed in London, which I desire you and your friends would have, and recommend most earnestly. 'Tis the best thing of its kind I ever saw. You would think the author had been at Cambuslang.'

1742: 'The most serious and judicious, both ministers and Christians, have looked upon it to be, *in the main*, a genuine work of God, and the effect of that effusion of the Spirit of grace which the faithful have been praying, hoping, longing, and waiting for'.[1] One of the signatories of this statement was Thomas Foxcroft, senior pastor of the same First Church where Chauncy also ministered.[2]

Anonymity was likewise used in the first direct answer to Edwards' *Distinguishing Marks*. In *The Late Religious Commotions in New England considered, An Answer to the Reverend Mr. Jonathan Edwards's Sermon Entitled, The distinguishing Marks* .. , the writer gave twenty pages to refuting Cooper's preface to Edwards' printed sermon, and forty to answering the sermon itself, point by point. The author (thought to be William Rand, a ministerial friend of Chauncy) believed that the churches were better off before the revival.

This book had scarcely appeared in Boston's shops in March 1743 when to the chagrin of its supporters, Edwards' major work, *Some Thoughts Concerning the Present Revival*, was also published. Not without a touch of sarcasm, on March 16 Chauncy wrote to his cousin, the Reverend Nathanael Chauncy of Durham, Connecticut:

Mr Edwards' book of 378 pages upon the *good work* is at last come forth; And I believe will do much hurt; and I am the rather inclined to think so, because there are some good things in it. Error is much more likely to be propagated, when it is mixed with truth. This hides its deformity and makes it go down the more easily. I may again trouble myself and the world upon the appearance of this book. I am preparing an antidote. . . .[3]

Chauncy's 'antidote' was his *Seasonable Thoughts on the State of Religion in New England*. A Treatise in five parts, it was a work of

---

[1]From the Attestation prefixed to *A Display of Special Grace* [Jonathan Dickinson], Boston, 1742. Dickinson's name only appeared in the second edition published the next year in Philadelphia.

[2]Foxcroft (1696–1769) was one of the strongest supporters of the revival and a close friend of Whitefield. His usefulness and leadership in the First Church had, however, been diminished by a paralysis which he suffered in 1736.

[3]*New England Historical and Genealogical Register*, X, 332. Quoted by E. S. Gaustad, *The Great Awakening in New England*, pp. 89–90.

424 pages and a 30-page Preface. His case was that fanatical extravagances were the main part of 'the late religious stir', and by so concentrating upon these allegations (from pp. 35 to 332) he caricatures the whole awakening. Only in his last thirty pages does he attempt an answer to Edwards' *Thoughts Concerning the Present Revival* which he virtually dismisses as a mere repetition of his *Distinguishing Marks*. Trumbull in his *History of Connecticut* speaks strongly against the dependability of Chauncy's work: 'The great body of those who were subjects of the divine operations at that time, were humble, prayerful, sober christians; loved and adhered to their ministers, and were strict in their morals.' Chauncy 'took up reports against his brethren, not at the mouth of two or three witnesses, and without inquirying whether they were friends or enemies'.[1]

Chauncy's volume was ready in September, 1743. Opposition to the revival had, however, already come out into the open before it was published. A Convention of ministers of 'the Province of Massachusetts Bay', meeting in Boston in May 1743, published a full list of errors and disorders 'which have of late obtained in various Parts of the Land', and refrained from any positive assertion on the existence of a true revival. Attention was drawn solely to chaff.

Edwards was present at this Convention and he may have been among those ministers who attempted to speak against the procedure which was adopted: 'They were', says Joshua Gee, of Boston's Second Church, 'interrupted in a rude way and treated with open contempt. . . . Many earnest pleas for their being heard were stifled in clamor and opposition'.

Believing that the Convention's 'Testimony' misrepresented the position, Gee and others called a counter-Convention for July 7 which exceeded (by twenty) the ministerial attendance at the first Convention, and in its own Testimony professed the belief that an extraordinary work of the Spirit had been seen in many parts of the land 'after a long time of great decay and

[1] *History of Connecticut*, 2, pp. 201–2. Although only a child at the time of the Great Revival, Benjamin Trumbull (1735–1820) grew up under the ministries of Edwards' friends, Pomeroy and Wheelock and, of course, had first-hand knowledge of the abiding change which the awakening brought. Eleazer Wheelock was probably optimistic in believing that Chauncy's work was 'never vendible' except among a handful of Connecticut Arminians.

deadness'. 'The present work', some sixty-eight ministers declared, 'appears to be remarkable and extraordinary, *On account of the numbers wrought upon.* We never before saw so many brought under soul concern. . . . *With regard to the suddenness and quick progress of it.* Many persons and places were surprised with the gracious visit together, or near about the same time. . . . *Also in respect of the degree of operation,* both in a way of terror and in a way of consolation.'[1]

This Testimony was supported by attestations received from a further forty-five ministers, and among their names is 'Jonathan Edwards of Northampton'.

By the summer of 1743 the clergy of New England were thus openly divided, and opposition and defence reached their crescendo in a welter of publications which continued to appear well into the following year.[2]

Any assessment of this division requires the consideration of a number of separate issues all of which are important to an understanding of Edwards' writings during the Awakening.

In the first place something must be said on the reasons for the strength of the opposition, and at once a distinction must be made between those who were opposed to *some* features present in the revival and those who were virtually committed to opposing the whole. Of the four hundred ministers in New England it has been conjectured that possibly one hundred and thirty belonged to this latter category. How is the strength of their hostility to be explained?

Firstly, they were offended by the 'new' type of preaching which became common in the awakening. The preaching of Whitefield, Tennent, Edwards and their associates, was too different from the customary pulpit exercises of many ministers to avoid appearing as a challenge. The 'New-Light' preachers, as opponents now called them, were quite open in comparing what preaching ought to be with what it too commonly was. Speaking of the spirit with which ministers of the gospel should

[1]See Tracy, *The Great Awakening*, p. 296.
[2]Without question, the most important of these was *The Christian History*, containing 'Accounts of the Revival and Propagation of Religion in Great Britain and America', edited by Thomas Prince, Jr. This was the first specifically religious magazine to be published in America and it may have owed its existence to a suggestion made by Edwards (1.429).

be clothed Edwards wrote in *Some Thoughts concerning the Present Revival*:

They ought indeed to be thorough in preaching the word of God, without mincing the matter at all; in handling the sword of the Spirit, as the ministers of the Lord of hosts, they ought not to be mild and gentle; they are not to be gentle and moderate in searching and awakening the conscience, but should be sons of thunder. The word of God, which is in itself sharper than any two-edged sword, ought not to be sheathed by its ministers, but so used that its sharp edges may have their full effect, even to the dividing asunder soul and spirit, joints and marrow (1.401).

This was disturbing enough to men who felt it was a reflection upon their own ministries, but Tennent and Whitefield went further in declaring their belief that the pulpit inadequacies of the age could be traced to a yet more serious deficiency. 'The body of the clergy', said Tennent, were 'as great strangers to the feeling experience' of the new birth as Nicodemus 'who talked like a fool about it'. 'Isn't this the reason', he asked, 'why a work of conviction and conversion has been so rarely heard of, for a long time, in the churches, till of late, *viz*. That the bulk of her spiritual guides were stone-blind and stone-dead'.[1] It was one thing for Tennent to preach this, as he did, in the Middle Colonies, another for Whitefield to apply the same sentiments to the New England clergy themselves. When the Englishman's *Seventh Journal* was published after his first visit in 1740, all the occupants of the parsonages of Massachusetts and Connecticut were alert when they read of New England:

On many accounts, it certainly excels all other provinces in America; and, for the establishment of religion, perhaps all other parts of the world. The towns all through Connecticut, and eastward towards York, are well peopled. Every five miles or perhaps less, you have a meeting-house; and, I believe, there is no such thing as a pluralist or non-resident minister in both provinces. Many, nay most that preach, I fear, do not experimentally know Christ; yet I cannot see much worldly advantage to tempt them to take up the sacred function.[2]

It need hardly be said that some who read these words were

[1] *The Danger of an Unconverted Ministry* (preached at Nottingham, Pennsylvania, March 8, 1740), Philadelphia, 1740, p. 13.
[2] *Journals*, p. 482.

incensed and never forgot the charge.

Without condoning all Whitefield's words, to which we shall return later, it may be said, secondly, that hostility to the Awakening cannot be separated from an opposition to experimental Christianity itself: 'There is naturally a great enmity in the heart of man against vital religion', writes Edwards, 'and I believe there would have been a great deal of opposition against this glorious work of God in New England if the subjects and promoters of it had behaved themselves never so agreeably to Christian rules' (1.408). It was this 'vital religion' which, after years of much formal Christianity, the Awakening revived, and it was bound to distinguish those who preferred the former state of things from those who now rejoiced in the change. The words of Thomas Boston, another eighteenth-century pastor, are apposite:

When winter has stripped the trees of their verdure it is hard to distinguish those that have life from those that have not; but when the spring approaches, then they are easily known by their spreading leaves, while those that are dead still continue the same; thus when religion is in decay, the saint can scarcely be distinguished from the sinner; but when a time of refreshing comes, then will they blossom and bring forth fruit abundantly.[1]

After a cautious survey of the differences which emerged between men as a result of the Great Awakening, Archibald Alexander concludes: 'I cannot doubt that, in a good degree, the contest between the parties was between the friends and the enemies of true religion.'

A third reason for opposition to the Awakening was the dislike of a number of the clergy and others to the historic Calvinism which was suddenly seen to gain such new strength. As we have already noted this theology was already on the wane in New England at the beginning of the eighteenth century. In 1740 it had no representatives at Harvard, and, though Thomas Clap, Rector at Yale, adhered to it, it is said that Arminianism prevailed among the Yale trustees. Puritan authors were discounted: Whitefield reported that he found at

[1] *The Fourfold State*, quoted in W. H. Foote, *Sketches of North Carolina*, 1846 (reprinted 1966), p. 352.

Harvard in 1740 that 'Tillotson and Clarke are read instead of Shepard, Stoddard, and suchlike evangelical writers'.[1] No longer looking to their original spiritual leaders, New England progressives were being drawn to emulate the Arminianism fashionable in England and none was more energetic in promoting this than Timothy Cutler, ex-Rector of Yale, and his fellow Anglicans who were seeking to hasten doctrinal change in the colonies.

Nothing could have been more contrary to the opinions of this school of thought than the convictions proclaimed by the leaders in the Awakening. The latter asserted that the revival was a glorious manifestation of the sovereignty of divine grace: the large number of converts of varying ages and backgrounds, the contrast in the response between one place and another, the differing results attending the same sermons – all these they traced back to God himself. Any other divinity, they claimed, was helpless in explaining the phenomenon. 'Now is a good time', said Edwards, 'for Arminians to change their principles' (1.423). Nor was this all. The friends of the revival not merely claimed a place for the old divinity, they positively blamed Arminianism for the carelessness and superficiality which resulted from the belief that conversion is a matter which can be determined by the human will. Arminianism had encouraged the common opinion of the unregenerate man that it is in his own power to decide upon his salvation. A typical example of this 'natural' type of thought occurs in David Brainerd's Diary where he speaks of his pre-conversion experience:

I read Mr Stoddard's *Guide to Christ*, which I trust was, in the hand of God, the happy means of my conversion, and my heart rose against the author; for though he told me my very heart all along under convictions, and seemed to be very beneficial to me in his directions; yet here he failed, he did not tell me anything I could *do* that would bring me to Christ, but left me, as it were, with a great gulf between, without any direction to get through. For I was not yet effectually and experimentally taught that there *could* be no way prescribed, whereby a *natural* man could, of his own strength, obtain that which is *supernatural*, and which the highest angel cannot give (2.318).

[1] *Works*, 4, p. 213.

By 1740 Brainerd had discovered the same truth which the leaders of the revival were then preaching with one voice. While declaring that faith in Christ is man's duty, they took care not to hide the necessity of regeneration by divine power in order for such faith to be saving. 'Faith' exercised where there was no re-birth would prove to be only the temporary response of a 'stony-ground' hearer. Speaking of Tennent's preaching in Boston, Thomas Prince writes:

It was not merely, nor so much his laying open the terrors of the law, and wrath of God, or damnation of hell (for this they could pretty well bear, as long as they hoped these belonged not to them, or they could easily avoid them) as his laying open their many vain and secret shifts and refuges, counterfeit resemblances of grace, delusive and damning hopes, their utter impotence, and impending danger of destruction; whereby they found all their hopes and refuges of lies to fail them, and themselves exposed to eternal ruin, unable to help themselves, and in a lost condition. This searching preaching was both the suitable and principal means of their conviction.[1]

The author of *A Letter from a Gentleman in Boston to Mr George Wishart* complained bitterly of Tennent and especially his view that 'all were Pharisees, hypocrites, carnal unregenerate wretches, both ministers and people, who did not think just as he did, particularly as to the Doctrines of Calvinism'. Timothy Cutler – unlike Chauncy, the probable author of that letter – was ready to dismiss that theology and abominated what he called Tennent's 'impudent and noisy' preaching, but, after all, it might have been expected from a Presbyterian whose only training was a 'log college'![2] What was utterly unexpected was a priest in holy orders from Oxford, who could gather an estimated 20,000 on Boston Common and tell the Harvard faculty, 'Gentlemen, I profess myself a Calvinist as to principle, and preach no other doctrines than those which your pious ancestors, and the founders of Harvard College, preached long before I was born!'[3] And Whitefield's Calvinism was just as

[1]Gillies, *Historical Collections*, p. 352.

[2]Writing to a friend in England of Tennent's preaching, Cutler says, 'In the most dreadful winter I ever saw, people wallowed in snow, night and day, for the benefit of his beastly brayings' (Quoted in Luke Tyerman, *Life of Whitefield*, 2, p. 125).

[3]*Works*, 4, p. 225.

practical in effect as Tennent's. In a previous chapter we quoted from Nathan Cole's account of his rush, with his wife and one horse to bear them, to hear the Englishman at Middletown. But it is relevant at this point to refer to the result of that sermon in Cole's case. Far from being brought at once to Christ and peace with God, he came under a distress of soul which, he tells us, 'lasted almost two years'. Cole's sketch of what happened once they arrived in Middletown is as follows:

When I saw Mr. Whitefield come upon the scaffold he looked almost angelic, a young, slim, slender youth, before some thousands of people and with a bold, undaunted countenance . . . it solemnized my mind and put me in a trembling fear before he began to preach for he looked as if he was clothed with authority from the Great God. Hearing him preach gave me a heart wound [so that], by God's blessing, my old foundation was broken up and I saw that my righteousness would not save me, then I was convinced of the doctrine of election and went right to quarrelling with God about it because all that I could do would not save me. . . .

Both in the Middle Colonies and in New England the revival preachers were nicknamed 'New-Lights' or 'New-Side' by their critics. The cry was raised, 'How comes it to pass that we hear so much of these things of late, which former times and ages knew so little about?'[1] In reply to this it was not difficult for the preachers to show that it was not they who were guilty of inventing *new* things, and a dramatic and popular return to the reading of older writers gave demonstration to their claim. Speaking of the recovery brought by the Great Awakening, Samuel Blair writes: 'Excellent books that had lain by much neglected, were then much perused, and lent from one to another: and it was a peculiar satisfaction to people to find how exactly the doctrines they heard daily preached, harmonized with the doctrines maintained and taught by great and godly men in other parts and former times'.[2] Blair wrote of the Middle Colonies but in Boston Thomas Prince observed the same thing: 'The people seemed to have a renewed taste for those old pious and experimental writers, Mr Hooker, Shep-

[1] For one effective response see Jonathan Dickinson, *Display of God's Special Grace, Sermons and Tracts*, Edinburgh, 1793, p. 403.
[2] Gillies, p. 345.

ard, Gurnall, William Guthrie, Joseph Alleine, Isaac Ambrose, Dr Owen and others. The evangelical writings of these deceased authors ... were now read with singular pleasure; some of them reprinted, and in great number quickly bought and studied.'[1]

Speaking of the origin of the term 'New Lights', Lyman Atwater believed that it was used principally because of the new kind of preaching which characterized the revival leaders. He quotes Professor Fisher who says, 'The boldness with which they declared in the pulpit the terror of the gospel, and the force of their appeals to the conscience, in contrast with what had been usual, made their sermons exciting and effective'. 'This was more especially true,' comments Atwater, 'of the elder Edwards and Bellamy, who gave emphasis to the terrors of the Lord at a time when a prevalent reticence in regard to them, into which preaching in quiet times is always apt to subside, rendered such emphasis startling and potent. But this is no peculiarity of any new system of theology, in contrast with the old; it simply pertains to ministerial prudence and fidelity.'[2]

Certainly the awakening brought a revived orthodoxy into collision with ideas which had been slowly replacing it and the 'New-Side' leaders were unanimous in believing that it was an unwillingness to abandon error which sometimes made their critics so determined. David McGregore, preaching at Benjamin Colman's Brattle Street Church in Boston on November 3, 1741, declared, 'I believe that the *principal* and *most inveterate Opposers* are Men of *Arminian* and *Pelagian* principles'.[3] When Edwards' *Distinguishing Marks* came out later that same month, the Preface by William Cooper included the same suggestion. 'There are those,' he wrote, 'who may dislike the present work because it supports and confirms some principles which they have not yet embraced. ... For it is certain these fruits do not

[1] *Ibid.*, p. 353.
[2] *The Biblical Repertory and Princeton Review*, vol. 30 (1858), p. 603: 'The whole class were called New Lights, rather with reference to the unusually startling and awakening character of their preaching, and the extravagances which marred the revival of which they were the leading promoters, than to any theological tenets at variance with the old Calvinism.'
[3] Part of McGregore's sermon, entitled, 'The Spirits of the Present Day Tried' is printed in *The Great Awakening*, Documents Illustrating the Crisis and Its Consequences, Alan Heimert and Perry Miller, 1967, pp. 215–227.

grow on Arminian ground' (2.259). Mild compared with McGregore's, these words of Cooper nevertheless drew the fire of the anonymous writer of *The Late Religious Commotions*. The fact is that the same theology which had been responsible for driving Puritans out of the Old England in the 1630's was found by the Great Awakening to be established in the New.

*   *   *

Clerical opposition was not, however, the only difficulty attending the revival. Nor does it explain important issues which still remain to be considered. If true revival, by definition, does not depend upon human support, how was it that by 1742, after such remarkable progress, there came an ebb to the flood? 'Had it continued of this unmixed character', writes Dwight, 'so extensive was its prevalence and so powerful its operation, it would seem that in no great length of time it would have pervaded the western world' (1.lxx). Why did it not continue? A modern writer suggests that 'it declined simply because it had to, because society could not maintain itself in so great a disequilibrium'. This was not Edwards' view. For him the reason was much more profound or, to use his word, 'mysterious'. He came to believe that there was one principal cause of the reversal, namely, the unwatchfulness of the friends of the Awakening who allowed genuine and pure religion to become so mixed with 'wildfire', and carnal 'enthusiasm', that the Spirit of God was grieved and advantage given to Satan.

The origins of a fanatical element in the revival cannot be traced with any distinctness but by the latter half of 1741, and very clearly in 1742, its presence was plainly to be seen in many places. In his New Haven sermon of September 1741 Edwards admitted that 'imprudencies, irregularities' and a 'mixture of delusion' were observable amidst the revival, and warned: 'Satan will keep men secure as long as he can; but when he can do that no longer, he often endeavours to drive them to extremes, and so to dishonour God, and wound religion in that way' (2.271). In the same month Daniel Wadsworth noted in his diary, 'The great awakening &c. seems to be degenerating into Strife and faction'.[1]

---

[1] *Diary of Rev Daniel Wadsworth*, Hartford, 1894, 71 (Entry for Sept 1, 1741) quoted by Winslow, *op. cit.*, pp. 199–20.

Similarly, Eleazer Wheelock, after attending a service at Voluntown, Connecticut, on October 21, 1741, wrote in his diary: 'There is a great work in this town, but more of the footsteps of Satan than in any place I have yet been in: the zeal of some too furious: they tell of many visions, revelations, and many strong impressions upon the imagination.'[1]

Trouble first appeared in connection with the cases of sudden physical collapse, of outcries, and of swoonings which were witnessed in many congregations from the summer of 1741 onwards.[2] The scene of great distress which occurred when Edwards preached at Enfield in June of that year was not untypical. In Edwards' view such evidences of shock were not *proof* of any saving work of the Spirit: people might indeed be overwhelmed and prostrated by sudden alarm when savingly convicted by God, but he also knew that the same outward effects could accompany feelings prompted by the truth in the unregenerate while under the slavish fear of God. The presence of such phenomena might even be the result of hysteria, yet his own experience in the summer of 1741 led him to believe that in most cases there was no need for friends of the revival to be alarmed if congregations were disturbed by signs of physical distress. When a certain Deacon Lyman of Goshen, Connecticut, clearly concerned about the unusual phenomena, wrote to him, Edwards replied on August 31, 1741,

In my prodigious fullness of business, and great infirmity of body, I have time to write but very briefly concerning those things you mention. Concerning the great stir that is in the land, and those extraordinary circumstances and events that it is attended with, such as persons crying out, and being set into great agonies, with a sense of sin and wrath, and having their strength taken away, and their minds extraordinarily transported with light, love and comfort, I have been abundantly amongst such things, and have had great opportunity to observe them, here and elsewhere, in their beginning, progress, issue and consequences; and however there may be some mixtures of natural affection, and sometimes of temptation, and some imprudences and irregularities, as there always was, and always will be in

[1]Quoted in Tracy, *The Great Awakening*, p. 201.
[2]These phenomena do not appear to have been present at the beginning of the Great Awakening. Thomas Prince remembered nothing of the kind under the preaching of Whitefield or Tennent (Gillies, p. 351).

this imperfect state, yet as to the work in general, and the main of what is to be observed in these extraordinary things, they have all the clear and incontestable evidences of a true divine work. If this ben't the work of God, I have all my religion to learn over again, and know not what use to make of the Bible.[1]

But Edwards also believed, as he made clear in his New Haven sermon, that physical responses during a service should not be encouraged. People 'should endeavour to refrain from such outward manifestations . . . to their utmost, at the time of their solemn worship' (2.271). It was just here that differences began to enter. Some, confident that they could identify the Spirit's work, began to encourage the idea that the greater the outcries and the commotion, the more glorious was the evidence of God's power, and once this idea was accepted the door was open to all manner of excess. No authority on earth could have stopped some of the scenes which occurred under powerful preaching in the Great Awakening, any more than human authority could have pacified the distressed multitude at Pentecost, yet there were occasions when disorder *could* have been stopped if it had been remembered that excitement, *as such*, is not necessarily a blessing from heaven. Far from attempting to restrain themselves, people sometimes wilfully gave way to sheer emotion. One example of this occurred in the church of Edwards' cousin, Solomon Williams, at Lebanon. The presence of George Whitefield had drawn many people from other districts to the Lebanon meetinghouse. When Whitefield's sermon from the text, 'Take not thy Holy Spirit from me', was over, and the service concluded, Whitefield and Williams left the building. Many who had remained, however, reported an eye-witness, 'became so perfectly frantic – jumping, dancing, singing and praying, that the scene seemed to form a sort of Bedlam'. The outcome was as follows:

Good Deacon Huntington – Dr Williams' right hand man – having continued in the church, as a witness to what passed, went straight to his pastor to see if he could not do something to quell the disorder. Dr Williams and Mr Whitefield both hastened to the church; and, on entering, such was the noise and tumult on every side, that the presence of the two ministers was not immediately observed. They

[1] Printed in full in J E (Yale), 4, pp. 533–4.

went forward to the Deacon's seat, and Mr Whitefield, stamping his foot with great violence on the floor, exclaimed with a voice of thunder – 'What means all this tumult and disorder?' Instantly there was silence through the house; but some of them quickly remarked that they were so much delighted to see and hear their spiritual father, and were so filled with the Spirit, that they could not forbear their demonstrations of joy. Whitefield replied to them with great mildness of manner – 'My dear children, you are like little partridges, just hatched from the egg. You run about with egg shells covering your eyes, and you cannot see and know where you are going'.

The effect of his gentle expostulation was that the disorder entirely ceased, and they withdrew quietly to their several homes.[1]

This event occurred after the Great Awakening was over. When the spirit of fanaticism was at its height it was often far more difficult to deal with than on this occasion at Lebanon. Edwards himself, by 1742, had considerable difficulties at Northampton: 'A great deal of caution and pains were found necessary to keep the people, many of them, from running wild' (1.lix). He dates the beginning of the trouble to the arrival of 'a number of the zealous people from Suffield' at the time of Buell's visit in January-February 1742. Amidst the great blessing attending Buell's preaching, instances of phenomena which were not God-honouring 'soon became very apparent' and members of the Northampton congregation became influenced by the assumption that noise, excitement and spiritual power were all one. Writing of this in December 1743 he says:

With respect to the late revival of religion amongst us for three or four years past, it has been observable, that in the former part of it, in the years 1740 and 1741, the work seemed to be much more pure, having less of a corrupt mixture than in the former great outpouring of the Spirit in 1735 and 1736. Persons seemed to be sensible of their former errors, and had learned more of the tendency and consequences of things. They were now better guarded, and their affections were not only stronger, but attended with greater solemnity, and greater humility and self-distrust, and greater engagedness after holy living and perseverance: and there were fewer errors in conduct. But in the latter part of it, in the year 1742, it was otherwise: the work continued more pure till we were infected from abroad: our people hearing of, and some of them seeing, the work in other places, where there was a

[1] *Annals of the American Pulpit*, W. B. Sprague, 1, p. 325.

greater visible commotion than here, and the outward appearances were more extraordinary, were ready to think that the work in those places far excelled what was amongst us, and their eyes were dazzled with the high profession and great show that some made, who came hither from other places.

That those people went so far beyond them in raptures and violent emotions of the affections, and a vehement zeal, and what they called *boldness for Christ*, our people were ready to think was owing to far greater attainments in grace, and intimacy with heaven: they looked little in their own eyes in comparison with them, and were ready to submit themselves to them, and yield themselves up to their conduct, taking it for granted that every thing was right that they said and did. These things had a strange influence on the people, and gave many of them a deep and unhappy tincture from which it was a hard and long labour to deliver them, and from which some of them are not fully delivered to this day (1.lxi).

In some places ministers found themselves almost wholly unable to restrain unruly emotionalism. David Hall, Edwards' close friend, having seen ninety-eight added to his church, later lost many of his people when he tried to restrain wild-fire. The case of Joseph Fish, another friend of the revival, who ministered at North Stonington, was even worse. Seeing a number in his quickened congregation laying emphasis upon 'violent agitations and outcries, ecstasies, visions, trances, and inward impressions, he greatly feared that many would be deceived as to the nature of true religion and in consequence perish'. But when he began to speak on the subject, so strong was the false zeal, that the majority of the congregation left him and he 'with grief and anxiety saw his church gradually dwindling away.'[1]

Such separations from congregations became commonplace in 1742–43, especially in eastern Connecticut, and as a result nearly a hundred 'Separatist' churches came into being.[2] Without doubt these separations were justified in some instances, but too often, as in the cases of Hall and Fish, they were the result of people exercising an unwarranted judgment upon their ministers. It was at this point that the precedent of

[1]Sprague, *op. cit.*, pp. 360–61.
[2]They are listed by C. C. Goen in *Revivalism and Separatism in New England*, 1740–1800, pp. 302–27.

denouncing unconverted ministers, set by Tennent and White-field, two years earlier did such damage. Not that the evil did not merit denunciation but these evangelists had spoken so authoritatively respecting the numbers of such men that the idea got into circulation that it was not a difficult thing to determine whether preachers were true Christians, irrespective of their orthodoxy. By the time the two men recognized their mistake the damage was done. With characteristic humility, Whitefield was to write later, 'Alas, alas! how can I be too severe against myself, who, Peter like, have cut off so many ears, and by imprudencies mixed with my zeal, have dishon-oured the cause of Jesus?'[1]

Separations did not come alone. Preachers were required for the new congregations and in many instances they could only be found among a new class of self-appointed lay-preachers or exhorters who too often thought that a man needed no 'book- learning' provided he could preach 'in the Spirit'. Benjamin Colman of Boston speaks of these 'many poor and miserable exhorters who have sprung up like mushrooms in a night, and in the morning thought themselves accomplished teachers and called of God to be so'. And he prays that they might 'awake at length out of their dream, or rather delirium.'

Gilbert Tennent, replying to a letter of Edwards, expresses the same concern

As to the subject you mention, *of laymen being sent out to exhort and to teach*, supposing them to be real converts, I cannot but think, if it be encouraged and continued, it will be of dreadful consequence to the church's peace and soundness in the faith. I will not gainsay but that private persons may be of service to the church of God by private, humble, fraternal reproof, and exhortations; and no doubt it is their duty to be faithful in these things. But in the meantime if christian prudence and humility do not attend their essays, they are like to be prejudicial to the church's real well-being. But for ignorant young converts to take upon them authoritatively to instruct and exhort publicly, tends to introduce the greatest errors and the grossest anarchy and confusion. The ministers of Christ should be apt to teach and able to convince gainsayers, and it is dangerous to the pure

---

[1] *Works*, 2, p. 214. See also p. 144, 'In how many things have I judged and acted wrong'.

church of God, when those are novices, whose lips should preserve knowledge.

I know most young zealots are apt, through ignorance, inconsideration, and pride of heart, to undertake what they have no proper qualifications for: and, through their imprudences and enthusiasm, the church of God suffers. I think all that fear God, should rise up and crush the enthusiastic creature in the egg. Dear brother, the times we live in are dangerous. The churches in America and elsewhere are in great hazard of enthusiasm: we have need to think of the maxim, *principiis obsta.*[1] May Zion's King protect his church! I add no more, but love, and beg a remembrance in your prayers. (1.liv-v)

Edwards was of the same mind as Colman and Tennent as is clear from the following letter written to a young man in Goshen, Connecticut.

Northampton, May 18, 1742

My Dear Friend,

I am fully satisfied by the account your father has given me, that you have lately gone out of the way of your duty, and done that which did not belong to you, *in exhorting a public congregation.* I know you to be a person of good judgment and discretion, and therefore can with the greater confidence put it to you to consider with yourself what you can reasonably judge would be the consequence, if I and all other ministers should approve and publicly justify such things as laymen's taking it upon them to exhort *after this manner?* If one may, why may not another? And if there be no certain limits or bounds, but every one that pleases may have liberty, alas! what should we soon come to? If God had not seen it necessary that such things should have certain limits and bounds, he never would have appointed a certain particular order of men to that work and office, to be set apart to it in so solemn a manner, in the name of God: the Head of the church is wiser than we, and knew how to regulate things in his church.

'Tis no argument that such things are right, that they do a great deal of good for the present, and within a narrow sphere; when, at the same time, if we look on them in the utmost extent of their consequences, and on the long run of events, they do ten times as much hurt as good. Appearing events are not our rule, but the law and the testimony. We ought to be vigilant and circumspect, and look on every side, and, as far as we can, to the further end of things. God may if he pleases, in his sovereign providence, turn that which is most wrong to do a great deal of good for the present; for he does what he pleases. I hope you will consider the matter, and for the future avoid

[1] 'Check the first symptoms' (Ovid).

doing thus. You ought to do what good you can, by private, brotherly, humble admonitions and counsels; but 'tis too much for you to *exhort public congregations*, or solemnly to set yourself, by a set speech, to counsel a room full of people, unless it be children, or those that are much your inferiors, or to speak to any in an authoritative way. Such things have done a vast deal of mischief in the country, and have hindered the work of God exceedingly. . . . [1]

Had all the ministerial friends of the Awakening been of this mind from the outset the wild-fire of separatist preaching might have been curbed, but instead a few (whose association with Whitefield added to their standing) gave their support to excesses. One of these was Jonathan Barber, who was minister at Oyster Ponds, Long Island, until the spring of 1740 when two texts, forcibly 'impressed' upon his mind, convinced him that he should leave his pastorate and itinerate. Whitefield met him in Rhode Island in September 1740 and thereafter Barber travelled with Whitefield so that he was also at the Northampton parsonage the following month during the Whitefield visit to Edwards which we have already described. Believing that he saw an unhealthy element in Barber's fervour, Edwards dealt 'plainly with him', at which, says Edwards, 'he seemed to be displeased and replied with earnestness and zeal.'[2]

Barber's presence in New England was short-lived, as two months later he went to assist at Whitefield's Orphanage in Georgia. Much worse than Barber was to follow. New-Haven trained, grandson of a famous Puritan, the Rev. James Davenport was to ignite and direct fanaticism as no one else. Like Barber he also left a Long Island pastorate in the spring of 1740. In June of that year we find him with the Tennents in Philadelphia, and in October with Whitefield in New York. It seems evident that his ministry at this time was used to the awakening of many and that there was nothing which could be objected to in the content of his sermons. But the root of much future trouble was already present. Davenport seems to have believed that the Holy Spirit can give such direct guidance to ✓ Christians by 'impressions' made upon their minds that they may be infallibly sure of the will of God. The strength of an

[1] Printed in *The Bibliotheca Sacra*, vol. xxviii, 1871, pp. 95–6.
[2] *Copies of the Two Letters Cited by the Rev. Mr Clap*, Edwards, 1745, p. 7.

'impression' was enough to prove its authenticity. The effect of this error, in the high tide of emotion accompanying the Great Awakening, was to encourage Christians (and others) to accept any powerful subjective impulse as the 'special leading' of the Spirit.

The first major controversy over Davenport came in the summer of 1741 when the same prostrations, accompanied by conviction of sin, were to be seen under his preaching in Connecticut as were already evident under other ministries. His preaching was undoubtedly blessed with many conversions[1] but disturbing features became increasingly apparent. Bodily agitations and outcries in services he took as marks of the Spirit's saving work, and he seems to have begun to pronounce upon the number of converts. After a service at New London on July 18, 1741, Davenport, it is alleged,

went into the broad aisle, which was much crowded, and there he screamed out, 'Come to Christ! come to Christ! come away!' Then he went into the third pew on the women's side, and kept there, sometimes singing, sometimes praying; he and his companions all taking their turns, and the women fainting and in hysterics.[2]

In the meetinghouse at Groton he continued the service until two o'clock in the morning. Not surprisingly, not all the meetinghouses remained available for his use, and when two godly ministers declined their support Davenport pronounced them to be unconverted. At New Haven, Joseph Noyes admitted him to his pulpit (just a few days after Edwards had preached there on *The Distinguishing Marks of a Work of the Spirit of God*) but this did not save Noyes from the same condemnation! 'Guided' by the words of Psalm 115, 'He will bless the house of Aaron', Davenport believed that blessing upon the 'house of Aaron', in New England must mean the conversion of many ministers, and this he expected to happen, in part, through his own plain speaking. But when pastors did not recognize his 'divine commission', nor heed his warnings, he called the people to immediate separation. This frequently

---

[1] See Tracy, *The Great Awakening*, Chapter 14, and Webster, pp. 531–45.
[2] *Diary of Joshua Hempsteed of New London, Connecticut*, quoted by Goen, *Revivalism and Separatism*, p. 21.

entailed further disturbance and high-feelings. One Connecticut layman, writes Ola Winslow, 'went axe in hand to the
meetinghouse, chopped out the sheep-pen pew in which he and
his family had sat ever since the meetinghouse was built, and
transferred it "root and branch and all in all" to his own attic.
The uprooted pew became the rallying ground for other
aggrieved members, and soon a new church was formed.'

On January 13, 1742, Aaron Burr wrote to Joseph Bellamy
from Newark: 'I can join with you in expressing a very great
value for that eminent man of God, Mr Davenport. But I dare
not justify all his conduct, nor can I see through it. Our dear
brother, Mr Edwards, tells me in a letter, he thinks he does
more towards giving Satan and other opposers an advantage
against the work than any one person'.[1]

By the summer of 1742 Davenport's career was approaching its crisis and, as though sensing it himself, his testimony
now developed an apocalyptic note. He professed to have been
taught by the Spirit that the end of the world was very near,
though he knew not the exact time. In June he was brought
before the General Assembly of the Church meeting at Hartford, his heroic and defiant bearing raising such a fervour
among his supporters that a guard of forty armed men was
deemed necessary. After two days the ministers reached their
conclusion, 'Davenport is under the influence of enthusiastical
impressions and impulses and thereby disturbed in the rational faculties of his mind'. They ordered that he be sent back
to his own church on Long Island. Thus Davenport left
Connecticut, yet before the end of the same month, to the
consternation of the ministers of Massachusetts, he had arrived in Boston and commenced preaching, as Whitefield and
Tennent had done, on the Common. The *Boston Evening-Post*
reported on July 5,

Were you to see him in his most violent agitations you would be apt to
think that he was a madman just broke from his chains: But especially
had you seen him returning from the Common after his first
preaching, with a large mob at his heels, singing all the way through
the streets, he with his hands extended, his head thrown back, and his
eyes staring up to heaven, attended with so much disorder that they

[1]Quoted in Webster, p. 538.

look'd more like a company of Bacchanalians after a mad frolick, than sober Christians who had been worshipping God!

An association of pastors of Boston and Charlestown, who had met with Davenport a few days earlier, spoke more moderately in a Declaration they published on July 1. They believed him 'to be a man truly pious' but his actions 'we can by no means approve of or justify, but must needs think very dangerous and hurtful to the interests of religion'. The response from Davenport was inevitable: some of the ministers he named as unconverted and the rest were all 'like Jehoshaphat in Ahab's army'. In mid-August, when still in the vicinity of Boston, he was charged before a Grand Jury for uttering 'many slanderous and reviling speeches' but he was acquitted on the grounds that when he spoke he was *non compos mentis*.

Davenport was back on Long Island during the winter of 1742–3; but in March 1743 when at New London, Connecticut, there was a final act of fanaticism. He had come to the town at the invitation of separatists to organize a new church, and his first act – based, he believed, on a message from God – was to purify the company from the idolatrous love of worldly things. Accordingly, it is alleged, he listed a number of items to be given up and committed to flames; they included cloaks, breeches, hoods, gowns, rings, jewels, and necklaces. This done, more subtle 'evils' were to be destroyed, namely, a number of religious books. On March 6 his followers carried a quantity of books – some of John Flavel's *Works* and other Puritan books among them – to a wharf where they were burned amidst songs of praise![1]

It is a characteristic of religious fanaticism that, once given its head, it may be uncontrollable, and so it proved in New England. Although from this date the exhausted Davenport withdrew from the public eye (to re-emerge a chastened and wiser man in the 'Retractions' he published in July 1744)[2] the

[1] See Tracy, *op. cit.*, pp. 349–51.

[2] It should be said that this, and other allegations, came from Chauncy's pen and frequently unsupported by any other testimony. Davenport, as Richard Webster rightly complains, is only remembered for the short period of his excesses. 'Few men were more highly eulogized, living or dying, by the wisest and best of his own day. But the sneers of Chauncy have been adopted for true, as though the professed opponent of the doctrines and results of the Great Revival could be safely relied on for candour' (*A History* etc., p. 531).

spirit which he had epitomized continued in many places and wrought havoc which few would have imagined possible back in the summer of 1741. Sometimes the extravagances were mere follies. At a private meeting in the parish of Solomon Williams at Lebanon, for instance, two children of about ten or twelve years of age fell into trances and simultaneously, they alleged, had a vision of heaven. In the Lamb's Book of Life they saw the names of a number of their friends, some in large letters, but the name of Solomon Williams was so small as to be scarcely readable and was crowded down to the very bottom of the page! Yet from folly of this type an impetus was given to a form of religious experience which was well able both to confuse believers and to attract excited unregenerate men. On this subject the convictions of Joseph Bellamy – who travelled widely in New England during the Awakening – coincided exactly with those of Edwards. 'Whereas', writes Sprague, 'at one period, he had seemed to regard the signs of the times as indicating the dawn of millennial glory, he was afterwards deeply pained to notice the spread of a fanatical and censorious spirit, which seemed to put in jeopardy the best interests of the Church. He was especially concerned at the intrusion of ignorant and conceited men into the place of public teachers; at the disregard, and even contempt, of evangelical order, which was often manifested; and, above all, at the rapid progress of a spurious religion, under the guidance of pride, ignorance, and spiritual quackery.'[1]

Before we turn from this narrative of events certain conclusions need to be noted. Without question, the rise of the fanatical element coincided with the decline of the spiritual power of the Awakening. Those who spoke most loudly of being led by the Spirit were the very persons responsible for quenching the Spirit's work. As Edwards puts it,

The cry was, 'O, there is no danger, if we are but lively in religion, and full of God's Spirit, and live by faith, of being misled! If we do but follow God, there is no danger of being led wrong! 'Tis the cold, carnal, and lifeless, that are most likely to be blind, and walk in darkness. Let us press forward, and not stay and hinder the good work, by standing and spending time in these criticisms and carnal

[1]*Annals*, 1, p. 405.

reasonings!' etc., etc. This was the language of many, till they ran on deep into the wilderness, and were taught by the briers and thorns of the wilderness (1.cl).

For Edwards the turning point in the revival came when men thus failed to guard against excesses. Thomas Prince similarly dates the turning point in Boston to the arrival of Davenport in the summer of 1742. Davenport's condemnation of the ministry (in a place where the ministerial supporters of the revival out-numbered the rest by three-to-one!), and his call for separation, 'diverted the minds of many from being concerned about their own conversion to think and dispute about the case of others'. 'This', Prince continues, 'not only seemed to put an awful stop to their awakenings, but on all sides to roil [stir up] our passions and provoke the Holy Spirit, in a gradual and dreadful measure, to withdraw his influence. Now a disputatious spirit most grievously prevailed amongst us'.[1] Whitefield (who was absent from New England from October 1740 until October 1744) was to come to the same conclusion: 'I found . . . that the work of God had went on in a most glorious manner for near two years after my departure from New England, but then a chill came over the work through the imprudence of some Ministers who had been promoters and private persons who had been happy subjects of it.'[2]

So, in the words of Dwight, the revival's 'worst enemies were found among its most zealous friends'.

The effects of fanaticism did not stop, however, with the divisions caused between men who had originally stood together. The same fanaticism gave occasion for those to speak who hitherto had been doubters, silent onlookers, or secret opponents. In 1740–41, although rumours were heard that the Awakening was all 'the effect of an heated imagination, or mere enthusiasm and disorder', no spokesman for such opinions was to be found in the land. An awe came upon men and stilled every tongue. The general consciousness that the work was of God was so strong that, as we have seen, when criticism at length began to be heard it needed the cover of anonymity. All this was changed by the emergence of an undeniable fanati-

[1]Gillies, p. 357.
[2]*Journals*, p. 529.

cism. Was it not possible, men could now ask, that, the 'enthusiastical impressions' which had seized Davenport, were in fact the cause for *all* that had been attributed to divine operation? Was the Awakening, in reality, just a form of natural excitement similar to such other excitements as may agitate communities from time to time? 'Some persons of very good sense were once inclined to think God was doing wonders in this place', wrote the author of *The State of Religion in New England* in 1742, 'But that was at a time when the superstitious panic ran very high, and bore down everybody that was not well fixed and established, either by a natural steadiness of temper, or by strong reason and reflection'. Only 'as the Passions of the People subsided' could better judgments be reached by a larger number.

This argument was not without a degree of plausibility at a time when many had good reason to recoil from the excesses of Davenport. Fanaticism thus gave rise to a greater danger – the danger that opportunity was being given not merely to condemn excess but to undermine faith in the Holy Spirit and in the nature of true religion. Orthodoxy instead of being established in the land by the Awakening might accordingly be discredited. For Edwards this was the most serious challenge of the 1740's and we cannot move on with his personal history until we pause in the next chapter to look at his literary response to the danger.

THE DEFENCE OF EXPERIMENTAL
RELIGION

Some Thoughts

Concerning the prefent

Revival of Religion

I N

NEW-ENGLAND,

And the Way in which it ought to be
acknowledged and promoted,

Humbly offered to the Publick, in a

TREATISE on that Subject.

In Five PARTS ;

PART I. Shewing that
the Work that has of
late been going on in
this Land, is a glori
ous Work of GOD.

PART II. Shewing the
Obligations that all are
under, to acknowlege,
rejoice in and promote
this Work, and the
great Danger of the
contrary.

.RT III. Shewing in
many Inftances, where

in the Subjects, or zea-
lous Promoters, of this
Work have been inju-
rioufly blamed.

PART IV. Shewing what
Things are to be cor-
rected or avoided, in
promoting this Work,
or in our Behaviour
under it.

PART V. Shewing pofi-
tively what ought to
be done to promote
this Work.

By *JONATHAN EDWARDS*, A. M.
iftor of the Church of CHRIST at *Northampton*.

Ifai. 40. 3. *Prepare ye the Way of the Lord, make ftrait
in the Defart a high Way for our God*

BOSTON : Printed and Sold by S. *Kneeland*
and *T. Green* in *Queen-Street*, 1742.

Title page of Some Thoughts Concerning the Present Revival

An intemperate, imprudent zeal, and a degree of enthusiasm, soon crept in and mingled itself with that revival of religion; and so great and general an awakening being quite a new thing in the land, at least as to all the living inhabitants of it, neither people nor ministers had learned thoroughly to *distinguish* between solid religion and its delusive counterfeits. Even many ministers of the Gospel, of long standing and the best reputation, were for a time overpowered with the glaring appearances of the latter.

JE (2.321)

12

he Great Awakening, and its aftermath, gave rise to the most important of Edwards' writings, the seed-thoughts of which are all in his published sermon of September 1741, *The Distinguishing Marks of a Work of the Spirit of God*. This was followed, as we have seen, by the first title which he wrote specifically as a book, *Some Thoughts concerning the Present Revival of Religion in New England in 1742*, and, in 1746, by another book, *A Treatise concerning Religious Affections*. Linked with these volumes, and bearing closely on their over-all theme, was his last major work of the 1740's, *The Life and Diary of David Brainerd* (1749).

The first of these works appeared when Edwards was thirty-eight years of age, the last when he was forty-six. They show that while his theology remained basically the same, a considerable variation gradually emerged in its emphasis and in its application. It was not only the revival which was 'an unexpected, surprising overturning of things', other surprises belonged equally to the 1740's, and his assessment of New England's needs underwent corresponding modifications.

A difference is already apparent when his *Distinguishing Marks* of 1741 is compared with the volume which he wrote in the following year. The former is a cogent defence of the Awakening, having as its starting point the words of 1 John 4.1, 'Try the spirits whether they are of God'. The only safe means to do this, Edwards argued, was by the Word of God itself, taking what Scripture gives as the 'distinguishing marks' of the

Holy Spirit's activity and comparing them with what was then being witnessed in the land. The Spirit's true work can be distinguished from that which is false because we know that he always (1) causes a greater esteem for Christ (2) operates against the interest of Satan's kingdom 'which lies in encouraging and establishing sin' (3) promotes greater regard for the truth and the divinity of the Holy Scriptures (4) brings men to the light of truth (5) excites love to God and man, making the attributes of God, manifested in Christ, 'delightful objects of contemplation'.

Such are the 'heads' which Edwards elaborates and in the light of these tests he regards the failure of some to support the revival as inexcusable: 'We must throw by our Bibles and give up revealed religion if this be not in general the work of God'. He believed that the hyper-caution, or 'pretended prudence', of those who stood aside and questioned the revival brought *their own* religious experience into question. 'When the Spirit of God came to be poured out so wonderfully in the apostles' days', he reminds his readers, 'many who had been in reputation for religion and piety had a great spite against the work because they saw it tended to diminish their honour and to reproach their formality and lukewarmness.'

Certainly Edwards admitted the existence of 'imprudences and irregularities', but 'imprudences will not prove a work to be not of the Spirit of God', for such things were to be found even in the New Testament churches themselves. Their presence in New England was a reaction 'after a long-continued and almost universal deadness'. To wait to see a work of God without blemishes and faults, is to be like a fool 'waiting at the river side to have the water all run by'. 'A work of God without stumbling-blocks is never to be expected.'

Distinguishing Marks is a slender piece compared with *Some Thoughts concerning the Present Revival.* How Edwards managed to write the larger work amidst all the engagements of 1742 is cause for wonder. Yet several things pointed to the need for this volume. First, as already noted, the opposition had become articulate by 1742; thus the grounds upon which some men based their denial of any revival were now clarified and required an answer. Second, the strength and the number of 'imprudencies' had become much more significant and the need for a discouragement of fanaticism correspondingly more imperative. In 1741 Edwards had spoken of the devil's tactics in introducing excess and confusion into a work of God, but he had not attributed anything in the present revival explicitly to that source. 'I see no need of bringing in the help of the devil', he had written with respect to the understanding of one phenomenon. In 1742 his mood had changed and the revival, in his view, had reached a stage when it was essential to recognize an unseen warfare. The over-reaction might be explicable in terms of the previous deadness and of the inexperience and youthfulness of a number of the leading preachers, but he was now certain that the devil was involved in it. A new note thus emerges in *Some Thoughts concerning the Present Revival*:

There being a great many errors and sinful irregularities mixed with this work of God, arising from our weakness, darkness, and corruption, does not hinder this work of God's power and grace from being very glorious. . . . How unreasonable is it that we should be backward to acknowledge the glory of what God has done, because the devil, and we in hearkening to him, have done a great deal of mischief! (1.380)

. . . If we look back into the history of the church of God in past ages, we may observe that it has been a common device of the devil to overset a revival of religion; when he finds he can keep men quiet and secure no longer, then he drives them to excesses and extravagances. He holds them back as long as he can; but when he can do it no longer, then he will push them on, and, if possible, run them upon their heads. And it has been by this means chiefly that he has been successful, in several instances, to overthrow most hopeful and promising beginnings. Yea, the principal means by which the devil was successful, by degrees, to overset the grand religious revival of the world in the primitive ages of Christianity, and in a manner to overthrow the christian church through the earth, and to make way for the great Antichristian apostasy, that masterpiece of all the devil's works, was to improve the indiscreet zeal of Christians, to drive them into those three extremes of *enthusiasm, superstition,* and *severity towards opposers*; which should be enough for an everlasting warning to the christian church.

Though the devil will do his diligence to stir up the open enemies of religion, yet he knows what is for his interest so well, that, in a time of revival of religion, his main strength shall be tried with the friends of it; and he will chiefly exert himself in his attempts to mislead them. . . .

It is a grand error for persons to think they are out of danger from the devil and a corrupt, deceitful heart, even in their highest flights, and most raised frames of spiritual joy. For persons, in such a confidence, to cease to be jealous of themselves, and to neglect watchfulness and care, is a presumption by which I have known many woefully insnared. However highly we may be favoured with divine discoveries and comforts, yet, as long as we are in the world, we are in the enemies' country, and therefore that direction of Christ to his disciples is never out of date in this world [Luke 21.36], 'Watch and pray always, that you may be accounted worthy to escape all these things, and to stand before the Son of man'. It was not out of date with the disciples to whom it was given, after they came to be full of the Holy Ghost, and *out of their bellies flowed rivers of living water*, by that great effusion upon them that began on the day of Pentecost. And though God stands ready to protect his people, especially those that are near to him, yet he expects of all great care and labour, and that we should put on the whole armour of God, that we may stand in the evil day.

To whatever spiritual privileges we are raised, we have no warrant to expect protection in any other way; for God has appointed this whole life to be all as a race or a battle; the state of rest, wherein we shall be so out of danger as to have no need of watching and fighting, is reserved for another world. I have known it in abundance of instances, that the devil has come in very remarkably, even in the midst of the most excellent frames. It may seem a great mystery that it should be so; but it is no greater mystery than that Christ should be taken captive by the devil, and carried into the wilderness, immediately after the heavens had been opened to him, and the Holy Ghost descended like a dove upon him, and when he heard that comfortable, joyful voice from the Father, saying, 'This is my beloved Son, in whom I am well pleased' (1.397–98).

Edwards' basic view of the revival is unchanged, it was 'a very great outpouring of the Spirit', but some differences between his *Thoughts concerning the Present Revival* and his *Distinguishing Marks* are noticeable. When he wrote in 1741 he almost seemed to regard as unthinkable the possibility that a true Christian might be among the opposers of the work. Twelve months later he is ready to warn that the critical attitude of some may be due to the 'prejudices they have received from the errors that have been mixed with this work', as well as to other reasons, and 'to determine how far opposing this work is consistent with a state of grace is, as experience shows, a very difficult thing . . . I have seen what abundantly convinces me that the business is too high for me; I am glad that God has not committed such a difficult affair to me' (1.416).

More than this, it can be said that even between the time when Edwards started to write the larger work in 1742 and its conclusion (it was published in March 1743) some variation in his assessment is observable. The reason undoubtedly lay in the events recorded in the last chapter. The writing of *Thoughts concerning the Present Revival* was proceeding at the very time when Davenport's excesses in Connecticut were receiving such publicity in the summer of 1742. The situation was clearly changing and the unknown factor to Edwards, as he pressed on with his book in Northampton, was whether this wild-fire could be contained and arrested. In the earlier part of the volume he entertains the hope that the Awakening in 1742 was still only at its *beginning* and that all which they had seen thus far was but 'the dawn' of that age of general revival which, he believed, Scripture promised for the latter days: 'The very uncommon and wonderful circumstances and events of this work seem to me strongly to argue that God intends it as the beginning or forerunner of something vastly great' (1.383). By the time, however, that he came to write the closing section of the same book a note of uncertainty was appearing. 'Great' though the Awakening had been, perhaps, after all, it was not 'the dawn'. A closing recommendation is introduced with the words: 'One thing more I would mention, which, if God should still carry on this work, would tend much to promote it . . . ' (1.429). Similarly, the final paragraph contains the warning: 'God is giving us the most happy season to attempt an universal reformation that ever was given in New England. And it is a thousand pities that we should fail of that which would be so glorious for want of being sensible of our opportunity.'

When Edwards commenced writing *Thoughts concerning the Present Revival* he knew that he had to engage in a debate on two fronts. On the one side there were those whose attitude had become one of decided opposition, and, on the other, those who saw no danger at all provided men displayed enough spiritual zeal. The structure of his book gives some grounds for believing that in the course of its composition his uppermost concern shifted from the opponents of the revival to the excesses of those who proclaimed that they were its best friends. The unequal length of the five main divisions into which the book is divided points in this direction. The headings of the five parts, with the number of pages they contain in the Edinburgh edition of 1743 are as follows:

1. Showing that the Extraordinary work which has of late been going on in the land is A Glorious Work of God (50 pages); 2. Showing the Obligations that all are under to Acknowledge this Work, and The Great Danger of the Contrary (34 pages); 3. Showing, in many instances, Wherein the Subjects, or zealous Promoters, of this Work, have been Injuriously Blamed (23 pages); 4. Showing what things are to be Corrected or Avoided in Promoting this Work, Or in Our Behaviour under It (84 pages); 5. Showing positively, What Ought to be Done to Promote this Work (31 pages).

Part 4 – by far the longest part – deals solely with cautions to friends of the revival and Edwards' justification for that proportion of space is plainly stated: the excesses of one 'truly zealous person', he writes, 'may do more (through Satan's being too subtle for him) to hinder the work than a hundred great, and strong, and open opposers' (1.398). By the time the book went to the press Edwards was plainly convinced that the continuance or the ending of the revival depended, more than anything else, on whether the wild-fire and fanaticism could be curbed. It was an emergency which demanded action and he felt the weight of his responsibility. 'If some elder minister had undertaken this', he says in the Preface, 'I acknowledge it would have been more proper; but I have heard of no such thing like to be done. . . . If others would hold forth further light to me in any of these particulars, I hope I should thankfully receive it. I think I have been made in some measure sensible, and much more of late than formerly, of my need of more wisdom than I have' (1.365).

It must not, however, be supposed that the year 1742 marked Edwards' first recognition of the danger from 'friends of the revival'. In some measure he had anticipated it much earlier. Speaking of this subject to William M'Culloch (whose parish of Cambuslang, Scotland, had been visited by a great revival in 1742) he writes on May 12, 1743:

We live in a day wherein God is doing marvellous things: in that respect, we are distinguished from former generations. God has wrought great things in New England, which, though exceedingly glorious, have all along been attended with some threatening clouds; which, from the beginning, caused me to apprehend some great stop or check to be put to the work before it should be begun and carried on in its genuine purity and beauty, to subdue all before it, and to prevail with an irresistible and continual progress and triumph; and it is come to pass according to my apprehensions (1.lxxii).

Proof that Edwards was apprehensive 'from the beginning' was later to emerge in an unexpected manner. Towards the end of 1744, when critics of the late revival were making Whitefield their chief target, Thomas Clap, Rector of Yale, published a letter in which he sought to include Edwards among those who were critics of Whitefield. According to Clap, when he and his wife were riding to Boston in May 1743 they had met Edwards on the road, travelling to the same destination, with Sarah, his eldest daughter, sitting behind him on his horse. They proceeded together and, in the conversation on the revival in which they engaged, Clap claimed that Edwards and he were 'well agreed to condemn many Errors'. Further, with respect to Whitefield, Clap now divulged an extraordinary piece of information. The Yale Rector gave Edwards as his source for an alleged statement by Whitefield to the effect that he wanted the people to be encouraged to turn 'the bigger part of the ministers of New-England' out of their pulpits and that he would see them replaced by young converted men from Britain! With this in print (with the obvious intent of damning Whitefield) Edwards was forced to reply. He categorically denied either reporting such words or having ever heard them from Whitefield. 'The relation you give of the conversation that passed between us as we rode together through Leicester is one of the most amazing things to me that ever I met with in my life'. Wherever Clap obtained his false rumours it was not from him, and, given the wide difference between them on the subject of the revival, was it likely, Edwards asked, that he would have shared any confidence with him on Whitefield?

There was little in our conversation, in the journey Mr Clap speaks of, to draw me to such a confidence in him as to choose him above all the world to reveal my greatest secrets to: for he immediately fell upon me, as he knows, as soon as ever we began to ride the road together, about some passages in my book, *Concerning the Revival of Religion*, greatly blaming me, earnestly disputing, I suppose, for hours together.[1]

Clap's publication was damaging to Edwards as well as to Whitefield for in his *Thoughts concerning the Present Revival of Religion* Edwards had openly commended 'the great things that Mr Whitefield has done' (1.424). If Clap's report was correct the implication was that either Edwards had changed his judgment or that his private conversations differed from his published statements. It was this which forced Edwards, replying to Clap in 1745, to state a criticism of the evangelist which he had, on occasion, shared with a few friends. He had first spoken of the matter to Whitefield himself, at the very beginning of the Awakening, when the two had met at Northampton in October 1740. The controversial point which they had then discussed was not that of displacing ministers or of dividing churches, but the danger – as Edwards saw it – of following purely subjective impulses as though they were the sure guidance of the Holy Spirit. Upon this point Edwards admitted to Clap:

I indeed have told several persons that I once purposely took an opportunity to talk with Mr Whitefield alone about impulses: and have mentioned many particulars of our conference together on that head: That I told him some reasons I had to think he gave too great heed to such things: and have told what manner of replies he made; and what reasons I offered against such things. And I also said that Mr Whitefield did not seem to be offended with me: but yet did not seem to be inclined to have a great deal of discourse about it: And that in the time of it he did not appear to be convinced by any thing I said.

This subject which Edwards had anticipated in 1740 was subsequently to become the talking-point of the whole country and central to the controversy which developed. Whitefield's judgment on the subject had changed by the time that Edwards answered Clap, but at the beginning of the Awakening the visitor to New England had evidently not seen the danger. What that danger was Edwards stated clearly in his New

[1] *An Expostulatory Letter from the Rev. Mr Edwards of Northampton to the Rev. Mr Clap*, 1745, p. 15.

Haven sermon of September 1741. At a time of revival, when Christians have a 'strong and lively sense of divine things', all their faculties are invigorated – the mind is more intense, the 'affections' are heightened, and the imagination, also, may be more active. It is easy, in this condition, argued Edwards, to regard a strong impression made upon the imagination, and explainable by natural causes, as a direct leading of the Spirit. The 'impressions' or 'impulses' which he criticized were varied in character. Sometimes they involved an element of the visionary. Sometimes they appeared to provide foreknowledge of future events. And sometimes they were accompanied and apparently supported by random texts of Scripture – for example, Davenport's 'call' to itinerate was based upon the words of the Philistines to Jonathan and his armour-bearer in 1 Samuel 14.12, 'Come up to us'. Whatever their form, the result was that the person who trusted these impressions was assured of God's help in a manner not customary among Christians. And when such experiences were simultaneous with genuine revival, it was comparatively easy for their subjects to believe that they owed them directly to the Holy Spirit.

Against this belief Edwards argued that a Christian might indeed have a 'holy frame and sense from the Spirit of God' but the 'imaginations that attend it are but accidental' and not directly attributable to the Spirit. His reasons for so believing were twofold:

First, his reading of history and his own observation had convinced him that where Christians based their actions or plans upon subjective impulses, unsupported by the clear teaching of Scripture, they were liable to be greatly disappointed: 'Many godly persons have undoubtedly in this and other ages, exposed themselves to woeful delusions by an aptness to lay too much weight on impulses and impressions' (2.265). In this connection it is interesting to note that it was further experience which brought Whitefield to realize what he could not see in 1740. Prior to the birth of Whitefield's only child in October 1743, he declared his belief that the child would be a son and that he would be a preacher of the gospel. Four months later the infant who, as Whitefield 'fondly hoped', 'was to be great in the sight of the Lord', died, and Whitefield at once recognized his mistake saying: 'I misapplied several texts of Scripture. Upon these grounds, I made no scruple of declaring "that I should have a son, and that his name was to be John".[1] When back in New England, in 1745, he could say feelingly of what had happened there, 'Many good souls, both among clergy and laity, for a while, mistook fancy for faith, and imagination for revelation'.[2] As Edwards was pointing out early in the 1740's, texts accompanying impulses were no safe guide if wrenched from their original and only true meaning. The announcement of the birth of John the Baptist did not contain a 'special' message for Whitefield any more than the call of the Philistines constituted a call from God to Davenport.

Secondly, Edwards held that for impulses to contain direct 'messages' from God they must necessarily partake of the nature of those extraordinary gifts which, he believed, were unique to the infancy of the apostolic church. Such impulses, if truly from the Spirit, 'are properly inspiration, such as the prophets and apostles and others had of old' (2.274). Edwards' arguments against the continuing existence of the extraordinary gifts of the Spirit are too extended to be covered here; suffice it to say that he was not thoughtlessly following the standard reformed view. The Quakers, the French Prophets, and other groups had given cause enough for the scriptural evidence to be re-examined. There were even some orthodox Christians in New England who believed that a glorious revival in the latter days 'would partly consist in restoring those extraordinary gifts of the Spirit'. For Edwards that belief was erroneous and dangerous, and its existence, in his view, was partly responsible for the readiness of some to treat 'impulses' as God-given. He saw it as dangerous because a wish for the restoration of extraordinary gifts suggested a wrong view of what are indeed the great and abiding influences of the Spirit in the Church.[3] The extraordinary gifts had no necessary connection with the power of godliness; indeed, he asserts, a man might have them 'and go to hell'. The glorious work of the Spirit is that in which

[1] *The Works of the Rev. George Whitefield*, 1771, vol. 2, p. 51.
[2] *Ibid.*, 73.
[3] For Edwards on the cessation of extraordinary gifts, see his *Charity and Its Fruits*, pp. 38, 44–47, 306–324; *Works* 1, p. 274 and vol. 2, pp. 274–5. For a full treatment of the 'mischievous principle' that God guides his saints in these days by immediate revelation, see 1: pp. 404–5.

he imparts regenerating and sanctifying grace to the soul, revealing Christ's divine beauty and communicating his nature to the believer. Such influences of the Spirit, Edwards says, 'I had rather enjoy one quarter of an hour than to have prophetical visions and revelations the whole year'. 'It does not appear to me that there is any need of those extraordinary gifts to set up the kingdom of God through the world; I have seen so much of the power of God in a more excellent way, as to convince me that God can easily do it without' (2.275).

The above quotations on 'impulses' were written in 1741, in 1742 he speaks still more decidedly:

One erroneous principle, than which scarce any has proved more mischievous to the present glorious work of God, is a notion that it is God's manner in these days to guide his saints, at least some that are more eminent, by inspiration, or immediate revelation. . . .

This error will defend and support errors. As long as a person has a notion that he is guided by immediate direction from heaven, it makes him incorrigible and impregnable in all his misconduct. . . .

And why cannot we be contented with the divine oracles, that holy, — pure word of God, which we have in such abundance and clearness, now since the canon of Scripture is completed? Why should we desire to have any thing added to them by impulses from above? Why should we not rest in that standing rule that God has given to his church, which, the apostle teaches us, is surer than a voice from heaven? And why should we desire to make the Scripture speak more to us than it does? Or why should any desire a higher kind of intercourse with heaven, than by having the Holy Spirit given in his sanctifying influences, infusing and exciting grace and holiness, love and joy, which is the highest kind of intercourse that the saints and angels in heaven have with God, and the chief excellency of the glorified man Christ Jesus? (1.404).

In speaking in this way Edwards knew that he was in danger of isolating himself from the two parties which had wide support. With the sanction which Whitefield had given and with Davenport not yet generally discredited, it was possible for some to regard Edwards as a critic of the very thing which they saw as one great proof of God's work!

Even when the pro-revival Boston ministers warned against Davenport's error in their Declaration of July 1742 they by no means carried all the supporters of the Awakening with them.

The Rev. Andrew Croswell, who had been associated with Whitefield, and was pastor at Groton, Connecticut, immediately replied, condemning them for criticizing a ministry which God had so much used, and defending Davenport's view of the Spirit's guidance:

I remember that Mr Whitefield looks upon the impression that was occasioned on Mr Barber's mind by the application of a passage of the Holy Scriptures to himself and Mr Whitefield, to be really from God. Nor have Mr Davenport's impressions done him any harm as yet: and to expect danger from that quarter, is fearing where no fear is; especially if we consider the uncommon sanctity of the man, and his trembling at the appearance of evil.[1]

At the other extreme, the view which was gaining ground that the 'aptness to take the motion of their own minds for something divinely extraordinary' was characteristic of all who claimed to see a great work of God in the land. Those of this opinion believed that the excitement of the so-called 'revival' only added up to a delusion. What men called 'the out-pouring of the Spirit' was nothing more than enthusiasm! Such was the case which, as we have seen, Chauncy was to argue openly in 1743.

Edwards certainly felt the difficulty of standing in between the parties represented by Croswell and Chauncy. As he later noted, when parties are divided, 'Satan leads both far out of the right way, driving each to great extremes, one on the right hand, and the other on the left, till the right path in the middle is almost wholly neglected' (1.235). Yet although the positions of Croswell and Chauncy were so much opposed Edwards saw that they were both guilty of the same mistake. Both refused to distinguish parts from the whole. Ardent supporters of the revival such as Croswell argued that if God's hand was already present in the revival then the *whole* must be regarded as of God, and that if God designed to bless and use the ministries of his servants it was not for men to criticize any part of ministries so divinely owned. Therefore, to censure Davenport amounted to a criticism of the providence of God.[2]

From an opposite standpoint Chauncy argued with a similar

---

[1]Quoted in Tracy, *The Great Awakening*, p. 245.
[2]Edwards answers this argument forcefully (1.409).

show of logic. If parts of the so-called revival could be proved to be the effects of the 'enthusiastical spirit', if upholders of 'the work' at times resembled Quakers or French Prophets, then the *whole* was to be rejected.

In reply to this, Edwards urged that distinctions have to be made, because 'darkness mixed with light, and evil with good, is always to be expected'. Such was to be found even in the apostolic church, 'in that great effusion of the Spirit', when they were under 'the care of infallible guides' (1.372). The 'bad things' were not 'the revival' (as Chauncy argued) but were only incidental to it. So one of Edwards' opening sections in *Thoughts concerning the Present Revival* demonstrates the principle, 'We should distinguish the good from the bad, and not judge of the whole by a part.'

Edwards saw the consequences of both extremes as perilous. The Awakening had revived true heart religion across the land and for this revived religion to be opposed *in toto* by those who claimed to be Christians was tantamount to the disapproving of the Christianity portrayed in the New Testament itself. To treat all the renewal of love, holiness and joy seen in New England as being of the same nature as 'the distemper that is become so epidemical in the land' was, in effect, writes Edwards in 1742, 'to create a suspicion of all vital religion, and to put the people upon talking against it and discouraging it, and knocking it on the head as fast as it rises'. What would be left of real Christianity if all felt spiritual experience was rejected?

What notions have they of religion, that reject what has been described, as not true religion! What shall we find to answer those expressions in Scripture – 'The peace of God that passeth all understanding; rejoicing with joy unspeakable and full of glory, in believing in and loving an unseen Saviour; – All joy and peace in believing; God's shining into our hearts, to give the light of the knowledge of the glory of God in the face of Jesus Christ; With open face, beholding as in a glass the glory of the Lord, and being changed into the same image, from glory to glory, even as by the Spirit of the Lord; – Having the love of God shed abroad in our hearts, by the Holy Ghost given to us; – Having the Spirit of God and of glory rest upon us; – A being called out of darkness into marvellous light; and having the day-star arise in our hearts:' – I say, if those things which have been mentioned do not answer these expressions, what else can we find out that does answer them? Those that do not think such things as these to be the fruits of the true Spirit, would do well to consider what kind of spirit they are waiting and praying for, and what sort of fruits they expect he should produce when he comes (1.378).

The line which Chauncy was to urge, Edwards rightly saw, would lead to a mere formal Christianity, akin to the rationalism which was already influential in eighteenth-century Deism. But in warning of that danger he did not assume, like Croswell, that the best support for true Christianity was an advocacy of the opposite extreme. That extreme also was perilous because it failed to make a distinction between 'vital religion' and 'enthusiasm'. Those uncritical friends of the revival, who saw no need to guard against excesses and errors, were going to awake, he believed, with a sad surprise and then the danger would be of a swing to an opposite position! In a moving passage addressed to the supporters of the work, Edwards concludes Part 4 of his *Thoughts concerning the Present Revival*:

The devil has driven the *pendulum* far beyond its proper point of rest; and when he has carried it to the utmost length that he can, and it begins by its own weight to swing back, he probably will set in, and drive it with the utmost fury the other way; and so give us no rest; and if possible prevent our settling in a proper medium. What a poor, blind, weak and miserable creature is man, at his best estate! We are like poor helpless sheep; the devil is too subtle for us. What is our strength! What is our wisdom! How ready are we to go astray! How easily are we drawn aside into innumerable snares, while in the mean time we are bold and confident, and doubt not but we are right and safe! We are foolish sheep in the midst of subtle serpents and cruel wolves, and do not know it. Oh how unfit are we to be left to ourselves! And how much do we stand in need of the wisdom, the power, the condescension, patience, forgiveness, and gentleness of our good Shepherd! (1.420)

*   *   *

It would have given pleasure to some to have seen a division between Edwards and Whitefield. Edwards never expressed any public criticism of Whitefield except briefly in his letters to Clap quoted above. Those same letters contained far more in

Whitefield's commendation although written at a time when opposition to the Englishman was the prevailing fashion in the public press (1744–45). The friendship of the two men was sealed by a second Whitefield visit to Northampton for a week in July 1745, this time accompanied by his wife Elizabeth. Whitefield had arrived in New England in the previous October. Speaking of Whitefield's reception, Edwards wrote to a friend in Scotland:

Many ministers were more alarmed at his coming than they would have been by the arrival of a fleet from France, and they began soon to preach and write against him. . . . I question whether history affords any instance paralleled with this, as so much pains taken in writing to blacken a man's character and render him odious. . . . Many that when he was here before durst as soon eat fire as speak reproachfully of him, the regard of the people in general was so great to him, now have taken liberty of opposing him most openly and without restraint. . . . It was a kind of miracle that Mr Whitefield should appear so little moved by all that he met with, and should in the midst of all possess himself with so much courage and calmness. . . .

Concerning Whitefield's second visit to his home, Edwards continues:

He behaved himself so that he endeared himself much to me; he appeared in a more desirable temper of mind, and more solid and judicious in his thoughts, and prudence in his conduct, than when he was here before. . . . In the eastern parts of Connecticut . . . he very boldly, plainly and abundantly testified against the opinions and way of the wild and extravagant people there, and has there done a great deal of good; a considerable number have been reclaimed by him. But yet the big part are obstinate, and condemn Mr Whitefield, as they do other ministers that oppose them.[1]

Whitefield undoubtedly had a greater appreciation of Edwards' insight in 1745, and shortly after, he gave eloquent warning against the two extremes which his friend had discerned in 1742. In a sermon on 'Walking with God' first published in 1746, in a volume prefaced by Gilbert Tennent, he declares:

[1]'Extract of a Part of the Reverend Mr Jonathan Edwards's Letter . . .' in *The Christian Monthly History*, December, 1745, pp. 259–63.

Though it is the quintessence of Enthusiasm to pretend to be guided by the Spirit without the written Word, yet it is every Christian's bounden duty to be guided by the Spirit in conjunction with the written Word of God. Watch, therefore, I pray you, O believers, the motions of God's blessed Spirit in your souls, and always try the suggestions or impressions that you may at any time feel, by the unerring rule of God's most Holy Word. And if they are not found to be agreeable to that, reject them as diabolical and delusive! By observing this caution, you will steer a middle course between the two dangerous extremes many of this generation are in danger of running into; I mean, Enthusiasm, on the one hand, and Deism, and downright infidelity, on the other.[1]

[1] *Six Sermons*, George Whitefield, 3rd Edition, London, 1750, p. 92.

13

'THE RELIGIOUS AFFECTIONS'

*An idealised impression of the centre of
Northampton below Meetinghouse Hill. Houses
were undoubtedly closer together.*

I would say, though it is an exaggeration, I would like to sit at Jonathan Edwards' feet, to learn what is true religion, and at Thomas Boston's, to learn how I am to get it . . . but between Boston and Edwards there is no contradiction, and they are important to each other . . . I would like to see a divine arise in whom Jonathan Edwards and Thomas Boston were thoroughly welded into one.

DR. JOHN 'RABBI' DUNCAN
In the Pulpit and at the Communion Table, 1874, p. 63, 34,
and *Colloquia Peripatetica*, 1907, p. 86.

he indications are that Edwards' series of sermons on 1 Peter 1.8, 'Whom having not seen, ye love; in whom, though now ye see him not, yet believing, ye rejoice with joy unspeakable and full of glory', preached in 1742 and in the early part of 1743, underwent major revision before their publication in 1746 as *A Treatise Concerning the Religious Affections*. While the concerns which gave rise to the book are patently rooted in the Awakening the standpoint in time has changed; it is no longer 'the present revival' but 'the late extraordinary season' or 'the late great revival'. To use Edwards' own illustration, when he spoke in 1742 it was 'spring-time' and he viewed 'the multitude of blossoms'. In 1746 the view was no longer like that of the month of May; it was October, and the actual 'fruit' resulting from the blossoms which had all appeared 'fair and beautiful' told another story. He uses the same illustration more than once:

It is with professors of religion, especially such as become so in a time of outpouring of the Spirit of God, as it is with blossoms in the spring; there are vast numbers of them upon the trees, which all look fair and promising; but yet many of them never come to anything. . . . It is the mature fruit which comes afterwards, and not the beautiful colours and smell of the blossoms, that we must judge by.[1]

[1] *The Religious Affections, Select Works of J E*, Banner of Truth, 1961, pp. 113–4. While the text of this work is, of course, contained in the two-volume edition of Edwards, I am here, and in the following pages, quoting from this more easily read reprint which remains currently available. Hereafter I will refer to this title in this edition as *RA*. See also J E (Yale) vol. 2.

But, leaving aside the metaphor, how is one to judge genuine Christian experience? Or, to put the question in the words Edwards uses in his Preface, 'What is the nature of true religion? and wherein lie the distinguishing notes of that virtue which is acceptable in the sight of God?' These sentences introduce the theme of *The Religious Affections* and Edwards never gave closer and more careful thought to anything than he did to this.

Edwards' statement of the nature of true religion, in the first place, bears against those who would not recognize the revival of 1740–42 and who did not believe that 'there has been so much to be seen of the operations of the Spirit of God of late'.[1] As he anticipated in 1742, the minority view represented by Chauncy that religion lies in 'reason and judgment' and in dutiful behaviour, had now become more widely credited because of the uncritical praise of everything which had recently gone under the name of experience and emotion. The pendulum had indeed swung back so that in 1746 he could speak of 'the prevailing prejudices against religious affections at this day in the land.'[2]

Because many who, in the late extraordinary season, appeared to have great religious affections did not manifest a right temper of mind, and ran into many errors, in the time of their affection and the heat of their zeal . . . religious affections in general are grown out of credit with great numbers, as though true religion did not at all consist in them. Thus we easily and naturally run from one extreme to another. A little while ago we were in the other extreme; there was a prevalent disposition to look upon all high religious affections as eminent exercises of true grace, without much inquiring into the nature and source of those affections and the manner in which they arose; if persons did but appear to be indeed very much moved and raised, so as to be full of religious talk, and express themselves with great warmth and earnestness, and to be filled, or to be very full, as the phrases were; it was too much the manner, without further examination, to conclude such persons were full of the Spirit of God, and had eminent experience of his gracious influences. This was the extreme which was prevailing three or four years ago. But of late, instead of esteeming and admiring all religious affections without distinction, it is a thing much more prevalent to reject and discard all without distinction. Herein appears the subtlety of Satan. . . . This he knows is the way to bring all religion to a mere lifeless formality, and effectually shut out the power of godliness, and every thing which is spiritual, and to have all true Christianity turned out of doors.[3]

[1]*RA*, p. 90.   [2]*RA*, p. 50.   [3]*RA*, pp. 48–9.

Far from wanting to avoid the charge that he gave undue importance to the emotions or 'affections', Edwards meets the opposition head-on with a series of arguments to prove that 'holy affections do not only necessarily belong to true religion but are a very great part of it'.[1] 'If we be not in good earnest in religion, and our wills and inclinations be not strongly exercised, we are nothing'. His starting-point is an analysis of the human personality. While warning that 'language here is somewhat imperfect', he justifies the usual distinction between the faculty of 'understanding' (which perceives, views and speculates) and the 'heart', the exercises of which are called the sphere where the 'will' and 'inclinations' are operative – 'either in approving and liking, or disapproving and rejecting'. This delineation, he proceeds to show, harmonizes with the scriptural portrayal of real religion. Christian experience cannot reside in the understanding *alone*: 'He that has doctrinal knowledge and speculation only, without affection, never is engaged in the business of religion. . . . The holy Scriptures do everywhere place religion very much in the affections: such as fear, hope, love, hatred, desire, joy, sorrow, gratitude, compassion, and zeal'.[2] Among the proofs which he gives for this proposition are the scriptural accounts of the religion of 'eminent saints' (David, Paul and John) and the example of Christ himself – 'the greatest instance of ardency, vigour and strength of love, both to God and man, that ever was.'

He draws a further argument for the vital place occupied by the affections in true Christian experience from the biblical account of heaven:

The way to learn the true nature of anything is to go where that thing is to be found in its purity and perfection. If we would know the nature of true gold we must view it, not in the ore, but when it is refined. If we would learn what true religion is, we must go where there is true religion, and nothing but true religion, and in its highest perfection, without any defect or mixture. . . . If we can learn anything of the state of heaven from the Scripture, the love and joy that the saints have there is exceeding great and vigorous; impressing the heart with the strongest and most lively sensation of inexpressible sweetness, mightily moving, animating, and engaging them, making them like a

[1]*RA*, p. 29.
[2]*RA*, pp. 30–1.

flame of fire. And if such love and joy be not affections, then the word *affection* is of no use in language. Will any say that the saints in heaven, in beholding the face of their Father and the glory of their Redeemer, and contemplating his wonderful work, and particularly his laying down his life for them, have their hearts nothing moved and affected by all which they behold or consider?[1]

With no references to Chauncy and, comparatively few to contemporary events, the reader of *The Religious Affections* is apt to forget that Edwards was writing in the midst of a major controversy. Academic considerations were altogether out of his view, he wrote for the sake of a cause. He wanted to answer, with all the earnestness and ability God might give him, those who by rejecting the importance of religious affections were stunning 'the life and power of religion'. His censures lose nothing in force because they were not personal for he does not hide the contemporary relevance of his convictions: 'Let it be considered that they who have but little religious affection have certainly but little religion. And they who condemn others for their religious affections, and have none themselves, have no religion.'[2]

It is, however, in bringing his case to bear against those at the other extreme that Edwards enters most fully into the nature of true religion. And it is here that a major difference appears between his assessment in 1742 and the view to which he had now come. At the time of the Awakening, as we have seen, Edwards identified the element of wild-fire with mis-guided, incautious young Christians – pushed on by the devil. But by 1746 other factors had emerged and had given rise to the question why many so-called converts had failed, and why much blossom had produced no permanent fruit. 'It has been a common thing in the church', he writes, 'for bright professors, that are received as eminent saints among the saints, to fall away and come to nothing'.[3] The 1740's had proved to be no exception.

Edwards offered two explanations for this disappointment. The first was the theological argument that a distinction is to be

[1]*RA*, 121, p. 43.
[2]*RA*, p. 50.
[3]*RA*, p. 111.

made between the operations of the Spirit of God which are saving and those which are only common. By 'common' he meant such influences of God's power as may sober, arrest and convict men, and which may even bring them to what at first appears to be repentance and faith, yet these influences fall short of inward, saving renewal. People under such influences may, like Herod Antipas, do 'many things' (Mark 6.20); they may, as the 'stony-ground hearers', receive the word 'with joy' (Matt. 13.20), tasting 'the good word of God and the powers of the world to come' (Heb. 6.5), and escaping 'the pollutions of the world through the knowledge of the Lord and Saviour Jesus Christ', but for all this prove in the end to be nothing more than unregenerate, temporary believers. In his Preface, Edwards indicates that while in his *Distinguishing Marks* of 1741 he had included both the Spirit's 'common and saving operations', he intended now to distinguish between these more closely. This he does repeatedly in the pages which follow.

But this does not mean that professed 'converts' who had borne no permanent fruit, had all relapsed into their previous worldliness and unconcern. In Edwards' judgment something 'worse' than that had happened to many of them and this is the second theme which he expounds in explaining the aftermath of the Awakening. In addition to the work of the Holy Spirit, Satan had been powerfully active in producing a counterfeit religion – a religion which was 'evangelical', which made much of 'experience', of 'discoveries of Christ' and of 'the fulness of the Holy Spirit'. The devil, Edwards argues, does not trouble to counterfeit valueless things – 'there are many false diamonds and rubies, but who goes about to counterfeit common stones?'[1] – he employs his subtlety in making imitations of the most excellent things.

In 1746, as in 1742, Edwards believed that fanaticism had been the great stumbling-block in the revival, but now, instead of simply identifying that excess with young Christians, he was convinced that it had been more commonly promoted by persons who were deluded with a false 'evangelical' experience. Four years after the Awakening these people had not relapsed into the world. On the contrary, they were often the persons

[1]*RA*, p. 73.

most prominent in wanting to 'prolong' the revival, yet, unlike true Christians who had also been involved in excess, they did not repent of censoriousness, of following 'impulses', and of needless divisions. The fact was that the extreme, from which Davenport and others had withdrawn, had now hardened into a type of religion which, in Edwards' view, was frequently a counterfeit of true Christianity. He does not actually name the separatists but, without question, he viewed them as the people chiefly responsible for this state of things.[1]

Quotations from one succinct passage will show his thought. In a false conversion, he writes, a man may have 'the corruption of nature only turned into a new channel instead of its being mortified'. Instead of returning to former profaneness, such men, 'from the high opinion they have of their experiences, graces and privileges', may 'gradually settle more and more in a self-righteous and spiritually proud temper of mind'. He continues:

When it is thus with men, however far they may seem to be from their former evil practices, this alone is enough to condemn them, and may render their last state far worse than the first. For this seems to be the very case of the Jews of that generation that Christ speaks of (Matt. 12.43–45). They had been awakened by John the Baptist's preaching, and brought to a reformation of their former licentious courses, whereby the unclean spirit was as it were turned out, and the house swept and garnished; yet, being empty of God and of grace, full of themselves, and exalted in an exceeding high opinion of their own righteousness and eminent holiness, they became habituated to an answerable self-exalting behaviour. They changed the sins of publicans and harlots for those of the Pharisees; and in the issue, had seven devils and were worse than at the first.[2]

*   *   *

Although *The Religious Affections* is eminently a 'practical' and experimental book, it proceeds from a definite doctrinal conviction, namely, that holiness is necessarily involved at the outset of true Christian experience. Grace planted in the heart

[1] Later, when there were no prospects of separatists being reclaimed, he does name them (e.g. 2:33, 452).
[2] *RA*, p. 314.

in the new-birth is 'a principle of holy action or practice' and it always produces an abiding change of nature in a true convert. Therefore, wherever a profession of conversion is not accompanied by holiness of life it must be understood that the individual concerned is not yet a Christian.

If this basic conviction of Edwards (and reformed theology) respecting the permanent nature of regeneration is not granted, the alternative is to argue that persons can be renewed and, then, ultimately, lose both their holiness and their salvation. For John Wesley this alternative was the obviously true explanation of what had happened in New England. In his greatly abridged version of Edwards' *Religious Affections*, published in 1773, Wesley thought it necessary to warn the readers of the author's fundamental mistake:

The design of Mr. Edwards in the treatise from which the following extract is made, seems to have been chiefly, if not altogether, to serve his hypothesis. In three preceding tracts he had given an account of a glorious work in New England. . . . But in a few years a considerable part of these 'turned back as a dog to the vomit'. What was the plain inference to be drawn from this? Why, that a true believer may 'make shipwreck of the faith'. How then could he evade the force of this? Truly, by eating his own words, and proving as well as the nature of the thing would bear, that they were no believers at all.

In order to this, he heaps together so many curious subtle, metaphysical distinctions, as are sufficient to puzzle the brains, and confound the intellects, of all the plain men and women in the universe, and to make them doubt of, if not wholly deny, all the work which God had wrought in their souls.[1]

There is clearly a serious difference between Edwards and Wesley and it does not simply relate to the perseverance of believers. Wesley's charge is that 'Christian' experience is so basically simple that it is needless to attempt distinctions between the real and the false in those who claim to be rejoicing in Christ. If a person who has assurance of salvation later loses it, and abandons the Christian practice which he once followed,

---

[1] Wesley's *Works*, 14, pp. 283–4 (1831) 'Out of this dangerous heap,' Wesley adds, 'wherein much wholesome food is mixed with much deadly poison, I have selected many remarks and admonitions which may be of great use to the children of God.'

— he is plainly a case of a person losing his salvation. So Wesley thought. Edwards would have been almost nonplussed by such an approach. For him it was axiomatic that there are *apparent* conversions, accompanied, it may be, with joy, zeal and love, which time may prove to have been the result of influences other than the *saving* work of the Holy Spirit. The ways in which men are misled are 'so many that no philosophy or experience will ever be sufficient to guide us safely through this labyrinth and maze, without our closely following the clue which God has given us in His Word.'[1]

However much we may regret it, Edwards believed that the problem involved in recognizing true Christian experience is a fact. Simplistic judgments, for example, the view of those who — would make a certain *type* of conversion the proof of a genuine experience, are therefore thoroughly dangerous. Difficulties are inevitable both because of the variety and mystery of the Holy Spirit's work and because of the complexity of the human personality, yet he believed that the Scriptures do give us directions and that it is only when men neglect them that they will be 'bewildered, confounded and fatally deluded'.

Edwards argues that there are always certain things *missing* from the 'affections' of those who have no true grace. Humility is missing. Thus he regarded much talk of 'great experiences' as no mark of real godliness.[2] 'There are some persons that go by the name of high professors . . . I do not believe there is an eminent saint in the world that is a high professor. Such will be much more likely to profess themselves to be the least of all saints. . . . Such is the nature of grace and of true spiritual light that they naturally dispose the saints in the present state to look upon their grace and goodness [as] little and their deformity [as] great. . . . The more grace a person has, the more the smallness of his grace and love appear strange and wonderful: and therefore he is more ready to think that others are beyond him.'[3] An abiding sense of sin is missing. 'All gracious

[1] *RA*, p. 281.

[2] *RA*, p. 247. 'The true saint, when under great spiritual affections, from the fulness of his heart, is ready to be speaking much of God and his glorious perfections and works . . . but hypocrites, in their high affections, talk more of the discovery, than they do of the thing discovered.' *RA*, p. 178.

[3] *RA*, pp. 248–50.

affections are broken-hearted affections',[1] for repentance in genuine Christian experience is life-long, 'True saints are spoken of in Scripture not only as those that have mourned for sin, but as those that do mourn, whose manner it is still to mourn' (Matt. 5.4).[2] Accordingly, those who lack 'gracious affections' have no reverential fear, they are 'familiar' with God in worship and 'bold, forward, noisy and boisterous' with men.[3] In Scripture, Edwards argues, rejoicing is not the opposite of 'godly fear' but it is ever joined with it.

There is always a true balance missing from the seeming grace of an unregenerate 'evangelical' professor of Christ. The real Christian, enjoying assurance of salvation, has 'holy boldness' but he also 'has less of self-confidence and more modesty. . . . He is less apt than others to be shaken in faith, but more apt than others to be moved with solemn warnings, and with God's frowns, and with the calamities of others. He has the firmest comfort, but the softest heart. Richer than others, he is the poorest of all in spirit: the tallest and strongest saint, but the least and tenderest child among them'.[4]

It is true that as Edwards works out these differences at some length, an effort is sometimes required to keep with him. *The Religious Affections* is deep and profound. The content was originally preached, it should be remembered, not to the young converts of 1735, but to those who had, or professed to have, much spiritual experience seven years later. Yet Edwards' basic and recurring theme is straightforward enough. The love and the pursuit of holiness is *the* enduring mark of the true Christian. Though the Holy Spirit may influence the unregenerate 'many ways', he writes, 'yet he never, in any of his influences, communicates himself to them in his own proper nature'. On the other hand, while the experience of a young Christian may be 'like a confused chaos', he will follow holiness, and true religious affections differ from false affections

[1] *RA*, p. 266.
[2] *RA*, p. 294.
[3] *RA*, p. 288. Censoriousness is often joined with this: 'The humble Christian is more apt to find fault with his own pride than with other men's . . . the proud hypocrite is quick to discern the mote in his brother's eye' *RA*, p. 261.
[4] *RA*, p. 292.

in that the true are always related to holiness. 'Natural men have no sense of the goodness and excellency of holy things, at least for their holiness' but, for the saints, holiness 'is the most amiable and sweet thing that is to be found in heaven or earth'.[1] When persons are possessed of 'false affections', and 'think themselves out of danger of hell, they very much put off the burden of the cross, save themselves the trouble of difficult duties, and allow themselves more of the enjoyment of their ease and their lusts.' 'Some of these,' he adds, 'at the same time make a great profession of love to God, and assurance of his favour, and great joy in tasting the sweetness of his love.'[2]

In Edwards' own short manuscript notes on 'Directions for Judging of Persons' Experiences', he writes, 'See to it that they long after holiness and that all their experiences increase their longing. . . . See to it, whether their experience makes them long after perfect freedom from sin, and after those things wherein holiness consists.' This is the point which is so fully expanded in *The Religious Affections*. Where 'joys and other religious affections are false and counterfeit', he writes:

individuals, once confident that they are converted, have no more earnest longings after light and grace . . . they live upon their first work, or some high experiences that are past, and there is an end to their crying and striving after God and grace. But the holy principles that actuate a true saint have a far more powerful influence to stir him up to earnestness in seeking God and holiness. . . . The Scriptures everywhere represent the seeking, striving, and labour of a Christian, as being chiefly after his conversion, and his conversion as being but the beginning of his work. And almost all that is said in the New Testament, of men's watching, giving earnest heed to themselves, running the race that is set before them, striving and agonizing, wrestling not with flesh and blood but principalities and powers, fighting, putting on the whole armour of God, and standing, pressing forward, reaching forth, continuing instant in prayer, crying to God day and night; I say, almost all that is said in the New Testament of these things, is spoken of and directed to the saints. Where these things are applied to sinners' seeking conversion once, they are spoken of the saints' prosecution of the great business of their high calling ten times.[3]

[1] *RA*, p. 188.
[2] *RA*, pp. 286–7.
[3] *RA*, pp. 306–7.

John Wesley was, like Edwards, concerned for holiness, indeed for 'Christian perfection' in Christians, but a fundamental difference between the two men has to do with what happens to an individual in regeneration and conversion. Edwards believed, as already said, that a renewal in holiness is basic to conversion. For the Christian, holiness is the beauty of the God whom he has been brought to know and, having now a principle of holiness in his own nature, he delights in God and seeks to be like him. 'There is a holy breathing and panting after the Spirit of God to increase holiness which is as natural to a holy nature as breathing is to a living body.'[1] The true believer loves God, 'in the first place, for the beauty of his holiness'. Instead of being something separable from salvation, holiness is the very purpose of salvation. Once a person is renewed, a life of holiness is instantly begun and 'a transformation of nature is continued and carried on,' he writes, 'to the end of life, until it is brought to perfection in glory.'

Surveying evangelical history since Edwards wrote his *Religious Affections* it is evident that his viewpoint – the viewpoint of the reformers and Puritans – has commonly been *No?* exchanged for that of Wesley. Arminian beliefs inevitably depreciate the radical nature and the full significance of the rebirth, and, where such beliefs are accepted, the experimental divinity of Edwards will always receive the kind of criticism which Wesley gives it above. But there is something more which also needs to be said here by way of explanation for the neglect of the convictions outlined above. An argument which was already gaining ground when Edwards published *The Religious Affections* has since obtained much wider support. It is the claim that if holiness is made *necessary* for salvation then the gospel of salvation through simple faith in Christ *alone* is being undermined. Further, it is said, that if assurance of salvation is related to personal holiness instead of to faith in Christ, or to direct experiences of the Holy Spirit, then a system of 'legalism' is being advanced. These were charges which evangelical 'enthusiasts' and separatists were bringing against Protestant orthodoxy in the 1740's and Edwards answers them. To the first charge – if holiness is inseparable from salvation then

[1] *RA*, p. 307.

justification by faith alone is undermined – his reply was that, while faith is the means by which we rest on Christ for salvation, it never exists apart from regeneration. Certainly the sinner is not to wait for some sign of God's work in him before he believes; nonetheless it is the *sight* of Christ, given by the light of the Spirit in regeneration, which is the immediate cause of faith.[1] Such faith which rests upon Christ alone is therefore faith accompanied by the presence of the Holy Spirit *in* the believer and it must coincide with newness of life. Christ's work, and not the work of the Spirit in renewing the sinner, is the sole basis of justification, yet the work of Christ and the work of the Spirit are inseparable parts of salvation.

To the further charge that when men look for signs or evidences of holiness in their lives they have fallen into a 'legal' way of seeking assurance, Edwards gives more extended treatment. His main answer is to marshal the sheer weight of scriptural evidence

that holy practice is the principal evidence that we ought to make use of in judging both of our own and others' sincerity . . . This evidence is ten times more insisted on as a note of true piety throughout the Scriptures, from the beginning of Genesis to the end of Revelation, than anything else. . . If we make the Word of Christ our rule, then undoubtedly those marks which Christ and his apostles did chiefly lay down and give us that we might try ourselves by them, those same marks we ought especially to receive, and chiefly to make use of, in the trial of ourselves.[2]

But that the worthiness of nothing in us recommends us and brings us to an interest in Christ, is no argument that nothing in us is a sign of an interest in Christ.[3]

The freeness of grace, and the necessity of holy practice, which are thus from time to time joined together in Scripture, are not inconsistent one with another. Nor does it at all diminish the honour and importance of faith that the exercises and effects of faith in practice should be esteemed the chief signs of it; any more than it

---

[1] 'The Scripture is ignorant of any such faith in Christ of the operation of God, that is not founded in a spiritual sight of Christ. . . . That faith which is without spiritual light is not the faith of the children of light, but the presumption of the children of darkness' *RA*, p. 104.

[2] *RA*, pp. 356–59.

[3] *RA*, p. 376.

lessens the importance of life, that action and motion are esteemed the chief signs of that.[1]

Edwards and his brethren who were leaders in the Great Awakening realized that the new danger among the professedly orthodox was Antinomianism. Its advocates were repeating – probably unbeknown to themselves – the very errors which sectaries had raised in England and New England in the previous century. The Antinomians made particular experiences, understood in terms of emotions ('affections'), *the* basis of assurance. Sometimes the experience on which they rested was that of 'conversion'. An example of this occurred in the alleged teaching of the Rev. Philemon Robbins in the same year that *The Religious Affections* was published. Against Robbins it was charged that

He has publicly taught that it is as easy for persons to know when they are converted as it is to know noon daylight from midnight darkness; making the only sure evidence of conversion to consist in inward feeling, and a sense of their love to God.

He has declared in public, that believers never doubt of their interest in Christ, after conversion; and if they do, it is the sign of an hypocrite; rendering sanctification no evidence of conversion or justification, and that believers are never in the dark.[2]

In this view, assurance is of the essence of salvation and therefore once 'saved', the convert need never doubt it, no matter how he lives. In his concern to avoid this error, Edwards' disciple, Joseph Bellamy, went to an opposite extreme and tended to deny that there is any real assurance to be obtained simply by a convert's first faith in Christ; assurance must always be grounded on the inward marks of regeneration which the believer finds in himself.[3] But Edwards is more careful to avoid this extreme. There *is* assurance through direct faith in Christ and it was here that Thomas Boston, facing a different spiritual situation in Scotland, put his emphasis in 'the Marrow controversy'. Edwards likewise believed that faith

[1]*RA*, p. 379.

[2]See Trumbull's *History of Connecticut*, 2, p. 171 ff. Trumbull believed that these views were unjustly credited to Robbins.

[3]'While we are justified simply on the account of Christ's righteousness, we can know that we are in fact justified merely by a consciousness of our own inherent graces'. *Works of J. Bellamy*, 1853, vol. 1, p. 492. Bellamy does, however, qualify this (p. 492).

in Christ is enough (in a young convert) for assurance, but he held that religious conditions necessitated putting emphasis upon another strand of biblical truth, namely, the spiritual change which is always to be found in true believers. The mistake of Bellamy was to absolutize the 'marks of regeneration', just as Antinomians (and such followers of Boston in Scotland as the Rev. David Wilson) absolutized the place of faith.[1] A few years later two Boston ministers, Alexander Cumming and Andrew Crosswell, were to be in contention for this same reason.[2]

In passing, it should be noted that the question whether a young convert can have assurance upon his first believing is not the same as the question of how Christians may have confidence in *another's* assurance when it is untested by time. Even in 1735 Edwards had been hesitant to speak of the number of conversions and all his subsequent experience, and that of other leaders in the Great Awakening, underlined the danger of that practice. When a superficial friend of Whitefield professed to know 'when persons are justified,' the preacher commented: 'It is a lesson I have not yet learnt. There are so many stony-ground hearers which receive the word with joy, that I have determined to suspend my judgment, till I know the tree by its fruits.' Likewise, when sudden conversions were reported to Whitefield he would say, 'I shall wait until we see how the physic works'.[3]

The danger of Antinomianism in Edwards' mind, however, was not simply restricted to the question of conversion. More often it related to an assurance claimed through an experience of the 'immediate witness' of the Holy Spirit – 'immediate' in the sense that it was wholly unrelated to graces of the Spirit *in* the believer. Such an assurance, it was asserted, was more

---

[1]Dr. John Duncan shrewdly says: 'If I met a man from New England, I would say to him – "Read the Marrow-men". If I met a Marrow-man, I would say to him – "Read the New-England Men". They are the complement of each other. Men like Wilson on the one hand, and Bellamy on the other, are extreme; but between Boston and Edwards there is no contradiction, and they are important to each other.' On the same subject he also observes: 'When the doctrine of Assurance being necessarily contained in faith (as as to be essential to it) gets into a Church, *in the second generation it gets habituated to the use of the highest appropriating language by dead, carnal men.*' In the Pulpit and at the Communion Table, 1874, pp. 34, 63.

[2]Webster, p. 615.

[3]*The Life and Times of George Whitefield*, Robert Philip, 1838, p. 398.

evangelical, more honouring to grace, and more worthy of the Holy Spirit than that hitherto preached in the churches. Edwards was familiar with these claims, personally in New England, and, by correspondence, in New Jersey where there were 'flagrant errors concerning the witness of the Spirit, imparting immediate knowledge of our acceptance with God'.[1] The pretensions of such teaching he viewed with alarm:

There is a sort of men, who indeed abundantly cry down works, and cry up faith in opposition to works, and set up themselves very much as evangelical persons in opposition to those that are of a legal spirit, and make a fair show of advancing Christ and the gospel and the way of free grace, who are indeed some of the greatest enemies to the gospel way of free grace, and the most dangerous opposers of pure humble Christianity. . . .[2]

Edwards' conviction was that the New Testament teaches no *one* experience as being the permanent source of the believer's assurance. One 'witness of the Spirit' is not enough any more than one 'experience' at the supposed time of conversion is enough. For assurance is never to be enjoyed on the basis of a past experience. There is need of the present and continuing work of the Holy Spirit. And this inward work of the Spirit, giving assurance, is not an alternative to the assurance obtained through resting in Christ, or through one 'immediate witness', rather it is the basis of all true spiritual comfort – a comfort which may exist in many varying degrees of strength. Further, Edwards insists, from Scripture, that *action* on the part of the believer is involved in order to assurance. Walking in obedience to God and the comfort of the Holy Spirit belong together (Acts 9.31) and, therefore, such assurance as is maintained permanently, without any regard or care for holiness of life, is false assurance.[3] Antinomians, in wanting to

---

[1] Webster, pp. 147–8, 448.

[2] *RA*, pp. 244–5.

[3] 'A true assurance is not upheld but by the soul's being kept in a holy frame, and grace maintained in lively exercise'. When a Christian lapses into spiritual decay it is as impossible to keep alive 'a holy and Christian hope in its clearness and strength as it is to maintain the bright sunshine in the air when the sun is gone down. Distant experiences, when darkened by present prevailing lust and corruption, will never keep alive a gracious confidence and assurance' *RA*, p. 103; 107–8; 121–22 etc.

base assurance solely on 'experience' of Christ and the Holy Spirit, Edwards asserts, make an unbiblical distinction between inward experience and outward behaviour: 'Indeed, all Christian experience is not properly called practice, but all Christian practice is properly experience. . . . Holy practice is one kind or part of Christian experience and both reason and Scripture represent it as the chief and most distinguishing part of it. . . . "This is the love of God, that we keep his commandments" (1 John 5.3); "This is love, that we walk after his commandments" (2 John 6).'[1]

At first sight, it is perhaps surprising that Edwards, the theologian of revival, should oppose as he does the separatists' emphasis upon the 'immediate witness'. On this point he speaks extensively. It is not his purpose to deny what he personally knew, namely, large and glorious communications of the Holy Spirit. The believer, receiving 'the earnest of the Spirit' may know 'such unutterable and glorious joys' as are 'too great and mighty for weak dust and ashes'.[2] 'And who shall limit God in his giving this earnest, or say he shall give so much of the inheritance and no more?' There is indeed a work of the Spirit in witnessing or sealing and, he says, 'this seal of the Spirit is the highest kind of evidence of the saints' adoption that ever they obtain'.[3] His objection is to the word 'immediate', as though the believer receives a witness 'by immediate suggestion or revelation'. Rather the 'witness' or 'seal' is the Spirit's 'holy stamp, or impressed image, exhibiting clear evidence to the conscience that the subject of it is a child of God'[4] – a witness which so enlivens faith and love in the believer that there is such an evidence to the reality of salvation as can never be imitated by the devil. Yet although this be 'the highest sort of witness of the Spirit which is possible', it is not a once-and-for-all experience, as the separatist teachers made it. An increase of assurance is ever to be sought in on-going communion with God: 'A man, by once seeing his neighbour,

[1] *RA*, p. 271.
[2] *RA*, p. 60.
[3] *RA*, p. 161; p. 374.
[4] *RA*, p. 160. Edwards' teaching on 'the witness of the Spirit' needs to be read with care, even Whitefield appears to have misunderstood him, see below pp. 489–90.

may have good evidence of his presence; but by seeing him from day to day, and conversing with him in various circumstances, the evidence is established'.[1] For Edwards, glorious as the witness of the Spirit is, it is *part* of his whole care for the children of God,[2] and he was alarmed that errorists spoke of 'immediacy' in a way which belittled the Spirit's general and constant work. There can be no true assurance of any kind for the believer without the work of the Spirit. By separating 'the witness' from the evidence of grace in the heart and life, Antinomians were rejecting the main emphasis of the New Testament: 'It is greatly to the hurt of religion for persons to make light of, and insist little on, those things which the Scripture insists most upon as of most importance in the evidence of our interest in Christ, under the notion that to lay weight on these things is legal.'[3]

However we assess the greatness of Edwards' *Religious Affections* as compared with his other works, there should be no question as to its first-place in enduring relevance. The troubles of the 1740's were thus the means of bringing forth what is unquestionably one of the most important books possessed by the Christian church on the nature of true religion.

[1] *RA*, p. 374.
[2] He points out, for example, that the context of Romans 8.15–17 'has a more immediate respect to what Christians experienced, in their exercises of love to God, in suffering persecution' *RA*, p. 375.
[3] *RA*, p. 380. Edwards' strongest words concerning error over an 'immediate witness' were to be written later at the conclusion of his *Life of Brainerd* (2. pp. 248–50).

14

CHANGES AT NORTHAMPTON AND BEYOND

Training-Day on the Market-Place

One of the leaders in the militia, and a prominent figure
in Northampton, was Edwards' friend, Colonel Timothy
Dwight. Dwight's son, 'Ensign Dwight' (see p. 313)
was to marry Mary Edwards. His grandson was to be
President of Yale and his great-grandson (S. E. Dwight)
Edwards' biographer.

People at a distance have been more ignorant of our former imperfections, and have been ready to look on Northampton as a kind of heaven upon earth.

J E to the Council at Northampton, December 26, 1749, Dwight, *Life of President Edwards*, p. 350.

I have found the work of the ministry among you to be a great work indeed, a work of exceeding care, labour, and difficulty. Many have been the heavy burdens that I have borne in it, to which my strength has been very unequal. God called me to bear these burdens, and I bless his name, that he has so supported me as to keep me from sinking under them.

J E on July 1, 1750 (1.cciv).

14

At the same time as Edwards was publicly engaged in controversy with opponents of revival inclining to rationalism on the one hand and with men heedless of the danger of 'enthusiasm' on the other, he was also being drawn into a personal theological problem of his own. Until 1743–44 he had admitted individuals into the communicant membership of the church on much the same basis as the one introduced by his grandfather. That is to say, provided that a baptized member of the church possessed an adequate knowledge of the Christian Faith, and that there were no open inconsistencies in his conduct, nothing further was necessary to qualify for admission to the Lord's Table. An individual was required to make a general profession of the Christian Faith rather than give any testimony to his *own* personal faith in Christ.

In order to understand how this view had become established in Northampton, and also how Edwards himself had accepted it for so long a time, it needs to be said that Stoddard's intention had not been to lower the biblical qualifications for full church membership. It is probable that his primary concern was to help individuals lacking assurance who could, nevertheless, be regarded by others 'in the judgment of charity' as true Christians. All such doubting Christians, he argued, should participate in the Lord's Supper even if it was not clear to them that 'a work of saving conversion' had been wrought in their souls. In other words, Stoddard was making a distinction between 'professing faith' in Christ and possessing an assurance that the faith professed was *saving* faith. There was nothing novel in such a distinction but the problem was that, in seeking to accommodate weak *Christians*, Stoddard went further and argued that, even supposing a communicant to be unregenerate, his unregeneracy was no bar to the sacrament, for the unregenerate 'need to learn what God teaches in this ordinance and to profess what Christians profess, viz. their need of Christ and the saving virtue of his blood'. 'If unregenerate persons have no right to the Sacrament,' he argued, 'then those who come must have assurance'. And if assurance must precede participation at the Lord's Table then how could the sacrament be what all Protestants professed it to be, a help to Christian assurance?

No

At first sight, Stoddard's case on the basic requirement for the admission to the Lord's Table is not patently erroneous. If it had been so, it would not have become so generally acceptable in New England. Yet it has also to be said that its acceptance owed at least something to its obscurity. A. V. G. Allen is surely right in saying: 'Mr Stoddard's position was not a clearly defined one, and was easily liable to misapprehension'.[1] It was for this reason – in part – that Edwards could subsequently differ widely from his cousins over the question of what their grandfather actually taught. Modern writers have added to the confusion. Ralph Coffman says that after 1677 Stoddard changed to his new scheme in which 'All were equal in God's eyes. . . . For the first time a resident of the town could claim church membership as a right'.[2] Yet on evidence which the same author himself quotes this is clearly false. At the Massachusetts Synod of 1679 Stoddard opposed the need for communicants to 'make a relation of the work of God's Spirit upon their hearts' but he voted for 'The making of a profession of their faith and repentance'. Communicant figures in Northampton in 1706, already quoted, show no considerable change from the earlier position. In 1707 Stod-

---

[1] *Life and Writings of Jonathan Edwards*, p. 258 fn.

[2] *Solomon Stoddard*, pp. 69–70. 'Stoddard, at this time,' Coffman further says, 'implicitly rejected the conversion experience as the central datum of covenant theology'. The truth is that Coffman is all at sea in attempting to follow the experimental Christianity of the Puritans.

dard himself complained that in his congregation 'there be four to one that do neglect the Lord's Supper, as if it did not belong to them.' Convinced this situation was wrong, Stoddard now urged that it was better for those concerned religious people who stayed away from the Lord's Table to participate even *supposing* they were still unregenerate 'because this ordinance has a proper tendency in its own nature to convert men'. In a sermon on Exodus 12.47, 48, in 1707, he argued that 'sanctification is not a necessary qualification to partaking in the Lord's Supper'[1] and yet, in response to opposition from Increase Mather, Stoddard could still maintain in his *Appeal to the Learned* (1709), 'My business was to answer a case of conscience and direct those that might have scruples about participation of the Lord's Supper . . . not at all to direct the churches to admit any that were not to rational charity true believers'.

The obscurity in Stoddard's teaching is bound up with a basic inconsistency, namely, that only those who in the judgment of probability are Christians should be admitted to the Table, yet, he added, the absence of regeneration should not debar men from Communion just as it did not debar Israelites from the Passover. Later Edwards put his finger on this inconsistency when he asked, Why should the church regard it as a duty to exclude the unregenerate if God intends the Lord's Table to be a means to their conversion?

Whatever the obscurity of ideas, the practical tendency of Stoddard's scheme was to open the Lord's Table to a much larger number. If the unregenerate may benefit from being communicants it was charitable to make qualifications for admission broad enough to include them. Provided an individual could profess the Faith, although not 'professing godliness', it was sufficient.

Edwards' concern over this subject did not arise suddenly.

[1] Preached at Northampton, December 17, 1707, Coffman, p. 131. This published sermon is so rare that Dwight could obtain no sight of it when he wrote his biography of Edwards but he does summarize Increase Mather's reply, *Life of President Edwards*, pp. 301–2 fn. There are important quotations from Stoddard in Edwards' *Works* (e.g. 1.437, 492 fn). Edwards seems to regard a reconciliation of his grandfather's conflicting statements as impossible, 'I must confess myself at a loss'. The misunderstandings of others are hardly therefore surprising!

He wrote in 1749: 'I have had difficulties in my mind, for many years past, with regard to the admission of members into the Church who made no pretence of real godliness'.[1] His difficulties arose in part from the situation he observed in his own congregation. Due to the accepted mode of admitting members there existed in the church two

different bodies of professing saints, one within another, openly distinguished one from another, as it were by a visible dividing line. One company consisting of those who are *visibly gracious* Christians, and open *professors of godliness*; another consisting of those who are *visibly moral* livers, and only profess common virtues, without pretending to any special and spiritual experiences in their hearts, and who therefore are not reputed to be converts (1.479).

The existence of this condition was clear enough before the years of revival but when the revival came the anomaly of the situation must have become clearer to Edwards as numbers in the congregation professed conversion who for a long time previously had tacitly professed to feed by faith on the body and blood of Christ. Furthermore, during the Great Awakening, when Edwards was examining more closely the nature of true conversion and distinguishing it from a mere temporary change in those convicted or awakened, he must have seen how the ready admission of those in the latter condition into full church membership was liable to mislead them. When the awakened lost their convictions they would revert to the mind of the world and swell the number of unconverted communicants. By December 1743, with such persons in mind, Edwards could write of being 'much afraid lest there be a considerable number that have woefully deceived themselves' (1.lxi). Further, he

[1] Dwight, *Life of President Edwards*. This quotation is from the commencement of Edwards' Journal on the Communion controversy which is given in full in Dwight. The complete omission of the Journal in Hickman's abridgement of Dwight is singularly unfortunate and leaves the reader without an essential source of information. While Edwards says that he conformed to his grandfather's practice it is clear from his *Narrative of Surprising Conversions*, where he speaks of the admission of new communicants in 1735, that he thought he had 'very sufficient evidence of the conversion of their souls, through divine grace, though it is not the custom here, as it is in many other churches in this country, to make a credible relation of their inward experiences the ground of admission to the Lord's Supper' (1.350).

could no longer resist the conclusion that he was himself a party to this deception in the manner in which he had admitted some 550 communicant members during his pastorate.[1] In tolerating qualifications for membership broader than those allowed by Scripture, considerable additions of the world into the church had undoubtedly occurred. Nevertheless, Edwards' change of view was slow and evidently involved him in a considerable personal struggle. He knew that any change from the received view would be interpreted as opposition to his grandfather and that it would be unwelcome to many both in Northampton and beyond. Speaking of the doctrine to which he was later to adhere he says, 'I believe I myself am the person, who, above all other upon the face of the earth, have had most in my circumstances to prejudice me against this doctrine' (1.479).

By 1744 Edwards had reached a point of personal conviction where he could no longer receive any candidate for full < membership without the profession and appearance of Christian grace and piety. New Testament evidence on the membership of the Christian church was the fundamental objection which he now saw to his old view but there were also four Old Testament texts which laid an irresistible constraint upon his conscience: 'Her priests have violated my law, and have profaned mine holy things: they have put no difference between the holy and the profane' (Ezek. 22.26; also Lev. 10.10; Jer. 15.19; and Ezek. 44.6–8).

Speaking of his change, Edwards writes, 'I came to this determination, that if any person should offer to come into the church without a profession of godliness, I must decline being active in his admission.' Recalling this, a few years later, Sarah Edwards writes, 'Not very long after Mr Edwards had admitted the last person that ever was admitted into this church who made no profession of godliness, he told me that he would not dare ever to admit another'.[2] Yet, at the same time, Edwards' mind was not wholly made up. While, lest he should be accused of rejecting any further candidate for communion out of personal prejudices, he made his change of view known to

[1] The figure given in Solomon Clark, *Historical Catalogue of the Northampton First Church*, 1891, pp. 40–67.
[2] Mrs Edwards' letter of testimony on this subject will be found in Appendix 3.

some in Northampton, he resolved to 'continue a diligent search' in the matter. He brought it up for discussion at a meeting of the Hampshire Association and also determined that whenever the request of another candidate for communion came before him he would have a full discussion of the issue with his uncle, Colonel John Stoddard.

Surprisingly, five years – 1744 to near the end of 1748 – were to pass before any individual did request admission to the Lord's Table and full church membership. After all great revivals there is frequently a period of re-action but in the case of Northampton there were some more specific reasons for the comparative spiritual stand-still of these years.

The first was a matter of discipline which arose in 1744 and which was not brought to a satisfactory conclusion. In March of that year, Moses Lyman reported to his minister that a 'bad book' was in circulation among some of the young people. Apparently it was a handbook for midwives, harmless enough in itself but an occasion for excitement and obscene talk for those who found it a matter of entertainment. Edwards has been blamed for not approaching these 'children', or their parents, privately, and for creating a needless public controversy. But the matter was not so simple; the leaders were not 'children', they were young men in their twenties and apprentices away from parental oversight. Convinced that the matter required public action, Edwards preached a sermon on a relevant text (Hebrews 12.15–16), and called for a church meeting to follow the service. At this meeting, concerned at what they heard, the members readily agreed to a committee of enquiry to assist their pastor. Only after its composition and time of meeting at the parsonage in King Street was agreed, did Edwards read a list of the names of the young people whom he required to be present. It was startlingly large and, says Dwight, 'through mere forgetfulness or inadvertence on his part', Edwards failed to distinguish between names of suspects and those who were to be called simply to give information. The list of names which Edwards had in his hand that morning still survives and his marks against certain names seem to indicate that the young people were not all in the same category. But no distinction was conveyed to the meeting. The youth of almost every prominent family in the church appeared to be involved, or related to those who were, and before many of the members were back in their own homes they repented of ever having supported a committee of enquiry. 'The town', in Dwight's words, 'was suddenly all in a blaze' (1.cxv).

For the next two months the case absorbed attention. Observing their seniors to be disunited, the ringleaders gathered confidence and their disdain of the minister and of the committee of the church became more serious than their initial offence. Called to the parsonage in order to express penitence, some engaged in playing 'leapfrog' in the yard while waiting to be interviewed, while another climbed to an upstairs window to view a few girls who were also waiting to see the Committee. Simeon Root was overheard to say to his companions, 'What do we here? We won't stay here all day long,' while his brother, Timothy, commenting on the dress of the minister and certain members of the committee, declared, 'They are nothing but men moulded up of a little dirt; I don't care a — for any of them'. The matter was closed by June 3rd when the two Root brothers were required to confess their 'scandalously contemptuous behaviour towards the authority of this Church' but it would seem that the action was ineffective. Edwards appears to have been impeded by lack of support and thereafter his leadership was impaired.

Referring to this failure, Dwight writes:

This was the occasion of weakening of Mr Edwards' hands in the work of the ministry, especially among the young people, with whom, by this means, he greatly lost his influence. It seemed in a great measure to put an end to his usefulness at Northampton. . . . He certainly had no great visible success after this; the influences of the Holy Spirit were chiefly withheld and stupidity and worldly-mindedness were greatly increased among them (1.cxv).

At the same time as the 'bad book' case, another issue was also putting a strain on relations between Edwards and some in his congregation. It concerned the delicate matter of his salary. Due to the unsettled state of New England currency at this period, Edwards' salary was not fixed but determined annually. From the initial figure of £100 per year in 1726 it was steadily increased, yet in 1740 Edwards, with increasing family expenses, had to ask for more. Increments given then, and again in 1742, still left him, however, with a salary slightly less in value due to the depreciation of Massachusetts currency from inflation. The position had improved by 1748 when he was being paid £700 per year with an extra £170 'to support his family and buy books'.

But the actual salary figure was not the only problem. The money for ministerial support was commonly raised in New England by rates on the parish which were collected by constables. This system could well lead to delays in the payment of all that was due. As early as 1734 Edwards had to complain, 'I never have been at so much difficulty to get in my Salary as I have been this year.' Ten years later the problem remained and the same month, as the discipline issue erupted, Sarah Edwards – exercising her managerial role in the household – wrote to one of the town officials or constables

Northampton March ye 26
1744

Sir

Mr Sheldon jest now informs me that you cannot Send all the money at the time Mr Edwards is Rid out and therefore I write to Desire you to Send Some as much as you Possibbly can for Mr Edwards is under Such obligations that he cant Possibbly do without it and therefore mustr up all possible Pains to procure it.

This from your friend and Ser^{vt}

SARAH EDWARDS

While this question was resolved by 1748 there was a larger underlying problem which was not removed. The parish acceded to Edwards' requests but with a reluctance born in part out of the changing social conditions of the age. Solomon Stoddard had been a comparatively wealthy man and no one had questioned his position or manner of life. It was long understood that in a society marked by distinctions of 'superiors' and 'inferiors', the ministers belonged among the gentry. But as the eighteenth century progressed, and the possibilities of acquiring wealth became more general, everyone hoped to prosper. Northampton itself reflected the change. By the 1740's it had become a trading centre for other new villages to the north and west. The day was passing when one blacksmith, one tanner, one hat shop and one general store could meet the needs of all. And with barges now able to navigate the Connecticut to a point much closer to the town, tradesmen had a new advantage. The population also was growing so that it was no loss to the church or town when Southampton, ten miles to the south-west, sprang up with its own church in 1743.

It is clear that the 1740's brought a general increase of wealth to Northampton and as a result people began to spend money in a way unknown before. No longer were white shirts, hooped skirts, or china tea services the privileges of a very few. Edwards believed that expenditure ought to be related to status and position. What was fitting in one place would be unjustifiable in another. 'We in this town are evidently got to a great excess,' he warned his people. 'Boston is extravagant beyond London. And we, considering all things, I think beyond them . . . how far below we fall short in rank . . . state . . . education and our situation in the world. . . . Such excess in gaiety and costliness of apparel is a manifestation of great vanity of mind.'[1]

Justified or not, it is unlikely that this stricture was well received by a number, for the very criticism that was aired about Edwards, when his salary was debated in the 1740's, was that the parsonage spending was lavish and excessive. The increase in his salary in 1742 had been accompanied by 'great uneasiness in the town' on this point. To allay such criticism it appears that Edwards in 1743 gave details of his family budget but with no beneficial result. The fact was that the Edwards of set purpose kept their own 'station', they wore Boston-cut clothes, gave their daughters a superior finishing education away from home, kept a number of servants, and so on. 'A cheap Minister is the great Article in the desire of too-many,' declared another New England minister.[2] The Northampton people thought that their pastor was certainly not a 'cheap Minister'.

[1]Notes of a sermon on 1 Peter 3.19, 20, in Grosart, p. 209.

[2]Frequently ministers' salaries did not rise with the rising cost of living. In 1735 Timothy Edwards was forced to draw his congregation's attention to a careful comparison between the price of commodities then and in 1695 when he had settled at East Windsor. Of the ministers in New England and northern Long Island between 1680 and 1740, 12 per cent were involved in serious financial disputes with their congregations. See Richard L. Bushman, *From Puritan to Yankee*, 1970, p. 157.

Edwards himself appears to have had no doubts on the question of his use of his salary. Ministers of the gospel were constantly in public view, always giving generous hospitality, and he believed that their office warranted the position it had long been given in Protestantism. When he officiated at the ordination of young ministers he was prepared to tell the congregation what was proper in the way of material support. But he viewed ministerial difficulties relating to salaries as involving more than a mere matter of figures. There was a spirit in the age which needed to be resisted and more than the office of the ministry was involved. When an outlying district of Northampton was formed into a new precinct and congregation in 1743 Edwards' sermon on the ordination of Jonathan Judd, the first minister of Southampton, included the words:

There are some professors, in some of our towns, that are anti-ministerial men; they seem to have a disposition to dislike men of that order; they are apt to be prejudiced against them, and to be suspicious of them, and talk against them; and it seems to be as it were natural to them to be unfriendly and unkind towards their own ministers, and to make difficulty for them. But I don't believe there is a true Christian on earth that is of this character; on the contrary . . . everyone that receives Christ, and whose heart is governed by a supreme love to him, has a disposition to receive, love and honor his messengers.

Later, speaking to his own congregation on the nature of Christian humility, he was to say:

Humility will further tend *to prevent a levelling behaviour*. Some persons are always ready to level those above them down to themselves, while they are never willing to level those below them up to their own position. But he that is under the influence of humility will avoid both these extremes. On the one hand, he will be willing that all should rise just so far as their diligence and worth of character entitle them to; and on the other hand, he will be willing that his superiors should be known and acknowledged in their place, and have rendered to them all the honours that are their due. He will not desire that all should stand upon the same level, for he knows it is best that there should be gradations in society; that some should be above others, and should be honoured and submitted to as such. And therefore he is willing to be content with this divine arrangement, and, agreeable to it, to conform both his spirit and behaviour to such precepts as the following: 'Render therefore to all their dues: tribute to whom tribute is due; custom to whom custom; fear to whom fear; honour to whom honour' (Rom. 13.7); 'Put them in mind to be subject to principalities and powers, to obey magistrates, to be ready to every good work' (Titus 3.1).

*   *   *

Although local conditions thus concerned Edwards in the mid-1740's they by no means occupied him wholly. He had now settled into a habit of writing for publication and, once his sermons on 'the Religious Affections' were revised and ready for the press, he turned his attention to the subject which for the rest of his life he was to regard as a special danger to the future of Protestant Christianity. We have seen that in the 1730's there were those in New England who regarded any warnings over Arminianism as needless; in their view, the advocates of such beliefs were a mere handful. Edwards had disagreed. While there were certainly no well-known proponents of those errors in the country, he correctly read a changing attitude to orthodoxy. There were too many young men in the ministry whose 'open-mindedness' suggested no sense of obligation to any doctrinal position. Charles Chauncy was representative of this number who were ready for change. He has been described as 'dull, liberal, Arminian, and a profound scholar', but the words are not applicable to his early career. Ordained the same year as Edwards, and colleague of the orthodox Colman at Boston's First Church, Chauncy was initially traditional enough. Even his opposition to Edwards in the Great Awakening was from the stand-point of an alleged defence of the *status quo* against unbiblical innovation and emotionalism.

But the truth is that the Great Awakening had accelerated a readiness for doctrinal change among those who were basically unsympathetic, and even some who were at first sympathetic now distanced themselves from the position of Edwards and Whitefield. Ebenezer Gay of Hingham was typical of the latter. Orthodox in general, and welcoming Tennent to his Massachusetts pulpit, following the Awakening, says his biographer: 'Gay began to define much of his theology by what he renounced and found unacceptable. . . . Gay had no solid commitment to Calvinistic orthodoxy; he detested creeds and tried to remain determinedly open to truth. . . .' [1]

In the mid-1740's, Chauncy, Gay, Jonathan Mayhew and others, found much help towards the change to which they were 'open' in fashionable theological literature coming out of England, particularly in the works of Daniel Whitby, Samuel Clarke and John Taylor. These authors professed a more scholarly approach to Scripture, 'returning to the original language of a text to determine nuances of particular words before attempting an explication of a particular doctrine'. Chauncy took up this 'new' approach and, says a recent writer,

begin to explore a wide range of doctrinal issues using it. The results of his sustained inquiry were ultimately to lead him to refashion much of the Puritan theology he inherited. But for the time being he left his conclusions in manuscript form, referring to them collectively as 'the pudding'. He did discuss his reformulated views with selected associates, but remained content to wait for a 'seasonable' time to release 'the pudding' to the public. [2]

Edwards knew what was happening although he was to be dead for many years before some of Chauncy's 'pudding' was served up in Boston bookshops. He believed that it was low views of God and high views of human abilities which lay behind the movement for change and that to confront Arminianism was therefore the principal need of the hour.

In a letter to Bellamy of January 15, 1747, Edwards advises the younger man on the best theological reading: 'Take Mastricht for divinity in general, doctrine, practice and controversy, or as an universal system of divinity; and it is much better than Turretine or any other book in the world, excepting the Bible, in my opinion.' His own work, however, he goes on to say, presently had to do with very different authors:

I have been reading Whitby, which has engaged me pretty thoroughly in the study of the Arminian controversy, and I have written considerably upon it in my private papers . . . I have got so deep into this controversy that I am not willing to dismiss it till I know the

---

[1] *The Benevolent Deity*, Robert J. Wilson III, 1984, p. 120.

[2] *Seasonable Revolutionary*, The Mind of Charles Chauncy, Charles H. Lippy, 1981, p. 61. This deviation from Scripture, in the name of a professed advance in biblical understanding and with a studied care not to make their findings prematurely public, has a close parallel in nineteenth-century liberalism.

utmost of these matters. . . If you could enquire of Dr. Johnson or Mr. Beach, or some other, and find me what is the best book on the Arminian side, for the defence of their notion of Free will . . . . [1]

*   *   *

At this same period, Edwards' concern for the preservation of the truth was a factor which led him into closer association with his ministerial friends in New Jersey where so much had happened since his visit in 1735. Beginning in 1739, the great revival had prevailed as widely there as in New England. 'The alteration in the face of things is altogether amazing,' Dickinson could write in 1740. No churches benefited so largely from Whitefield's ministry as did the Presbyterian and Whitefield's circle of friends in the Middle Colonies became the same as Edwards'. One of the younger men in that circle was Aaron Burr, who, while a student at Yale, had discovered,

I had spent my life in a dream . . . but then I was brought to the footstool of sovereign grace . . . before this I was strongly attached to — the Arminian scheme.

Graduating in 1735, Burr was settled at Newark, New Jersey in 1738, where, the next year, he commenced a long and close friendship with Whitefield with whom he had so much in common. At about the same time Burr became a correspondent with Edwards and, later, a regular visitor to his home.[2]

The zeal of these Presbyterians for evangelism did not stop with the white population. In 1740 Dickinson, Pemberton and Burr, moved by 'the deplorable and perishing condition of the Indians', had written to the Society in Scotland for Propagating the Gospel and been appointed 'correspondents', with authority to act on behalf of the Society in employing missionaries.

---

[1]*New England Quarterly*, 1928, pp. 229–31. Mastricht = Peter Van Mastricht and the reference is to his *Theoretico – practica Theologia*. Turretine = Francis Turretine whose great work, *Institutio Theologiae Elencticae*, as that of Mastricht, still awaits an English publisher.

[2]In a letter (now lost) of Dec. 14, 1740, Edwards had told something of his own spiritual experiences to Burr. It has been surmised that this letter was the origin of Edwards' 'Personal Narrative', finished sometime in 1739 or 1740, but Dwight's assertion that the 'Narrative' was written 'near twenty years' after his conversion 'for his own private benefit' (1.xii) is more likely. The MS of his 'Personal Narrative' has not survived.

There had been divisions also in the Middle Colonies, so much so that in 1741 the Presbyterian Church was split. Thereafter the 'Old Lights', with some exceptions, continued in the Synod of Philadelphia, while the men who were chiefly prominent in the awakening subsequently came together in the Synod of New York. With fast-growing congregations, the need for more ministers was more urgent than ever, and the New-Side men fulfilled a widely-shared desire in the founding of the College of New Jersey, which received its first charter in 1746. Jonathan Dickinson was made the first president and the work officially began in his home at Elizabethtown in 1747. Other New Englanders involved in the new college were Jonathan Belcher, acting governor of New Jersey, John Pierson of Woodbridge and Jacob Green, a Harvard student who had come from Boston with Whitefield in 1745. Edwards heartily encouraged the development from afar,[1] but when Dickinson died suddenly in October, 1747, there were several, including, it seems, Belcher, and certainly Aaron Burr, who wanted the pastor of Northampton as the new president. In 1748, Burr, who was the acting-president, put the possibility to Edwards while visiting Northampton and pointed out that such a removal would set him free from any impending controversy on the communion issue.[2] In the event, Burr himself was finally appointed. Whether Edwards actually declined to be nominated is not clear, but as letters from Belcher show, he remained in close touch as a valued adviser of the College trustees. In one letter Belcher writes to Edwards:

As to our embryo college, it is a noble design, and if God pleases, may it prove an extensive blessing. . . . I thank you, Sir, for all the kind hints you have given me for the service of this excellent undertaking . . . I shall exert myself to advance its future welfare . . . a relish for true religion and piety being great strangers to this part of America. The accounts I receive from time to time, give me too much reason to fear that Arminianism, Arianism and even Socinianism, in destruction to the doctrines of free grace, are daily propagated in the New England colleges (1.cii).

---

[1] It was from Edwards' pen that the first news of the College was heard in Britain, *The Christian Monthly History*, Nov. 1745, p. 239.
[2] See Sarah Edwards' Letter, Appendix 3.

*　　　*　　　*

At this point in time, when the College of New Jersey was only in its infancy, there could be no certainty that it would have a future. These were years when the whole of Protestant North America was threatened by Europe's major Catholic powers. Spain traditionally was an harassment to Britain's North American colonies in the South, but when France also declared war upon England in 1744 the danger concentrated in the North. French ships threatened all the coast of New England and brought a virtual end to the fishing industry. To meet this offensive New England boldly determined to take France's chief fortress, Louisburg, on Cape Breton Island. Command- <
ing the entrance to the Gulf of St. Lawrence, Louisburg was a key to the French supply lines. Early in 1745 five thousand men, including 'above twenty' from Northampton, left home to reduce the French arsenal. Edwards' sermon notes for April 4, 1745, are marked with the words, 'Fast for success in the expedition against Cape Breton'.

As we have seen, Edwards had already developed a connection with Britain (especially Scotland) through the Great Awakening. The European and Catholic danger now deepened the sense of a trans-Atlantic common cause among English Christians.[1] From Edwards' pen *The Christian Monthly History* in Glasgow (started to carry news of revival) now provided different information. A long letter from Edwards in 1745 was packed with military facts on the Cape Breton expedition and with news of its ultimate success. It was published in full. By the time this letter left Northampton Edwards had heard of the landing of the Catholic Charles Edward Stewart in Scotland, through French aid, and by the time it arrived in Britain 'the Young Pretender' was marching with 5,000 men in rebellion on London. Prayer now rose for Britain as Protestants on both sides of the Atlantic faced the possibility of a 'common calamity'. When Edwards wrote another letter of May 12, 1746, also published in *The Christian Monthly History*, he had not heard of the battle of Culloden (April 16, 1746) but he did know

---

[1] Edwards appears to have thought of himself as English: 'I will take the liberty of an Englishman' (1.424). The term 'American' originally applied only to the Indians.

[285]

of the Pretender's retreat 'and that the rebellion is almost wholly suppressed . . . for which not only you, but we, and all Protestants, have great cause of thankfulness; especially all within the British Dominions, which must all have fallen together under the calamity, if the Pretender had gained his purpose'.

Two more years were to pass before there was peace with France in 1748 and in the meantime Northampton itself was not immune to aggression. War in Canada always revived the fears of marauding bands of Indians – with French support – returning to the Connecticut valley to kill, scalp and burn. It had happened on a small scale in 1720's; the peril was now more widespread. On September 19, 1745 Edwards preached on a Fast-Day marking the Proclamation of war with the Indians. Militia training days under the eye of Colonel Stoddard now took on a new earnestness. Once more the town was fortified and 'watch houses' were built on the outskirts, including one in Edwards' own garden.

Such precautions were not unnecessary. In a postscript to his letter to Scotland of May 12, 1746, Edwards says, 'We have almost daily news of mischief done by them [Indians], surprising particular persons, and some families, killing and taking captive, burning houses and killing cattle . . . the French are greatly enraged by our taking Cape Breton.' In the summer of 1746 a note in Samuel Hopkins' Journal reads: 'Northampton, Tuesday 26. Came here to-day. Lodge at Mr. Edwards's. The Indians killed five men and a girl at Deerfield yesterday.'

While Northampton men who went to Cape Breton were to return safely in due course, several townsmen were to die at home in surprise attacks by the Indians. Elisha Clark was one of them, killed by Indians while threshing in his barn in August, 1747. Edwards marked the event with a sermon on Isaiah 9.13–14. Most of the fighting with Indians, however, was to occur some thirty miles away from Northampton. In 1748 and the year following nearly 150 persons were either killed or captured by Indians in Western Massachusetts.

The extent to which Edwards was interested in political and military events at this period was not, in his view, a diversion from his biblical beliefs. God rules in history and he knew that the outcome of events with regard to the great Catholic powers would have a close bearing upon the future advancement of the church in the world. Even the disturbance of war falls within divine providence and is related to the prayers of God's people (Rev. 8.4–5). 'Great shakings and commotions,' he writes to M'Culloch, 'have commonly preceded glorious changes in the state of the Church of God, as there were great shakings of nations preceding the establishment of God's people in their rest in Canaan'.

Both locally at Northampton and in the English-speaking world at large, Edwards viewed the mid 1740's as a time for humiliation. He was not, however, as some have alleged, 'melancholy' or pessimistic. He unwaveringly believed, as we shall see, that the cause of Christ had indeed a glorious future. And if, in the meantime, Christians were humbled by divine providence, it would 'be better to them in the end than their elevations and raptures' (1.lxxix).

Woodbury March 25. 1745

— I sold my Tea-kittle to Mr. Jo. Woodbridge, and an Iron kittle to Mr. Tim. Woodbridge.. both which amounts to something more than it round, which is owing them to pay to you for the School. If that succeed, I hope you will use the money that way, if not you are welcome to it your self.

As to my Blankett I desire Mr Woodbridge to take the trouble of throwing them into the Beer skins. If he has not done it, I wish he would and save the skins to Mr. Hopkins, or it might be to Mr Bellamy.

I am, Sir, in greatest hast

your obedient humble servt

David Brainerd

Revd Mr John Sergeant

A note from David Brainerd to John Sergeant

THE INTERNATIONAL UNION AND
MISSIONARY VISION

Brainerd's grave at Northampton. 'Sacred to the memory of the
Rev. David Brainard. A faithful and laborious Missionary of the
Stockbridge, Delaware and Susquehannah Tribes of Indians, who
died in this town, October 10, 1747, aged 32.'

The church of God in all parts of the world is but one, the distant members are closely united in one glorious head. This union is very much her beauty, and the mutual friendly correspondence of the various members, in distant parts of the world, is a thing well becoming this union (at least when employed about things appertaining to the glory of their common head, and their common spiritual interest and happiness). . . .

I should have more hope from the union, fervency, and unfailing constancy of the prayers of God's people, with respect to the religious affairs of the present day, than anything else; more than from the preaching and writing of the ablest and best friends to the work of God's Spirit. . . .

from 'Mr. Edwards's Letter to his Scots
Correspondent' in *The Christian Monthly History*,
Nov. 1745, pp. 234–254

15

n the mid – and later – 1740's difficulties were only a part of Edwards' experience. Simultaneously he had two of the greatest encouragements of his ministry, both of which were to lead to the writing of major books.

The first of these encouragements began in the form of correspondence from across the Atlantic. While Edwards' *Faithful Narrative* had been reprinted in Scotland in its first year of publication (1737) it was only in 1742 that his reputation as a theologian was established in that country. In the latter year John M'Laurin of Glasgow and James Robe of Kilsyth, two of the leading evangelical preachers in the Church of Scotland, wrote to him and received replies. In 1743 Edwards extended the correspondence to William M'Culloch of Cambuslang. Thomas Gillespie of Carnock became a correspondent in 1746, and, most significantly of all, John Erskine in 1747. Erskine, belonging to a family of Scottish nobility, was destined for the legal profession when he was converted during his student days in Edinburgh. In opposition to family opinion, he entered the ministry at Kirkintilloch in 1744, moving to Culross in 1753 and finally to Edinburgh in 1758. In the Scottish capital he was to exercise great influence till his death in 1803. John Erskine was some twenty-six years of age when he first wrote to Edwards. The correspondence was not only to be lifelong but, continuing with one of Edwards' sons and then a grandson, it extended through a period of fifty-six years. Erskine was also to become the first editor of

Edwards' books in Britain and certainly the most dedicated overseas promoter of his writings. It was through Erksine's influence that William Carey carried an Edwards volume with him to India in 1792 for he was to be a key link between Edwards and the missionary movement which commenced in Britain before the end of the eighteenth century.

Some of Edwards' extensive Scottish correspondence is now lost but the letters which are to be found in Dwight's *Life* and elsewhere are of great value. The correspondence with Scottish evangelicals obviously meant much to Edwards as the number and length of his letters indicate. It was also carried on despite the slowness of communications. As much as a year could pass between the despatch of a letter and the arrival of a reply. Such delays were not always excusable. His ministerial friend Thomas Prince took care of correspondence addressed to Northampton on its arrival at Boston but his forgetfulness tried Edwards' patience. On one occasion Edwards explains to M'Culloch that the last letter from Cambuslang

lay a long while at Mr Prince's in Boston before I received it. . . . It seems he had forgotten that he had any such letter, and when I sent a messenger to his house, on purpose to inquire whether I had any letter lodged there for me from Scotland, he told him 'No', when I suppose this letter had been long in his house. And I should probably never have had it at last, had not one of my daughters had occasion to go to Boston, who made a visit at the house and made a more full inquiry (1.xci).

Yet these obstacles did not deter Edwards from maintaining the correspondence. In January, 1747 (before he had started to hear from Gillespie or Erskine), he wrote to M'Culloch of having two other regular correspondents in Scotland, but 'The time seems long since I have received a letter from you. . . . Our correspondence has been to me very pleasant and I am very loth it should fail'.

The Scottish mail, as well as being heartening to Edwards, had other important spiritual results. It established an international bond in prayer. References to prayer, such as, 'Desiring that we may meet often at the Throne of Grace', normally concluded letters but the subject of prayer, far from being treated as an addendum to other more important themes, was itself a chief interest. In October, 1744 a group of evangelical ministers in Scotland, among whom Edwards' correspondents were the leaders, formed a prayer union for intercession on behalf of the world-wide extension and prosperity of the kingdom of Christ. It was proposed among them that some part of every Saturday evening and Sabbath morning, and the whole or part of the first Tuesday of every quarter (beginning the first Tuesday of November and at three month intervals thereafter), should be given to 'united extraordinary supplications to the God of all grace . . . earnestly praying to him that he would appear in his glory, and favour Zion, and manifest his compassion to the world of mankind, by an abundant effusion of his Holy Spirit on all the churches and the whole habitable earth, to revive true religion in all parts of Christendom and to deliver all nations from their great and manifold spiritual calamities and miseries, and bless them with the unspeakable benefits of the kingdom of our glorious Redeemer . . .' (2.282).

Being international in its objective, news of this union, or 'concert' as it was called, was passed to John Wesley in England who in turn proposed that ministers in North America might also be invited to join. Writing to a Scottish correspondent (Lord Grange) on March 16, 1745, Wesley asks, 'Might it not be practicable to have the concurrence of Mr Edwards in New England, if not of Mr Tennent also, herein? It is evidently one work with what we have seen here. Why should we not all praise God with one heart?'[1]

By the time that Wesley's opinion was passed on in Scotland, Robe or M'Culloch had already sent word of the concert in prayer to Northampton. Edwards' response, when received in Scotland, was immediately published in *The Christian Monthly History* for November, 1745.[2] After initial comment on other matters, Edwards proceeds:

One thing that has been very joyful to me, that I have been informed

---

[1] *The Letters of John Wesley*, ed. John Telford, 2, p. 33. Grange's letter to Wesley will be found, in abridged form, in Wesley's *Journal*, ed. N. Curnock, 3, p. 178ff.

[2] The date given for Edwards' letter, 'Nov. 20, 1745', is either a printer's error or the *History* for November, 1745, was issued several months after its publication date. Probably it was the latter. The letter is reprinted in J E (Yale) 5, pp. 444–460.

of in the letters I have received from you, and my other correspondents, your dear neighbours and brethren, is that Concert that is come into, by many of God's people in Scotland and England, for united prayer to God for the pouring out of his Holy Spirit on his church and the world of mankind. Such an agreement and practice appears to me exceeding beautiful, and becoming Christians; and I doubt not but it is so in Christ's eyes. And it seems to me a thing peculiarly becoming us, in the state that things are in at the present day. God has lately done great things before our eyes, whereby he has shown us something of his wonderful power and mercy; but has withal so disposed things that events have tended remarkably to shew us our weakness, infirmity, insufficiency, and great and universal need of God's help; we have been many ways rebuked for our self-confidence, and looking to instruments, and trusting in an arm of flesh, and God is now shewing us that we are nothing, and letting us see that we can do nothing. . . . It is apparent that we can't help ourselves, and have no where else to go, but to God, 2 Chron. 20.12, *'We know not what to do; our eyes are upon thee.'*

Edwards goes on to say that letters from Scotland on this subject he had taken with him into the pulpit to read parts to his people, 'using many arguments with them to comply with the thing proposed'. Despite what seems to have been a rather poor initial response in Northampton and its neighbourhood, Edwards was convinced that something of real importance was at stake and he continued to hold the proposal before his congregation. To John M'Laurin of Glasgow, acknowledged by his friends as 'the chief contriver and promoter' of the union for prayer, he wrote on May 12, 1746: 'With respect to the Concert for Prayer for the pouring out of the Spirit of God, the people of this town have of late more generally fallen in with it. Before the last quarterly season, I preached on a subject tending to excite to the duty of united prayer for a general outpouring of the Spirit. . . . What was delivered seemed to have a great influence on the congregation and the first Tuesday of February last was pretty generally observed, in whole or part, as a day of prayer, in private societies, for the forementioned blessing'.[1] The next year, at a Tuesday lecture,

[1] Elsewhere Edwards speaks of the people's 'several religious associations in various parts of the town' (1.lix); these were probably the same as the 'private praying societies' which he exhorted the congregation to attend (1.ccvii).

February 3, 1747, he pressed the same theme from the words of
Zechariah 8.20–22: 'Thus saith the Lord of hosts: It shall yet
come to pass, that there shall come people, and the inhabitants
of many cities: and the inhabitants of one city shall go to
another, saying, Let us go speedily, to pray before the Lord,
and to seek the Lord of hosts: I will go also. . . . '

Meanwhile, in Scotland, the 'Concert for United Prayer',
originally proposed for two years, was renewed for another
seven in 1746. At the same time a short 'Memorial' concerning
its purpose was drawn up by Scots ministers, and approaching
500 copies sent to New England. Following his Zechariah
sermon, in February, 1747, Edwards also determined to
enlarge upon the same subject in writing and he had fulfilled
this purpose by the time that he next wrote to William
M'Culloch on September 23, 1747. Referring to the Concert
and to his forthcoming book, he says:

The propagation of it is but slow, but yet so many do fall in with it,
and there is that prospect of its being further spread, that it is a great
encouragement to me. I earnestly hope, that they that have begun
extraordinary prayer for the outpouring of the Spirit of God, and the
coming of Christ's kingdom, will not fail, or grow dull and lifeless, in
such an affair but rather that they will increase more and more in their
fervency. I have taken a great deal of pains to promote this concert
here in America, and shall not cease to do so, if God spares my life, as I
have opportunity, in all ways that I can devise. I have written largely
on the subject, insisting on persuasions, and answering objections;
and what I have written is gone to the press (1.xci).

The printers were slow with Edwards' much enlarged sermon
on Zechariah 8.20–22.[1] It appeared at last from the press of a
Boston printer in January, 1748, with a title which so well
expressed the purpose of the author that we must give it in full:

*An Humble Attempt to Promote Explicit Agreement and Visible Union of
God's People in Extraordinary Prayer, For the Revival of Religion and
the Advancement of Christ's Kingdom on Earth, pursuant to Scripture –
Promises and Prophecies concerning the Last Time*

It seems that the size of the book exceeded the printer's initial

[1]The original sermon notes, an outline rather than a full MS, consist of 20
small pages, $3\frac{1}{2}$ by $4\frac{1}{2}$ inches.

advertisement (which had invited subscriptions) in *The Boston Weekly News-Letter*, for it was proposed to print it in octavo in 'about 12 sheets', and, unless it should prove larger, 'at six shillings a piece, old tenor, stitched and covered with blue paper'. In its first British edition of 1789, which we shall have occasion to notice again, the *Humble Attempt* runs to 168 pages.

Samuel Miller writes: 'Instead of making his *Humble Attempt* a pamphlet of twenty or thirty pages, as most men would have done, he made it a volume; rich, instructive, carefully reasoned and of permanent value. . . . On all subjects, he wrote, not for his contemporaries alone, but for posterity.'[1] No one in recent times appears to agree with this estimate of Miller's yet, with qualification, it does merit support. While Edwards' aim was to promote earnest prayer he handles this practical duty in a theological framework. The kingdom of God, he argues, advances by the power of the Holy Spirit accompanying the gospel. And that kingdom has by no means yet reached its world-embracing scope for 'a very great part of the world is but lately discovered and much remains undiscovered to this day' (2.286). A far greater day is coming. Reviewing the biblical evidence for this belief, Edwards concludes with Romans 11:

The Apostle, in the 11th of Romans, teaches us to look on that great outpouring of the Spirit, and ingathering of souls into Christ's kingdom, in those days, first of the Jews and then of the Gentiles, to be but as the first-fruits of the intended harvest, both with regard to Jews and Gentiles, as a sign that all should in due time be gathered in . . . the Apostle speaks of the fulness of both Jews and Gentiles, as what shall hereafter be brought in, distinctly from the ingathering from among both, in those primitive ages of Christianity. . . . These things plainly show that the time is coming when the whole world of mankind shall be brought into the church of Christ; the fulness of both, the whole lump . . . . (2.286)

This final period of world-wide blessing, which will attain its height after the conversion of Israel, is for Edwards 'the latter day glory' or the millennium of Revelation chapter 20.

Stephen J. Stein, the Editor of Edwards' *Apocalyptic Writings* in the Yale edition of his Works, charges him with a major reversal of view in *The Humble Attempt*. 'Some five years after he

[1] *Life of Jonathan Edwards*, p. 93.

had published the bold prediction about the imminence of the millennium,' says Stein, 'Edwards withdrew the conjecture'.[1] For proof of this criticism Stein refers to a passage in *Thoughts Concerning the Present Revival of Religion in New England* (1743), where, he thinks, 'Edwards expressed in public his private commitment to millennialism'. But a comparison of what Edwards says on unfulfilled prophecy in these two works reveals no such retraction. In 1743 Edwards did speak of 'the latter-day glory' (he did not use the word millennium) but his belief on that subject, far from being hitherto a 'private' opinion, was in the Confession of Faith owned by all the New England Churches.[2] Only at one point had he introduced a novelty and it was not on a point of biblical interpretation. In the work of 1743 (written before that date) he had, with some measure of caution, expressed a view which was quickly seized on and distorted: 'It is not unlikely that this work of God's Spirit' – that is to say, the present revival in New England – 'so extraordinary and wonderful, is the dawning, or, at least, a prelude of that glorious work of God, so often foretold in Scripture' (1.381). Again, 'What is now seen in America, and especially in New England may prove the dawn of that glorious day' (1.383). Edwards does not say – as Chauncy reported that he did – that the millennium had *begun*,[3] nor that it was surely imminent, only that he believed the revival to be the forerunner of greater events which were to follow, as the dawn is prelude to the day. That belief he does not withdraw in his *Humble Attempt* of 1747, on the contrary he restates it:

That the Spirit of God has been of late so wonderfully striving with such multitudes – in so many different parts of the world and even to this day in one place or other continues to awaken men – is what I

[1] J E (Yale) 5, pp. 45–6.
[2] *The Savoy Declaration*, 1658.
[3] 'It has been,' he tells M'Culloch in 1744, 'slanderously reported and printed concerning me, that I have often said that the Millennium was already begun, and that it began at Northampton' (1.lxxix). Chauncy quoted an unnamed 'worthy gentleman' who said that Edwards claimed that 'the millennium began when there was such an awakening at Northampton eight years past – so that salvation is gone forth from Northampton and Northampton must have the praise of being first brought into it' (*Seasonable Thoughts*, p. 372n.).

should take encouragement from that God was about to do something more glorious, and would, before he finishes, bring things to a greater ripeness, and not finally suffer this work of his to be frustrated and rendered abortive by Satan's crafty management. And may we not hope that these unusual commotions are the forerunners of something exceeding glorious approaching, as the wind, earthquake, and fire at Mount Sinai, were forerunners of that voice wherein God was in a more eminent manner? (1 Kings 19.11, 12). (2.294)[1]

It is true that in 1747, unlike 1743, Edwards expresses no special hope respecting North America yet his expectation, as such, is unchanged.

Edwards never entertained the view that calculations as to the date of future blessings are a necessary prelude to earnest prayer for those blessings.[2] The reason why he does take up considerable space with unfulfilled prophecy in his *Humble Attempt* is because of the prevalence of certain views which he saw as discouragements to prayer. There were, for instance, a number who believed that the darkest hour for the church – the slaying of the two witnesses (Rev. 11) – was still to come and that the age of general blessing spoken of in Revelation chapter 20 was therefore a long way off.[3] Against this, Edwards argues that the symbolism of Revelation 11 was already filled in the desolation of the pre-Reformation church. He shared the view of Moses Lowman (1680–1752) that history is as far advanced as the pouring out of the sixth vial (Rev. 16.12). But he is critical of Lowman for his date-setting, and particularly critical of his argument that the end of Antichrist's reign would not be

[1]See also 2.310.

[2]Thus he writes to M'Culloch in 1747, 'I expect no certainty as to these things, or any of the various conjectures concerning the time of the calling of the Jews, and the fall of the kingdom of the beast, till time and fulfillment shall decide the matter' (1.xcii).

[3]When Thomas Prince of Boston sought Whitefield's opinion on Revelation, chapter 11, the latter replied: 'What flourishing days are coming on I know not – I have little or not insight into them, and therefore am no judge of Dr Mr Edwards his opinion concerning the slaying of the witnesses – However, I should be glad to see what he wrote, and can heartily join with all those who pray for the coming of the latter day glory.' Letter of Mar.25 1748 (MS, Boston Public Library), quoted by Stein in J E (Yale), 5, p. 87. Here, and in another quotation, Whitefield is sceptical of all date-setting, but not of Edwards' views as Stein implies.

until after the year two thousand. Edwards does not counter this with other conjectures but rather he urges that instead of expecting things to happen 'at one stroke' we should expect a more gradual progress. The overthrow of unbelief in Christendom, the conversion of the Jews, and the full enlightenment of all Mahomedan and heathen nations, will not, he asserts, be accomplished 'in one great conflict' (2.306).[1] Rather such great things will come to pass, in answer to prayer, through successive revivals – a succession in which the Awakening of 1740 played its own notable part. Thus, he argues:

If God does not grant that greatest of all effusions of his Spirit so soon as we desire . . . there will be all reason to hope that we shall receive some blessed token of his acceptance. If the fall of mystical Babylon, and the work of God's Spirit that shall bring it to pass, be at several hundred years' distance, yet it follows not that there will be no happy revivals of religion before that time, which shall be richly worth the most diligent, earnest, and constant prayer (2.310).

The 'historicist' interpretation of the Apocalypse, and the differences within that school of interpretation, are unlikely to re-assert the place they held in the church two-hundred years ago. Some of the exegetical argumentation is almost certainly flawed by wrong general principles of interpretation and this must qualify any statement on the modern value of the *Humble Attempt*. Nonetheless it remains a remarkable work. While it does not contain the superficial optimism of some nineteenth-century writers,[2] Edwards believed beforehand in the great missionary advance and saw, by faith, the gospel of Christ 'throughout all parts of Africa, Asia, America and Terra Australis' (2.306). It is arguable that no such tract on the hidden source of all true evangelistic success, namely, prayer for the Spirit of God, has ever been so widely used as this one. In the 1820's, over seventy years later, when for the first time

---

[1]Here, and elsewhere in the two-volume edition of Edwards some of his material (for the sake of space) has been put by editors into footnotes of incredibly small print. The reference I here quote can be far more easily read in J E (Yale), 5, p. 410.

[2]Nathaniel Porter, for instance, was to assert in 1822, 'In half a century there will be no Pagans, Jews, Mohomedans, Unitarians, or Methodists'. Sprague *Annals*, 2, p. 56.

world-wide missionary endeavour was becoming a reality, S. E. Dwight could speak of his grandfather's book as having, 'through the Divine blessing . . . exerted an influence, singularly powerful, in rousing the church of Christ'. Unquestionably Edwards' words were used to implant his own faith in the world-wide success of the gospel in others, and this conviction, Dwight could say, 'has been a prime cause of the present concentrated movement of the whole church of God to hasten forward the reign of the Messiah' (1.xciii).

Credit for any foresight would have been the last thing to occur to Edwards had he lived to see the new age of world mission which dawned at the end of his century. He viewed the unity in prayer in the mid 1740's as God-given: the set backs which had attended and followed the Great Awakening were all a part of providence so that the church might better learn, in prayer, to wait upon God alone. Far from being disillusioned by the post-revival difficulties in Northampton and elsewhere, Edwards' own faith was strengthened. He knew that any present lack of visible success was no indication of God's ultimate purposes. As he writes to one Scottish correspondent: 'Jacob and the woman of Canaan met with great discouragements while they were wrestling for a blessing, but they persevered and obtained their request.'

*　　　*　　　*

On Thursday, May 28, 1747, possibly a day on which Edwards was busy preparing the *Humble Attempt* for the press, David Brainerd rode into the parsonage yard at Northampton. The two men were comparative strangers, having met only once before at the Yale Commencement of 1743, but the friendship of the summer which followed Brainerd's coming to Northampton was to prove the second great encouragement for Edwards at this period. It was also to lead to a permanent and far-reaching result in the best-known of all Edwards' literary works, *The Life and Diary of the Rev. David Brainerd*.

Except for that one meeting four years earlier, no personal communications seem to have passed between the two men, yet Edwards did have, he tells us, 'much opportunity, before this, of particular information concerning him from many who were well acquainted with him' (2.378). It was as a result of such information that the pastor of Northampton had been one of the sympathetic advisers who had stood by Brainerd at the Commencement of 1743 when the Connecticut student, instead of appearing at the head of his Yale class, was refused his degree by the governors of the College. Brainerd's fault was that as a young convert in the winter of 1741–42, at the height of the excitement of the Great Awakening, he had spoken critically of the spiritual character of one of his tutors. For this offence – considered enough to brand a man as a separatist – he had been expelled (2.321). At the Commencement of 1743, Brainerd had petitioned that his degree might be conferred, and made what Edwards observed as 'a truly humble and Christian acknowledgement of his fault'. The petition was refused.

Prior to this final refusal of his degree, Brainerd had been invited to New York by Dickinson, Pemberton and Burr. These correspondents of the Society in Scotland for Propagating Christian Knowledge interviewed him as a missionary candidate in November, 1742, and, regarding him as the man for whom they had been looking, appointed him to begin missionary work among the Indians in April, 1743 (2.330).[1]

Brainerd's first location had been at 'Kaunaumeek', twenty miles from a dot in the wilderness recently named 'Stockbridge', on the borders of Western Massachusetts and New York. John Sergeant, earlier mentioned as one who studied at the Northampton parsonage, was already engaged in work among the Indians at Stockbridge and it was he who assisted Brainerd in language study in the winter of 1743–44. Notes in Brainerd's Diary give some idea of what those frequent twenty-mile rides to Stockbridge entailed. They include such

[1] It appears that Thomas Clap of Yale complained of their receiving a man under the censure of his college, and the correspondents accordingly encouraged Brainerd to make apology and seek the conferring of his degree at the 1743 Commencement. It was almost certainly they who also sought Edwards' help. The attitude of Yale in this matter had long-term consequences. Burr says, 'If it had not been for the treatment received by Mr. Brainerd at Yale, New Jersey College would never have been erected'. On which Alexander comments, 'How many influences are made to combine and operate when Providence has the design of giving existence to an institution which has affected and will still affect the happiness of thousands!' *The Log College*, p. 70.

sentences as 'was nearly overdone with the extreme cold', and, 'Much fatigued with my journey . . . much exposed and very wet by falling into a river' (2.340–41).

After a year of no apparent success, Brainerd had received a unanimous call to the pastorate of the congregation at East Hampton, back in New England, which he declined. Later he was to say, 'I never, since I began to preach, could feel any freedom to "enter into other men's labours", and settle down in the ministry where the gospel was preached before'.[1] Receiving 'orders' from the Society to proceed to Indians on the Delaware River in Pennsylvania, Brainerd persuaded his few Kaunaumeek Indians to re-settle under Sergeant's care at Stockbridge while he moved on. Amidst his nomadic life and hardships, he could write, 'There appeared to be nothing of any considerable importance to me but holiness of heart and life, and the conversion of the heathen to God'. In May, 1744, he was above the Forks of Delaware where he spent most of the summer before a visit west to the Susquehanna River in October. In these areas there was much preaching by Brainerd, and still more prayer, though with little visible result. A year later, in May, 1745, when he had just completed a journey of 350 miles, he was 'sometimes much discouraged and sunk in his spirits through the opposition that appeared in the Indians to Christianity' (2.358). If there was 'no better prospect of better special success' he was almost resolved to quit at the end of the year rather than be a burden on the Society in Scotland who paid his salary.

But a marvellous change came in the hot, dry summer of 1745, and as Edwards was later to say, 'at a time, in a place, and upon subjects that scarce ever entered into his heart'. At Crossweeksung, in New Jersey, 'God was pleased to display his power and grace', and a work of conviction, awakening and conversion began among the Indians which closely resembled what had earlier occurred among the civilized citizens of New England during the Great Awakening. Here was a 'revival' among the heathen and judging by the record in Brainerd's Journal it was one of the most remarkable in Christian history.

[1]Despite this fact, and Brainerd's own words, Norman Pettit asserts that Brainerd wanted 'a settled ministry' and that he was 'a missionary by default' J E (Yale) 7, pp. 54, 63.

Not surprisingly, despite his worn-out body, Brainerd found new energies. By November, 1745, he had ridden over three thousand miles in nine months – averaging twenty hours a week in the saddle. Nevertheless, despite some wider blessing, it was the Indians of Crossweeksung who became his 'own congregation' of whom he could write: 'I have oftentimes thought that they would cheerfully and diligently attend divine worship twenty-four hours together if they had an opportunity to do so . . . I know of no assembly of Christians where there seems to be so much of the presence of God, where brotherly love so much prevails. . . .'

In 1745 Edwards had not been long in hearing this good news from New Jersey. On November 20 of that year he wrote to a Scottish correspondent: 'Mr Brainerd, a missionary employed by the Society in Scotland for propagating Christian Knowledge, to preach to the Indians, has lately had more success than ever. This Mr Brainerd is a young gentleman of very distinguishing qualifications, remarkable for his piety, and eminent zeal for the good of souls, and his knowledge in divinity, and solidity of his judgment, and prudence of conduct. And I hope he will be improved to be a great blessing.'

In 1746 Edwards heard more of the awakening among Brainerd's New Jersey Indians. Brainerd was then preparing his Journal for the years 1745–46 for the printers. Part of it Edwards saw in advance of publication as he tells M'Laurin in a letter of May 12, 1745, 'I have lately seen a Journal of Mr Brainerd's, Scots missionary to the Indians in Pennsylvania and New Jersey, giving indeed a very remarkable and wonderful account of his success among these poor ignorant people the last summer and fall'.

What Edwards did not know on the day the missionary arrived, probably unannounced, at his home in 1747 was that his life and ministry were almost over. By the winter of 1746–47 the tuberculosis from which Brainerd was suffering was so far advanced that almost all his work – save prayer – had ended. Setting out for New England, he had spent the winter months with Jonathan Dickinson, President of the College of New Jersey, before making slow progress northwards in the spring. But Brainerd's spirit on the day he came to Northampton was such that it belied his real condition. The twenty-nine-year-old was cheerful, 'vastly better than by his account he had been in the winter,' says Edwards, 'indeed so well that he was able to ride twenty-five miles in a day and to walk half a mile' (2.377).[1]

After their first weekend together Edwards invited his friend Dr. Samuel Mather to the parsonage to examine his guest.

On June 9, 1747, encouraged by the doctors to continue riding, Brainerd temporarily left Northampton as Edwards explains to Joseph Bellamy in a letter of June 11:

Mr. Brainerd is far from being so broken in his understanding as I have heard. He is capable of conversing very agreeably, and praying in the family most admirably. He is now gone to Boston with my daughter Jerusha. She intends to stay in Boston about a fortnight while Mr Brainerd goes to the eastward and then he is to return with her hither again. Mr Brainerd is a very desirable man indeed; I am glad I have had such an opportunity of acquaintance with him. Physicians speak of the state of his bodily constitution as very dangerous and difficult, and Dr Mather of this town gives him over, but Dr Pynchon is not so positive that he will not recover. For my part I cannot but have some hopes of his recovery. . . .[2]

These hopes were dashed by letters from Jerusha Edwards at Boston at the end of June, 'He is extremely weak. . . . He says, it is impossible for him to live, for he has hardly vigour enough to draw his breath' (2.380). Yet in these weeks at Boston Brainerd wrote an introduction to a work of Thomas Shepard's which was about to be reprinted and also some letters of great value (2.438–39). To his brother John, also a missionary among the Indians of New Jersey, he writes:

My soul longs that you should be fitted for, and in due time go into, the work of the ministry. . . . Do not be discouraged because you see your elder brothers in the ministry die early, one after another. I declare, now I am dying, I would not have spent my life otherwise for the whole world.

To another youth, preparing for the ministry, Brainerd writes, 'Read Mr Edwards' piece on the *Affections*, again and again, and labour to distinguish clearly upon experiences and affections in religion, that you may make a difference between the gold and the shining dross.'

[1]Brainerd, born 1718, was twenty-nine on April 20, 1747. The age given on his grave-stone (see above p. 289) is thus incorrect.
[2]*The New England Quarterly*, 1928, p. 235.

Somewhat recovered, Brainerd, with Jerusha Edwards, was in Northampton again on Saturday July 25, in time for the Lord's Day when Brainerd wrote in his Diary, 'This day I saw clearly that I should never be happy, yea, that God himself could not make me happy, unless I could be in a capacity to "please and glorify him for ever".' Longing for heaven because of 'a sense of the excellency of a state of perfection' was a thought he often expressed. 'Nothing so refreshes my soul as when I can *go to God*,' he wrote one Lord's Day, 'yea, to God my exceeding joy'. He rode to the meetinghouse for the mid-week lecture on the first Wednesday in September, and 'it was,' notes Edwards, 'the last time that ever he went out at our gate alive'.

Brainerd rose from his bed for the last time on September 29, 1747. Recalling the evening of that day, Edwards was soon to tell his people at Brainerd's funeral:

A little before his death, he said to me, as I came into the room, 'My thoughts have been employed on the old dear theme, the prosperity of God's church on earth. As I waked out of sleep (said he) I was led to cry for the pouring out of God's Spirit and the advancement of Christ's kingdom, which the dear Redeemer died and suffered so much for: it is that especially makes me long for it.' But a few days before his death, he desired us to sing a psalm concerning the prosperity of Zion which he signified his mind was engaged in above all things, and at his desire we sang a part of the 102d Psalm. And when he had done, though he was then so low that he could scarcely speak, he so exerted himself, that he made a prayer, very audibly, wherein, besides praying for those present, and for his own congregation, he earnestly prayed for the reviving and flourishing of religion in the world (2.35).

David Brainerd died in the Edwards' home, 'towards day, about six o'clock in the morning,' on Friday, October 9th, 1747.

The coming of Brainerd to Northampton was an event of far-reaching importance in Edwards' life. While the opposite result might have been expected, the presence of a dying man, through many weeks, was uplifting to Edwards. For five years past he had been particularly occupied with the nature of true godliness and it was as he advanced in this subject that he became not only isolated from many ministerial neighbours but also from others in his own congregation. Without question, Edwards felt the loneliness. In Brainerd, though almost a stranger on his arrival, there was an instinctive unity of mind and spirit. Edwards' spirit was stirred and comforted. Although unable to help Edwards by any public duties in the meetinghouse, Brainerd's very presence was enlivening (2.378). 'I never had an opportunity to hear him preach, but I have often heard him pray and think his manner of addressing himself to God almost inimitable, such (so far as I may judge) as I have very rarely known equalled' (2.33).

Strong in his insistence upon doctrinal purity and upon the need for the special influences of the Holy Spirit,[1] Brainerd also felt as keenly as Edwards the danger of such wild-fire as had marred the Great Awakening.

Knowing there were those there who needed to hear words of warning, Edwards told the great congregation that assembled for Brainerd's funeral:

He detested 'enthusiasm' in all its forms and operations, and abhorred whatever in opinion or experience seemed to verge towards antinomianism [such] as: the experiences of those whose first faith consists in believing that Christ died for them in particular, and their first love, in loving God, because they supposed they were the objects of his love, and their assurance of their good estate from some immediate testimony, or suggestion (either with or without texts of Scripture) that their sins are forgiven, that God loves them, etc., and the joys of such as rejoiced more in their own supposed distinction from others, in honour, and privileges, and high experiences, than in God's excellency and Christ's beauty, and the spiritual pride of such laymen that are for setting up themselves as public teachers, and cry down human learning, and a learned ministry. He greatly disliked a disposition in persons to much noise and show in religion, and affecting to be abundant in publishing and proclaiming their own experience; though he did not condemn but approved of Christians speaking of their experiences, on some occasions, and to some persons, with modesty, discretion, and reserve. (2.33)

Edwards poured his heart into Brainerd's funeral sermon on the subject, 'True Saints, When Absent From The Body, Are Present With The Lord'. Eight neighbouring ministers and 'a great concourse of people' listened as Edwards concluded, 'Oh

---

[1] In his last weeks, says Edwards, 'He dwelt much on the great importance of the work of gospel ministers; and expressed his longings that they might be "filled with the Spirit of God"' (2.384).

that the things that were seen and heard in this extraordinary person, his holiness, heavenliness, labour, and self-denial in life, may effectually stir us up to endeavour that in the way of such a holy life we may at last come to so blessed an end.'

But the event which was, in God's providence, for ever to bind the names of Edwards and Brainerd together followed Brainerd's death. Only then did Edwards examine all the personal papers which Brainerd had spared from destruction upon the grounds of his trust in Edwards who records: 'I might dispose of them as I thought would be most for God's glory and the interest of religion' (2.315).[1]

Edwards had no doubt that God had 'laid in' his way the publishing of Brainerd's life. By the end of August, 1748, he was able to send John Erskine a 'Paper of Proposals' (*i.e.* an advertisement) of the volume, more than three hundred pages long, which came out in 1749, *An Account of the Life of the Late Reverend Mr. David Brainerd.*

This was the first biography printed in America to gain international recognition and the first full missionary biography ever to be published. At the very time that Edwards was thinking, writing and praying about the coming era of world missions, a flesh and blood trail blazer of that future age had come to his door. Edwards knew that this was an example which had to be given to the world. Without hesitation he laid aside other writing projects, 'diverted', as he tells John Erskine, 'by something else that divine providence unexpectedly laid in my way' (1.xcv). If the *Humble Attempt* promoted intercession, few books have done so much to prompt prayer and action as the *Life of Brainerd.* Yet, surprisingly, it is probable that Edwards did not himself anticipate what was to be the book's main impact upon posterity. The truth is that Edwards had another purpose chiefly in view and one which he considered to be yet more basic and relevant. He wanted Brainerd to be read and known not simply as an example of a true missionary but as an example of a real Christian, showing what the power of

---

[1]Despite these words, Pettit criticizes Edwards for doing a normal editor's work on the Brainerd diaries. His charge that Edwards' 'tampered' with his friend's writings and 'took great liberties throughout' bears no relation to the facts. J E (Yale) 7, pp. 22, 24, 79. Similar inaccuracies mar Pettit's Introduction to this volume of Edwards' Works.

godliness and 'vital religion' truly is. The Christian life is God-centred living; it means giving reverence to all the commands of God and it is 'not rapture but habit'. The Christian has an experience of God which is 'of an increasing nature', even when 'a general deadness returned' in the land, but the motivation is to be 'conformity to God', not a longing for experiences as such.

Edwards' pages of 'Reflections and Observations' on Brainerd give the substance of both men's views on the essence of experimental Christianity (2.447–458). They are among the most important descriptive pages on the Christian life which Edwards ever wrote, and their absence from, or severe abridgement in the shortened reprints of Edwards' *Life of David Brainerd* has seriously curtailed Edwards' original purpose.

Edwards does not idealize Brainerd. He was aware of a brooding introspection and an occasional melancholy in him which was related to his physical condition. Brainerd's example is not uncritically commended. Nor is the biography a full portrait. It could not be, because, except for those few months together in 1747, Edwards was almost wholly dependent upon Brainerd's diary. There was an attractive human element in Brainerd which is never in sight except when Edwards could finally write as an eye-witness. We are almost surprised therefore when, speaking of their meeting in May 1747, Edwards reports: 'I found him remarkably sociable, pleasant and entertaining in his conversation . . . far from any stiffness, moroseness, or affected singularity in speech or behaviour' (2.378).

From the many instances of the subsequent influence of Edwards' *Life of Brainerd* – unquestionably the most widely read of all Edwards' works – we here give but one from the pen of another New Englander, Adoniram Judson Gordon. When, more than a century after Edwards, Gordon was called to the difficult task of ministering in a largely Unitarian Boston, he writes of how he read and re-read the Brainerd volume and never forgot the impression of a winter's day visit to the missionary's grave in Northampton:

Does it savor of saint-worship or superstition to be thus exploring old graveyards, wading through snow-drifts, and deciphering ancient headstones on a cold day in midwinter? Perhaps so, on the face of it;

but let us justify our conduct. What if the writer confesses that he has never received such spiritual impulse from any other human being as from him whose body has lain now for nearly a century and a half under that Northampton slab? For many years an old and worn volume of his life and journals has lain upon my study table, and no season has passed without a renewed pondering of its precious contents. 'If you would make men think well of you, make them think well of themselves,' is the maxim of Lord Chesterfield, which he regarded as embodying the highest worldly wisdom. On the contrary, the preacher and witness for Christ who makes us think meanly of ourselves is the one who does us most good, and ultimately wins our hearts. This is exactly the effect which the reading of Brainerd's Memoirs has on one. Humiliation succeeds humiliation as we read on. 'How little have I prayed! how low has been my standard of consecration!' is the irresistible exclamation; and when we shut the book we are not praising Brainerd, but condemning ourselves, and resolving that, by the grace of God, we will follow Christ more closely in the future.[1]

* * *

There is one epilogue to the story of Edwards and Brainerd which needs to be added. Before the winter which began with the death of Brainerd was over, Jerusha Edwards herself fell ill and, after only five days, died on February 15, 1748. She was 'esteemed the flower of the family' her father was to write to John Erskine (1.xcv), and he tells Bellamy that Brainerd 'looked on her not only as a saint, but as a very eminent saint'. Her grave was to lie side by side with Brainerd's, bearing the text chosen by her parents, 'I shall be satisfied, when I awake, with thy likeness' (Psalm 17.15).

It was probably from the near proximity of those two graves that a legend grew in later years, the legend that Brainerd and Jerusha were betrothed to one another in that short summer of 1747, and even that it was a romantic attachment to her which had first brought Brainerd to the Edwards' parsonage. For such opinions there is not a trace of evidence. The fact is that Brainerd arrived in need of immediate care, at a time when there was another minister staying at the parsonage who was

[1] *A. J. Gordon*, A Biography, Ernest B. Gordon, 1909, p. 85.

'very poorly',[1] and when Sarah Edwards had given birth to their tenth child, Elizabeth, only a few weeks earlier. Clearly Jerusha, who was already a mature Christian, was the best available nurse in the family and thus, as Edwards says, she was constantly 'with him as his nurse, 19 weeks before his death'. The friendship between them was the friendship of Christians: 'She looked on him as an eminent servant of Jesus Christ' (2.385 fn.) but, as far as natural relationships were concerned, Brainerd could say five days before his death that he loved his brother John 'the best of any creature living'.

The idea of romance as an explanation for Brainerd's coming to Northampton has to be set aside. It may be that Dr. Mather's medical reputation had attracted him and that, bereaved of both his parents in his former Connecticut home, the known warmth of the Edwards' household encouraged him first to call and then to stay. What is clear is that the dying missionary, who could write, 'Oh, how I long for the holiness of that world,' had no definite plans for those last months of his life. 'He was at a loss for some time,' says Edwards, 'which way to bend his course next'. But on that October day of Brainerd's funeral, as Edwards surveyed the empty bedroom and the manuscripts entrusted to his care, he could indeed say with the friend whose unexpected stay had brought him so much encouragement, 'I have learned, in a measure, that all good things, relating both to time and eternity, come from God'.

In these troubled years in his own parish Edwards was thus led to take long-term views. With correspondents in Scotland he found the communion of saints to be international. In the 'Concert for Prayer' they looked forward in hope. And, after the two new graves in the cemetery in Bridge Street, the bonds were closer with heaven itself. Despite the sorrow, Jonathan and Sarah Edwards knew that they were rich.

[1] Eleazar Wheelock, so Edwards tells Bellamy in a letter of June 11, 1747. It was uncertain, he wrote, whether Wheelock would ever preach again. He recovered and became President of Dartmouth College.

THE COMMUNION CONTROVERSY

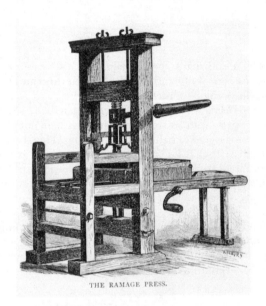

THE RAMAGE PRESS.

*The so-called Ramage Press, built in London
about 1650 and brought to Boston in 1717.
By such means the subject in controversy in
Northampton came to a much wider public.*

A minister by his office is to be the guide and instructor of his people. To that end he is to study and search the Scriptures and to teach the people, not the opinions of men – of other divines or of their ancestors – but the mind of Christ. As he is set to enlighten them, so a part of his duty is to rectify their mistakes, and, if he sees them out of the way of truth or duty, to be a voice behind them, saying, 'This is the way, walk ye in it.' Hence, if what he offers to exhibit to them as the mind of Christ be different from their previous apprehensions, unless it be on some point which is established in the Church of God as fundamental, surely they are obliged to hear him. If not, there is an end at once to all the use and benefit of teachers in the church in these respects – as the means of increasing its light and knowledge, and of reclaiming it from mistakes and errors. This would be in effect to establish, not the word of Christ, but the opinion of the last generation in each town and church, as an immutable rule to all future generations to the end of the world.

From J E'S Journal on the Communion
Controversy, Dwight, *Life of President Edwards*, p. 358

It often comes to pass in this evil world, that great differences and controversies arise between ministers and the people under their pastoral care . . . and although contests and dissensions between persons so related are the most unhappy and terrible in their consequences, on many accounts, of any sort of contentions, yet how frequent have such contentions been!

J E, July 1, 1750 (1.ccii)

16

It is an evidence of the esteem in which the Edwards held uncle John Stoddard that when he lay seriously ill in Boston in June, 1748 Sarah hastened there to assist in his nursing despite having to leave thirteen-month-old baby Elizabeth ('Betty') at home. In a purely domestic letter – which shows him well abreast of all the household affairs – Edwards wrote to his wife:

Dear Companion,

I wrote you a few lines the last Sabbath day by Ensign Dwight, which I hope you will receive. By this I would inform you that Betty seems really to be on the mending hand; I can't but think she is truly better, both as to her health and her sores since she has been at Mrs Phelps's. The first two or three days, before she was well acquainted, she was very unquiet; but now more quiet than she used to be at home. This is Lecture day morning, and your two eldest daughters went to bed last night, both sick; and Rose beat out, and having the headache. We got Hannah Root to help them yesterday in the afternoon, expect her again today. How Sarah and Esther will do today I cannot tell, for they are not up. We have been without you almost as long as we know how to; but yet are willing you should obey the calls of Providence with regard to Col. Stoddard.

If you have money to spare, and it isn't too late, I should be glad if you would buy us some cheese in Boston, and bring it with other things if it can be safely:– give my humble service to Mr Bromfield and Madam and proper salutation to other Friends.

I am your most affectionate
Companion
Jonathan Edwards

Northampton June 22, 1748

The letter was scarcely written when news came that Colonel Stoddard had died of apoplexy and on June 26 Edwards preached his funeral sermon at Northampton. The sermon, 'God's Awful Judgment in the Breaking and Withering of the Strong Rods of a Community' gives a high view both of Edwards' convictions on civil government and of the character of his uncle:

Perhaps never was there a man that appeared in New England to whom the denomination of *a great man* did more properly belong. . . . He was a most faithful friend . . . He was thoroughly established in those religious principles and doctrines of the first fathers of New England usually called *the doctrines of grace* (2.39).

John Stoddard's death was a real personal loss for Edwards for, as Hopkins says, he 'greatly strengthened' Edwards' hands in the work of the ministry. First citizen of Northampton in both rank and wealth, and Chief Justice of the County, there would be no open criticism of Edwards as long as Stoddard sat appreciatively in his pew beneath the pulpit in the meeting-house Sunday by Sunday. Stoddard was gone before Edwards could obtain his counsel when the next applicant for communion came forward at Northampton, and with his passing, despite the many relatives remaining in the neighbourhood, support for Edwards from the wider family circle in Hampshire County virtually ceased.

The troubles now developing at Northampton remind us that few controversies in the Church have been exclusively concerned with theological issues. However it is to be explained, no small part of the opposition which Edwards met with originated with his own relations. The hostility of Israel Williams – now indeed 'the monarch of Hampshire' on the death of Stoddard – had deepened with the years and since 1744 he had become 'the confidential adviser of the disaffected party' in the Northampton congregation. From Hatfield, only five miles away, where he had his grand residence, this role was easy enough to maintain. 'In this course,' writes Dwight, 'he had the countenance of other members of the family, of a character superior to his own'[1] – a reference which would probably include Israel's brother, Solomon, seventy miles away in the Connecticut parish

[1] *Life of President Edwards*, p. 307.

of Lebanon and his half-brother, Elisha, who had tutored Edwards at Yale. But there were more Williamses in Hampshire itself. Four of the clergy of Hampshire, says Dwight, 'were connected with the ——[Williams] family and accustomed to act with them'.[1] As noted earlier, they included Jonathan Ashley of Deerfield and also Chester Williams of Hadley.

Still closer to hand was Edwards' aunt Rebekah in Northampton, widowed by the suicide of her husband, Joseph Hawley, in 1735. Perry Miller has no problem in explaining the part of the Hawley family in the future course of events. Joseph, he asserts, was 'thrown into despondency by Edwards' preaching' and his son, Joseph Jr., was therefore motivated by a desire to 'get even with his father's destroyer'. Like so much else in Miller, the accusation is false. Both father and son were victims of an hereditary depressive condition, though in the case of the son (Edwards' cousin) it was not yet apparent in the 1740's. Hawley, Jr. (1724–1788), graduated from Yale in 1742, after which, it is said, he studied theology with Edwards and was licensed to preach. Of his relationship to his uncle Jonathan at this date he was later to say, 'I was not only under the common obligations of each individual of the society to him, as a most able, diligent, and faithful pastor, but I had also received many instances of his tenderness, goodness and generosity to me as a young kinsman, whom he was disposed to treat in a most friendly manner' (1.cxxvi).

The next thing we know of Joseph Hawley Jr. was that he was one of the Northampton men on the Cape Breton expedition in 1745 where it appears that he formed a close friendship with another of the town's citizens, Major Seth Pomeroy (1706–1777), who served with the 4th Massachusetts Regiment. Referring, in a letter to Scotland, to the number of Northampton men at Cape Breton, Edwards makes particular mention of these two – 'a Major of one of the Regiments and the General's Chaplain, both worthy pious men'.[2] He did not then know that both his cousin Joseph and Seth Pomeroy were in a few years to become leaders in the opposition to his ministry.

[1] *Live of President Edwards*, p. 436.
[2] 'Mr. Edwards's Letter to his Scots Correspondent', Nov. 20, 1745 *The Christian Monthly History*, No. viii, Nov., 1745, p. 240.

As already mentioned, the Pomeroys had long been a leading family in the town, with Seth's brother, Ebenezer Pomeroy Jr., serving as one of Edwards' deacons since 1739. The origin of the breach between the Pomeroys and Edwards cannot be traced but it may have been connected with another problem of discipline in the church. In 1747 an unmarried mother in Northampton had borne twins and named Joseph Hawley's brother, Elisha, as the father. The woman privately agreed to give up all future claims for maintenance in return for a substantial sum of money but Edwards believed that more than reparation for 'outward injury' was involved. 'The order, decency and health of human society in general', required that the parents should be married. Hawley declined and when a council of local churches was convened in June 1749 'to hear a matter of grievance between the Church and Lt. Elisha Hawley' Edwards' view was not upheld. The Council advised that the decision be left to Hawley's own conscience and that he be received back into the Church upon repentance for his fornication. The fact that Elizabeth, daughter of Deacon Ebenezer Pomeroy, and niece of Major Seth, married Elisha Hawley in 1751 suggests a family view of this whole affair different from that of Edwards.

Joseph Hawley was a little later than Seth Pomeroy in returning to Northampton after army service. He had laid aside his chaplaincy and in 1748 was studying law in Suffield before taking up practice, the next year, in his home town. Whether out of sympathy with his brother or for other reasons, Hawley's attitude to Edwards was already different in the year of his return (1749) and the date is significant because it was now that the controversy on the qualifications required for communicant membership broke out in full force. In December 1748 Edwards had told an applicant for membership that he must profess to be a Christian before he could become a communicant. After consultation with others, the individual refused. 'He hoped he could make a profession of godliness', Edwards notes in his Journal on the controversy, but 'he did not think that he was obliged to make it in order to admission into the Church'.

The report of this, says Edwards, 'made great uneasiness in the town'. In the hope of alleviating it, he proposed to the

Committee of the Church in February 1749 that he should explain from the pulpit the reason for his change of mind. 'The prevailing voice seemed to be zealously against this course of action', he writes, although the need for the church to be informed of his reasons 'seemed to be allowed by all'. Accordingly a proposal that these reasons should be prepared for publication was agreed. Edwards immediately began to write what was to become a book. At the same time, regarding the view of the Committee as no more than an opinion, he did not exclude the possibility of preaching on the subject.

Shortly after this, feeling was further raised over the case of Mary Hulbert, a young woman, who applied to Edwards for admission to communicant membership:

> She gave me a hopeful account of her religious experience, and the operations of Divine grace upon her mind; and manifested herself ready publicly to make a profession of religion, agreeably to what she had now professed in private. I then desired her to prepare for examination with respect to her doctrinal knowledge, and to come to me again, and I would draw up a profession, agreeably to what she had expressed to me.[1]

After some time Mary Hulbert returned for this second visit but, perhaps intimidated by others, 'said that she was afraid, by what she had heard, that there would be a tumult if she came into the church in that way, and she did not desire to be the occasion of a tumult'. She did, however, agree to make profession of faith in the words which Edwards had drawn up if the Committee of the Church would consent to it. But only three out of the fifteen members of the Committee were ready to consent when the Committee met in April 1749, the rest arguing that the acceptance of such a change in admission to the church would pre-judge the issue upon which they were presently in disagreement with their pastor.

Edwards saw only one way to break the deadlock and he took it by giving the Church Committee a written promise in the

---

[1] Edwards' proposal was that new candidates should make formal public commitment to Christ and to the obedience required of Christians in Scripture: he was not asking for an extempore rehearsal of their religious experience before the church.

following words:

> I, the subscriber, do hereby signify and declare to such as it may concern, that if my people will wait till the book I am preparing for the press, relating to the admission of members into the church, is published, I will resign the ministry over this church, if the church desires it, after they have had opportunity pretty generally to read my said book, and after they have first asked advice of a council mutually chosen. The following things also being provided; viz., that none of the brethren be admitted to vote on this affair but such as have either read my said book, or have heard from the pulpit what I have to say in defence of the doctrine that is the subject of it; and that the society will engage that I shall be free from all rates, and also that a regular council approve of my thus resigning my pastoral office in this church. Northampton, April 13, 1749   JE

Soon after this date, his book, upon which so much depended, went to the printer in Boston with a note from the author 'urging him very much not to delay the printing'. Edwards was under no illusions as to the seriousness of the controversy and its possible outcome for himself. Not only was it possible for opponents of his view to represent him as being against his revered grandfather, and against the prevailing practice in New England, but the issue had obvious implications for existing communicants who gave no evidence of Christian holiness. Their standing within the church could scarcely escape questioning once Edwards' position on the grounds for admission to the Lord's Table was accepted.

In a long letter of May 20, 1749, to John Erskine in Scotland (mainly to do with advancing mission work among the Indians) Edwards concludes with this note about his personal affairs:

> A very great difficulty has arisen between my people, relating to qualifications for communion at the Lord's table. My honoured grandfather Stoddard, my predecessor in the ministry over this church, strenuously maintained the Lord's Supper to be a *converting ordinance*, and urged all to come who were not of scandalous life, though they knew themselves to be unconverted. I formerly conformed to his practice but I have had difficulties with respect to it, which have been long increasing, till I dared no longer to proceed in the former way, which has occasioned great uneasiness among my people, and has filled all the country with noise (1.cv).

[318]

Towards the end of July 1749, when there was still no word of
the arrival of Edwards' book, the suspicion was raised that their
pastor was simply playing for time, and without his consent
there was 'a meeting of the members of the church, or at least of
many of them, to determine whether to wait any longer for my
book'. But by mid-August the book had arrived, a quantity
being carried home by Colonel Dwight on his return from
business in Boston. It bore a typically Edwardean title, *An
Humble Inquiry into the Rules of the Word of God concerning the
Qualifications requisite to a Complete Standing and Full Communion in
the Visible Christian Church.* Speaking of the controversy, Edwards
wrote in his Preface:

I can truly say it is what I engage in with the greatest reluctance that
ever I undertook any public service in my life. . . . I am conscious, not
only is the interest of religion concerned in this affair, but my own
reputation, future usefulness, and my very subsistence, all seem to
depend on my freely opening and defending myself, as to my
principles . . . (1.432).

From the arrival of Edwards' book until October 'there
seemed to be less noise in the town'. In the meantime Edwards'
regular ministry was continued and the work of the pulpit still
received his first attention. A sermon on 1 Peter 3.19, 20 in June
1749 was as impressive as any that he had preached during the
Great Awakening. The 'doctrine' of the sermon was, 'Those
wicked men who lived before the flood, and went to Hell in
Noah's time, are still there'.[1] Edwards noted a change in
thought during the summer among some of the young and 'two
or three instances of hopeful conversion' (1.cxxii). It was
probably these persons, and perhaps some others, who were the
occasion of more controversy in October 1749. Several persons,
says Edwards, not yet in the church, now privately made a
credible profession of godliness and wished to become communicants.

Edwards, who had the support of the church for a Fast Day
to be held on Thursday October 26th ('to pray to God that he
would have mercy on this church . . . that he would forgive the
sins of both minister and people . . . '), asked that the three

---

[1] Edwards' notes of this sermon are printed in Grosart, *op. cit.*, pp. 203–9.

local ministers who were invited for the services of that day should advise on 'the admission of such persons as are able and willing to make a credible profession of true godliness'. This was proposed only as a temporary solution 'until our present unhappy controversies can be brought to an issue'. Strong objection was made to such a step in a church meeting and Edwards' opponents now introduced the debate into the Precinct meeting (the town meeting) where it was at once urged that a separation should be sought between Edwards and the church if he failed to give up his principles. In a short time this became an approved resolution, in Edwards' words, 'That, if I persist in my principles, I ought not to continue the Pastor of this Church'.

As a minister could not be dismissed without the judgment of Council, the calling and composition of such a Council soon became another major subject of controversy. Edwards believed that it would be premature for a Council to be convened because the church had as yet neither heard nor read his convictions and that, until they had done so, there should not be any decision on a separation. All he asked was for a 'fair hearing' of his answer to the question, 'whether any adult persons but such as are in profession and appearance endowed with the Christian grace or piety, ought to be admitted to the Christian sacraments' (1.434).

Edwards' complaint that he had not been heard was well grounded. His friend Colonel Dwight who had carried the copies of a *Humble Inquiry* from Boston reported that only twenty copies were sold in Northampton. Relating this in his Journal, Edwards proceeds:

Many of those who might have read even these, have showed an utter aversion to reading it. One of my most strenuous opposers declares that the people are in no way to be informed of the reasons of my opinion for two years to come; while others have asserted that they are never likely to be generally informed. Numerous witnesses declare that some have altogether refused to read it, and that others have said that they would not even let the book come into their houses. . . . Before the publication of my pamphlet, they would not consent that I should preach, on the ground that it was best I should publish; and now I have published, they will not read.

[320]

The above words occur in a lengthy statement which Edwards made to a Council of local ministers which convened at Northampton on December 26, 1749. He concluded his statement:

The laws of nature, and the laws of Christ, require me to love this people, to whom I have been so related, and to value their charity and esteem. I have reason also to think, that there are many of my spiritual children, who are God's dear children, in this congregation, who now entertain hard thoughts on account of my opinion. Now I ought not to be driven from hence, without opportunity to exhibit a testimony for myself before them, and so with the people at large.

The next morning Edwards delivered to the Council a statement basically the same as his promise made to the Church Committee the previous April. Abandoning any hope that his book would be read, and perhaps having some doubts whether the contents were too taxing for the ordinary reader,[1] Edwards now asked the Council to advise the people to 'hear me deliver the reasons of my opinion from the pulpit' and to lay aside all further public agitation until the Spring. At that time, he said, if the controversy was unresolved, a further Council should be called, and if it failed to secure any accommodation, and the people declared their unwillingness that he should continue as pastor, 'I will resign my pastoral office'.

There was only one new element in Edwards' proposal. As the weight of ministerial opinion in Hampshire County (from which the Council was formed) was clearly against him, he asked both that he should have an equal hand in the choice of a future Council and that he should be allowed to 'go out of the county into the other parts of New England for my choice'.

But Edwards' main request, that the Council advise the people to hear him preach, was not granted. The Williams family were known (among the ministers at least) to be against that procedure, alleging that it would 'make for parties'. Thus December 1749 ended as it had begun. Edwards wrote to his friend Joseph Bellamy on December 6th:

Things are in great confusion: the tumult is vastly greater than when

---

[1] Referring to his book, Edwards says, 'My people complain, many of them, that on this subject they cannot understand me'.

you was here, and is rising higher and higher continually. The people have got their resentments up to a great height. . . . There have been abundance of meetings about our affairs since you was here, society meetings, and church meetings, and meetings – of Committees, of Committees of the Parish and Committees of the Church, Conferences, Debates, Reports, and Proposals drawn up, and Replies and Remonstrances. . . . I have been openly reproached in Church meetings, as apparently regarding my own temporal interest more than the honour of Christ and the good of the Church.

> You may easily be sensible, dear sir, that this is a time of great trial with me, and that I stand in continual need of the divine presence and merciful conduct in such a state of things as this. I need God's counsel in every step I take and every word I speak; as all that I do and say is watched by the multitude around me with the utmost strictness and with eyes of the greatest uncharitableness and severity, and let me do or say what I will, my words and actions are represented in dark colours, and the state of things is come to that, that they seem to think it greatly concerns them to blacken me and represent me in odious colours to the world to justify their own conduct – they seem to be sensible that now their character can't stand unless it be on the ruin of mine. They have publickly voted that they will have no more sacraments; and they have no way to justify themselves in that but to represent me as very bad. I therefore desire, dear sir, your fervent prayers to God. If He be for me, who can be against me? If He be with me, I need not fear ten thousands of the people. But I know myself unworthy of his presence and help, yet would humbly trust in his infinite grace and all sufficience.[1]

When the same Council as met in December re-convened on February 7, 1750, the main debate was first over the composition of a future Council which would decide the issue. Then once more the question was raised by Edwards, 'Whether it was the duty of my people to hear the reasons of my opinion from the pulpit'. All along Edwards emphasized that the one reason he had not exercised his right to preach on the issue was for the sake of peace. 'The state of the people has been most obviously such, that, if I had taken any opportunity on the Sabbath, without their previous consent, it would have been the occasion of tumult on that holy day, to the extreme dishonour of Christ, and wounding the interests of religion . . .

[1] *Jonathan Edwards, Representative Selections*, Clarence H. Faust and T. H. Johnson, 1962, pp. 387–89.

I thought it the most prudent course to wait for a more favourable opportunity.'[1]

It was in the interests of securing a calm hearing that Edwards now again asked for the support of the Council, but once more they failed to give it. Reporting this critical juncture, Edwards writes:

I then made a declaration before the members of the Council, and also in the presence of the Committee of the Church, to the following purpose: 'I judge that there is a great prospect of our controversy issuing in a separation between Pastor and People; and, on long and mature consideration, I have determined that I cannot leave this people, without first making trial, *Whether my people will hear me give the reasons of my opinion from the pulpit*, unless I am advised to the contrary by a Council'.

Put this way Council members were in difficulty. Clearly they did not want to be placed in the position of silencing Edwards, nor did they want to approve his proposal. It was expedient that they should leave such a controversial decision for him to take alone. Accordingly they offered him no guidance either way,

Upon which I declared, That I judged that I had a right to preach on the subject on the Sabbath; but, that I might do it in the way which would least offend, I should first make trial whether my people would hear me on Lectures appointed for that end, and that I proposed to have my first Lecture the next Thursday, Feb 15, at 2 o'clock, p.m.; and, if I found that my people would not hear me on Lecture days, I would reserve liberty to myself to do it on the Sabbath.

Matters were now at their head. The meeting house was packed by the early afternoon of the following Thursday; even the justices of the County Court, then sitting in Northampton, adjourning their proceedings to attend the Lecture – much to the annoyance of Israel Williams, the Clerk of the Court. From the pulpit, however, Edwards saw a congregation widely different from his normal Sunday attendance: 'My first lecture was thinly attended by [my] own people, but there were present a very great number of strangers'. Angry that Edwards was being heard by some, two of his chief opponents, Deacons

[1] *Life of President Edwards*, p. 362.

Noah Cook and Ebenezer Pomeroy,[1] tried to get a church meeting held after church the next Sunday. When Edwards refused to call a meeting they, and others, appealed to the ministers of the Hampshire Association, in a letter addressed to Chester Williams, minister of Hadley. Professing alarm at the tone of this communication, Williams urged the attendance of the ministers at his house the next Thursday:

> I hope you will come, for you can't easily think what posture things are in. And unless we do not concert some measures, we are in danger of being overrun; and Northampton will proceed to extreme measures, being conducted by some gentlemen not over tender of ministers or churches; which may prove of pernicious consequence to us, and all our churches.

It was a clear appeal to self-interest. Williams was suggesting that if men such as Pomeroy took things into their own hands in Northampton, there were not lacking others in the Connecticut Valley who might be encouraged to do the same whenever other church controversies arose. So the Hampshire Association men, or many of them, met in Chester Williams' parsonage in Hadley the same day that Edwards delivered his second lecture. Again, says Edwards, it was 'attended thinly by my own people, but by a great number of strangers'. Long after it was over the ministerial brethren continued their deliberations at the Hadley parsonage. The next day, Edwards notes, 'after long considerations, they broke up and did nothing'.

*　　　*　　　*

Edwards gave five Thursday lectures in all on the communion question, his opponents – lacking any intervention from the County ministers – deciding to give their minister the opportunity for which he had asked. For most of them it could scarcely have been called a 'hearing'. Impatiently they waited for Edwards to announce a church meeting on the first Sunday after his last lecture. This he did on Sunday March 25,

[1] Except for John Clark (ordained 1730, died 1768) these men were now the only deacons. Stephen Wright, ordained with them in 1739, appears to have left Northampton in 1740. Ebenezer Wright (ordained 1704) had died in 1748.

appointing a meeting for 1 o'clock the next day. The meeting quickly proved that the lectures had achieved little. When Edwards asked for those 'who were of the same principles on which the Church had proceeded in their former practice' to show it by raising their hands 'it appeared that there was a great majority still of those principles'. Much discussion then followed on the decisive Council which had to be called. But Edwards, knowing well the situation in Hampshire County, would agree to proceed to a Council only if he were free to choose half the members of the Council and three of these from outside the County. This latter proviso was refused by a majority vote. 'After some discourse,' writes Edwards, 'I told them that I stood ready to yield to have but two of the Council from abroad, unless the Council consisted of more than ten'. Adjourned, the meeting continued the next day with Major Seth Pomeroy putting fresh pressure on Edwards and the meeting again voting not to allow any members of the Council 'from abroad'.[1] With no consent possible, Edwards proposed to dissolve the meeting, whereupon 'there was much earnest talk about the power of the Church to act without me, and to call a Council themselves'.

The meeting ended with greater disorder in the meeting-house than had ever been seen before. This was on March 27th 1750. At the next meeting on April 16th the result was precisely the same, 109 voted against allowing any members from outside the County, with fifty-six for it. During these weeks the turmoil was incessant. Meetings of the Precinct, and committees of the Precinct (with Major Pomeroy active in them all) carried on independently of Edwards. To Thomas Gillespie, Edwards wrote on April 2: 'I have had no leisure or opportunity to write by reason of my peculiar and very extraordinary circumstances. . . . This controversy, in the progress of it, has proved not only a controversy between me and my people, but between me and a great part of New England; there being many far and near who are warmly engaged in it.'

On April 17, 1750 (the day after the last Church meeting

[1]'The people,' Edwards writes, 'insisted that the Council should be wholly of the neighbourhood, undoubtedly because they supposed themselves most sure that their judgment and advice would be favourable and agreeable to them . . . the neighbouring ministers were all youngerly men.'

mentioned above) Edwards had to leave Northampton for 'a journey down the country'. This gave the opposition opportunity to hold two church meetings in Edwards' absence, Major Pomeroy being voted Moderator. Yet another committee was appointed by the Church and when it failed to obtain any agreement there was, at last, an acceptance of the condition for which Edwards had asked a month earlier, namely, that two ministers or churches out of the proposed Council might be chosen from outside Hampshire. This was finally agreed at a church meeting over which Edwards presided on May 3rd and with his account of that meeting Edwards' journal on the controversy suddenly breaks off. Perhaps he judged that the outcome was so well-known that nothing further was required by way of a record.

The decisive Council met in Northampton on June 19, 1750, and terminated on June 22 after pronouncing its majority-decision that the pastoral relation between Edwards and his people should be dissolved. Each church represented at the Council, sent its minister and one messenger. But one church within the County which Edwards had asked to represent his interests declined to do so, though the minister himself, Jonathan Billing, attended in a private capacity and was allowed to vote. As each messenger voted in the same way as his minister, if Billing had been accompanied by a messenger the Council would have been exactly divided, for all five churches nominated by the congregation voted one way, and the four, plus one minister, nominated by Edwards, the other. The vote of the Church itself, however, was by no means so evenly balanced, as Edwards informs John Erskine. It is evident from his letter of July 5, 1750, that his young cousin, Joseph Hawley, took over the lead role in presenting the Church's case to the Council:

The people, in managing this affair on their side, have made chief use of a young gentleman of liberal education and notable abilities, and a fluent speaker, of about seven or eight and twenty years of age, my grandfather Stoddard's grandson, being my mother's sister's son; a man of lax principles in religion, falling in, in some essential things, with Arminians, and is very open and bold in it. He was approved as one of the agents for the church, and was their chief spokesman before the council. He very strenuously urged before the council the

[326]

necessity of an immediate separation; and I knowing the church, the most of them, to be inflexibly bent on this event, informed the council that I should not enter into the dispute, but should refer the matter wholly to the council's judgment; I signified, that I had no desire to leave my people, on any other consideration, any other than their aversion to my being their minister any longer. . . . When the church was convened, in order to the council's knowing their minds with respect to my continuance, about twenty-three appeared for it, others staid away, choosing not to act either way; but the generality of the church, which consists of about 230 male members, voted for my dismission. My dismission was carried in the council by a majority of one voice. (1.cxx)

The minority in the Council entered a protest, particularly against the hastiness of the people, and, says Hopkins, 'some of that part of the Council who were for the separation, expressed themselves surprised at the uncommon zeal manifested by the people in their voting for a dismission'. But the deed was done. David Hall, a member of the Council who was sympathetic to Edwards, noted in his diary Edwards' reaction to the decision:

That faithful witness received the shock, unshaken. I never saw the least symptoms of displeasure in his countenance the whole week but he appeared like a man of God, whose happiness was out of the reach of his enemies and whose treasure was not only a future but a present good, overbalancing all imaginable ills of life, even to the astonishment of many who could not be at rest without his dismission.

How far the inability of any female communicants to vote affected the outcome cannot, of course, be determined. Timothy Dwight regarded the spirituality of New England female communicants as putting 'our own sex to shame' and certainly in Northampton, as elsewhere, their numbers exceeded the male communicants. He writes, 'were the church of Christ stripped of her female communicants, she would lose many of her brightest ornaments, and, I fear, two thirds of her whole family'.[1]

On July 1, 1750, nine days after the Council had dispersed, Edwards preached his 'Farewell Sermon'. The text was 2 Corinthians 1.14, 'As also ye have acknowledged us in part, that we are your rejoicing, even as ye also are our's in the day of

---

[1] *Travels*, 4, p. 474.

the Lord Jesus'. Even in cold print at this distant date it is a moving sermon and the reader can well understand why Edwards could report of its reception: 'Many in the congregation seemed to be much affected, and some are exceedingly grieved. Some few, I believe, have some relentings of heart that voted me away.' In the course of the sermon, which directed attention far more to the concerns of eternity than to those of time, Edwards said:

It was three and twenty years, the 15th day of last February, since I have laboured in the work of the ministry in the relation of a pastor to this church and congregation . . . I have spent the prime of my life and strength in labours for your eternal welfare. You are my witnesses that what strength I have had, I have not neglected in idleness, nor laid out in prosecuting worldly schemes, and managing temporal affairs, for the advancement of my outward estate and aggrandizing myself and family; but have given myself to the work of the ministry, labouring in it night and day, rising early, and applying myself to this great business to which Christ has appointed me. . . .

How exceeding beautiful, and how conducive to the adorning and happiness of the town, if the young people could be persuaded, when they meet together, to converse as Christians and as the children of God. This is what I have longed for: and it has been exceedingly grievous to me when I have heard of vice, vanity and disorder among our youth. And so far as I know my heart, it was from hence that I formerly led this church to some measures, for the suppressing of vice among our young people, which gave so great offence and by which I became so obnoxious. . . .

A contentious people will be a miserable people. The contentions which have been among you, since I first became your pastor, have been one of the greatest burdens I have laboured under in the course of my ministry – not only the contentions you have had with me, but those which you have had one with another, about your lands and other concerns – because I knew that contention, heat of spirit, evil speaking, and things of the like nature, were directly contrary to the spirit of Christianity and did, in a peculiar manner, tend to drive away God's Spirit from a people. . . .

Let the late contention about the terms of Christian communion, as it has been the greatest, be the last. I would, now I am preaching my farewell sermon, say to you, as the apostle to the Corinthians, 2 Cor. 13.11: 'Finally, brethren, farewell. Be perfect, be of one mind, live in peace; and the God of love and peace shall be with you.'

May God bless you with a faithful pastor, one that is well

acquainted with his mind and will, thoroughly warning sinners, wisely and skilfully searching professors and conducting you in the way to eternal blessedness. . . .

And let me be remembered in the prayers of all God's people that are of a calm spirit, and are peaceable and faithful in Israel, of whatever opinion they may be with respect to terms of church communion. And let us all remember, and never forget our future solemn meeting on that great day of the Lord; the day of infallible decision and of the everlasting and unalterable sentence. Amen. (1.cxcviii ff)

Edwards' 'Farewell Sermon' gives us a vivid impression of his character. He does not hide from his people that he had been plunged 'into an abyss of trouble and sorrow', yet his words are singularly free of blame or accusation. His notebooks indicate that he had first done some preparation on a different text for this occasion, namely, Jeremiah 25.3, where the prophet speaks of twenty-three years of ministry (the precise time of Edwards' own at Northampton) and concludes, 'but ye have not hearkened'. This text Edwards laid aside, mentioning it only briefly in the sermon which he did preach, leaving unquoted the rebuke with which the verse ends, and assuring the people, 'I am not about to compare myself with the prophet Jeremiah'.

As a young Christian Edwards had prayed for the graces of patience and gentleness. 'A wonderful calmness of mind' was one of the traits which he had admired in his future wife in 1723. Now that calmness shone in Edwards. In his last official duty to his flock it is *their* needs rather than his own which are uppermost in his mind as he longs that they and he, 'now parting one from another as to this world . . . may not be parted after our meeting at the last day'. No congregation was ever spoken to more tenderly than the people of Northampton on July 1, 1750. Some, at least, as they made their way sadly home that summer's morning, would have thanked God for the grace which they *saw* in their former pastor. Unconsciously he exemplified what he had told them years before – the real Christian is the 'tallest and strongest saint, but the least and tenderest child among them'.

BEHIND THE CONTROVERSY

*Memorial plaque by Herbert Adams erected in the First
Church of Christ, Northampton, in 1900. Edwards'
church stood until the early 1800's. It was followed
by another in 1812. When this was destroyed by fire
in 1876 the present building of the First Church was
erected on a new site in Main Street.*

It is most evident, that godly reforming divines have in their doctrine *unanimously* taught, and in their practice (many of them) endeavoured, a *strict selection* of those who should be admitted to the Lord's supper.

JONATHAN MITCHEL (1624–64) quoted by
Thomas Foxcroft, 1749, J E (1: p. 482)

The question in controversy, between Mr Edwards and his people, was one of vital importance to the purity and prosperity of the Christian Church. Wherever the lax method of admission has prevailed, all distinction between the church and the world has soon ceased, and both have been blended together. This question had never been thoroughly examined; and it needed some mind of uncommon power, to exhibit the truth with regard to it, in a light too strong to be ultimately resisted.

SERENO E. DWIGHT
Life of President Edwards, p. 445

The letting go this principle, particular churches ought to consist of regenerate persons, brought in the great apostasy of the Christian Church.

JOHN OWEN

17

Even though he saw it coming, and could speak so calmly in his Farewell Sermon, Edwards was undoubtedly shocked by the strangeness and the finality of his dismissal. Five days after that sermon he wrote to William M'Culloch in Scotland: 'I am now separated from the people between whom and me there was once the greatest union. Remarkable is the providence of God in this matter. In this event we have a striking instance of the instability and uncertainty of all things here below' (1.cxxii).

While Edwards finally resolved his dismissal in terms of the overruling providence of God, his theology of providence did not lead him to ignore 'second causes'. There were *reasons* for what had happened, some of which he himself records.

In the first instance, he was convinced that his opponents had achieved considerable success in misrepresenting and confusing the question at issue. From the outset of the disputes when he proposed to a candidate for communion that his public profession of faith should include the words, 'That he believed the truth of the gospel with all his heart,' he reports that, 'many of the people cried out that this amounted to a profession of absolute perfection' (1.491 fn.). In the Preface to the published version of his Farewell Sermon, Edwards speaks of 'gross misrepresentations' which had been 'abundantly and industriously made': 'such as . . . that I have undertaken to set up a pure church, and to make an exact and certain distinction between saints and hypocrites' (1.cxcviii). In the sixteenth century the Elizabethan separatist, Robert Browne, had been charged with the theory that the church consists only of the regenerate, and with proposing such high tests for admission as would effectively exclude all others. This same view seems to have been revived by the New England separatists but it was one which Edwards constantly denied.

In his Preface to his *Humble Inquiry* he rejects the separatists' 'notion of a "pure church" by means of "a spirit of discerning"' (1.432). He believed as firmly as the Westminster divines that 'The purest churches under heaven are subject both to mixture and error', and that to be *sure* of an individual's regeneration is no part of a minister's duty. Accordingly, stating the real point at issue in the controversy on qualifications for communion, he writes:

The question is not, whether Christ has made converting grace *itself* the condition or rule of his people's admitting any to the privileges of members in full communion with them. . . . It is the credible *profession* that is the church's rule. . . . God has given those who are to admit persons no *certain rule*, whereby they may know whether they [i.e. candidates for communion] believe or [have] any inward moral qualification whatsoever. These things have all their existence in the soul, which is out of our neighbour's view. Not therefore a certainty, but a profession and visibility of these things, must be the rule of the church's proceeding (1.434–5, 469).

Similarly, Edwards says that a minister may have 'suspicions and fears' about a particular candidate for communion and yet have no sufficient ground to debar him from membership. Or again, an individual may have no assurance about his own salvation and yet be received 'however he himself might scruple his own conversion' (1.488). He denies as a falsehood the claim that he 'insisted on persons being assured of their being in a state of salvation in order to my admitting them into the church' (1.cxcviii).

But notwithstanding these, and many other similar statements, when Solomon Williams took the role of the defender of the church's action at Northampton, and the upholder of Stoddard's reputation, by answering his cousin in *The True State of the Question concerning the Qualifications necessary to Lawful*

Communion in the Christian Sacraments, he built a large part of his case on the very misrepresentation which Edwards had already repudiated.

Williams argued that a profession of godliness had *always* been required for membership at Northampton but that the change which Edwards had sought had to do with the *degree* of evidence for the 'saintship' of those admitted. 'Mr Edwards seems to suppose', he wrote, that it 'must be the *highest* evidence a man can give' (1.488). Edwards was subsequently to reply to this with a sharpness which suggests that he believed Solomon Williams was deliberately distorting the position. 'Mr W. is bold to suggest that what I insist on, is a *certainty* of others' regeneration. . . . He is abundant, from one end of his book to the other, in representing as though I insisted on judging men *by their inward and spiritual experiences*' (1.490). On the contrary, says Edwards, 'I freely grant, and show abundantly in my book, it is never to be expected that all unsanctified men can be kept out, by the most exact attendance on the rules of Christ, by those that admit members' (1.511).

Although it was much too late to affect the issue, Edwards was to re-assert against Williams the real question which occasioned the controversy. Reminding Williams that he had himself admitted three-quarters of the present Northampton membership, and had been acquainted with every member admitted by Stoddard who had been alive in the previous twenty-three years, he insists that a profession of godliness was *not* the norm at Northampton. Williams had mis-stated both Stoddard's view and the practice which had long existed. Writing two years after his dismissal, Edwards says:

The controversy was, Whether there was any need of making *a credible profession of godliness* in order to persons being admitted to full communion; whether they must *profess having faith*, or whether *a profession of common faith* were not sufficient; whether persons must be *esteemed truly godly*, and must be taken in under that notion, or whether if they *appeared morally sincere*, that were not sufficient?. . . There was no suggestion that the dispute was only about *the degree of evidence*, but what was the thing to be made evident, whether *real godliness* or *moral sincerity* (1.487).

So the issue was not whether the unregenerate would sometimes still be admitted. On occasions they would, as Edwards agreed, but it must not be with the church's cognisance. Persons should no more be permitted to make the kind of broad profession which was *designed* to allow the entrance of the unregenerate. The mode of admission to New Testament churches, Edwards argued, was not designed to permit the entrance of the unsanctified. '*Natural* and *graceless* men were not admitted designedly, but *unawares*' (1.453). Church members, in the New Testament are addressed as persons who, in the judgment of charity, possessed a 'visibility of godliness'. No such judgment had been required in Northampton. The customary, long-established, public profession had ceased 'to be of the nature of any profession of gospel faith and repentance' (1.cxcix).

Probably the very length of Edwards' writings on qualifications for communion did not encourage readers and thus contributed to a continued misunderstanding. More than a hundred years later even such a theologian as Charles Hodge is still to be found charging Edwards with the principles of 'the Brownists'. Hodge alleges that Edwards confuses two 'very different' things, namely, to profess to be a Christian and to be, in the judgment of the church, godly.[1] But Edwards is not confused. His whole case is that the church must not allow a separation between a profession of Christ and conduct which supports that profession, because a profession of the *essence* of Christianity which should be required of candidates *includes* such truths as repentance and gospel holiness. If the church accepts a profession from those who evidently 'live still under the reigning power of the love of the world' it nullifies its meaning. 'Piety of heart, in the more essential things belonging to it, is as clearly revealed as the doctrines concerning the nature of God, the person of the Messiah, and the method of his redemption' (1.448). To the response that a man's opinions can be tested but his heart cannot be, Edwards would say that actions do reveal something about a man's will and his heart. Professing Christ implies being subject to him in practice, it entails the promise of universal obedience to him.

---

[1] *Systematic Theology*, vol. 3, 1873, p. 569. The same misrepresentation continues today. David Harlan, for instance, writes, 'Edwards tottering on the brink of separation, pleaded his vision of a pure church.' *The Clergy and the Great Awakening in New England*, 1980, p. 93.

Truly pious persons . . . submit to the *laws* and *orders* of Christ's <
school, such as, *to love their Master supremely; to love one another as brethren;*
and *to love their book*, i.e. their Bible, more than vain trifles and
amusements, yea, above gold and silver; to be faithful to the interest of
the Master. . . . (1.461).

There are two competitors for the kingdom of this world, Christ and
Satan; the design of a public profession of religion is to declare on
which side men are. And is it agreeable to the custom of mankind in
such cases, to make laws that no other than ambiguous words shall be
used or to accept of such in declarations of this kind? There are two
competitors for the kingdom of Great Britain, King George and the
Pretender: is it the constitution of King George and the British
Parliament that men should take oaths of allegiance, contrived in
words of indeterminate signification, to the end that men who are in
their hearts enemies to King George, and friends to the Pretender,
may use them and speak true? (1.497–8).

As we have seen, Edwards accepts a distinction between
profession and reality, a distinction which takes into account
the difference between the 'apparent probability' and 'the
certainty' that a communicant is a Christian. But he will not
accept a legitimate distinction between 'professing Christ' and
'professing godliness'. 'None profess to be on Christ's side, but
they who profess to renounce his rivals'. To profess Christ is to
profess to be on his side, it is to profess to prefer him to the world
and self (1.448). Whoever therefore regards Christ rightly, even
supposing he still lacks assurance of his own salvation, will
show by his life whether his profession is credible.[1] Godliness is
not first of all a matter of speech, and therefore in accepting a
profession of godliness the church must be concerned with
more than speech. 'I call that a profession of godliness which is
a profession of the great things wherein godliness consists, and
not a profession of his own opinion of his good estate' (1.488).

---

[1]Hodge himself says, 'It is impossible that the faith which this sacrament
demands should exist in the heart without producing supreme love and
gratitude to Christ, and the fixed purpose to forsake all sin and to live devoted
to his service' (*Ibid.*, p. 624). Hodge's real difference with Edwards seems to
be over the extent to which the church should attempt to receive only true
believers to the Lord's Table. He repeats with approval the words of Paraeus,
'In church reformation, 'tis an observable truth that those that are for too
much strictness, do more hurt than profit the Church' (*Ibid.*, p. 572). This was
not, however, the danger in Edwards' situation.

Edwards had thus come to a position in which he was certain in his own mind of the biblical teaching. Through the fallibility of men, the unconverted might enter apostolic churches but the public profession of Christ in the New Testament is not designed to accommodate the worldly and the lukewarm. And no such lax profession is 'worth regarding', rather it is 'a mere sham of a solemn public profession of Christianity, and seems to be wholly without warrant from the word of God, and greatly to his dishonour' (1.448).

The extent to which Edwards was misrepresented was undoubtedly a major factor in the outcome of the controversy.

*　　*　　*

In further explaining the action of the Northampton church against their pastor, it has to be observed that Edwards' proposal that there should be visible evidence of godliness in communicants was bound to be offensive to the unconverted who were already members. A lowered standard of admission had existed for too long for any change to be implemented without trouble. In the words of Dwight: 'The lax mode of admitting members into the church had prevailed about forty-five years, and though both Mr Stoddard and Mr Edwards had been most desirous of the prevalence of vital religion in the church, yet, a wide door having been thrown open for the admission of unconverted members, *as such*, it cannot but have been the fact, that, during this long period, many unconverted members should, through that door, have actually obtained admission into the church. . . . The consequences of Mr Stoddard's error fell with all their weight on *his own grandson*.'[1]

All the evidence supports this conclusion. Real grace in the congregation was not as great as many supposed, nor even as great as Edwards had once supposed. Thus, in addressing the congregation in which nearly all adults and some younger people were members,[2] he could say in his Farewell Sermon, 'I have reason to fear I leave multitudes in this large congregation in a Christless state' (1.ccv).

[1] *Life*, pp. 308, 447.
[2] Dwight puts the membership figure at this date at 'more than seven hundred', p. 433.

In attempting to change the long-established practice on admission Edwards was bound to have the opposition of unconverted communicants, for a change on this point would be the equivalent of a rejection of their legitimate status as church members. It would, as Dwight says, be tantamount to asking them 'to relinquish the only resting place, which human ingenuity had discovered, in which an unconverted person might – for a time at least – remain unconverted, both securely and lawfully'.[1]

Ola Winslow is surely right in drawing a parallel between the opposition aroused by Whitefield in 1740 and by Edwards in 1749. 'Whitefield's greatest mistake, in terms of his own popularity, had been his attempt to purify the ministry. To attempt to purify the membership was to invite mutiny'.[2]

The above remarks, however, need to be qualified. It would not be true to suggest that the majority of those who opposed Edwards were unbelievers. Such an interpretation would necessarily imply the worthlessness of the many conversions both in the revival of 1735 and at other times. That supposition does not trouble modern writers who frequently affirm it both as a fact, and as a fact which Edwards himself came to acknowledge. Edwards' biographer, H. B. Parkes writes, 'The majority of the conversions had not, he freely confessed, been true conversions'.[3] And Patricia J. Tracy repeats the same, 'By now, of course, he knew that most of those conversions had not been genuine'.[4] This misrepresents Edwards. Possibly his last expressed view of the year 1735 in Northampton, written as late as 1751, was that it saw a 'very glorious work of God': 'there were numerous instances of saving conversion; though undoubtedly many were deceived and deceived others; and the number of true converts was not so great as was then imagined' (1.cxxxiii).[5]

[1] *Ibid.*, p. 307.
[2] *Jonathan Edwards*, p. 243.
[3] *Jonathan Edwards*, p. 170.
[4] *Jonathan Edwards, Pastor*, 1980, p. 174.
[5] Speaking of the whole of New England, and of the 'awakened' rather than of professed converts, Edwards writes in 1752, 'How small a proportion are there of the vast multitude, that in the time of the late religious commotion through the land had their consciences awakened, who give hopeful abiding evidences of a saving conversion to God' (1.504 *fn*).

Not a little of the pain Edwards must have felt was caused by the opposition of Christians who, in the words of Hopkins, once 'looked upon it as one of their greatest privileges to have such a minister, and manifested their great love and esteem of him'. Many of them undoubtedly believed what they had for so long regarded as biblical, namely, that the Lord's Supper may be a means of grace to the unconverted, and they therefore saw Edwards' proposed change for admission to the Table as something which might be a serious spiritual loss – a loss equivalent to any proposal to remove the right of baptism from their children. As a nineteenth-century editor of Edwards writes, 'A false principle, therefore, betrayed them into warmth and obstinacy of opposition, rather than a deliberate love of sin, or a total want of respect to their minister'. This interpretation has Edwards' support. It was because he believed that he was dealing, in part, with a misunderstanding that he was so much concerned that his arguments should be heard by his people. This was the reason why he had told the Council of local ministers in December 1749, that the supposition that 'most of the leading men in the Church' had read his book was not enough. He wanted more, because 'the controversy on this subject is between me and the Church, and not between me and the leading men of the Church'.

There is little doubt that the existing prejudices of tradition, backed by the misrepresentations stirred up by leaders in the Church and some whom Edwards calls 'crafty designing men', account for the sad way in which many Christians acted. 'The great power of prejudices from education, established custom, and the traditions of ancestors and certain admired teachers, and the exceeding unhappy influence of bigotry, has remarkably appeared in the management of this affair' (1.cxix). Persuasive leaders in the Church, 'professors of religion yet not the most famed for piety . . . used their utmost endeavours to engage the minds of the common people in this controversy'. Still more significant in Edwards' judgment was the influence from without: 'My opposers have also been assisted and edged on by some at a great distance, persons of note . . . ' (1.cxxxiii); 'There are many in the neighbouring towns to support their resolution, both in the ministry and civil magistracy, without whose influence I believe the people never would have been so violent as they have been'. Some were so confused, he says, that, 'without check of conscience', they came 'to look on their zeal against me as virtue' (1.cxxxiii).

Certainly the whole controversy is striking evidence of the fallibility of Christians and of Churches. 'Of all unsafe places for truth to live and breathe,' says one writer, 'the excitement of good men is one of the most unsafe'.[1]

*   *   *

Edwards' fundamental explanation of what had happened was that God had permitted such weaknesses in order to expose the evil of spiritual pride:

The people have, from the beginning, been well instructed; having had a name, for a long time, for a very knowing people; and many have appeared among them, persons of good abilities; and many, born in the town, have been promoted to places of public trust: they have been a people distinguished on this account. These things have been manifestly abused to nourish the pride of their natural temper, which had made them more difficult and unmanageable. . . . In latter times, the people have had more to feed their pride. They have grown a much greater and more wealthy people than formerly, and are become more extensively famous in the world, as a people that have excelled in gifts and grace, and had God extraordinarily among them; which has insensibly engendered and nourished spiritual pride, that grand inlet of the devil in the hearts of men, and avenue of all manner of mischief among a professing people. Spiritual pride is a most monstrous thing. If it be not discerned, and vigorously opposed, in the beginning, it very often soon raises persons above their teachers, and supposed spiritual fathers, and sets them out of the reach of all rule and instruction, as I have seen in innumerable instances. And there is this inconvenience, attending the publishing of narratives of a work of God among a people, (such is the corruption that is in the hearts of men, and even of good men,) and there is great danger of their making it an occasion of spiritual pride. There is great reason to think that the Northampton people have provoked God greatly against them, by trusting in their privileges and attainments. And the consequences may well be a warning to all God's people, far and near, that hear of

---

[1] Dr John Todd in *The Memorial Volume of the Edwards Family Meeting, 1870*, 1871, p. 128. In Dwight's *Life*, pp. 346–7, there are valuable words of Edwards on the power of religious prejudice.

them (1.cxxxi).[1]

This is not to say that Edwards attributed all the blame for the separation to the people. He was ready to speak of his own failure. One failure, in particular, on his part, has been persistently mentioned by later writers. During Edwards' twenty-three years at Northampton, given his practice, already mentioned, not 'to visit his people in their own houses unless he was sent for by the sick', it was inevitable that he should appear more remote and more absorbed in study than is usual among parish ministers. In the eyes of some, he dwelt apart as though he had no time for the common, everyday interests of his people. This certainly lent itself at the time of the communion controversy to the charge that he was 'stiff and unsociable'. It should, however, be remembered that at this period 'the minister rarely visited'[2] and it is interesting to note that Hopkins – his only biographer who was an eye-witness – does not criticize Edwards at this point although he draws attention to the matter. Edwards' practice, Hopkins asserts, was not due to any disinterest towards his people – 'they had a great interest in *his* affection . . . for their good he was always writing, contriving, labouring; for them he had poured out ten thousand fervent prayers; and they were dear to him above any other people under heaven' (1.cxxiv). His custom with regard to visitation was a considered decision, arrived at in the light of his own gifts and circumstances. Hopkins writes:

He did not neglect visiting his people from house to house because he did not look upon it, in ordinary cases, to be one part of the work of the Gospel minister. But he supposed that ministers should, with respect to this, consult their own talents and circumstances, and visit more or less, according to the degree in which they could hope hereby to promote the great ends of the Gospel ministry. He observed that some ministers had a talent at entertaining and profiting by

---

[1] In a valuable letter on 'Is it a fact that faithful parochial Ministers, as they advance in Life, frequently lose the Esteem they had obtained, and decline in apparent Usefulness?' Thomas Scott argues that one reason why this occurs is that 'many pious and even eminent ministers have so humoured and indulged their people, as to render them captious, self-conceited, and ready to take offence at every faithful and needful reproof and expostulation'. *Letters and Papers of Thomas Scott*, Ed. John Scott, 1824, p. 315.

[2] Webster, p. 535.

occasional visits among their people. They have words at will, and a knack at introducing profitable, religious discourse in a free, natural, and, as it were undesigned way. He supposed such had a call to spend a great deal of their time in visiting their people. But he looked on his talents to be quite otherwise. He was not able to enter into a free conversation with every person he met with, and in an easy manner turn it to what topic he pleased, without the help of others. . . . And as he was settled in a great town, it would take up a great part of his time to visit from house to house, which he thought he could spend in his study to much more valuable purposes. . . . It appeared to him, that he could do the greatest good to souls, and most promote the interest of Christ by preaching and writing, and conversing with persons under religious impressions in his study, where he encouraged all such to repair.[1]

There is no indication that Edwards himself ever considered that he had been wrong in this decision. He saw his deficiency as a limitation in his gifts rather than as a moral fault. The failures with which he charges himself lie elsewhere. 'God knows the sinfulness of my heart, and the great and sinful deficiencies and offences which I have been guilty of in the course of my ministry at Northampton.' In particular, he believed he had fallen seriously short in his work as a teacher. The emphasis in his sermons on *The Religious Affections* was needed earlier. He had been slow to see the danger to the Northampton people of their habit of treating the profession of a certain kind of conversion experience as a proof of a true conversion instead of looking more to 'the abiding sense and temper of their hearts'. All who professed to be Christians in Northampton believed in a *felt* religion but 'many of them never could be made to learn to distinguish between impressions on the imagination and living spiritual experience'. They were also too forward in religious talk, especially the rehearsal of their spiritual experiences 'in a light manner, without any air of solemnity.' Looking back from the vantage point of 1751 Edwards deplored his immaturity in the critical earlier years:

One thing, that has contributed to bring things to such a pass at Northampton, was my youth, and want of more judgment and experience, in the time of that extraordinary awakening, about sixteen years ago. Instead of a youth, there was want of a giant, in judgment and discretion, among a people in such an extraordinary

[1] *Life of Edwards*, 1765, p. 50.

state of things. In some respects, doubtless, my confidence in myself was a great injury to me; but in other respects my diffidence of myself injured me. It was such, that I durst not act my own judgment, and had no strength to oppose received notions, and established customs, and to testify boldly against some glaring false appearances, and counterfeits of religion, till it was too late. And by this means, as well as others, many things got footing, which have proved a dreadful source of spiritual pride, and other things that are exceedingly contrary to true Christianity. If I had had more experience, and ripeness of judgment and courage, I should have guided my people in a better manner, and should have guarded them better from Satan's devices, and prevented the spiritual calamity of many souls, and perhaps the eternal ruin of some of them; and have done what would have tended to lengthen out the tranquillity of the town (1.cxxxii).[1]

Before we leave this consideration of the reasons which lay behind Edwards' dismissal, there is at least one more factor in the church situation then existing in New England which requires notice. Edwards' problems, as we have seen, were heralded by a degree of failure in church discipline. In attempting to implement discipline within the congregation Edwards was supported by no office-bearers appointed for that purpose and accordingly he was partially isolated and exposed to the charge of possessing a 'tyrannical spirit'. Some church members believed that in asking for greater control of admission to communicant membership Edwards was aiming at investing himself with greater authority. Stoddard, as Edwards reminded them in 1749, was allowed to negative any application for communicant status, but they were unwilling to allow him the same liberty. The fact is that there was in the 1740's an unrest of far greater proportions in the churches over ministerial authority than had ever been known in Stoddard's day. But at least one factor which entered into this unrest had been foreseen. The Cambridge Platform of 1649 – a Confession of the church polity of the New England churches – laid down the need for ruling elders as essential for the normal working of a church. Yet even by the time of the Synod of 1679 it was clear that ruling elders were disappearing from the churches.

[1] Despite such admissions as the above, Norman Pettit alleges that Edwards 'was always sure of his views and never took a step that he later considered to be a mistake' J E (Yale) 7, p. 20. One can only wonder how far some editors of Edwards have actually read him.

Churches, said the 1679 Synod, were now 'generally destitute of such *Helps* in *Government*'. In Northampton, the office of ruling elder lingered until 1729 when its last representative, Ebenezer Strong, died on the same day as Solomon Stoddard. As noted earlier, the Synod of 1679 viewed the demise of eldership as a calamity, arguing that the only alternatives were that church government become 'prelatic' or 'popular'. By 'prelatic' they meant that a minister, assuming all power, would, in the later words of Cotton Mather, 'make himself a congregational pope'. To some extent occasional Councils lessened the dangers of both 'prelatic' and 'popular' authority. But it is clear that an uncertainty over ministerial authority had become built into the congregational system and the church government which had evolved was ill suited to deal with the problems which Edwards had to face in the late 1740's. Through circumstances for which he was not responsible he had to stand alone in the leadership of the congregation.

Edwards recognized the difficulty and he attempted to address himself to it.[1] For example, a sermon preached in June 1748 suggests that he saw that shared responsibility was necessary in order to achieve effective church discipline: 'It is the mind of God that not a mixed multitude but only select persons of distinguished ability and integrity are fit for the business of judging causes.' Whenever meetings of a whole church attempted to deal with such things, the practice, he believed, had been productive of 'wounds . . . contentions . . . quarrelling with their minister, quarrelling one with another'.[2] He certainly did not advocate

---

[1]He rejects as a misrepresentation the charge that 'I insisted on acting by my sole authority in the admission of members into the church' (1.cxcviii).

[2]Patricia J. Tracy, *Jonathan Edwards, Pastor*, 1980, p. 166. In his personal notes on 1 Corinthians 12.28 (which the Westminster *Form of Presbyterial Church-Government* uses as a proof text for 'Other Church-Governors') Edwards expresses the view that the gift of 'government' is not to be understood as warranting 'a distinct standing office' in the church (*Selections from the Unpublished Writings of Jonathan Edwards*, A. B. Grosart, 1865, p. 158). Dexter says that the 1679 Synod attributed the decline of the eldership to the existence of a doubt whether the New Testament appoints such an office *distinct* from the ministry of the Word. Another cause of the decline was said to be the 'inconveniences, whereunto many Churches have been plunged by Elders, not of such a Number, or not of such a Wisdom, as were desirable'. There was a 'penury of men well qualified'.

the 'popular' government which the 1679 Synod had also feared. Yet neither did he advocate a restoration of the eldership. He was, he says, 'far from supposing there ought to be such lay elders as used formerly to be in such independent churches'. There is an obscurity in Edwards' apparent position at this point, which might possibly be unravelled by a closer examination of his unpublished manuscripts. But what does seem to be clear is that in the month after this sermon, that is to say in July 1748, fifteen men were elected to assist the pastor for one year. This appears to be the body which, with their election renewed, was operative as the Church committee in 1749–50.

As far as we can judge, the operations of the Church committee were ineffective in the controversy. It was overshadowed by the Precinct meeting and acted with no more authority than is commonly accorded to committees in church matters. At the end of the day it seemed to be deacons who frequently exercised most influence, and the tangle of endless meetings of various kinds which marked the controversy indicated that the church had lost a structure designed for the maintenance of discipline within itself. Edwards must have had some reservations about the nature of the office of ruling elder within the Presbyterian Churches, but whatever these were they were not sufficient to prevent him writing to John Erskine on July 5, 1750:

You are pleased, dear Sir, very kindly to ask me, whether I could sign the Westminster Confession of Faith, and submit to the presbyterian form of church government; and to offer to use your influence to procure a call for me, to some congregation in Scotland. I should be very ungrateful, if I were not thankful for such kindness and friendship. As to my subscribing to the substance of the Westminster Confession, there would be no difficulty; and as to the presbyterian government, I have long been perfectly out of conceit of our unsettled, independent, confused way of church government in this land; and the presbyterian way has ever appeared to me most agreeable to the word of God, and the reason and nature of things; though I cannot say that I think that the presbyterian government of the church of Scotland is so perfect, that it cannot, in some respects, be mended (1.cxxi).[1]

[1] Edwards was clearly not in sympathy with the way controversy between congregationalists and presbyterians had sometimes been conducted in the previous century. 'It was, as I have heard, in those days real matter of question with some, whether a presbyterian, living and dying such, could be saved' (1.lxxvii).

*   *   *

Two things remain to be said as we conclude this summary of the controversy. First, there was never any hesitation in Edwards' mind over the serious nature of the truth involved. He came to the firm conviction that a wrong principle of admission to the Lord's Table imperils the whole nature of the church, for then the world and the church cease to be distinguished. Whenever persons are received who manifest no evidence of saving faith or of sanctifying grace, then Christians 'are obliged to receive those as their *brethren*, admit them to the *communion of saints*, and embrace them in the highest acts of Christian society . . . whom yet they have no reason to look upon otherwise than as *enemies of the Cross of Christ*' (1.478). Certainly Edwards never regretted the personal loss which he suffered on account of the controversy. He saw the opposition he incurred as deeper than mere misunderstanding. After it was all over, he wrote to Thomas Gillespie: 'I believe the devil is greatly alarmed by the opposition made to the lax doctrine of admission to the Christian church. . . . And God, for wise ends, has suffered him to exert himself, in an extraordinary manner, in opposition; as God ordinarily does, when truth is in the birth' (1.cxxxiii).

Speaking of Edwards' two works on qualifications necessary to participation in the Lord's Supper, Perry Miller writes: 'Today, the two books are the least rewarding of Edwards' works since the issue is utterly forgotten.' Forgotten perhaps, but not utterly. When the church does not bar unbelievers from her communion, and fails to keep the sacraments holy, she 'tramples her own glory in the dust' and falls to the level of the world. Such can only happen when the true nature of conversion itself is allowed to fall into obscurity. Once biblical convictions on what constitutes a true Christian are re- asserted, then the question of who participates at the Lord's Table will soon be treated with all the seriousness with which Edwards viewed it in 1749–50. Far from being a by-path in Edwards' thought, it was a direct consequence of the Great Awakening which, in Joseph Tracy's words, 'brought out and presented in bold relief, the idea, that conversion is a change ordinarily discoverable by its effects, so that he who exhibits no evidence of it, may with propriety be regarded as an unconverted man'. Such a person is unfit to be a communicant member of the Christian church.

Secondly, in this account of the controversy which ended Edwards' ministry at Northampton it needs to be noted that the last word came from the unhappy Joseph Hawley who was so prominent in the opposition. It seems that a letter from Hawley to Edwards in August 1754 (which is now lost) expressed repentance and asked for Edwards' comment on the controversy. In November 1754 Edwards replied, desiring to treat his cousin 'with true candour and Christian charity'. He also gave notice, that whatever Hawley's final thoughts, he intended to write on the subject no more: 'I have had enough of this controversy and desire to have done with it. I have spent enough of the precious time of my life in it heretofore. I desire and pray that God may enable you to view things truly, and as he views them, and so to act in the affair as shall be best for you, and most for your peace living and dying.'[1]

Hawley's sorrow was such that he was not satisfied until, in May 1760, a letter from him to Edwards' friend, David Hall, was published in a Boston newspaper. It confirmed that pride was indeed the cause of Northampton's spiritual fall:

In the course of that most melancholy contention with Mr Edwards, I now see that I was very much influenced by vast pride, self-sufficiency, ambition, and vanity. I appear to myself vile, and doubtless much more so to others who are more impartial. . . . Such treatment of Mr Edwards, wherein I was so deeply concerned and active, was particularly and very aggravatedly sinful and ungrateful in me, because I was not only under the common obligations of each individual of the society to him, as a most able, diligent and faithful pastor; but I had also received many instances of his tenderness, goodness and generosity to me as a young kinsman, whom he was disposed to treat in a most friendly manner. . . . I am most sorely sensible that nothing but that infinite grace and mercy which saved some of the betrayers and murderers of our blessed Lord, and the persecutors of his martyrs, can pardon me; in which alone I hope for pardon, for the sake of Christ, whose blood, blessed be God, cleanseth from all sin. (1.cxxv)[2]

[1] The letter is in Faust and Johnson, p. 392ff.
[2] Hawley's later public life was distinguished, though sadly the hereditary affliction of insanity ultimately overtook him. He died in 1788 and in the same tragic way as his father.

'But to Joseph Hawley,' writes H. B. Parkes, 'the pardon of infinite grace and mercy was denied. He was converted back to Calvinism'.[1] Which reminds us that falsehoods did not end with the year 1750.

[1] *Jonathan Edwards*, p. 208.

REMOVAL

The Mission House, Stockbridge. When John Sergeant (1710–1749) married Abigail Williams in 1739 he left his simpler home on the village street in Stockbridge for the above, built near to the home of Abigail's father, Colonel Ephraim Williams, on Prospect Hill. It is said that wood carvings for the house were brought by ox team from Connecticut. In the 1920's the house was moved down to its present location on Main Street.

June 22, 1750 Revd Jonathan Edwards was dismissed.

Note in the *Church Record* of the
Northampton First Church

God tries the graces of his people by persecutions, that the truth and
power of his grace in them may appear to his own glory, both before
men, angels and devils. One end is that by such a discovery of the
truth and strength of their faith and love, he may as it were triumph
over Satan; and make him to see what a victory is obtained over him,
by so rescuing those souls that were once his captives from his power;
and convince him of the real success of his design of redeeming and
sanctifying souls – notwithstanding all that he had done to [them],
whereby he thought he had utterly ruined mankind, and put them
past the possibility of cure. For this end God tried Job. God gloried in
Job as a perfect and an upright man, that did good and eschewed evil
[Job 1.8]. Satan don't own the truth of it, but charges that Job was a
hypocrite, and his service mercenary. But God tries Job with grievous
affliction for Satan's conviction. So it is in the church in general, their
trials being for Satan's conviction. . . .

Entry 52 in 'Notes on the Apocalypse'
J E (Yale) 5, p. 146

18

The year 1750 was one of light as well as shadow for Jonathan and Sarah Edwards. The family circle was completed in April with the birth of Pierrepont, their third son, and two months later – only two weeks before the dissolution of her father's pastoral connexion – their eldest daughter, Sarah, twenty-one, was married to Elihu Parsons. Then, in November, Mary married Timothy Dwight. The bride was sixteen and the groom – the six-foot-four-inches tall son of Edwards' friend and neighbour –was twenty-four. Throughout New England, justices of the peace were authorized to marry and on this occasion it is interesting to note that the ceremony was undertaken by Colonel Dwight. It was a marriage which was to leave a deep imprint upon history. Mary's first son, another Timothy, was – to be President of Yale and author of a hymn deeply expressive of the church-life in which his mother had grown up, 'I love Thy kingdom, Lord'.

> For her my tears shall fall,
> For her my prayers ascend,
> To her my cares and toils be given,
> Till toils and cares shall end.

It is said that after her father's dismissal Mary Dwight felt so strongly about the matter that she would not go into the meetingplace beyond the vestibule where she sat in sight of the pulpit but scarcely as a member of the congregation. On

Communion Sundays she would travel some twelve miles to the church at Norwich and to this church she was finally to transfer her membership in 1783.[1] At the same time it is important to note that Mary, like her father, was in no sense disillusioned with the Great Awakening. Her son, Timothy, undoubtedly reflected the view of the whole family when he subsequently wrote of the revival period: 'At this time, a vast multitude of persons united themselves to the christian church; and, with few exceptions, testified through life by their evangelical conduct the genuineness of their profession. The influence of this body of men, many of whom survived for a long time the peace of 1763, retarded essentially the progress of the evil. All vicious men felt that religion must be regarded with reverence, and life conducted with a good degree of moral decency.'

It was a grandson of Mary, Sereno E. Dwight, who became her father's principal biographer almost eighty years later.

While ready to see God's chastening hand upon himself in his dismissal, Edwards believed that it was adherence to a truth of Scripture which was the main cause of his trials. In 1888, when C. H. Spurgeon was in the midst of a controversy no less painful than the one we have reviewed, Andrew Bonar commented in his Diary: 'Much struck with all Mr Spurgeon is passing through because of his faithful testimony for the truth. Just like the Lord, however, in the case of one so abundantly honoured and used: the "thorn of the flesh", such as Paul needed, such as Moses at Meribah, and often, often in the case of others of his most honoured servants like Jonathan Edwards.'[2]

Edwards and his wife had already faced the question whether in severe trials they 'could cheerfully resign all to God' (i.lxvii), and the year 1750 brought confirmation to their faith. Tears shed for Christ's cause do not mean personal gloom, for he has promised, 'Blessed are ye when men shall persecute you'. But the nature of the practical difficulties which now faced them could hardly have been anticipated. For many years, he had possessed, in his own words, 'the largest salary of any country minister in New England' (i.cxli) and the indications are that he needed it for the care of a large family,

[1] *Timothy Dwight 1752–1817*, Charles E. Cunningham, 1942, p. 102.
[2] Andrew A. Bonar, *Diary and Letters*, 1894, pp. 367–8.

not to speak of other uses. Now his stated income was summarily ended and there was no source of relief at hand. In an era when girls married at sixteen, some already regarded Edwards as 'an old man'[1]. Ministers of his years were commonly settled in a parish until death. Four days after his Farewell Sermon of July 1, 1750, he wrote to John Erskine:

I am now, as it were, thrown upon the wide ocean of the world, and know not what will become of me and my numerous and chargeable family. Nor have I any particular door in view that I depend upon to be opened for my future serviceableness. Most places in New England that want a minister, would not be forward to invite one with so chargeable a family, nor one so far advanced in years – being 46 the 5th day of last October. I am fitted for no other business but study, I should make a poor hand at getting a living by any secular employment. We are in the hands of God, and I bless him, I am not – anxious concerning his disposal of us (1.cxx).

The next day he touched on the same subject more briefly in a letter to William M'Culloch: 'I have now nothing visible to depend upon for my future usefulness, or the subsistence of my numerous family. But I hope we have an all-sufficient faithful, covenant God, to depend upon' (1.cxxii).

Months after his dismissal Edwards was still without any regular means of support. An invitation from Erskine to consider Scotland was not rejected out of hand. 'As to my removing, with my numerous family, over the Atlantic, it is, I acknowledge, attended with many difficulties that I shrink at. Among other things, this is very considerable, that it would be on uncertainties, whether my gifts and administration would suit my congregation, that should send for me without trial; and so great a thing as such a removal had need to be on some certainty as to that matter.'

Meanwhile, strange though it seems, Edwards was still supplying the Northampton pulpit on frequent occasions. The manuscripts of twelve sermons which he preached in his former congregation between his 'Farewell' in July and mid-November, 1750, still survive. But this procedure did not represent any change of heart on the part of the majority. Only a month after his dismissal the Town had denied him the use of the meadow land on which he had been dependent for the grazing of his

[1]See below, p. 361.

sheep and other animals. At that time yet another committee had been formed and despatched to the parsonage 'to convince him (if they can) that he hath no right to that land'. When these men failed to convince Edwards, the Town settled their denial of the meadow land by vote.

The church's supply committee had different problems. Many attempts to find suitable candidates to supply the pulpit met with no success. 'They have exerted themselves very much', Edwards wrote to Erskine on November 15, 1750, 'but have hitherto been disappointed and seem to be very much nonplussed'. Accordingly, he says in this same letter: 'They have asked me to preach the greater part of the time since my dismission, when I have been at home; but it has seemed to be with much reluctance that they have come to me, and only because they could not get the pulpit supplied otherwise; and they have asked me only from sabbath to sabbath' (1.cxxii).

It was possibly about this date that an incident occurred one Sunday which became part of the folklore of Northampton. Two strangers stopped over the weekend in the town, men who were 'greatly prejudiced against Edwards' and who did not realize that he was to be in the pulpit for the services they were to attend. Having never seen Edwards before, when they took their places in the meetinghouse on Sunday morning they assumed that the slender figure who entered the pulpit was a visitor. After Edwards had taken the preliminary part of the service and had begun his sermon, one of the strangers whispered to the other, 'This is a *good* man.' And a little later, 'He is a *very* good man'. Finally, 'Whoever he may be, he is a *holy* man'.

If this happened in the latter half of 1750 it scarcely reflected the view of the congregation as a whole. Edwards was right in believing that many only heard him on sufferance. 'A great uneasiness was manifested by many of the people at his preaching there at all', says Hopkins, and it was at length agreed to continue without any preaching rather than to ask him further. This must have followed a note in the Town Book of November 19, 1750, which records the settling arrears of money owed to Edwards for supply: 'Voted to give the Revd Mr Edwards ten pound old ten^r per Sabbath for the time he has preached in this Parish since he was dismissed.'

Reviewing in 1754 what had happened earlier, Edwards wrote:

The people most manifestly continued in a constant flame of high resentment and vehement opposition for more than two years together; and this spirit, instead of subsiding, grew higher and higher, till they had obtained their end in my expulsion. Nor indeed did it cease then, but still they maintained their jealousy of me, as if I was secretly doing the part of an enemy to them, so long as I had a being in the town, yea 'till they saw the town well cleared of all my family. So deep were their prejudices that their heat was maintained, nothing would quiet them till they could see the town clear of root and branch, name and remnant.[1]

In a letter of November 15, 1750 to Erskine, Edwards had also said, 'I have as yet had no call to any stated business elsewhere in the ministry'. A few weeks later, with all ministry in Northampton finally concluded, an invitation at length came. It was not to one of the principal charges of New England but to Stockbridge, described to Edwards' Scots correspondents by Thomas Prince as 'an Indian town above 160 miles right out in the Wilderness West of Boston'.

Stockbridge was founded as a frontier settlement in 1737 and as the direct result of a meeting held in Colonel John Stoddard's home in 1734 which Edwards had attended. Stoddard had long had a friendly interest in the Indians. As Edwards recorded at his funeral, 'He had a far greater knowledge than any other person in the land of the several nations of Indians in these northern parts of America'. He was also better known by them than any other white man. John Stoddard had a vision of the day when the frontiers would no more need the militia but be secured by the good-will of Indians themselves. For such an inter-racial bond to come about, however, there needed first to be a unity in the knowledge of God. Conversion to Christ would bring blessings to nations as well as to individuals.

Stoddard was acting in this matter on behalf of the Commissioners for Indian affairs at Boston, which body was in turn an agent for the 'Society in London for Propagating the Gospel in New England'. As a result of the 1734 meeting, John Sergeant, already mentioned, was sent to the Housatonics or 'River

[1]Faust and Johnson, *op. cit.*, 394–5.

Indians'[1] and to aid the settlement of these semi-nomadic people, ground was secured to them and a school established at a site in the woods between two ranges of the Berkshire Hills. The Housatonics were few in number in Stockbridge (less than fifty when Sergeant first reached them in late 1734) but the numbers grew and, yet more important, as Stoddard had foreseen, there was the potential to reach out to larger tribes. The Mohawks were in the vicinity and they belonged to the mighty 'Six Nations' – the Iroquois – whose allegiance to France or to Britain could be decisive in settling the destiny of Canada.

Sergeant, clearly a hard-working missionary, died in 1749 at the age of thirty-eight, with no immediate successor apparent. An approach was made to Ezra Stiles, a young tutor at Yale, but Stiles was of a somewhat liberal turn of mind and it seems that he was not willing to have his orthodoxy examined by the Commissioners at Boston.[2] Samuel Hopkins, also approached, would not have found such an examination an ordeal, for he, like John Sergeant, had studied theology in the Edwards' parsonage. And Hopkins already had some acquaintance with the Housatonic Indians, having served a frontier church only an hour's ride from Stockbridge since 1743. But he declined the invitation of the Commissioners 'on the ground', writes Sprague, 'that he did not think himself adapted to the place, and at the same time he recommended Mr Edwards.'[3]

If Hopkins was not 'adapted' to the Stockbridge work, the Boston Commissioners might have considered one of New England's foremost theologians to have been still less suited. Nonetheless, an invitation went to Edwards early in December 1750, proposing that the Indian mission be combined with the pastorate of a small church of white people who had been permitted to form a village beside the Indian 'township'. Four

[1]'Housatonic' was the white man's name arising out of the location of their two 'townships' on the Housatonic River. The tribe was actually a remnant of the once great Mohicans, a branch of the Algonquins. Their own name for themselves meant 'the people of the ever-flowing waters'. In his *Religious Affections* Edwards had been one of the first to mention 'the Houssatunnuck Indians' in print (1.292).

[2]This curious story is well told by E. S. Morgan in *The Gentle Puritan*, A Life of Ezra Stiles, 1727–1799, 1962, p. 78ff.

[3]*Annals*, 1, p. 429.

white families, 'carefully selected', had been allowed to settle with Sergeant and another missionary companion in 1737, 'to aid them in their benevolent work'.

Edwards did not immediately accept the invitation nor did he set it aside. But obviously he was deeply interested, for instead of waiting for spring, he left home amid the snow of January 1751 to review the situation for himself at Stockbridge. He found there some two hundred Housatonics, including an effective school for their children run by a certain Timothy Woodbridge (one of the original settlers) and supported by a converted Indian of ability and evident piety. Woodbridge's Indian assistant was to be Edwards' main interpreter among them and even learning his name must have been a strong reminder of the linguistic difficulties to be faced on the frontier. He was John Wauwaumppequunnaunt, who had been the only — person with whom Brainerd could speak in English when he went to Kaunaumeek (2.335). By the time of Sergeant's death, forty-two of the Housatonnock Indians had become communicant members of the Stockbridge Church. In addition to this there was a separate boarding school for the Mohawks, intended, it seems, for young and old, and supervised by a Captain Martin Kellogg. Around the time of Edwards' visit in January 1751 and perhaps due to it, the number of Mohawks increased from twenty to about ninety, including several chiefs. Such a development Edwards viewed with great hope, and describing his two-month initial visit to Stockbridge, he later wrote, 'I spent much time with the Indians, particularly with the Mohawks under the care of Capt Kellogg'. Edwards' interpreter with the Mohawks was Kellogg's sister who had been taken prisoner by the Iroquois when a child and was thus a native speaker of their language.

On the near sixty-mile trail back to Northampton from Stockbridge in March 1751 Edwards had much on his mind. He intended, for one thing, to seek the assurance of the Governor that there was a commitment to the Indian settlement in this comparatively unprotected region. In the words of Ola Winslow, 'Fear he did not know, but he wanted reasonable assurance of the safety of his wife and children'. There was also a practical difficulty. The Stockbridge church provided no parsonage and indeed there was not even ground available on which to build one if he had possessed the money. But above these considerations another factor must have given Edwards serious misgivings as he contemplated a removal to the frontier. While all the white settlers at Stockbridge were united in one church, he had seen little evidence of any unity of spiritual purpose among them. Timothy Woodbridge, deacon and schoolmaster, was clearly concerned to serve the Indians but another family among the first settlers showed a questionable interest in the mission work. This family was both the most influential in the settlement and, still more disconcerting, they were part of the same large Williams clan which had so long been involved in opposition to Edwards. Ephraim Williams, head of the Stockbridge branch of the family, was an uncle of Solomon Williams (the writer of the reply to Edwards' *Humble Inquiry* on qualifications for communion). Since his arrival in 1737, this Williams (aided by his son, Ephraim Jr.) had made a name for himself both in frontier defence and in the acquisition of property. Despite a ruling to the contrary, his 150 acres, allotted in 1737, had grown to over 400 by the purchase of Indian lands. With his daughter, Abigail, married to John Sergeant, and Ephraim Jr., the town's representative to the General Court, Timothy Woodbridge was not alone in fearing that Colonel Ephraim Williams viewed Stockbridge as his private preserve.

There is no record of the conversations which Edwards must have had with these relatives on his visit to Stockbridge but he was aware of their attitude to his possible re-location in their midst. The Williamses had hoped for the settlement of Ezra Stiles. In a letter to Stiles of November 6, 1750, the widowed Abigail Sergeant had complained to him of the efforts of Timothy Woodbridge to secure Edwards' appointment:

I cannot forbear telling you that our worthy Deacon is going forthwith to push Mr Edwards immediately into the mission, although he has been entreated sufficiently to forbear. My father, Captain Kellogg, Mr Jones, etc. are very bitterly against it. . . . How unsuitable a person is Mr Edwards on almost every account for this business! I have not time so much as to mention a hundred things that I could talk a day upon. . . . Can't the commissioners be led to think it of the last importance that a gentleman should be young in order to be expert in the language; should be of a generous, catholic spirit, not only to recommend himself and mission to the prince and others abroad, but [to] do forty times as much good at home?

Mr Hopkins of Springfield is far from thinking his brother [in-law] proper to come here. He freely told Mr Woodbridge so. But he [Woodbridge] can get the Indians to say just what he bids them; and their humble petition with his earnest desire will be sufficient for the purpose. Our neighbor, Mr Hopkins, is deeply engaged with him. Mr Hopkins of Springfield is so nearly related, that I fear he will be loath to act against his brother [in-law]. . . . [1]

When Edwards' name was first broached for Stockbridge Ephraim Williams Jr. had taken care that Edwards should know the family opinion. In a letter to Jonathan Ashley of Deerfield, he reports:

he [Edwards] hears I have done all I can to prevent his coming. . . . Its true when they first talkd of settling him I was against it gave my reasons, & sent them to him like an honest fellow. . . .

    1. That he was not sociable, the consequence of which was he was not apt to teach.

    2. He was a very great Bigot, for he would not admit any person into heaven, but those that agreed fully to his sentiments, a Doctrine deeply tingd with that of the Romish church.

    3. That he was an old man, & that it was not possible for him to learn the Indian tongues therefore it was not likely he could be serviceable to the Indians as a young man that would learn the tongue. . . .

    4. His principles were such, If I had rightly been informed, I could by no means agree to, that I had taken pains to read his Book,[2] but could not understand it, that I had heard almost every gentleman in the county say the same, & that upon the whole I believd he did not know them himself.

The above reasons I sent to him by Lt Brown, who has since told me he deliverd to him verbatim, which I believe did not suit him.[3]

In the face of such comments, it was only the consideration that the Stockbridge invitation might be of God which had led

---

[1]Samuel Hopkins (1693–1755) of Springfield, married to one of Edwards' sisters, had been involved in the mission to the Housatonics from the outset. He does not appear to have been close to his brother-in-law.

[2]i.e. on qualifications for communion.

[3]Quoted in *Stockbridge*, 1739–1974, S. C. Sedgwick and C. S. Marquand, 1974, pp. 61–2.

Edwards to make the exploratory visit in the first months of 1751. By that time, it seems, the mood of the young Ephraim Williams was changing. Edwards would be best coming there, he tells Ashley, 'since they are so set for him', and because – from his viewpoint – the settlement of such a well-known figure in their district could prove a business asset in the future, 'raising the price of my land'. We do not know if the Williams family gave their distinguished relative a qualified welcome during his winter visit. It is probable that they did. Some of them at least had never known him personally before. Abigail Sergeant, in a letter to Ezra Stiles on February 15, 1751, freely confessed that he was not the man whom she had anticipated: 'Mr. Edwards is now with us. He has conducted [himself] with wisdom and prudence; and, I must confess, I am not a little disappointed in him. He is learned, polite, and free in conversation, and more catholic than I had supposed.' Despite any such change in attitude, Edwards certainly had grounds for remaining apprehensive of the Williamses' influence should he choose to settle. And anything that he heard from Timothy Woodbridge, who was a former friend of Brainerd's, would have confirmed his distrust.

By the end of his lonely road back to Northampton in March, 1751, Edwards had reached no conclusion as to his duty.

Notwithstanding the difficulties, he was drawn to Stockbridge. He may have felt that a ministry in that location would lead, in some measure, to be a fulfilment of his own long-continued prayer for the advancement of the gospel among the Indians. As Thomas Gillespie had written to him, 'Perhaps you are to be employed where the gospel has been little understood or attended to'.

Seeing his uncertainty, Edwards' friends in Northampton – led by Colonel Dwight and Dr. Mather – renewed their hopes of seeing him settled over there afresh. With that in view, they pressed for another Council to be held to consider the possibility of a second church in the town. While Edwards was averse to this proposal he considered that some purpose might be served by a further Council. Thus, while pursuing quietly his thoughts of a removal to Stockbridge and consulting the Governor of the Province, Sir William Pepperell, on the subject, he consented to the calling of the church Council which met in Northampton on May 15, 1751.

Once again, says Dwight, the town 'was put into a great tumult'. Edwards was accused by his enemies of seeking to re-establish himself in Northampton and the attack on him now became more directly personal. In the town tavern such characters as John Miller could be heard saying, 'It would be well if his head was seven feet underground but he thought six would do his turn, and Mr Edwards was just like his old cow lowing after a good mess' (i.e. a good salary). At another level, the church authorized a committee to draw up a 'Remonstrance' to lay before the Council. The heat and violence of this document may in part reflect an underlying fear in Hawley and others that a renewed Edwards ministry in the town would gather more support than they cared to recognize as possible. 'There is a number whose hearts are broken at what has come to pass', Edwards had written to Erskine in November 1751, 'there are more women of this sort than men, and I doubt not there is a number, who in their hearts are with me, who durst not appear, by reason of the great resolution and high hand with which things are carried in the opposition by the prevailing odium. Such is the state of things among us that a person cannot appear on my side without exposing himself to the resentments of his friends and neighbours, and being the object of much odium'.

Odium was certainly at its height in May 1751 when the church committee laid its 'Remonstrance' before the Council. On Joseph Hawley's own subsequent admission, this document contained much 'un-Christian bitterness'. The charges, he later confessed, were 'all founded on jealous and uncharitable mistakes, and so were really gross slanders'. Summarizing later what had happened at this Council in May 1751, Edwards wrote to Hawley:

I was charged with 'having a desire to be settled over a few of the members of the Church to the destruction of the whole, and that I set out on a journey with a certain gentleman to procure a Council to instal me at Northampton, and that I contrived to do it at such a time because I knew the Church was at that time about to send for a candidate, etc. that I might prevent their success therein, and that I was ready to settle in that place, and for the sake of it had refused an invitation to Stockbridge, that I had neglected this opportunity for the sake of settling over an handful, that I had a great inclination to continue at Northampton as a minister, at the expense of the peace and prosperity of the greater part of the town, yea that I was greatly engaged for it'.

Here is a heap of direct slanders positively asserted, all contrary to the truth of fact. I had not refused the invitation to Stockbridge, or neglected that opportunity. I had no inclination or desire to settle over these few at Northampton, but a very great opposition in my mind to it, abundantly manifested in what I continually said to them on occasion of their great and constant urgency.

It was much more agreeable to my inclination to settle at Stockbridge and, though I complied to the calling of a Council to advise in the affair, it was on these terms, that it should not be thought hard that I should fully and strongly lay before them all my objections against it . . . and what I said against it [i.e. the formation of a second church in Northampton] was the thing that did prevail against it and that only. I complied to the calling of the Council with a view to these two things. 1. To quiet the minds of those, who in so trying a time had appeared my steadfast friends, that they might not always think exceedingly hardly of me. And 2. The Country having been filled with gross misrepresentations of [the] controversy between me and my people, and the affair of my dismission, and the grounds of it, to the great wounding of my character at a distance, I was willing some ministers of chief note should come from different parts of the country, and be upon the spot, and see the true state of things with their own eyes.

As McGiffert says, 'There is something pathetic in the spectacle of America's premier theologian having to take measures to defend himself against the breath of scandal when he should be "cast on the wide world".' The Council which met on May 15 concluded four days later, the Committee which laid the Remonstrance having refused to appear to support any of their charges. The Council's decision was to advise Edwards to accept the call to Stockbridge. Accordingly he determined to leave the town where he had spent more than half his life and with which his name will ever be associated.

Unknown to Edwards, at the very time when he was reaching a final decision to go to Stockbridge, Presbyterians in Virginia were commencing strenuous efforts to secure his presence among them. Four years earlier the young Samuel Davies had become the first permanent pastor of evangelical persuasion in that colony and he had laboured almost single-handed amidst a powerful revival as well as against much opposition. Hearing of Edwards' difficulties, Davies' people raised funds for his support, and, without the least hesitation about placing the leadership in Virginia in Edwards' hands, Davies sought Joseph Bellamy's aid in accomplishing this purpose. A letter written by Davies to Bellamy, from Hanover, Virginia, on July 4, 1751, provides a clear idea of how Edwards was viewed by the Presbyterians of the Middle Colonies:

I assure myself, dear sir, of your most zealous concurrence to persuade him to [come to] Virginia. Do not send him a cold, paper message, but go to him yourself in person. If he be not as yet engaged to any place, I depend upon your word, and make no doubt but he will come. If he is engaged, I hope he may be regularly dismissed upon a call of so great importance. Of all the men I know in America, he appears to me the most fit for this place; and, if he could be obtained on no other condition, I would cheerfully resign him my place, and cast myself into the wide world once more. Fiery, superficial ministers will never do in these parts: they might do good; but they would do much more harm. We need the deep judgement and calm temper of Mr. Edwards among us. Even the dissenters here have the nicest taste of almost any congregation I know, and cannot put up with even the truths of the gospel in an injudicious form. The enemies are watchful, and some of them crafty, and raise a prodigious clamour about raving, injudicious preaching. Mr. Edwards would suit them both.

Edwards and Davies would have been a mighty combination in the furtherance of the gospel in the South but it was not to be. In a letter to Erskine, written in 1752, Edwards refers briefly to what might have happened in these terms: 'I was in the latter part of the last summer applied to, with much earnestness and importunity, by some of the people of Virginia, to come and settle among them in the work of the ministry; who subscribed handsomely for my encouragement and support, and sent a messenger to me with their request and subscriptions; but I was installed at Stockbridge before the messenger came' (1.cxlvi).

At about the same time as Edwards received the evidence of sympathetic interest and help from Virginia, there came yet larger encouragement from his friends in Scotland, among whom the news of his dismissal had been heard with deep concern. It led to plans for practical aid concerted with characteristic Scots generosity and 'canniness'. Funds in Edinburgh were gathered by William Hogg, a merchant, whose home on Castle Hill had long been a frequent rendezvous for evangelicals. This money, amounting to some thirty-five pounds, was forwarded to John MacLaurin in Glasgow who was responsible for co-ordinating the overall plans to send help. On February 11, 1751, MacLaurin wrote to Hogg to tell him that the total of contributions stood at sixty-three pounds, ten shillings.[1] Various discussions proceeded to take place in Glasgow concerning the most advantageous use of this money, it being agreed that if it were employed to purchase goods (such things as Bibles, white linen and tartan) to be shipped to New England, these could be sold in Boston with a profit of at least 20 per cent. A visitor to Glasgow (whose deceased wife had been a cousin of Edwards) suggested to MacLaurin that if the cargo were sent up the river Connecticut to Northampton, Mrs. Edwards, 'by her fitness to dispose of such things in places near her, might make possibly about 15 per cent more than would be got by selling to Merchants at Boston'. It was, however, eventually determined that the purchased cargo should go to Boston with Captain Lang, whose ship, 'the Boston Pacquet', after being hindered by the weather, left Glasgow towards the end of March, 1751.

Edwards had already left Northampton when he heard the news of what was being done for their help. Writing from Stockbridge on July 13, 1751, he addressed the following to 'Mr. William Hogg, Edinburgh':

Dear Sir,

The account which I have lately received from correspondents in Scotland, of the respect to me and my family, which you have in various ways testified, both by word and deed, may well deeply affect us with gratitude and excite our admiration [wonder]. And in the first place, we have reason to admire, and be most gratefully affected by, the providence of God which in the time of our peculiar and uncommon troubles has appeared for us in so wonderful and

---

[1] A subsequent gift from Christians in Paisley raised the amount to more than £70. MacLaurin's correspondence with Hogg on this subject will be found in the valuable supplement to Gillies' account of MacLaurin's life, entitled 'Friendship with Jonathan Edwards', *The Works of John MacLaurin*, Ed. W. H. Goold, vol. 1, 1860, xlvii-lix.

unexpected a manner, in that when, according to an human view of things, nothing was to be expected but difficulties and straits; and friends that were near at hand, which we formerly should have expected most from, stood at the greatest distance, and seemed to rejoice at our troubles, and to be ready, on every occasion, to increase them; others, who are perfect strangers, that we never so much as heard of, and at so great a distance, are raised up, have most friendly affections excited, and hearts enlarged towards us, to extend their kindness to our relief and bountiful supply, even beyond the ocean. How true in this instance does it appear to be, that God is, as he declares himself in his Word to be, an allsufficient and faithful God, and that his promise never fails; that we need not fear to trust him in the way of obedience to him: tho' according to an human appearance, we seem to run the greatest ventures by cleaving to him. In the next place, our gratitude is due to his people, to whom he has given the instruments of his bounty. I would by this, dear Sir, in particular, render thanks to you; to whom they are due, in some respects, in peculiar manner.

I, with my family, have for this two years past gone through many troubles: But I hope the Lord has not forsaken us, nor suffered us to sink under our trials. He has in many respects exercised a fatherly care of us in our distresses. A door seems to be opened for my further improvement in the work of the ministry in this place which is situated in the north western frontier of New England. . . . [1]

The letter proceeds to give an account of the Stockbridge mission and of his hopes 'of good things to be accomplished here for the Indians'. MacLaurin's correspondence with Hogg reveals other plans which the Scots had with respect to Edwards. The first of these plans did not succeed. It was that Edwards might come over to speak for the interests of the New Jersey College at the General Assembly of the Church of Scotland. But another proposal – apparently originating with MacLaurin – has earned the enduring gratitude of later ages. Writing to Hogg on January 21, 1751, the Glasgow minister pressed the value of such portraits as survived of the Reformers and of other Christian leaders and proceeded to argue that, 'As care has been taken to preserve to us the faces of so many other eminent authors and other persons, it seems a pity if no such respect is put on an author whose past and possibly some future composures may come to be

[1]This letter was first published by A. B. Grosart in *The Sunday at Home*, 1896–97, pp. 459–60.

more regarded when the world's taste mends'. MacLaurin's proposal was that a letter be sent to one of Edwards' friends in Boston who might 'prevail with him to let his picture be drawn'. Nor was this all, for he urged that a portrait of Sarah Edwards should also be secured. It was of Mrs Edwards, he reminds Hogg, that Dr Colman of Boston had written, 'that that person's face was reckon'd the best in British America, or words to that effect', and that she was the person whose experience – 'curiously concealed as not to tell whether it is man or woman' – was given in the passage in Edwards' *Thoughts on the Revival in New England* which had become well-known.

MacLaurin's proposal for portraits was taken up so speedily that by early November, 1751, a box containing the two pictures had arrived in Glasgow. The cost was five pounds sterling and MacLaurin had assurance from Abiel Walley (a Boston merchant who seems to have arranged the business) that 'they are done to the life, have a very exact resemblance'. Writing to William Hogg of this news, MacLaurin promised to send him the portraits, both because he thought that Hogg had the best right to them and also because he was eager to have 'some hundred prints cast off . . . I take it for granted you have by much the better engravers in your town'. In MacLaurin's view, several of the contributors to the help given to Edwards might receive a free copy of an engraving of the portrait while the sale of others, 'chiefly at London', would help defray the cost in which he and Hogg were sharing.[1] But if an engraving was done at this date in Edinburgh no copy of it appears to have survived. As for the oil portraits themselves, in due course they passed from Hogg to John Erskine, to be returned after Erskine's death to New England.[2]

The Stockbridge ministry, which officially began with Edwards' installation on August 8, 1751, was certainly a very different beginning from the one he had experienced at Northampton. On Sundays, instead of the bell which for so many years he had heard gathering his large congregation, the baleful sound of an enormous conch-shell – blown like a horn – gathered few more than a dozen white worshippers. Although

---

[1] *The Works of John MacLaurin*, vol. i, lvii.
[2] They are now at Yale University.

their numbers were increasing as word spread of the land possibilities on the frontier, they were never more than eighteen families during Edwards' ministry. On Sundays they gathered to hear the man who, as Ephraim Williams thought, was 'so full of Divinity' and 'so empty of Politics'. But, with his Indian hearers who – for language reasons – gathered at different hours in the same church building, Edwards had a new and larger field of opportunity and it was from this source that he received his first encouragement at Stockbridge. In July 1751, the month prior to his settlement, the Boston Commissioners had appointed Edwards to meet with Mohawk chiefs at Albany, in New York province. Such was the success of this meeting that these Mohawks met the Commissioners at Stockbridge the week after Edwards' installation. Among his manuscripts a scrap of paper remains which was probably written by him for this occasion. The care that he took to prepare this welcome to the Mohawks indicates the importance which it had in his thoughts. His notes read:

Your Coming here will rejoyce the Hearts of all Good men as They will hope it will be a means of your coming into greater Light & Knowledge in the Xtian Religion and so be a means of your Et[ernal] salvation and Happiness.

We dont desire to keep you from the Kn[owledge] of the Bible the Word of G. as the French Priests do their Indians. We are willing that you could read the word of G. as well as we & know as much as we.

While I continue here I shall be willing to come from time to time & to do my utmost to instruct you in the true Xtian Relig[ion].[1]

At this conference the Mohawks were promised good education for their children at Stockbridge, although, in view of past failures on the part of the English, one chief asked the Commissioners 'to promise nothing but what the government would certainly perform'. Time was to show that the chief's request was not needless. For the moment, however, Edwards' first efforts among the Indians were full of promise.

Edwards' family situation at the time of his installation in Stockbridge was far from normal. Unsure of their future accommodation, he had left Sarah and the children at North-

---

[1]A pencil note by a modern hand on this manuscript (Beinecke Library, Yale) queries an earlier date, 'Jan. 1751'.

ampton. The disposal of the parsonage in King Street was also a complication in their plans. Happily it was their own property but it was a house which no one wanted to buy and for a lengthy period it was to be on the market. In October 1751 Edwards petitioned the General Court for permission to purchase land for a home in Stockbridge and also some wood-land on the outskirts of the settlement. As ever, wood was a necessity for heating. The same month he rejoined his family in Northampton for his last stay in the only home they had known together. He preached there (perhaps in Timothy Dwight's house) on October 13. With the maples turning yellow and scarlet it was Northampton's most beautiful month. It was also a month which recalled many memories from the past including Whitefield's first visit, Brainerd's death, and his own birthdays.

A chapter was finally closed as they shut the doors of the home of so many memories on October 16. Their recently married daughter, Sarah, was to stay with her husband, Elihu Parsons, for a while before they both followed to Stockbridge. Mary Dwight, now living on the next door plot, was to stay permanently and, at seventeen, it was no doubt she who felt the departure most keenly as her parents, four sisters and three brothers left on the road to the west. We could wish that a certain John Judd had recorded more in his diary than he did that day:

Oct. 16 Met Mr Edwards and family at Lonard Bartletts. Rode some miles.

At the end of their journey it was a very different home which awaited the family. For the time being, at least, Edwards had secured the little house where Sergeant had lived before he had moved to a better house up the hill where Abigail's parents and other whites lived. They were indeed in changed circumstances but he believed in a God who settles the bounds of the habitations of his people and in the text which may be seen today on a sundial which marks the site of the Edwards' homestead, 'My times are in thy hand'. 'My wife and I are well pleased with our present situation,' he could write to his father a few months later. 'They like the place far better than they expected. Here, at present, we live in peace; which has of long time been an unusual thing with us.'

[370]

STRIFE IN A FRONTIER VILLAGE

Edwards' home on Main Street, Stockbridge, as it appeared in the last century. Originally built by John Sergeant in 1737, and occupied by him until 1739, Edwards was to purchase the house after some hesitations. When it was demolished to make way for 'a modern residence' in 1900, a local author, R. De Witt Mallary, obtained a chair made out of its oaken beams. 'As oft as I sit in it,' says Mallary, 'I congratulate the world that it has escaped the tyranny of Edwards's theology.' (Lenox and the Berkshire Highlands, R. De Witt Mallary, 1902).

Contention is directly against that which is the very sum of all that is essential and distinguishing in true Christianity, even a spirit of love and peace. No wonder, therefore, that Christianity cannot flourish in a time of strife and contention among its professors. No wonder that religion and contention cannot live together.

J E, *Charity and Its Fruits*, p. 23

19

iven the circumstances already existing in Stockbridge, the initial peace could not last. Even the very appearance of the place was suggestive of a division in the community. Along the straggling street, running east and west on the flat beside the river, were seventeen houses of English style, all built and occupied by Indians. The English themselves, who gathered on Sundays in the church at the west end of the street, beside the green and the burial ground, mostly lived above on Prospect Hill. 'The people on the hill' was a euphemism which Edwards sometimes used of the Williamses, for it was their stately residence – a virtual fort – which dominated the valley. Indians looked up to it daily knowing that the first rays of sunshine which fell on the thick oak-planks of its west side indicated the arrival of the hour of noon. But there was more than curiosity over the time in some of the looks which Housatonics cast up at the Williams' home. Their misgivings were growing that the mission was, after all, only another stage in white expansion. Ephraim Williams had never enjoyed the trust which they showed towards Timothy Woodbridge, their teacher, and the known disagreements between the two men increased their unease as well as that of the Mohawks.

It is perhaps impossible at this point in time to assess the character of Ephraim Williams. Hard-headed and thrifty he certainly was, but whether he was as cynically opportunist as he has been made out to be – and as Ephraim Jr. seems to have been – is not altogether clear. At this date Williams' youngest son, Elijah, was studying under Aaron Burr at Newark and a few of his father's letters to him have survived. While these reveal something of the father's interests in land schemes they also indicate a man who treated religion seriously. 'Daily ply the throne of grace for pardon,' he tells his son. 'Go to Christ as an all sufficient fountain of all good.'[1]

Wittingly or unwittingly, Ephraim Williams was soon to cause trouble. Charles Chauncy described it as the 'family-foible' of the Williamses that they 'were all too apt to be governed in conduct by an undue regard to self, in one shape or another'.[2] In Woodbridge's view, Colonel Williams showed this same propensity. Woodbridge regarded Williams' attitude towards the Indians as a threat to the mission. To retain the trust of the Indians and especially of the Mohawks (when, Edwards noted, the French were busy 'to seduce them from the English interest') was supremely important. He questioned whether Williams had any such concern, while Williams, for his part, did not hide his low opinion of the mission teacher.

In the year of Edwards' arrival there seems to have been an open rupture between Williams and Woodbridge which was temporarily healed when Williams professed that 'he would no more speak ill' of Woodbridge. Yet by early 1752 relations again worsened and in S. E. Dwight's words, Williams' 'promises appeared to be wholly forgotten' (1.cxlii). The immediate cause of the dissension appears to have been the running of the Indian schools, formerly under the general supervision of Sergeant, Williams' son-in-law. It had not taken Edwards long to discover the incompetence and illiteracy of Captain Martin Kellogg (a confidant of Ephraim Williams) who had charge of the Mohawk boarding school – a mission funded by Isaac Hollis, a Baptist minister of means in England. Conscious that the Boston Commissioners for the Indian mission were unfamiliar with the real state of things in Stockbridge, Edwards had very soon recommended the need for a resident trustee who would co-ordinate the mission

[1] 'Some Old Letters', edited by J. F. Dwight, in *Scribner's Magazine*, New York, 1895, p. 247ff.
[2] Quoted by F. B. Dexter in *Biographical Sketches of the Graduates of Yale College, 1701–1745*, 1885, p. 635.

activities. The Commissioners agreed and, with Edwards' approval, appointed a Brigadier-General Joseph Dwight. Dwight arrived during the winter of 1751–52, full of enthusiasm at the opportunity to sit under the ministry of Edwards for whom he had long professed a high regard. It was at Dwight's home in Brookfield that we noted Sarah Edwards staying in 1744. But a short time at Stockbridge saw a remarkable transformation in Dwight. As other men had done before him, he fell to the charm of the high-spirited widow Abigail Sergeant and before long they were married. Edwards' biographer writes of Joseph Dwight, 'Although Mr Edwards had never had a word of difference with him, or his new connexions, his whole conduct was suddenly and entirely changed and he had sided with them [the Williamses], in all their measures of opposition' (1.cxliii).

In the view of S. E. Dwight, the Williamses' earlier attitude to Edwards had re-asserted itself.[1] Perhaps Ephraim Williams Sr. had at first been restrained by a sense of his weakened influence at the time of Edwards' arrival. Now the full support of his son-in-law, General Dwight, in the disagreements with Woodbridge, had strengthened his hand and – more than that – there was news from London which confirmed his hopes of regaining his old authority in all Stockbridge affairs despite Edwards' presence. His nephew, Elisha Williams, had been in London during 1749–50 where he had been treated as something of a celebrity. Among honours conferred upon Yale's former rector, was his appointment to the board of the Society for the Propagation of the Gospel in New England (the body which, with the Boston Commissioners, governed the Stockbridge mission). Thus, unknown to Edwards at the time of his installation, Elisha Williams had already been appointed as one of his overseers. And further, at Elisha Williams' recommendation, his uncle, Ephraim Williams, was appointed as well.

Along with this surprising news, which can scarcely have been welcome to Edwards, was word of more advice which Elisha Williams had given to the London board. It had been

[1]This was, of course, Edwards' own view. See what he says of the unnamed 'family of some note . . . to whom my settlement at Stockbridge was very grievous', in a letter to M'Culloch, Nov. 24, 1752 (1.cliii).

decided that a female school should also be started in Stockbridge with another Williams as its head (Abigail Dwight), to whom a year's salary was to be paid in advance.

It was the issue of the Mohawk boarding-school which, early in 1752, hastened an open confrontation. When the young and able Gideon Hawley arrived, sent by the Boston Commissioners to take over this school which Kellogg had proved himself unable to run, Kellogg objected and insisted that he was still the superintendent and in charge of the finances for which, he seemed to think, he was answerable only to Hollis, three thousand miles away in England.

This whole situation Edwards now brought to the attention of the Boston Commissioners for the first time in a letter of February 18, 1752. Six days later he wrote also to Joseph Paine, an official for the London Society. Summarizing the latter letter, Ola Winslow writes: it 'sets forth the conflict between commercial and religious interest, the waste of public moneys, the duplication of effort by rival missionaries, and outlines a plan of centralized effort, with education the main objective, which sounds more like missionary planning a century later than that of pre-Revolution days.' Edwards had, she believes, 'a grasp of the larger aspects of the missionary problem surprising for the mid-eighteenth century'. 'He had the detachment of the administrator, and saw the problem which lay underneath the details of a given situation'.[1]

It seems that Kellogg's utter failure and greed were manifest to all save the Williams-Dwight clique. Under Kellogg's administration the Mohawks had complained bitterly of the lack of food, blankets and Bible teaching at the school. Gideon Hawley, on the other hand, was popular with the Indians. For a time the dispute remained unsettled until Kellogg's continued interference produced so much confusion that by April 1752 half of the Mohawks left Stockbridge in disgust. Later a friend of Kellogg entered Hawley's school and unprovoked hit a Mohawk child on the head with his heavy cane, an event which 'excited the universal indignation of the remaining Iroquois'.

In the summer of 1752, when Elisha Williams himself arrived at Stockbridge, fresh from his recent voyages, it is no

[1] *Jonathan Edwards*, pp. 280–1.

wonder that Edwards refused to deal with him. Edwards argued that he was responsible to all the trustees and commissioners as a body and not to any single member of the boards in London or Boston. His cousin Elisha's threat to inform the Society in London made no difference. In fact, charges against Edwards were already being laid and they were of the same nature as those written by Ephraim Williams Jr. to Jonathan Ashley before Edwards had gone to Stockbridge. Knowing something of the endeavours being made to remove him, Edwards confided in his friend, the Speaker of the General Court of Massachusetts, in a letter of August, 1752, that the whole purpose of his opponents was 'to establish a dominion of the family of Williams's over Stockbridge affairs'.

These were not Edwards' only difficulties in his first year at Stockbridge. His salary was now considerably reduced and financial problems were to be with them until their Northampton home and some land they possessed were sold. In a letter to his father in January 1752, he deeply regretted his inability to give monetary help to his sister, left a widow a few years earlier and now also bereaved of two children: 'We are much affected with sister's great and heavy afflictions'.[1] He later explains that 'by reason of lately marrying two children, and the charge of buying, building, and removing' he was about £2000 in debt. In June 1752 he confessed to his friend Colonel Dwight in Northampton to be 'in greater need of money than I expected'. It seems that to ease his situation he had petitioned the Court that the house which he had personally paid to erect 'be purchased as a parsonage'. This was denied, due, Edwards tells Colonel Dwight, to the intervention of Ephraim Williams who was 'constantly busy with the representatives' of the Court, and supplying them with 'his lime-juice punch and wine'. Edwards adds, 'Objections were made against the petition which could come from none but he.'[2]

Edwards' second son, Jonathan, seven-years-of-age at this

---

[1] His sister, Eunice, three years his junior, had married the Rev. Simon Backus in 1729. Backus, chaplain to the Connecticut Regiment which went to Cape Breton, had died there in Feb. 1746.

[2] The reference is to Ephraim Jr. who was the Stockbridge representative to the General Court. He was also to be remembered as 'Colonel Williams' but for the sake of clarity I have reserved that title for his father.

time, was still to remember his parents' financial difficulties over forty years later. S. E. Dwight also notes that the debt which Edwards incurred 'subjected them for a time to very serious pecuniary embarrassments'. The daughters now found a source of revenue in lace-making, embroidery and the making of fans with silk paper which they then painted. Such items found a ready market in Boston. Edwards had always been economical in the use of paper but at this period his note-books (as always, a vital part of his method of study), were made up of all sorts of sheets and scraps of unwanted paper sewn together in various shapes and sizes and including even the trimmings from his daughters' fan-making. Printer's proofs, old proclamations of intended marriages from Northampton days, envelopes, letters and much else, could all be utilized, even if there was only room on the margins or the bottoms of sheets. A French book sent by John Erskine on 'Frequent Communion' was taken to pieces to enable him to employ the margins and blank spaces for his own writing – his French being too imperfect for the book to be used as Erskine had intended!

Notwithstanding all these pressures, it was during these same months (from late Spring to July 1752) that Edwards somehow also accomplished his final work on the communion controversy. This was his one-hundred-and-fifty-page reply to Solomon Williams, to which we have already referred, entitled, *Misrepresentations Corrected, and Truth Vindicated.* Far removed from Boston printers, Edwards had a special concern for the one copy of his manuscript which began its journey in the hands of his son-in-law who was travelling to Northampton. From that point Edwards depended upon Colonel Timothy Dwight as he explains in a note addressed to him:

Sir,

I have just sent the Copy of my Answer to Mr Williams by my son Parsons, to be conveyed by you to Mr. Foxcroft. I need not tell you that extraordinary Care had need be taken in the Conveyance. There are many Enemies who would be glad to destroy it. I know not how in the world it can be well got to Mr. Foxcroft's Hand, especially by Reason of the small Pox, but I desire you would do the best you can.

Besides the sending of his last work on the communion controversy to the press, the summer of 1752 was also noteworthy for the marriage of the Edwards' third daughter, Esther. It was probably one of the most talked-of marriages of that year, not least because of its unexpectedness. In this summer the thirty-six-year-old Presbyterian minister of Newark, and president of the New Jersey College, Aaron Burr, made one of his periodic visits to Edwards but this time it was to ask the hand of twenty-year-old Esther. Burr's famed gaiety of temperament probably helped to bridge the difference in years. At any rate, as we shall see, it was a love-match from the outset and he had long been known in the family. In the later words of Ezra Stiles, Burr was widely regarded as 'an excellent divine and preacher, pious and agreeable, facetious and sociable, the eminent Christian'. Unlike the weddings of Sarah and Mary, the Edwards-Burr marriage was not a family affair for it took place at Newark with only Esther's mother present to represent the family. Perhaps one reason why Edwards was not at the wedding was that he had already promised to be present in New York (150 miles from Stockbridge) in September for a meeting with the correspondents of the Society for Propagating Christian Knowledge. He could scarcely have made the journey twice. When September came he stayed with Esther and Aaron in Newark, shared in a meeting of the College trustees at the time of the Commencement and at the Presbyterian Synod of New York preached what was possibly the last sermon which he ever wrote in full, 'True Grace distinguished from the Experience of Devils' (1.41–50).

This visit to New Jersey in September, 1752, gave Edwards much encouragement. As he later wrote to Erskine and M'Culloch, he there met a number of able young ministers, found the College of New Jersey in 'flourishing circumstances', and heard of 'some small movings and revivals'. Such uplift was a necessary preparation for a period of further trials which lay ahead as he returned to Stockbridge in October. These commenced with a time of greater family sickness than they had ever known before. Sarah Edwards was so ill that for a while her death seemed imminent. Sarah Parsons (his married daughter) was also 'very sick', and his youngest girl, Betty, weak since birth, 'was brought nigh unto death' (1.cliii).

The Williamses' attempt to get control of affairs was also now at its height. Ephraim Williams Sr. made a desperate bid to buy the land titles of the white residents friendly to Edwards (1.cxlviii), while his son-in-law, Joseph Dwight, sent a report to the General Court of Massachusetts, 150 miles away in Boston, with the intention of securing the termination of Edwards' position. Happily Timothy Woodbridge was also at Boston at the time and able to defend the true interests of the mission. But the representations against Edwards were widespread. Woodbridge heard that the Williamses had influenced the Governor, Sir William Pepperell, to use his authority in London for Edwards' removal from the mission. This information compelled Edwards to place his own account of affairs before the Governor. In a letter to Pepperell of January 30, 1753, he writes: 'There has for many years appeared a prejudice in the family of the Williams's against me and my family, especially ever since the great awakening at Northampton 18 years ago'. He proceeded to detail the facts which read, as summarized by Dwight,

that they deeply engaged themselves in the controversy at Northampton, on the side of his opposers, upholding, directing, and animating them, in all their measures; that two of them, especially, had been the confidential advisers of the opposition, in procuring his dismission; that when his removal to Stockbridge was proposed, the whole family, there and elsewhere, opposed it, with great vehemence, though, when they saw an entire union and universal engagedness in all the rest of the inhabitants, both English and Indians, for his settlement there, and that there was no hope of preventing it, they appeared as though their minds were changed; – that the author of the Report [Joseph Dwight], during the whole controversy at Northampton, in direct opposition to the family with which he was now connected, had remained his zealous friend and advocate; that he warmly advocated his removal to Stockbridge, and expressed a strong desire of living under his ministry; (for the evidence of which facts, he refers Sir William to two of the most respectable gentlemen in the province;) that this confidential friendship lasted until his connexion with that family, and then was suddenly changed, first into secret, and afterwards into open opposition.

This letter concluded with these moving words:

Now, Sir, I humbly request, that, if you had resolved on endeavouring to have me removed from my present employment here, you would once more take the matter into your impartial consideration. And I would pray you to consider, Sir, what disadvantages I am under; not knowing what has been said of me in conversation; not knowing, therefore, the accusation, or what to answer to. The ruin of my usefulness, and the ruin of my family, which has greatly suffered in years past, for righteousness' sake, are not indeed things of equal consideration with the public good. Yet, certainly, I should first have an equal, impartial, and candid hearing, before I am executed for the public good. I must leave the matter, dear Sir, to your justice and christian prudence; committing the affair to Him who knows all the — injuries I have suffered, and how wrongfully I now suffer, and who is the Great Protector of the innocent and oppressed; beseeching him to guide you in your determination, and mercifully to order the end (i.clv).

There is no indication that Edwards exaggerated the extent of the opposition which he and the mission now faced. In February 1753 the building used by Gideon Hawley for the Mohawk school, and where he also lived, was suddenly and unaccountably burned to the ground. Every item of Hawley's personal possessions was lost. 'It was supposed', writes S. E. Dwight, 'with some grounds, to have been set on fire by design'. Hawley left for pioneer missionary work in April, and the majority of the remaining Mohawks departed, yet the opposition continued, with Abigail Dwight still striving to be headmistress of the girls' school. In October 1753 Edwards concluded a letter to Thomas Gillespie (for whom faithfulness to the Word of God had brought deposition from the Church of Scotland ministry by its General Assembly the previous year) with these words:

As to my own circumstances, I still meet with trouble and expect no other as long as I live in this world. Some men of influence have much opposed my continuing a missionary at Stockbridge and have taken occasion abundantly to reproach me, and endeavour my removal. But I desire to bless God, he seems in some respects to set me out of their reach. He raises me up friends, who are exerting themselves to counteract the designs of my opposers; particularly the commissioners for Indian affairs in Boston with whom innumerable artifices have been used to disaffect them towards me but altogether in vain. Governor Belcher, also, has seen cause much to exert himself, in my behalf, on occasion of the opposition made to me. My people, both English and Indians, stedfastly adhere to me, excepting the family with whom the opposition began and those related to them; which family greatly opposed me while at Northampton. Most numerous, continued, and indefatigable endeavours have been used, to undermine me, by attempting to alienate my people from me; innumerable mean artifices have been used with one another, with young and old, men and women, Indians and English: but hitherto they have been greatly disappointed. But yet they are not weary.

As we, dear Sir, have great reason to sympathize, one with another, with peculiar tenderness, our circumstances being in many respects similar, so I hope I shall partake of the benefit of your fervent prayers for me. Let us then endeavour to help one another, though at a great distance, in travelling through this wide wilderness; that we may have the more joyful meeting in the land of rest, when we have finished our weary pilgrimage (1.clxi).

The storm, however, was almost spent. There were too many who knew the truth of the matter for the misrepresentations of Edwards to succeed. All the white settlers in Stockbridge, outside the Williams family circle, were witness that it was Edwards' opponents who had so mishandled and alienated the Indians with their greed, their land-grabbing and their incompetence. The Boston Commissioners stood by Edwards; Abigail Dwight's appointment was never ratified: and, in February 1754, the control of all money from the private benefactor (Hollis) in England was put in Edwards' hands. The dominion of the Williamses had at last altogether failed. In a final outburst against the man whom she never wanted at Stockbridge, Abigail Dwight, wrote:

They [our difficulties] are altogether of an ecclesiastic kind, too many to be enumerated, too base to be named. Mr Edwards and his abetters, by these deep-concerted schemes, have induced Mr. Hollis to submit himself with his whole charity and yearly donations into the hands of Mr. Edwards, to be disposed of entirely agreeable to the judgment and humour of his own mind.

The latter stages of the Williamses' opposition to Edwards at Stockbridge was carried on by the younger members of the family as Colonel Williams, in poor health, had removed to Deerfield in 1753. It may be that one or two of his children were more responsible for maintaining the controversy than the father, possibly to the point of affecting the regularity of their presence in church. When Elijah Williams, the younger son, had returned to Stockbridge after his father's departure, the latter exhorted him by letter, 'I must beg you to be close in your attendance on the public worship of God'. And in one of his last letters before his death in 1754, Ephraim Sr. wrote again: 'I long to hear the unhappy differences at Stockbridge were happily ended, then I should hope the God of Love and Peace would be and abide with you all. Pray for it earnestly daily and commit all your ways to God.'

A sketch of the Stockbridge Church, 1739–1785.

*North American Indians, from an engraving
by John Boydell, 1775.*

'Tis worth the while to take a great deal of pains to learn to read and understand the Scriptures.

I would have you all of you think of this.

When there is such a book that you may have, how can you be contented without being able to read it?

How does it make you feel when you think there is a Book that is God's own Word? . . .

Parents should take care that their children learn . . .

This will be the way to be kept from the Devil. . . . Devil can't bear [the Bible.] Kept from Hell. To be happy for ever.

But if you let the Word of God alone, and never use, and you can't expect the benefits of it. . . .

You must not only hear and read, etc, but you must have it sunk down into your heart. Believe. Be affected. Love the Word of God.

Written in your heart.

Must not only read and hear, but DO the things. Otherwise no good; but will be the worse for it.

And you should endeavour to understand. To that end to learn the English tongue.

If you had the Bible in your own language, I should not say so much Consider how much it is worth the while to go often to your Bible to hear the great God Himself speak to you.

There you may hear Christ speak.

How much better must we think this is than the word of men.

Better than the word of the wisest man of the world.

How much wiser is God than man.

Here all is true; nothing false

Here all is wise; nothing foolish.

J E in notes of a sermon on 2 Timothy 3.16 to the Indians at Stockbridge, in A. B. Grosart, *Unpublished Writings of Jonathan Edwards*, 1865, 195

20

n 1754, just as everything in Stockbridge was at last coming under Edwards' leadership, there was a new blow to the mission prospects. French-British relationships, ever tense in North America, exploded into further war. The French, moving south from Canada, were establishing a chain of forts from north to south in the interior for a thousand miles or more, with the design of linking their settlements in Canada and Mississippi and thus restricting the British to the east-coast side of the Appalachian Mountains. Though their own forces were far out-numbered, compared with the British, French influence and control among many Indian tribes proved as significant as New England had always feared. Moreover, lack of co-ordination among the two million Britons in the 13 Colonies was a major weakness compared with the unification of the French under their governor of Canada. 'We are divided,' Edwards observed, 'into a great many distinct governments, independent one of another, and, in some respects, of clashing interests: interests which unspeakably clog and embarrass our affairs and make us, though a great, yet an unwieldy, unmanageable body, and an easy prey to our vigilant, secret, subtle, swift and active, though comparatively small, enemy' (1.clxviii).

Once again, with hostilities impending, the whole New England frontier was thrown into a state of alarm. The reality of the danger was brought home to Stockbridge one quiet Sunday morning in September, 1754. 'Some Indians from

Canada,' writes Edwards, 'doubtless instigated by the French, broke in upon us on the Sabbath, between meetings, and fell upon an English family and killed three of them; and about an hour later killed another man.'

At this time Edwards was suffering from serious ill-health. He had made a will on March 14, 1753, 'having much in the infirmity of my constitution to put me in mind of death and make me sensible of the great uncertainty of my life'. In the summer of 1754 he entered upon what he calls 'the longest and most tedious sickness that ever I had in my life: it being followed with fits of ague[1] . . . for a long time very severe, and exceedingly wasted my flesh and strength, so that I became like a skeleton' (1.clxv). It is no wonder that Hopkins, visiting him, found him depressed. Writing to Bellamy, on September 3, 1754, and in the midst of rumours of Indian attacks, Hopkins says:

The dire alarm we have had is like to prevent the proposed journey of myself and wife; yet I shall come down next week, if it can be thought prudent to leave my family. You will doubtless rejoice with me when you hear that the first news we had from Stockbridge was not true; that good Mr. Edwards is yet alive, and as we hope, safe. His fits of the fever and ague had left him some time ago, but are now returned again, and he has a fit every day. I made him a visit last week. He seemed to be more dejected and melancholy than I ever saw him before; is quite [depressed], and pines at the loss of so much time.

The following month, October, 1754, Edwards had planned to be in Boston. He left home with that intention in view but entries in Hopkins' diary suggest he may not have reached his destination. At Bethlehem (home of Bellamy) Hopkins notes on October 13, 'Mr. Edwards not being able to travel, I am yet with him at Mr. Bellamy's'. On October 18, at Waterbury, he writes further, 'Having done my business at Waterbury, and Mr. Edwards continuing to have a severe fit every day, I left Mr. Edwards at Waterbury, and set homewards to-day.' There is no record of the date of Edwards' return to Stockbridge. He was there on November 18, 1754, when he replied to the enquiry, earlier mentioned, from the penitent Joseph Hawley.

[1] Probably malaria, intermittent high fevers with shivering.

[388]

In this letter he tells his cousin, 'I am still so weak that I can write but with a trembling hand, as you may easily perceive'. The ague attacks were to continue until mid-January, 1755.

The Indian threat had also brought new household difficulties. Following the deaths mentioned above, soldiers had been rushed to Stockbridge and a fort was built around the Edwards' home as a suitable place for retreat for others in the event of further attacks. This brought its own problems as Sarah Edwards expended time and money in supplying the needs of troops. In February 1755 Edwards had to write to an officer in charge of troops in that area to inform him, 'We have not lodgings so as to board and lodge more than four soldiers'.

By September 1755, when danger was again mounting, it seems that all troops had departed. With reluctance Edwards must have taken up his pen on September 5 to write to his cousin, Israel Williams (successor to John Stoddard as Colonel of the Militia), telling him that they were 'easy and open prey to our enemies'. The Connecticut soldiers, he wrote, were all gone, and General Shirley 'by his urgency had persuaded away almost all the Indian inhabitants fit for war, who objected much against going on account that the departure of so many would leave the town, and their wives and children too, defenceless'. Edwards concludes, 'We hope that the troops may be forwarded immediately, for, having no adequate means of repelling an attack, we have no security for a single day.'

Despite 'dreadful ravages' by Indians further south, Stockbridge was to be preserved. Not so, however, all its former inhabitants. Ephraim Williams Jr. died from French-Indian bullets on the frontier in 1755. Before that date there is reason to believe that he was no longer the same man who had appeared to be so indifferent to the welfare of the Indian mission five years earlier. In his will he had ordered that any wrongs inflicted upon the Indians at Stockbridge should be righted and that the bulk of the inheritance of lands received from his father should be left for the public good by endowing a 'Free School'.[1] The same year Elisha Williams, Edwards' old tutor at Wethersfield and nephew of Colonel Ephraim Williams, also died.

Edwards says very little of the Stockbridge opposition in his

---

[1] The evangelical 'Williams College' of a later day.

letters to Scotland, but one sentence to John Erskine well summarizes his feelings in 1755: 'The business of the Indian Mission, since I have been here, has been attended with strange embarrassments, such as I never could have expected, or so much as once dreamed of: of such a nature, and coming from such a quarter, that I take no delight in being very particular and explicit upon it' (1.clxv).

Although Edwards was only entering upon his fifties at this date he was deeply conscious of the brevity and uncertainty of his life. The resolution of his early Christian life 'never to lose one moment of time' was stronger than ever, but ill health and other hindrances impeded its fulfilment. Everything extraneous to his main concerns he laid aside. When his cousin, Jonathan Ashley, sought to have the last word in the debate on terms of communicant membership in a series of published sermons on *Churches Consisting of Saints*, the book was 'generally thought by those that oppose Mr. Edwards to be the best thing that has been published, and even unanswerable'. So Hopkins writes to Bellamy. Edwards utterly ignored it. 'Mr. Edwards,' Hopkins regretted, 'will not deign so much as to read Ashley's performance'.

But even at this juncture in his life, when Edwards had in view 'my own departure hence', he followed political and military events with close attention. Much more than their own personal safety was involved in his considerations. He was concerned for the North American Indians and for the glory of God in the American nation of the future. If French ambitions were successful, the Indians would be beyond the reach of gospel preaching and the whole prospect for the English-speaking colonies and for Protestantism would be darkened. In his letters there are shrewd observations on French and British policy and he clearly had something of his uncle Stoddard's broad grasp of Indian affairs. When he wrote to Erskine in April, 1755 the danger of the powerful 'Six Nations' going over to the French was much before him,

which there is the greatest reason to expect, unless the English should exert themselves, vigorously and successfully, against the French in America this year. They seem to be waiting to see whether this will be so or no, in order to determine whether they will entirely desert the English and cleave to the French. And if the Six Nations should forsake the English, it may be expected that the Stockbridge Indians, and almost all the nations of Indians in North America, will follow them. It seems to be the most critical season with the British dominions in America that ever was seen, since the first settlement of these colonies; and all, probably, will depend on the warlike transactions of the present year. What will be done I cannot tell. We are all in commotion, from one end of British America to the other (1.clxv).

It was well that the contest would not be settled in 1755 for the year was to see General Braddock's forces cut to pieces in an Indian ambush as they sought to advance against the French on the Ohio. 'The ministry at home,' says Edwards to Erskine (referring to the British government), 'miss it very much, in sending over British forces to fight with Indians in America, and in sending over British officers to have command of our American forces. Let them send us arms, ammunition, money, and shipping, and let New England men manage the business in their own way, who alone understand it.' What Edwards did not know, and did not live to see, was that a Seven Years' War had begun which was not to end until French power had been swept from North America. The unexplored West was destined to be the possession of the English-speaking race.

Although the frontier danger now made the arrival of visitors to Stockbridge much less likely there were still some who came. Hopkins, now long attached to the Edwards' home, was there frequently, occasionally with Joseph Bellamy. The subject of books generally figured in Hopkins' diary notes on these visits:

February 12, 1755. Mr. Bellamy came to my house last Tuesday, with whom I went to Stockbridge, and staid there two nights and one day to hear Mr. Edwards read a treatise upon the *Last End of God in the Creation of the World*. Returned home today. . . .

March 9. Went to Stockbridge to-day to borrow some books and returned. . . .

September 2, 1756. Rode to Stockbridge to-day on an important secret errand and returned.

More occasionally his friends called at Great Barrington:

September 3, Mr. Edwards and Madam, and their son Timothy at my house today.

*   *   *

Dwight conjectures what large good might have been done among the Indians by Edwards, supported by Woodbridge and Hawley, had it not been for the obstructions thrown in their way. The work among the Mohawks, for which initially there had been great hope, was especially frustrated. Yet clearly the mission was not wholly fruitless. Edwards notes in one letter to Erskine, 'Some of the Stockbridge Indians have of late been under considerable awakenings – two or three elderly men that used to be vicious persons' (1.clx). Until the Mohawks were scattered, Edwards appears to have taken four services every Sunday, one service for them, another for the Housatonics, and two for the white congregation. His surviving sermon notes reveal that he worked hard to adapt and simplify sermons for the Indians, dropping illustrations which he had used at Northampton and substituting others which were more familiar to their culture. While Edwards' white congregation was small, and clearly not wholly sympathetic to his ministry, there were times when they heard preaching equal to his best days in Northampton. In later years Dr. West of Stockbridge, who was a child in the congregation at this time, reported the following impression to Dwight:

On one occasion, when the sermon exceeded two hours in its length, he told me that from the time that Mr. Edwards had fairly unfolded his subject, the attention of the audience was fixed and motionless until its close, when they seemed disappointed that it should terminate so soon. There was such a bearing down of truth upon the mind, he observed, that there was no resisting it (1.clxxxix).

There were also regular week-day labours for Edwards both as a pastor and as a missionary. The children, both white and Indian, had classes on the Westminster Assembly's *Shorter Catechism* (which Edwards appears to have favoured instead of Watts' First Catechism previously used by Sergeant), and he was not averse to teaching them the rudiments of writing and spelling. Speaking of his father's work at this period, Jonathan Edwards, Jr. writes:

I remember that besides preaching on the Lord's day, he was wont to have an evening exercise, in the winter, at a private house, in which he gave them an account of sacred history, with practical reflections.[1]

[1] *Memoirs of Edwards*, Hopkins, edited by John Hawksley, 1815, p. 260.

[392]

*   *   *

Edwards' relations with the Stockbridge Indians refutes Ola Winslow's slander of Brainerd and his colleagues, 'These men had little interest in Indians except as souls to be saved'. *The Life of David Brainerd*, upon which Edwards had spent so much time, she tells us, 'is a tale which belongs to the annals of grim asceticism rather than in the annals of man's labours for his fellow man'. It is true that Winslow attempts to distance Edwards from Brainerd but any distinction between the two men in their attitude to the Indians is artificial. Both knew that true Christian love is practical and both cared for the Indians as people. They also knew that, despite the spiritual degradation of the Indians, there were qualities in their characters and cultures worthy of commendation. Edwards' grandfather Stoddard, and his uncle John Stoddard, both spoke of much that was to be admired among the Indians, especially their skilful adaptation to their environment. They were good hunters, farmers, artists, and boatmen, 'but the chief ornament of them was their hospitality'.[1] Winslow's statement that missionary work among the Indians 'proceeded on the hypothesis that only as the Indians lived according to the English fashion could Satan's kingdom be overthrown' is a slur.

Edwards showed much disinterested affection for the Indians. Indifference to their physical needs, as well as injustice in dealing with their grievances, incurred his anger. Possibly he got closer to them than to those in Northampton who complained of his 'unsociable' ways. Certainly his large family did not stand aloof from others and Edwards is obviously encouraged to be able to write to his father, 'The Indians seem much pleased with my family, especially my wife'. Many years later Jonathan Edwards, Jr., was to write of his memories of this period:

When I was but six years of age, my father removed with his family to Stockbridge, which, at that time, was inhabited by Indians almost solely, as there were in the town but twelve families of whites, or Anglo Americans, and perhaps one hundred and fifty families of Indians. The Indians being the nearest neighbours, I constantly

[1] Quoted by Ralph J. Coffman, *Solomon Stoddard*, 1978, p. 171.

associated with them; their boys were my daily schoolmates and play-fellows. Out of my father's house I seldom heard any language spoken but the Indian. By these means I acquired the knowledge of that language, and a great facility in speaking it. It became more familiar to me than my mother's tongue. I knew the names of some things in Indian that I did not know in English. Even all my thoughts ran in Indian; and, though the true pronunciation of the language is extremely difficult to all but themselves, they acknowledged that I had acquired it perfectly, which, as they said, had never been done before by any Anglo American. On account of my skill in their language in general, I received from them many compliments applauding my superior wisdom. This skill in their language I have, in a good measure, retained to this day.[1]

The value which Edwards placed upon work among the Indians is illustrated by his hopes that Jonathan Jr. might also be a missionary among them. Early in 1755, with the true heart of an evangelist, Gideon Hawley had set off deep into the territory of the Delawares, intending to station himself some two-hundred miles away at Onohoquaha on the Susquehanna river. Bellamy was afraid that Hawley was a man so 'venturesome' that he would 'fling away his life' yet Jonathan and Sarah Edwards had enough confidence to send nine-year-old Jonathan with Hawley, to learn the Mohawk language. Given the location to which the missionary and the boy had departed it is surprising that Edwards could expect a letter to reach them. He evidently did, as the following letter to Jonathan Jr. has survived to tell us:

Stockbridge, May 27, 1755

Dear Child:

Though you are a great way off from us, yet you are not out of our minds: I am full of concern for you, often think of you, and often pray for you. Though you are at so great a distance from us, and from all your relations, yet this is a comfort to us, that the same God that is here is also at Onohoquaha and that though you are out of our sight, and out of our reach, you are always in God's hands, who is infinitely gracious; and we can go to Him, and commit you to his care and mercy. Take heed that you don't forget or neglect Him. Always set God before your eyes, and live in his fear, and seek him every day with all diligence: for He, and He only can make you happy or miserable,

[1]Sprague, *Annals*, 1, 653–4.

as He pleases; and your Life and Health, and the eternal salvation of your soul and your all in this life and that which is to come depends on his will and pleasure. The week before last, on Thursday, David died; whom you knew and used to play with, and who used to live at our house. His soul is gone into the eternal world. Whether he was prepared for death, we don't know. This is a loud call of God to you to prepare for death. You see that they that are young die, as well as those that are old; David was not very much older than you. Remember what Christ said, that you must be born again, or you never can see the Kingdom of God. Never give your self any rest unless you have good evidence that you are converted and become a new creature. We hope that God will preserve your life and health, and return you to Stockbridge again in safety; but always remember – that life is uncertain; you know not how soon you must die, and therefore had need to be always ready. We have very lately heard from your brothers and sisters at Northampton and at Newark, that they are well. Your aged grandfather and grandmother, when I was at Windsor gave their love to you. We here all do the same.

> I am,
> your tender and affectionate father,
> Jonathan Edwards.

After nearly a year away, Hawley and Jonathan Jr. were back in Stockbridge early in 1756.

Letters such as the above indicate that, regardless of nationality, Edwards was fundamentally concerned with the spiritual welfare of others. But it was the same love which prompted that concern which also led him to attend patiently to the temporal needs of Indian youths. When war and the scattering of the Mohawk school nullified educational efforts at Stockbridge, Edwards arranged for some Indian boys to go to Bellamy for further help. In a letter accompanying these would-be pupils Edwards speaks of their need to learn arithmetic and continues:

I would also propose the following things, viz. that pains be taken with them to teach them the English tongue, to learn them the meaning of English words and what the name of everything is in English . . . and that they be taught to pray, that you write out for them various forms of prayer, and make them understand them, and turn them after into Indian. And to teach them the Assemblies' Catechism and endeavour as far as may be to make them to understand it. To ask them questions of the scripture history, not only the lessons they read, but the main things in the general history of the Bible in their order.

Edwards concludes with a few details about clothing and an admission that the boys were far from eager to make the trip to Bellamy, 'It is with a vast deal of difficulty that I have at last got the boys away, after manifold objecting, hiding and skulking to avoid going'.

Bellamy comments on these pupils in a letter of May 31, 1756 – a letter written chiefly to persuade Edwards to flee from the danger of the frontier and to join them in Bethlehem:

The Indian boys grow more and more easy and content, but they love to play too well – are very ignorant – and very stupid, as to the things of religion – and in arithmetic, when I would teach them anything that is a little difficult, they are soon discouraged, and don't love to try. So I take them off, and put them to writing again – designing, by little and little, to get them along. They will not endure hardship and bend their minds to business, like English boys. It seems they were never taught their catechism.

These extracts from Edwards and Bellamy are too brief to convey the amount of practical wisdom which both men favoured in handling children. Children's lessons, says Edwards elsewhere, must 'be rendered pleasant, entertaining and profitable', not a 'dull, wearisome task, without any suitable pleasure or benefit'. The teacher must create an appetite for knowledge, he must not allow the children to memorize without understanding, nor must he remain aloof from his class by adopting a superior manner. Familiar questions should be put to the child about the subjects of the lesson; and the child should be encouraged, and drawn on, to speak freely, and in his turn also to ask questions for the resolution of his own doubts.

We know enough of the record of the Stockbridge Indians in later years to have evidence that Edwards' work among them was not in vain. At the end of the century Timothy Dwight could write, 'Their reverence for him was very great and his family are still regarded by their descendants with peculiar respect'.[1]

[1] *Travels*, vol. 4, p. 383.

Some years after Edwards' day, it is recorded that Joseph Bellamy revisited Stockbridge 'during a revival of religion which extended, in some degree, to the Indians who resided in that neighbourhood, a considerable number of whom became hopefully pious'. After preaching at a Sunday afternoon service, Bellamy had just commenced a meal at the home where he was a guest when the sound of Indians singing psalms arrested him. Instantly he rose to leave the table and when, after some length of time he returned, he explained happily to his host, 'Do you think I can deny myself the pleasure of being in heaven for the sake of eating?'[1]

[1]Sprague, vol. 1, p. 409.

Culross, Scotland, the destination of Edwards' letters to John Erskine from 1753. Reproduced from an engraving by John Slezer (1669–1714).

THROUGH ESTHER'S EYES

New York in the late eighteenth century.

The female sex here hold an honourable station in society, and have an important influence upon its concerns. The first place at the table, in the family, in the social circle, and in every other situation where they are found, is given to them of course. On all occasions, they are treated with marked attention and respect, and the man who behaves rudely or insolently to a woman is considered as hardly meriting the name.

TIMOTHY DWIGHT
(nephew of Esther Edwards Burr) in *Travels in New-England and New York*, 1822, vol. 4, p. 475

hen Edwards' second daughter, Esther, re-moved to her new home at Newark, New Jersey, in 1752, it was a greater break with the family than any of the children had yet experienced. Her sister, Sarah, was close to her parents in Stockbridge and Mary only sixty miles away in the familiar surroundings of Northampton. But Newark was 150 miles distant and New Jersey a province sufficiently different to make Esther sometimes home-sick for New England. In her eyes New York, only a few hours by boat from Newark, offered a poor comparison with Boston. Its churches, shops and military defences ('but two guns that can be fired . . . so neglected that they are rusty and got quite out of order') did not impress Esther: 'I would not live here a fortnight for any money'. And not only was New Jersey behind Massachusetts in its development, but with many Indian, Dutch and other nationalities it was also more cosmopolitan. Newark had a local militia and noisy training days such as Esther had known in Northampton, but New England's long traditions and racial unity produced a fighting power which she believed could not be matched. Long enough in New Jersey to count herself one with the people, Esther, contemplating the French danger, wrote in 1755, 'Our people seem to know nothing what to do more than a parsle of Children would in such a case, nor half so much as New England Children would'. 'I could not help laughing heartily to see our people 3 days getting ready to go about 50 miles, and when they were ready wait a whole day for the Colonel who was afraid and wanted the Indians to go out of the way before he went'.

The Edwards also clearly felt the far-removed position of their daughter and especially when – so soon after her marriage – she was seriously ill in 1753. Her father wrote to her on March 28th of that year:

We are glad to hear that you are in any respect better but concerned at your remaining great weakness. I am glad to see some of the contents of your letter to your Mother and particularly that you have been enabled to make a free-will-offering of yourself to God's service, and that you have experienced some inward divine consolations under your affliction, by the extreme weakness and distressing pains you have been the subject of. For these you ought to be thankful, and also for that unwearied kindness and tender care of your companion, which you speak of. I would not have you think that any strange thing has happened to you in this affliction: 'Tis according to the course of things in this world, that after the world's smiles, some great affliction soon comes. God has now given you early and seasonable warning not at all to depend on worldly prosperity. Therefore I would advise . . . if it pleases God to restore you, to lot[1] upon no happiness here. Labour while you live, to serve God and do what good you can, and endeavour to improve every dispensation to God's glory and your own spiritual good, and be content to do and bear all that God calls you to in this wilderness, and never expect to find this world any thing better than a wilderness. Lay your account to travel through it in weariness, painfulness, and trouble, and wait for your rest and your prosperity 'till hereafter where they that die in the Lord rest from their labours, and enter into the joy of their Lord. You are like to spend the rest of your life (if you should get over this illness) at a great distance from your parents, but care not much for that. If you lived near us, yet our breath and yours would soon go forth, and we should return to our dust, whither we are all hastening. 'Tis of infinitely more importance to have the presence of an heavenly Father, and to make progress towards an heavenly home. Let us all take care that we may meet there at last.

Three years later Esther was to observe, 'I know what it is to be a stranger and among all strangers when sick'.

But despite Esther's distant location there were to be several factors which kept her close to her parents. Her father's

---

[1]To count on.

friendship with her husband, and his commitment to the College of New Jersey over which Burr was president, ensured the expectation of his presence from time to time. As already noted, Edwards was down for the College Commencement and for the Synod at New York only months after Esther's wedding. In 1754 Esther's mother was down for the birth of her first child – another Sarah ('Sally') – and the same year her sixteen-year-old brother, Timothy, had also arrived in Newark as one of Burr's students. Nor were the close ties with her sisters ended, for, besides letters, there were to be lengthy visits by Susannah ('Sukey'), Lucy ('Nabby') and Eunice.

What makes Esther of special interest, however, is her journal which has survived for the period October 1754 to September 1757.[1] This journal, from which we have already quoted above, is a hurriedly written narrative of day-to-day events, written by instalments for her close friend Sally Prince ('Fidelia') in far-off Boston.[2] While we could wish that Esther had still been at Northampton or Stockbridge when the journal was written, it nonetheless gives us in a unique way a sight of the human side of the Edwards family. What is missing from so many of the other documents upon which any biographer of Edwards is dependent, suddenly springs vividly to life in the 'conversation' on every-day affairs which was regularly despatched to Boston. 'I am grown such a Gossip,' Esther writes playfully at one point, and while 'gossip' is certainly not the purpose of the journal neither did the two friends intend to write anything beyond what was of immediate interest to each other. Much that would be of special interest to two young women in their mid-twenties, is to be found in these letters between 'Burrissa' and 'Fidelia'.

As Sally Prince was still single, and pursued by various suitors, it was inevitable that romance and marriage should be a recurring theme between them, and one can readily believe

[1] *The Journal of Esther Edwards Burr*, Ed. Carol F. Karlsen and L. Crumpacker, 1984.
[2] Daughter of Thomas Prince, minister of the Old South. The close friendship between the two girls began about 1751, and it was perhaps deepened by the fact that by 1754 Sally Prince had lost all three of her sisters. Esther had lost only one – the unforgotten Jerusha. Writing to Sally in 1754 Esther says, 'We, viz you and I never shall forget the friends we have lost by death. I mean our *Sisters.*'

that Esther is often reflecting something of her parents' views. Despite the apparent suddenness of her own marriage to Aaron Burr, the journal makes it abundantly clear that it was no marriage of convenience. The attraction of love, in Esther's opinion, is essential to a happy marriage and she warns Sally against any connection without love, no matter what other affinities might exist. Offering advice about one of Sally's suitors, Esther writes: 'The important point must turn here. If upon mature deliberation and serious consideration you find you cant think of spending your days with that Gentleman with Complaciency and delight, *say No* – but if on the contarary, I think you may venture to answer in the affermative'. Without this, the married state 'which aught to be a silken Cord of Mutial Love' becomes a chain. Where there is true love, although prudence and wisdom are also needed, marriage is essentially a state of happiness. Rejecting Sally's half-serious preference for the single state, Esther says, 'These poor fettered folks you seem to pity so much, I look upon as the happest part of the world', and two years later, with Sally still single, Esther abbreviates the whole discussion to, 'Marry and be happy'!

Without question, Esther first learned this attitude to marriage from her parents whom she specifically quotes at one important point in the protracted discussion on Sally's suitors. Sally did not want to marry a minister but she looked for a husband who would be a bright Christian. Thus a principal objection which she had to one young man was that he was not capable of 'religious conversation'. Obviously he was a church-goer. Esther, however, replied that any certainty as to a person's conversion is not *essential* to marriage. Answering Sally's objection she writes,

How knowest thou, O Woman, but thou mayest gain thy Husband. I think there is a good deal of reson to hope it as he has such a desire to have a relegious Wife.

I know it to be the opinnion of my Honored Parents that a person aught not to make concience of this matter. They say that some other things were more nesesary to happyness in a Married state, (which things you have mentioned of him) but when a Relegion meets those other things it Crowns all – tis proporly the Crown, but my dear this alone will not do – look around, you will soon see that tis not every good Man that you could live happily with in that state.

It seems that Esther's younger sister, Mary Dwight (who, of course, was not at Stockbridge when Burr visited in 1752) had some misgivings about Esther's 'way of marrying' but every visitor to the Newark parsonage could see how well-matched they were. Esther's feelings about her husband are frequently apparent in the journal, 'What would all the world be to me if he were out of it!' Others might speak off Burr's 'piercing intellect and commanding eloquence' but for Esther he was the < life and joy of the home and when absent, as he frequently was, she can write, 'Our house is very gloomy, as 'tis *always* when Mr Burr is gone.'

Esther ran the home much as her mother had done at Northampton and the house was quite as busy as the parsonage in King Street had ever been. It seems there was only 'Harry' as a permanent black servant, with kitchen help sometimes added. Most of the work was Esther's – cleaning, repairing, tailoring and endless cooking. With entries such as 'Dined eight minnisters', 'Dined 10 minnisters', it is not surprising that she was so much occupied. One day she writes: 'To morrow the Presbytery are to meet here, so you may think I am prety busy in the Citchin, making Mince-pyes and Cocoa-nut Tarts etc.' Or again, 'The Governor and Lady rode up this P.M. and made us a vissit, and the good gentleman as usual directs me what I shall get for his dinner, in jest – He says he must have a Pudding and a Roast Chicken – When they came I was at the Oven baking little Caks for Commencement. I brought them some of em, for the Governor loves such things. He and Madam Eat and commended em as good.'

One afternoon, 'there was Thirty, or Thirty one people came here, and most of 'em vissitors'. 'My days are to be spent in a hurry of business'. At one low point, suffering a bad headache after 'a vast deal of company', she writes to Sally, 'I am almost wore out and tired of *staying* here, for living I can't call it'. But on the whole, it was the kind of life with which she had grown up and she enjoyed it. She therefore objected to William Tennent's observation made one day as he looked at her, 'Poor creature, she is to have no comfort in life I see! but always be hurried to Death'. The occasions she seems to have appreciated most were the times of spiritual conversation. One frequent visitor to the home was the Rev. John Brainerd (brother to

David) whom she had first met in Northampton. After he and others had been visiting one 'Sabbath Eve', Esther writes, 'O my dear how Charming tis to set and hear such excellent persons convers on the experimentals of relegion. It seemed like old times'. And again, 'I esteem *relegious Conversation* one of the best helps to keep up relegion in the soul, excepting secret devotion, I dont know but the very best – Then what a lamentable thing that tis so neglected by God's own Children'.

One of Esther's most welcome guests was her husband's friend, George Whitefield, whom she had first met at the age of eight years in 1740. From that time Whitefield had remained in particularly close touch with the Presbyterians of the Middle Colonies. He had given unstinted encouragement to the College of New Jersey from the outset and promoted the interests of what he called the 'glorious plan' in England. Writing on the subject to a friend in 1750, Whitefield says: 'The present President Mr. Burr, and most of the trustees, I am well acquainted with. They are friends to vital piety.' It was Whitefield also who had pressed for the fund-raising visit to Britain of the two preachers, Samuel Davies and Gilbert Tennent, in 1753 – a visit which was successful despite the wonder of some at the prospect of a College standing for 'the exploded doctrines of Calvinism and experimental religion'.[1]

When Whitefield was back in America in 1754, Esther was afraid that he might not be able to stay in their home. 'I loted much on his company and conversation as well as preaching,' she writes to Sally Prince. But certainly she heard him preach for the Englishman was in Newark at the College Commencement in September, 1754, when he also preached at the meetings of the Synod. Reporting this to Lady Huntingdon, Whitefield writes: 'The Synod succeeded – But such a number of simple hearted, united ministers I never saw before. I preached to them several times, and the great Master of assemblies was in the midst of us.'[2]

---

[1] *Sketches of Virginia*, W. H. Foote, 1850, p. 256. Davies' journal of his British visit is printed in full in this volume.

[2] Whitefield's *Works*, 3, p. 104. When the Synods of New York and Philadelphia were re-united in 1758 there was a vast increase of numbers in the former. Philadelphia had only 20 ministers, while New York had seen 66 ordained and another 15 received from New England.

Luke Tyerman, Whitefield's Victorian biographer, comments on the 'almost unseemly haste' in exercising the powers of their charter with which the trustees of the New Jersey College acted in conferring the degree of M.A. on Whitefield at the Commencement of 1754. In any case, he adds, it was 'a dubious honour' for a man already possessing an Oxford B.A. But Whitefield did not view the infant College in that light. Already its work was vital and he believed in its great future. To the Marquis of Lothian he could write of Burr, 'there is not a ~ more accomplished deserving president in the world'.[1]

With the Commencement and Synod over, Burr and Whitefield together left for New England and Boston on October 1, 1754, where, among others, they expected to see Edwards. After their departure Esther writes of the kind of evenings which, she anticipated, her father and her husband were likely to be spending at the Prince home in Boston.

O my dear it seems as if Mr. Burr had been gone a little Age! and it is yet but one Fortnight! I dont know what I shall do with my self the rest of the time, I am out of patience already. I imagine now this Eve Mr Burr is at your house. Father is there and some others. You all set in the Middleroom, *Father* has the *talk*, and Mr Burr has the *Laugh*, Mr. Prince gets room to stick in a word once in a while. The rest of you set and see, and hear, and make observations to yourselves, Miss Janny amongst the rest, and when you get up stairs you tell what you think, and wish I was there two.[2]

This is certainly not the picture of the silent, unsociable Edwards which his detractors drew.[3] Despite the deferential position of females reflected in the above quotation Esther herself was not diffident when she had occasion to correct the opposite sex. John Ewing, one of the College tutors – 'a man of

[1] Whitefield was soliciting the aid of the Marquis in seeking a doctorate of divinity for Burr from the University of Edinburgh. For confirmation of this estimate, he adds, 'Your lordship might have testimonials enough from good Governor Belcher, Mr. Jonathan Edwards, *cum multis aliis*'. *Life of Whitefield*, L. Tyerman, vol. 2, pp. 342–3. For Tyerman's opinion on the 'worthless' New Jersey degree see p. 334.

[2] As noted earlier, on account of ill health Edwards may not have reached Boston at this date. If he did meet Whitefield it was their last meeting.

[3] In this same year, Timothy Cutler, the anti-evangelical Anglican minister of Boston, wrote of J E: 'I know the man: though more decent in his language than Mayhew and Prince, he is odd in his principles, stiff, haughty, and morose'.

good parts and lerning but has mean thoughts of Women' –
once ventured the opinion in her presence that women should
limit their conversation to 'things that they understood'. Did he
mean such things as 'fashions and dress' asked Mrs Burr? and
before any answer was forthcoming, the unfortunate tutor had
to listen to one who was quite evidently his equal in thought
and speech. 'My tongue, you know, hangs pretty loose,' Esther
reports to Sally, 'thoughts Crowded in – so I sputtered away for
dear life – I retorted several severe things upon him before he
had time to speak again. He Blushed and seemed confused. The
Gentleman seting by said little but when did speak it was to my
purpose and we carried on the dispute for an hour – I talked
him quite silent.'

It is, however, on spiritual issues that Esther Burr shows her
thought and discrimination most clearly. 'Her training is
reflected in every view she expressed,' says Ola Winslow. 'She
was so loyal to it that she did not know she was loyal'. But that
is not to do justice to the facts. Esther's judgments, as her
experiences, were clearly her own. That they might commonly
coincide with those of her parents was more than a matter of
education. On the question of preaching, for example, she is no
blind approver of anything that was orthodox. She wants more
than that from sermons. Her husband, she tells Sally, 'has been
remarkably stired up to be fervent in his preaching of late'.
John Brainerd, whom she often heard at Newark, lacked the
analytical gift of her father and her husband, 'He preached
well, tho' in the afternoon he indevoured to discribe true
Humility, and I thought he was a little confused'. Yet as a
preacher she prizes Brainerd, With reference to a Thursday
Fast Day she writes: 'I was at meeting all day and I think I
never heard Mr Brainerd pray and Preach so well. I believe he
had much of the presence of God with him.'

Esther Burr's spiritual thoughts are all the more valuable
because they are 'off-the-cuff' comments, found amidst the
narrative of daily events and problems. Like her mother, she is
far from the caricature of the sombre Puritan matron. The
numbers who enjoyed calling at the Newark parsonage were,
in part, a witness to the contagious cheerfulness of the
household. But basically life is serious:

Make it the business of life to prepare for heaven.

O pray for me that I may have a right temper of mind towards the ever blessed God!

That knowledge of God that does not produce a love to him and a desire to be like him is not a true knowledge.

God has ennabled me to trust in him and rely upon him – and tis my comfort and joy that he will be glorified what ever becomes of me.

I think God has been Near to me this eve – O how good tis to get near the Lord! I long to live near him always – nor is it living unless I do . . . I feel excdingly affraid of being left to distrust God as I have done for some weeks past – Nothing but the mighty power of God can keep me from it – I feel myself infinitely weak and unable to do the least thing of my self – And God appears all Sufficient – I have the Headache all day to day.

What a charming place this world would be of it was not for the inhabitants – O I long for the blessed and glorious times when this World shall become a Mountain of Holiness.

One 'Sabbath morn 6 o'Clock' she writes:

O that the Lord would be near to me this day and give me some sense of his glory and beauty as he is revealed in the gospel of his dear Son! I feel as dead as a stone – I have no zeal for God or his service – O why ant I sent down to the dark regions of dispare before this day? Why ant I deprived of all advantages for relegion for my horred abuse of them – tis of Gods mear good pleasure and infinite condesention that I be not now lifting up my Eyes in Eternal Torments insted of beholding one of the blessed days of the Son [of] Man.

I dont in the least doubt of God's Blessing both in Spirittuals and Temporals . . . I am ready to think that we loose much of the comforts of relegion, and G[od] looses much prais, by nor remarking small mercies – as we are apt to call 'em.

Esther obviously knew of the opposition to her father in Stockbridge, which was virtually over by the time her Journal commences. A cryptic line, 'I think Mr Dwight deserves to be licked' (Oct. 4, 1754) is probably a reference to Colonel Joseph Dwight.

A matter of great concern to Esther was the location of her parents' home at a time of renewed hostility with the French and the consequent danger of Indian attacks. News of the four deaths of white settlers at Stockbridge in the autumn of 1754 had reached Newark by October 31st. 'The topick of conversation was the mischeif done at Stockbridge (and war in general) I have avoided writing anything about My dear friends there because I should be two gloomy if I once begin. But O my dear friend tis impossible to conceive the anguish of my Mind on hearing the News first for it was told in the worst light it could be.' Rumours abounded. On November 8, 1754, Esther reports further to Sally:

Fryday
A gentleman from Albany has been here to day and brings the sertain news that all the Indians in Stockbridge have left the place except two or three famalys. He says they are much disgusted, and say the white people are jelous of em and they will not live among em any longar. He said farther that they had a mind to send for a neighbouring Tribe to assist em to kill all the people in Stockbridge. O my dear what a dismal aspect things have! I am almost out of my witts! What will become of my Dear father and his afflicted family! O help me to commit em to God who orders all things in mercy, and dont willingly afflict nor grieve any of his Children! I am ready to say some times, why is it? Why does God suffer his own most dear children to be hunted about in this manner! But this is a very wrong temper of mind. I hope I may be enabled to crush it by divine assistance. This day was our prepareation day for a recseption of the holy ordinance of the Lord Supper

The infrequency of news from Stockbridge added to Esther's anxieties. On April 2, 1755, she writes: 'I can only add that I have had the pleasure of hearing from Northampton, and that they are all well. Sister Dwight has another fine *Son*, which I suppose you have heard[1] Brother Dwight says he heard from Stockbridge some time in February, and my Mother had about that time had a very bad fall from a Horse, but was mending. This is all we have heard from there this five months.'

The defeat of General Braddock in July 1755 threw all the Middle Colonies into alarm. Esther decided against a proposed visit to Stockbridge and was nervous about the return to the frontier of Timothy and Susannah who were then with her:[2]

[1] Mary's second son, Sereno Edwards Dwight.
[2] Fourteen-year-old Susannah had come the previous November, both to help and to learn housewifery.

'My Brother and Sister talk of going home soon, but I am afraid it is not safe – I heard that a 100 Indians are gone from Stockbridge with Mr. Shirley.[1] I wonder what Mr Edwards does with himself. I reason he seems as if he had nothing to do.'

The last remark is a clear indication that she viewed her father primarily as a pastor and missionary and not as someone who aspired chiefly to literary work.

Despite what it would mean to have her parents much nearer at hand, Esther was against her father accepting a possible call to the Presbyterian church in New York at this time. In 1754 the church on Wall Street was again without pastors, following the removal of Ebenezer Pemberton, and his assistant minister, to Boston. The last years of Pemberton's pastorate had not been happy ones, despite the congregation's large growth. The English versus Scots difficulties of the 1720's had never been overcome and one point of controversy had been Pemberton's action in introducing the looser rendering of the Psalms in the < version of Isaac Watts for public worship. The Scots section of the congregation, in particular, wanted to retain the old version.

The vacancy in the New York church proved to be a long and troubled one. Initial enthusiasm was for a call to Joseph Bellamy, which was given and at length declined. Among other considerations, Bellamy knew that there was opposition to the convictions which he had come to share with Edwards over admission to the Lord's Table. One member had told him, 'If your sentiments with regard to church communion are such as Mr Edwards's, it would infallibly make the rent in our church much wider, as the bulk of our people are against it'.[2] Clearly, discussion on the Northampton controversy and Edwards' writings on qualifications for communion had gone on in the Jerseys. Possibly a change of conviction on this matter had added to Pemberton's problems on Wall Street, for, according to a later statement of Chauncy, 'Pemberton would go to the death for Edwards's

---

[1] Governor of Massachusetts, who succeeded Braddock in command of British Forces.
[2] Webster, p. 631.

distinguishing tenet:– refusing church privileges to the unregenerate'.[1]

After Bellamy's decision against moving to New York was
known, Esther Burr heard reports that there was a decision to
call David Bostwick, and should that fail, to turn to her father,
'which,' she writes, 'I should not like at all if I thought it
probable that he would come – he will by no means do for 'em if
he would come'. She knew, as a correspondent wrote to
Bellamy, 'those that opposed you would oppose Mr. Edwards
also', and she clearly believed that her parents had been
through enough battles.

Attitudes to Edwards among some in the New York congregation were not representative of the feelings of the ministers of
the Synod as a whole where it is clear that Edwards' counsel
had increasing influence. He was consulted on various matters
such as the breach with the Synod of Philadelphia and
measures to heal it, missionary affairs, assessments of ministers
for vacant charges, and the work of the College.

In September, 1755 Edwards was again invited to be the
guest preacher at the College Commencement – as Whitefield
had been the year before. Esther was expecting him to come by
Saturday, September 13, for on the next day the Sacrament of
the Lord's Supper was being celebrated in her husband's
church. When he did not arrive, she wrote:

> Saturday Ev. Still very hot.
> p.m. Went to hear a preparritory sermon to our saciment . . . a good
> practical discourse as Mr Brainerds sermons all are, but I want [was
> not] in a good frame to hear. It was so very hot in our close meeting-
> house that I could not attend, or at least I did'n't to my shame, tho' I
> heard enough to know it was a very good sermon.
>
> I am much disappointed by my fathers not coming to day as I fully
> expected. I fear he or some of the famaly are sick.

The week-end had passed before Edwards arrived at
midnight, 'very unexpectedly', on Tuesday, September 16th.
The following day he was probably awakened, as others in the

[1]Webster, p. 402. Dickinson and Burr were also showing the relevance of
this issue (Webster p. 528). In the 1730's, the Synod of Philadelphia had, it
would seem too ineffectively, exhorted ministers 'to use due care in examining
those they admit to the Lord's Supper' (p. 135).

household commonly were, by Sally prattling – 'like *other Birds* as soon as she is awake to singing . . . her Eyes sparkling like *diamonds*'. It was his first meeting with his infant grand-daughter. After three busy days, with, one supposes, later than usual conversations in the evenings, Edwards and Aaron Burr departed for the Synod at Philadelphia where important proposals for re-union were under discussion. Besides the sudden quietness in the household Esther was left with the possibility of having to appear in court as a witness in the prosecution of a man who, having verbally abused the Burrs, subsequently cut one of their horses. Esther's nerve failed her at this prospect: 'for I never was called before a Court in my Life, or so much as sworn. I dont know but I should faint if they call me to speak, for I am very bashful in such cases'.

In the event the two men were back a week later and before the court convened. Although they returned on a Saturday, in time for the duties of the next day, both were ill: 'Mr Edwards tired himself sick, and Mr Burr sick of a cold. I got something for their refreshment and have put 'em both to Bed.' In the event it was a happy Sunday for Esther:

Mr Edwards preached all day two charming sermons from those words, 'When a wicked man dieth his expectations perrish, and the hope of unjust men perrisheth'.

My Father seems much better to day but Mr Burr is very ill yet tho' he went out all day.

The next Tuesday the Burrs accompanied Edwards to New York, which involved a sail of four hours. With contrary winds on the Hudson there was some doubt about when he could sail north, and he employed some of his time attempting to pacify one of the leading protagonists in the controversy which still continued over what should be sung in public worship. Reporting her father's movements to Sally Prince, Esther writes,

he tells me that he dined at Loyer Smiths yesterday and he never saw a man in such a Rage as he is about the Psalms. He is quite beyond reason or anything but passion, and declares that if my father or any other Minnister in the Country should offer to set the Scotch Psalms he will get up immediately and go out of the house, and order all his famaly out, and will never again set his foot into that Meeting. My

Father said he indevoured to reason calmly with him and would have him consider if that method would be the most prudent that could be taken, but he would not hear him talk, and told him that it did not signify for him or any body elce to talk with him, for he was resolutely fixed, and would not be moved.[1]

The final outcome of the church troubles in New York was that Bostwick was settled in 1756 and the Scottish element in the congregation separated to form another congregation.

The Burrs were concerned at this same period for the future of the Newark congregation. As early as 1752 it had been decided – at the same Synod that Edwards had attended in New York – to move the College of New Jersey to a permanent location in the rural village of Princeton. While Newark was on the northern border of New Jersey, Princeton would be central to the whole state. But matters proceeded slowly, being dependent largely upon funds which had still to be raised in Britain.

By April, 1754 Samuel Davies could report 'most surprising success' in the mission to Britain. One of the leading figures in raising support had been William Hogg of Edinburgh – the same man who had come to Edwards' aid in 1751. 'Mr. Hogg and family' became special friends to Davies and Tennent, and in 1755 Hogg was in correspondence with Burr, indicating his persuasion that the collections in Britain and Ireland would not be less than £4000. Edwards' connection with the College, and the position of his son-in-law as president, had contributed to Hogg's readiness to believe Davies' representations of what Princeton could become, 'an extensive benefit to mankind, not only in the present but in future ages'.[2] In a letter of August 28,

---

[1] There was a party nick-named 'The Gentlemen' in the New York church, to which 'Lawyer Smith' seems to have adhered, who were men of wealth and influence, opposed to earnest preaching and to 'the Scotch party'. Smith was evidently incensed at a recent Synod decision that 'the Scotch Psalms be sung in the meeting in New York one half of the time' (see *Burr*, p. 143 fn. and p. 157). Edwards was in as good a position as any to reason with Smith, for although he held a high view of the importance of the metrical Psalter in public worship (1.240 and 554) he did not believe in an exclusive use of the Psalter: 'I am far from thinking that the book of Psalms should be thrown by in our public worship, but that it should always be used in the Christian church to the end of the world: but I know of no obligation we are under to *confine* ourselves to it' (1.396).

[2] Foote, *op. cit.*, p. 259.

1755, Hogg wrote to Burr: 'I notice your relation to the Rev. and worthy Mr. Edwards, by marrying a daughter of his. I have had for several years past a great regard for Mr. and Mrs. Edwards and their family, as he has been eminently useful by his labours in the ministry. I am heartily sorry for his present situation, but I would fain hope that the Lord will eminently appear in behalf of his people in North America and deliver them from their strong enemies.'[1]

In February, 1755 the trustees of the College of New Jersey were able to contract for a large building, to cost £4960, with the trustees themselves providing the stone and timber. As Princeton was a day's ride from Newark, Aaron Burr could no longer combine the pastorate with his presidency and his congregation were very reluctant to allow him to go full-time to the College. In March, 1755 the Presbytery dissolved the pastoral tie between Burr and the Newark Church, yet with nothing ready at Princeton, they continued to live at the parsonage with Burr frequently supplying the pulpit. With the preacher to whom they appear to have been closely attached still in their midst, it was hard for the people to address themselves to the necessary duty of giving another minister a call. The prospects of unanimity were also slim. Of one visiting preacher Esther says: 'He preached with a good deal of life and spirit. I liked him well, but I know by the countinances of people in general that they did not like him. Tis truth that this people are very whmsical about preachers.' In Esther's view, John Brainerd was the obvious man for Newark to call:

He is a very good man, and seems always much ingaged for the good of souls. I hope our people w'not be so foolish as to reject such a Man, and such a preacher – but Newark people are as diffecult as New York, and some w'not like this or the other man because such and such persons like him, etc. You know how people can act when they have got out of temper.

When Brainerd had preached for more than a year amongst them, and had still received no call, he decided to return to his earlier missionary work among the Indians. Esther was afraid the congregation might 'break all to pieces'.

The week after she had said farewell to her father in New

---

[1] *The Biblical Repertory*, 1840, p. 381.

York in October 1755, Esther made another visit to Princeton with her husband to view the progress of the building – Nassau Hall, as it was to be called. On this occasion they could climb to the top of the building where they believed the view to be enjoyed was 'the finest in the Province'. There was still, however, much work to be done before any removal would be possible. A further visit at the beginning of August, 1756, is recorded as follows:

. . . About 3 o'Clock it seemd a little cooler so set forward came safe to Princeton before sun set then walked to take a little view of the College for we had not patience to tarry till morning – Just looked at the Presidents House which is under cover – then returnd to our Lodgings, eat supper and tired almost to Death we were glad to go to Bed.

Teusday Morn, up very erly.
Soon after Breakfast went up to College to take a more petecular view of that and our House – the College is a Famous building I assure you and the most commodious of any of the Colleges as well as much the largest of any upon the Continent. There is something very striking in it and a grandure and yet a simpliscity that cant well be expressed – I am well pleased with the House they have begun for us.

As the move to Princeton would take them further still from Stockbridge there was a case for Esther making a visit home before the winter of 1756. She writes on August 6, 1756, 'Received Letters from Stockbridge, all well and extreamly urgent to have me make em a vissit before I go to Princeton'. Her parents had not seen their latest grandchild, Aaron Burr Jr, born the previous February. Baby Aaron was born prematurely when her husband was away from home. 'It had seemd very gloomy when I found I was actually in Labour,' Esther reported to Sally, 'to think that I was, as it were, destitute of Earthly friends – No mother – No Husband and none of my petecular friends that belong to this Town, they happening to be out of Town – but O my dear God was all these relations and more than all to me in the Hour of my distre[ss].'

Although not devoid of worries, Esther considered it her duty to make the difficult journey to Stockbridge with Aaron who was only six months old. She left Newark on Saturday, August 21st and spent an extremely hot three days in New York before the next sloop going up the Hudson left on the following Wednesday. The movement of soldiers which she observed was a reminder of the war which still continued in the interior. About an hundred miles up the river, Esther disembarked on the Saturday, August 28, for a further journey of fifty miles eastwards overland. A family acquaintance in the locality loaned a servant and a waggon to take her to Stockbridge. By Saturday evening they had reached a Dutch home 'in the woods' which, although 'a very inconvenient place to spend a Sabbath', was the only shelter available. 'The whole house is but one room, and a large famaly and no religion.' In addition to this difficulty, the servant loaned to her returned to his home, while fifty soldiers – recruits from Rhode Island – arrived unexpectedly in the evening and required board and lodgings. Notwithstanding, it was to prove a memorable day for Esther.

As soon as Breakfast was over I took an English Bible (which is rare among the Dutch) and walked about a quarter of a mile with some longing desires that I might meet God, and I hope I found him. O how good is God to an unworthy Worm that has forsook him to meet me this Morn – I said surely God is in this place, and I hope I shall never forget it – truly my dear I hant found such freedom and delight in Gods servise for many weeks past – God does not want for means nor place – I have been long seeking God in this and the other duty and ordinance – but it has pleased him to hide his face and disappoint me in my hopes and expecttations when I was ready to think him near – but how little did I think of meeting him here – last Sabbath I lost and I greived at the loos and I was affraid I should lose this – O what shall I render to the Lord for his goodness to me? I can render nothing but myself, my poor wicked sinfull self.

The next morning 'before sun rise', and on a 'very bad road', mother and child went on by waggon. They were only ten miles from Stockbridge when heavy rain commenced. 'We stopped as soon as we could find a convenient house which was about 6 miles from my Fathers. I could not bare to stop for all night, and our waggonner was urgent to go along so we set out wet to the skin as we were . . . in a half an hour I had not a dry thread abot me, but kept along and just as we got to my Fathers it left raining. We came in and surprised em almost out of their witts. Luck and Sucky were almost overcome. I need not tell you how glad they were to see us.' The journey had taken nine days; it is no wonder that Esther says elsewhere on the problems of travel, 'Why has not art contrived some method more commodious and quick?'

The joy of a home-coming after four years' absence was overshadowed by two things. First, as Mary Dwight was soon to deliver her third child, Sarah Edwards was due to leave for Northampton in a week's time. Esther's disappointment is understandable: 'On Tuesday My Mother sets out for Northampton. My sister Dwight is near her time, so I never said one Word against it altho' I am come 150 Miles to see my friends and am apt to think I shall not come again in many years if ever'. Despite plenty of other life in the household, Sarah Edwards was, in Esther's eyes, clearly the sun around which all else revolved.

> 7 Tuesday extream hot –
> This morn my mother set out for Northampton and hopes to return in about a month, but alas for me I shall not be able to wait her return. . . . My Mother gone! It adds double gloom to everything.

A week later her feelings were unchanged, 'You cant conceive how every thing alters upon my Mothers going away – All is Dark as Egypt.'

The second thing which troubled Esther was still more distressing. In mid-August the French under Montcalm had a further victory at Oswego on Lake Ontario, news of which was still coming through. In terms of personal safety she could hardly have been at Stockbridge at a worse time. The following entries in her journal to Sally tell their own story:

> Thursday and Fryday – 2–3
> Almost overcome with fear. Last night and Thursday night we had a watch at this fort and most of the Indians come to lodge here – some thought that they heard the enemy last night – O how distressing to live in fear every moment.

> Sabbath – 5
> Out all day. Heard 4 excellent sermons tho so Ill for want of sleep that I am hardly my self – I hant had a nights sleep since I left New York – Since I have been here I may say I have had none.

> 8 Wednesday still as hot as ever
> . . . This place is in a very defenceless condicion – not a soldier in it, the fighting Indians all except a very few gone into the Army, many of

the white people also, and this is a place that the enemy can easily get at, and if they do we cant defent our selves. 10 Indians might with all ease distroy us intirely. There has been a number seen at about 30 miles distance from this place.

Saturday – 11

Last night 17 soldiers came to Town to our assistance. The number is two small by much to defend three Forts. Some of em are to lodge here. Hope I shant be so much affraid as before tho' they are but little better than none.

The next day her father preached on a text relevant to the times from Amos 8.11 and Esther was helped, 'at night when retired felt calmed with the thought that God would be Glorified . . . the ever blessed God will loose none of his glory lett men or Devils do their worst.' Nonetheless, still deeply apprehensive, as well as homesick for her husband and 'Little Sally', she proposed to her father that she shorten her visit and leave the next week: 'But he is not willing to hear one word about it, so I must tarry the proposed time and if the Indians get me, they get me, that is all I can say, but tis my duty to make my self as easy as I can'.

In fact Esther seems to have kept busy. Her elder sister, Sarah Parsons, was close by and various other friends had to be visited besides callers to be entertained at the Edwards' home where Lucy, in charge of domestic arrangements was glad of extra help, 'Poor girl has her Head, hands, and Heart full now my Mother is gone.' Her father's work among the Indians also had her sympathetic interest: 'Vissit amongst the poor Indians, which excites in me a great concern for the poor cretures best interest.'

Although her journal makes no further comment upon it, Esther did shorten her visit, leaving by waggon at 5 p.m. on Wednesday, September 22. Of her last Sunday ever to be spent in her parents' home she writes as follows:

Sabbath – 19

Last eve I had some free discourse with My Father on the great things that concern my best intrest – I opend my diffeulties to him very freely and he as freely advised and directed. The conversation has removed some distressing doubts that discouraged me much in my Christian warfare – He gave me some excellent directions to be

[419]

observed in secret that tend to keep the soul near to God, as well as others to be observed in a more publick way – What a mercy that I have such a Father! Such a Guide!

On the return journey Lucy went with her for the first night, then she and Aaron were alone with the waggoner. The man was an 'honest Dutchman' but language problems made conversation with him almost as impossible as with the horses, 'but found I could convers with my God and did not think my self alone for he was present'. Arriving at Claverack, close to the Hudson, she found there was no sloop leaving for New York and had to spend Sunday among the Dutch whom she describes as 'very sivel (but not like the English). . . . The Sabbath here is no more than a play day.' The next day a suitable ship was to hand. By Thursday she was in New York and home at Newark in the early hours of the following morning.

If Esther Burr had ever dreamed that her private journal, sent to Sally Prince in Boston, would one day be examined by the world she would have told us more of her much-loved parents. But it is her utter unconsciousness of the eye of her future readers which contributes such value to what she has left on record. Although not intending anything for posterity, and frequently writing under a pressure which even hindered her from re-writing her 'scratchings', she opens a unique window on the whole Edwards family. With her journal we can at least guess how much more of the human story there was which remains hidden from view.

'MY GOD LIVES'

*The President's house and (left) part of Nassau Hall,
Princeton, 1764, as drawn by W. Tennent and engraved
by H. Dawkins.*

√ I Jonathan Edwards of Stockbridge, in the Province of the Massach-usetts Bay in New England . . . first of all, I give and commend my soul into the hands of God that gave it, and to the Lord Jesus Christ its glorious, all-sufficient, faithful and chosen Redeemer, relying alone on the free and infinite mercy and grace of God through his worthiness and mediation, for its eternal salvation; and my body I commend to the earth, to be committed to the dust in decent Christian burial, at the discretion of my executrix hereafter named; hoping, through the grace, faithfulness, and almighty power of my everlasting Redeemer, to receive the same again, at the last day, made like unto his glorious body.

J E's Last Will
March 14, 1753, in *Bibliotheca Sacra*, July, 1876

Christ has been sowing the seed of his word among you. Mr Edwards has been here a good while, sowing the word among you. He has sowed a great deal of good seed among you, and has watered it with his prayers and counsels, and tried to make it grow. But now he has done sowing the good seed among you, and is gone; and now you ought to sit down and consider what is become of the good seed that is sown.

SAMUEL HOPKINS preaching to the Indians at
Stockbridge 'the next Sabbath after Mr Edwards
left them'. *Works*, 1, p. 47

22

dwards' first biographers, Hopkins and Dwight, were in no doubt over the providence of God in his removal from Northampton. 'He was taken from that busy field at the best time of life, when his powers had gained their greatest energy', for a ministry of writing which would 'be a blessing to many thousands yet unborn'. 'The dismission of Mr Edwards' from Northampton', writes Dwight, 'proved in its ultimate consequences an essential blessing to the Church of God' (1.cxxvii).

In view of what we have already surveyed of Edwards' labours and difficulties in Stockbridge, it may seem strange for Hopkins to describe the place as 'a more quiet, and, on many accounts, a much more comfortable situation than he was in before'. But not only was he released from the constant demands of a large congregation, he was in a 'corner of the country' where there were far fewer daily interruptions. At Northampton, 'many of his friends, from almost all parts of the land, often made him pleasant and profitable visits', and his advice was frequently being sought by other churches. 'Here therefore', says Hopkins, 'he followed his beloved study more closely, and to better purpose than ever'.

The evidence for this assertion is clear enough in Edwards' Works. Whereas the bulk of his literary work had consisted previously in the revision of sermons for the press, it was at Stockbridge that he set himself more exclusively to write books. The first of these, his reply to Williams, which was published in

November 1752, we have already noticed. *Misrepresentations Corrected* is one of the most forceful of Edwards' writings and one of the best examples of his reasoning powers on spiritual issues. Given the obscurity into which this book has fallen, some further comment is needed. Edwards has been accused by modern writers of being unnecessarily strong in his response to his cousin. The explanation, however, lies in the way in which Solomon Williams had broadened the subject in dispute. In attempting to defend the reputation of their common grand-father, Williams had departed from Stoddard at a fundamental point. Stoddard taught that natural men cannot truly serve God for 'they are not subject to the law of God, neither indeed can be' (Rom. 8.7). *Before* they can be truly sincere, they must be renewed by divine grace. Williams, on the other hand, now argued that, at the level of 'moral sincerity' the unregenerate can consent to the gospel and that this can be an effective step to their receiving the saving grace of God.

Unregenerate communicants, possessed of such 'sincerity', were thus credited with being at least half-way to salvation, and acceptable to God as church members (1.502–506). It was this aspect of his opponent's case which led Edwards to append to his reply a letter to his former congregation in which he points out that Williams' book ('written and published very much by your procurement and expense') carries the controversy far beyond the original issue (1.529–31). While conceding that 'Men often do not see or allow the consequences of their own doctrines', Edwards argues that Williams' view amounted to a serious weakening of the whole doctrine of conversion. With Williams' teaching, the unconverted instead of being brought to the conviction that they were 'wholly under the power of enmity against God', were now given something 'to alleviate and smooth the matter' in their consciences. In being 'sincere' church members and communicants they might suppose themselves to be in a happier position than others:

I say if you believe Mr W you have been quite mistaken all your days, and were misled by your ministers. . . . If this book of Mr W with all these things, is made much of by you, and recommended to your children, as of great importance to defend the principles of the town, how far has your zeal for that one tenet, respecting natural men's right to the Lord's supper, transported you, and made you forget your value and concern for the most precious and important doctrines of Jesus Christ, taught you by Mr Stoddard, which do most nearly concern the very vitals of a religion!

Therefore let me entreat you to take the friendly warning I now give you, and stand on your guard against the encroaching evil. If you are not inclined to hearken to me, from any remaining affection to one whose voice and counsels you once heard with joy, and yielded to with great alacrity; yet let me desire you not to refuse, as you would act the part of friends to yourselves and your dear children.

I am, Dear Brethren, He who was once (as I hope through grace) Your faithful pastor, and devoted servant for Jesus' sake,   J E

It was not imagination which led Edwards to see in Solomon Williams' book a readiness to credit some powers to unregener- < ate men in accordance with the ideas of Arminianism. This was the error upon which Edwards had been seeking to write since 1746. In August, 1752 – immediately after the conclusion of his reply to Williams – he began to write his *Careful and Strict Inquiry into the Modern Prevailing Notions of that Freedom of Will which is supposed to be Essential to Moral Agency.* Three months later he reports to Erskine that he had made no progress because of 'extraordinary' duties and hindrances, but in December he resumed and by mid-April 1753 he can speak of the first draft of the work as 'almost finished'. Given the intensely theological (and philosophical) nature of the book it was necessary to raise 'subscriptions' to ensure the publisher against a serious loss. The first edition of Edwards *On the Will* came out in 1754 and contained a list of 298 subscribers, including forty-two from Scotland.

It is noteworthy that in taking up a defence of Calvinism, Edwards began with errors respecting the nature of the human will. The great purpose of his book was to show, both from reason and from Scripture, how the scriptural doctrine of human responsibility can be firmly held, and at the same time the Arminian belief in man's ability to determine his own will denied. If man is without the power to repent and turn to God, as the orthodox believed, how can he be held responsible for remaining in sin? If human inability were true, said the Arminians, then man is no longer a free agent, but acts under compulsion. Man is free, replies Edwards, in the sense that he has all natural faculties – mind, will, etc. – and this constitutes his responsibility. Man's utter incapacity to do spiritual good does not arise out of a physical lack of faculties, but altogether out of *the wrong moral disposition of those faculties.* In this way he explains how man, though totally corrupt in his nature, is still a responsible free agent. 'Doubtless common sense requires men's being the authors of their own acts of will, in order to their being esteemed worthy of praise or dispraise,' writes Edwards, and thus far all are agreed. The point of difference with the Arminians is his assertion that 'the acts of the will are rendered certain by some other cause than the mere power of willing.' The will, Edwards affirms, acts always at the dictates of man's moral nature. 'The will, in every instance, acts by moral necessity . . . a man is truly morally unable to choose contrary to a present inclination. . . .' Man's choice is therefore determined by his fallen nature; he is free to pursue his inclinations without restraint, but he is not free to choose what is contrary to those inclinations. This inability, far from being inconsistent with men's accountability, is that 'wherein their exceeding guilt and sinfulness in the sight of God most fundamentally and mainly consist.'

Subsequently some readers of Edwards *On the Will* suggested that if it is true that man has no power to change himself by his own choice then it were better that this should not be taught. To that view Edwards replies forcefully in a letter to a friend in Scotland:

By what I have heard, some think, that if it be really true that there is no self-determining power in the will, it is of a mischievous tendency to say anything of it; and that it is best that the truth in this matter should not be known by any means. I cannot but be of an extremely different mind. On the contrary, I think that the notion of liberty, consisting in a contingent self-determination of the will, as necessary to the morality of men's dispositions and actions, is almost inconceivably pernicious. . . . The longer I live, and the more I have to do with the souls of men, in the work of the ministry, the more I see of this. Notions of this sort are one of the main hindrances of the success of the preaching of the word, and other means of grace, in the conversion of sinners. . . . With respect to self-flattery and presumption, nothing can possibly be conceived more directly tending to it, than a notion of liberty, at all times possessed, consisting in a power to determine one's own will to good or evil; which implies a power men have, at all times, to determine them to repent and turn to God. And what can more effectually encourage the sinner in present delays and neglects, and imbolden him to go on in sin, in a presumption of having his own salvation at all times at his command? And this notion of self-determination and self-dependence, tends to prevent, or enervate, all prayer to God for converting grace; for why should men earnestly cry to God for his grace, to determine their hearts to that which they must be determined to of themselves. And indeed it destroys the very notion of conversion itself. There can properly be no such thing, or any thing akin to what the Scripture speaks of conversion, renovation of the heart, regeneration, etc., if growing good, by a number of self-determined acts, are all that is required, or to be expected. Excuse me, Sir, for troubling you with so much on this head. I speak from the fullness of my heart. What I have long seen of the dreadful consequences of these prevalent notions everywhere, and what I am convinced will still be their consequences so long as they continue to prevail, fills me with concern. (1.clxx-xxii).

The apparent speed with which Edwards wrote his major work *On the Will* and the two next titles which followed in the winter and spring of 1754–55, 'A Dissertation concerning the End for which God created the World' and 'A Dissertation concerning the Nature of True Virtue', has been a subject of comment. The achievement is the more remarkable when all the pressures of opposition, ill-health and war are kept in mind. At the same time it has to be remembered that the themes in all these works had been with him for many years.

This was particularly so with regard to the two 'Dissertations' on God's purpose in creation and on true virtue. Since his days at Yale he had been storing thoughts and meditations on these inter-related subjects. These two works represent an attempt on Edwards' part to enter the eighteenth-century debate of philosophers and deists on the subject of morality. According to the then prevailing school of opinion in Europe, while God was not to be wholly excluded, virtue, or morality, must be understood primarily as consisting in love for mankind in general. 'Some writers,' says Edwards, 'do not wholly exclude a regard to the Deity out of their schemes of morality but . . . they esteem it a less important and a subordinate part of true morality'. He argues that such an inversion of priorities renders their schemes 'fundamentally and essentially defective'. 'True virtue must chiefly consist in *love to God*'. Both

'Dissertations' are basically expansive arguments to prove this assertion.[1] In the first he seeks to show that God's purpose in creation was to have his excellency and glory delighted in by men. God acts out of supreme regard for himself and he communicates himself – his knowledge, his holiness, his happiness – to men in order that his perfections should be known. Far from depreciating man, this purpose of God is in man's highest interest. 'God acting for *himself*, or making himself his last end, and his acting for *their* sake, are not to be set in opposition; they are rather to be considered as coinciding one with the other, and implied one in the other' (1.101).

For redeemed man, increasing knowledge of God entails increasing love to him, joy in him, and participation in his moral excellence 'as truly as the brightness of a jewel, held in the sun's beams'. True morality, then, is that we conform to God's own design in making him our chief end: holiness consists 'primarily in love to God, which is exercised in a high esteem of God, admiration of his perfections, complacency in them, and praise of them'.

In these two works (published posthumously, as we shall later note) there is much of the distinctive genius of Edwards' mind. It is true that, in essence, he is saying nothing more than he taught the Indian children on 'man's chief end' from the first question of the Shorter Catechism, but his mind here soars like an eagle towards the sun and of all the experiences which Hopkins and Bellamy enjoyed with their friend there can have been few to equal that winter's day at Stockbridge in 1755 when they heard 'Mr. Edwards read a treatise upon the *Last End of God in the Creation*'.

Edwards' last work, begun in 1756 and finished by May 1757, was *The Great Christian Doctrine of Original Sin Defended*.

[1] I have given the conclusion of Edwards' argument, not the process by which he arrives at it through what Warfield calls the 'eccentric theory' that virtue is 'love to being in general'. As a true child of his time, says Warfield, he sought in these books 'to hale his adversaries to the court of reason' (*Studies in Theology*, 1932, p. 528f.). Yet it would be a mistake to regard Edwards as a rationalist in his apologetics: see *Works* 1.292–3. His emphasis is that for spiritual knowledge regeneration is indispensable: 'The Spirit of God not only directly evidences the truth of religion to the mind but it sanctifies the reasoning faculty and assists it to see the clear evidence there is of the truth of religion in rational arguments'. 'Miscellanies' 628, in Townsend, p. 251.

Both from human experience and from Scripture, it provides what William Cunningham calls 'the unanswerable establishment' of the truth 'that all mankind constantly in all ages, without fail in any one instance, run into moral evil.' Man has a universal tendency to disregard God and to disobey his law. While the book is essentially theological, and possibly the foremost ever written on this subject, Edwards' intention is unmistakably pastoral. He saw superficial views of the gravity of human corruption as the primary cause of the neglect of commitment to a *supernatural* redemption. 'I look on the doctrine as of great importance', he writes in the Preface. 'For if the case be such indeed, that all mankind are by nature in a state of total ruin, then doubtless, the great salvation by Christ stands in direct relation to this ruin, as the remedy to the disease. The whole gospel must suppose it and all real belief, or true notion of that gospel, must be built upon it.'

In particular, Edwards set out to answer John Taylor whose work *The Scripture – Doctrine of Original Sin Proposed to Free and Candid Examination* was first published in 1738. As noted earlier, it found a ready hearing on both sides of the Atlantic. In 1752 Edwards spoke of Taylor as 'that author who has so corrupted multitudes in New England' (1.530). Clyde Holbrook says that Taylor's work 'bore the marks of thorough scholarship and breathed an air of amiable open-mindedness'.[1] Certainly that was the intention which it was meant to convey but to Edwards the appearance of 'open-mindedness' was specious. It was his belief that Taylor, while appearing to honour Scripture and to express high opinions of the Apostle Paul, actually undermined the doctrines there revealed. Not that this was done openly and directly:

Hereby . . . incautious readers are prepared the more easily to be drawn into a belief that they, and others in their way of thinking, have not *rightly understood* many of those things in this apostle's writing which before seemed very *plain* to them. Thus they are prepared, by a prepossession in favour of these new writers. . . . They must understand that the first reformers, and indeed preachers and expositors in general, for fifteen or sixteen hundred years past, were too unlearned and short-sighted to be capable of penetrating into the sense, or fit to make comments on the writings of so great a man as this apostle . . . at

[1] J E (Yale), 3, pp. 2–3.

the same time it must be understood that there is risen up now at length, in this happy age of light and liberty, a set of men of more free and generous turn of mind, and of better discernment. . . . But their criticisms, when examined, appear far more subtle than solid. . . . The Holy Scripture is subtilized into a mere mist; or made to evaporate into a thin cloud, that easily puts on any shape, and is moved in any direction, with a puff of wind, just as the manager pleases (1.232–3).

A brief comparison of Taylor's work with that of Edwards might not suggest the difference between the two environments from which their books issued – the one written in the peace and comfort of Georgian England, the other in a lonely and threatened settlement among the Indians. But there is an international breadth in Edwards which is wholly missing in Taylor. If human nature has no native ignorance of God and has the ability to perform obedience to God's law, then what explanation, Edwards asks, has the Norwich divine got to offer for the condition of 'every Indian in America, before the Europeans came hither, and every inhabitant of the unknown parts of Africa and Terra Australis'? Nor can the answer be that the condition of men in paganism is simply due to a lack of means of knowledge, for access to knowledge is utterly inadequate in itself to change the tendency of the human heart as the English-speaking world proved:

To what a pass are things come in Protestant countries at this day, and in our nation in particular! To what a prodigious height has a deluge of infidelity, profaneness, luxury, debauchery and wickedness of every kind, arisen! The poor savage Americans are mere babes and fools (if I may so speak) as to proficiency in wickedness in comparison of multitudes that the Christian world throngs with.

Although situated in such comparative isolation, Edwards writes not as a parochial eighteenth-century scholar but as a pastor and evangelist, convinced that man's permanent and universal need is for biblical doctrine, applied by the Holy Spirit.

*   *   *

In June 1757 Edwards paid possibly his last visit to his parents

[430]

while on a visit to Boston. 'I look upon it as a great favour of heaven,' he had written to them in 1752, 'that you, my parents, are still preserved in the land of the living, to so great an age.' Timothy Edwards still preached at East Windsor until 1755,– when he was in his eighty-seventh year.

Describing a visit to East Windsor in 1756, Edwards had written to his son-in-law, Aaron Burr: 'I found my father more broken than ever I saw him, but yet he knew me, and was capable of some degree of conversation, and was able to walk a little; my mother infirm, but holds the powers of her mind unbroken.'

The letters between Burr and Edwards were never happier than in 1757. The Burrs had finally removed, with the students, from Newark to Princeton in November 1756, and 'not a china thing so much as cracked' Esther noted in her journal. Their lives were as busy as ever, with Aaron caring for a congregation two-thirds the size of his former charge at Newark, in addition to all the work now commenced in Nassau Hall with his seventy students. In February 1757 a sudden spiritual concern became evident among the students and of a nature which Esther had probably not seen since her childhood.

On February 8, 1757, she reports, 'There is a considerable awakening in College more general than has ever been since Mr Burr has had a care of it'. On February 14, Burr began a letter to Edwards on what was happening and there was more to add before he concluded on February 22 with the words, 'I never saw anything in the late revival[1] that more evidently discovered the hand of God'. Esther also wrote to her mother on the 'very remarkable and evident work of grace'. Her journal for this period has day-to-day information on the awakening including the following:

> Saturday Morn
>
> . . . the Concern is now become general in College – none of it in Town and several under very great distress of soul – O Help me to bless the Lord! Mr Burr is almost overjoyed. . . .
>
> Sabbath Eve
>
> Mr Spencer preached all day. . . . I never saw the scholars so attentive in my life. They really seemed as if they heard for their lives.

[1]The revival of 1740–42.

9 o'Clock – Mr Burr returned from College, Mr Spencer with him, and glorious things they relate – Mr Burr was sent for to the College about dark, and when he came their he found above 20 young Men in one room Crying and begging to know what they should do to be saved, 4 of them under the deepest sense of thier wicked Hearts and need of Christ. . . .

Monday Eve

9 o'Clock. No work carried on here, but only to get something to Eat. . . . Mr Tennent is astonished, and amazed, between joy, sorrow, hope, and fear and says he dont know what passion is uppermost, but he must call it an Awfull joy that he feels, which is the case with us all.

Teusday P.M. 2 o'Clock

This wonderfull pouring out of the spirit at this time just as the College is finnished and things a little settled looks to me exactly like Gods desending into the Temple in a Cloud of Glory, there by signifying that he did except of the House for his dwelling place and would Bless it. . . .

William Tennent, whose congregation at Freehold also experienced a revival at this date, visited Princeton and reported to Samuel Davies:

I went to the college last Monday, and saw a memorable display of God's power and grace in the conviction of sinners. The whole house was a Bochim. A sense of God's holiness was so impressed on the hearts of its inhabitants, that all of them, excepting two (esteemed religious) were greatly shaken as to the state of their souls. . . . This blessed work of the Most High so far exceeded all my expectations, that I was lost in surprise and constrained to say, Is it so? can it be so? Nor was my being eye and ear witness, from Monday till Friday, able to recover me from my astonishment. I felt as the apostles when it was told them the Lord had risen.[1]

Burr, mindful of what he learned from Edwards as well as observed for himself in former years, was cautious against any form of wild-fire or any announcement of numbers converted. Such things in the past had done more harm than the hostility of opponents. 'Much old experience', he writes to Edwards, 'has taught me to judge of these things more by the fruits than any account of experience for a short season. . . . There don't appear at present any signs of such imprudences as have too

[1]Webster, p. 263.

often attended the revival of religion.'[1]

This local revival of 1757 has important bearings on Edwards himself. One of the most dependable of modern writers on Edwards speaks of his 'early belief in, and later distrust of, revivals'.[2] If any proof that this was not the case is needed it is supplied by this revival at Princeton. Aaron and Esther Burr knew the eagerness there would be in Stockbridge to hear this news. And Edwards, far from distrusting their reports, hastened to pass on word to Scotland where it was included in an appendix to John Gillies' compilation of revivals, *Historical Collections relating to Remarkable Periods of the Success of the Gospel*.[3] In the first of two letters, he writes to John Erskine on April 12, 1757, 'Amidst the great darkness which attends the state of things in British America, God is causing some light to arise. We have news truly joyful concerning the college in New Jersey'. There follows a lengthy and enthusiastic account of the information he had received from his son-in-law and daughter. In his letter of July 28th Edwards confirms this report and urges a renewing of 'the concert for prayer'. It should be enlarged, he advises, to include participants from 'Holland, Geneva, Switzerland, etc.', and he promises, 'I stand ready to do my utmost to promote the affair in all parts of the British America, so far as I can do it by conversation and letters'. His faith in the possibility and in the necessity of true revivals was in no wise dimmed. Even before the awakening at Princeton had occurred he had recorded in one of his notebooks that 'the erecting of N. Jersey College' was a hopeful sign of the spread of the Gospel into the American world' in preparation for the 'glorious days' of the Church.[4]

Edwards' friends who were responsible for the College shared the same hope in the future and even Nassau Hall itself bore witness to it for although there were now only seventy students it was built to house one hundred and forty-seven. Changes were, however, soon at hand. Governor Belcher, one of the College's most influential helpers, died on August 31,

---

[1]Gillies, *Historical Collections*, p. 522.
[2]T. H. Johnson in *The New England Quarterly*, 1931, p. 356ff.
[3]Gillies, pp. 522–524.
[4]'History of the Work of Redemption', Notebook A, Folder 37, p. 35, Beinecke Library.

1758. Less than a month later, and not long after making a hurried visit to Stockbridge in very hot, sultry weather, Aaron Burr himself died at the age of forty-one, the life which had been 'a perpetual holocaust of adoration and praise' worn out with so many labours. A letter from the bereaved Esther carried the shock of the news to her parents whom she tells, 'God has seemed sensibly near in such a supporting and comfortable manner that I think I have never experienced the like'. With words which show how true theology kept her from a self-centred piety, Esther concludes:

O, I am afraid I shall conduct myself so as to bring dishonour on my God and the religion which I profess! No, rather let me die this moment, than be left to bring dishonour on God's holy name – I am overcome – I must conclude, with once more begging, that, as my dear parents remember themselves, they would not forget their greatly afflicted daughter, (now a lonely widow,) nor her fatherless children.

It seems that on the day when the news of his son-in-law's death reached him, Edwards was not at home but travelling in Massachusetts. That evening he stayed with his sister, Esther Hopkins, at the parsonage in West Springfield where his brother-in-law had died two years earlier. The newly-appointed minister, Joseph Lathrop, not yet married, was staying with Mrs. Hopkins at the time and at the hour for evening prayers asked Edwards to conduct the worship. 'But he declined,' a friend of Lathrop's later recorded, 'giving as a reason that his feelings were so intense as to forbid his utterance. He made the same request of him in the morning, and he complied with it: and Dr. Lathrop told me that his prayer, in respect to copiousness, appropriateness, tenderness and sublimity, exceeded any thing that he ever heard from mortal lips.'[1]

Four days after the death of Burr, the first Commencement of the College at Princeton took place and without any delay a successor was chosen. Seventeen of the twenty trustees present

---

[1]Sprague 1, p. 334. The recorder of this anecdote mistakenly supposed that the death by which Edwards was so affected was that of his daughter, Esther Burr. Of Lathrop's general impression of Edwards, the same writer recalls: 'He said that he was accustomed to look upon him even then, almost as belonging to some superior race of beings; though he mentioned one occasion – an interview with an Arminian clergyman – on which he so far forgot himself as to betray a good deal of impatience.'

at the meeting voted for Edwards. When this further news reached him it cannot have been an entire surprise. Edwards was the most prominent of the older men who had supported the College from its outset and despite his location he had remained in close touch with its work, as we have seen, in the succeeding years. He was, however, now ten years older than in 1748 when his friends had spoken of the desirability of his following Dickinson as President. It was true that his own health was stronger than it had been a few years earlier, in fact, about this time he had said to a friend that he was 'as well able to bear the closest study as he was thirty years before and could go through the exercises of the pulpit with as little weariness or difficulty' (1.44). But he was well settled into the quiet routine of Stockbridge and was content to remain at the outpost where he believed that God had led him.

Thus, notwithstanding his great interest in the College, Edwards considered that the Board should be looking elsewhere for their next President. In a long letter of October 19, 1757, he explains his reasons to the trustees. Taking the smaller difficulty first, he speaks of the temporal discomfort such an upheaval would involve 'when we have scarcely got over the trouble and damage sustained by our removal from Northampton'. The only property he had in the world was at Stockbridge and he saw no likelihood of his being able to sell it. Obviously his past financial difficulties, and the likelihood of their recurrence, was on his mind.

There were, however, much stronger objections:

The chief difficulties in my mind, in the way of accepting this important and arduous office, are these two: First, my own defects unfitting me for such an undertaking, many of which are generally known; beside others of which my own heart is conscious – I have a constitution, in many respects, peculiarly unhappy, attended with flaccid solids, vapid, sizy, and scarce fluids, and a low tide of spirits; often occasioning a kind of childish weakness and contemptibleness of speech, presence, and demeanour, with a disagreeable dulness and stiffness, much unfitting me for conversation, but more especially for the government of a college. This makes me shrink at the thoughts of taking upon me, in the decline of life, such a new and great business, attended with such a multiplicity of cares, and requiring such a degree of activity, alertness, and spirit of government; especially as succeeding one so remarkably well qualified in these respects, giving occasion to every one to remark the wide difference. I am also deficient in some parts of learning, particularly in algebra, and the higher parts of mathematics, and the Greek classics; my Greek learning having been chiefly in the New Testament.

To his second and final objection Edwards gives much more extended treatment. 'My engaging in this business will not well consist with those views, and that course of employ in my study, which have long engaged and swallowed up my mind, and been the chief entertainment and delight of my life.' He goes on to explain to the Princeton trustees how his method of study over the years had led to the accumulation of much material which he now wished to shape into a form suitable for publication. His heart, he tells them, was now 'much upon' subjects relating to

the prevailing errors of the present day which I cannot with any patience see maintained (to the utter subverting of the gospel of Christ). . . I have already published something on one of the main points in dispute between the Arminians and Calvinists; and have it in view, God willing, (as I have already signified to the public,) in like manner to consider all the other controverted points, and have done much towards a preparation for it. But beside these, I have had on my mind and heart (which I long ago began, not with any view to publication) a great work, which I call a *History of the Work of Redemption*, a body of divinity in an entire new method, being thrown into the form of a history; considering the affair of christian theology, as the whole of it, each part, stands in reference to the great work of redemption by Jesus Christ; which I suppose to be, of all others, the grand design of God, and the *summum* and *ultimum* of all the divine operations and decrees; particularly considering all parts of the grand scheme, in their historical order. The order of their existence, or their being brought forth to view, in the course of divine dispensations, or the wonderful series of successive acts and events; beginning from eternity, and descending from thence to the great work and successive dispensations of the infinitely wise God, in time; considering the chief events coming to pass in the church of God, and revolutions in the world of mankind, affecting the state of the church and the affair of redemption, which we have an account of in history or prophecy; till, at last, we come to the general resurrection, last judgment, and consummation of all things; when it shall be said, 'It is done. I am Alpha and Omega, the beginning and the end'.

In addition to this, he relates, 'I have also, for my own profit

[436]

and entertainment, done much towards another great work, which I call the *Harmony of the Old and New Testament*, in three parts,' which he proceeds to describe.

Thus, concluding his final objection, he writes: 'So far as I myself am able to judge of what talents I have for benefiting my fellow creatures by word, I think I can write better than I can speak. My heart is so much in these studies that I cannot find it in my heart to be willing to put myself into an incapacity to pursue them any more in the future part of my life.'

Edwards was insistent that he could never undertake the same role as Burr. At most, if he should see light to accept their invitation, he could only undertake a general supervision of the College and certainly not teach all classes and subjects. He would perform 'the whole work of a professor of divinity' but give no language instruction except in Hebrew.

If in the light of these objections and stipulations the trustees still wished to proceed, then Edwards would seek advice 'of such as I esteem most wise, friendly, and faithful'.

As Princeton did persist in their wish, Edwards proceeded to call a Council of friends to meet with him in Stockbridge on December 21st. They were to include Samuel Hopkins, John Brainerd, and Joseph Bellamy. Urging Bellamy's attendance, Edwards wrote, 'Don't fail of letting me see you here; for I never wanted to see you more.'

Meanwhile, in Princeton, Esther Burr had a further trial. A few weeks earlier her nineteen-year-old brother, Timothy (eldest son of the Edwards' family) who stayed with her while he studied at Princeton, had returned to Stockbridge on account of illness. No sooner had he left than Esther's infant son, Aaron, went down with an infection which brought him 'to the brink of the grave'.

Writing of this to her father on November 2, 1757, Esther says:

I did give myself and my children to God, with my whole heart. . . . A few days after this, one evening, in talking of the glorious state my dear departed husband must be in, my soul was carried out in such large desires after that glorious state, that I was forced to retire from the family to conceal my joy. When alone I was so transported, and my soul carried out in such eager desires after perfection and the full enjoyment of God, and to serve him uninterruptedly, that I think my

[437]

nature would not have borne much more. I think, dear Sir, I had that night a foretaste of heaven. This frame continued, in some good degree, the whole night. I slept but little, and when I did, my dreams were all of heavenly and divine things. Frequently since, I have felt the same in kind, though not in degree. This was about the time that God called me to give up my child. Thus a kind and gracious God has been with me, 'in six troubles and in seven.'

Edwards replied in a characteristic letter:

Stockbridge Novem. 20. 1757.

Dear Daughter,

I thank you for your most comfortable letter; but more especially would I thank God that has granted you such things to write. How good and kind is your heavenly Father! Indeed, he is a faithful God; he will remember his covenant forever; and never will fail them that trust in him. But don't be surprised, or think some strange thing has happened to you, if after this light, clouds of darkness should return. Perpetual sunshine is not usual in this world, even to God's true saints. But I hope, if God should hide his face in some respect, even this will be in faithfulness to you, to purify you, and fit you for yet further and better light.

As to removing to Princeton, to take on me the office of President I have agreed with the Church here to refer it to a Council of ministers, to sit here Decem. 21, to determine whether it be my duty. Mr. Tennent can inform you more of the matter. I with this, enclose a letter to him which I desire may be delivered to him as soon as possible. I have wrote more particularly about the Council in my letter to the Trustees. I know I can't live at Princeton, as a President must, on the salary they offer. Yet I have left that matter to their generosity – I shall have no money wherewith to furnish the house. I hope Mr. Tennent will exert himself to get a full Trustees meeting, to settle college affairs. I shall not be willing to come thither until that is well done. If the Trustees don't send me an account of their doings immediately by the Post to Claverack I wish you would do it and direct your letter to be left with Capt. Jeremiah Hoghoboom. I should be glad on some account, to have the letter before the Council. What the Council will do, I cannot tell. I shall endeavour as fairly and justly as possible to lay the matter before them with every material circumstance. Deacon Woodbridge is a coming man, and an eloquent speaker; he will strive to his utmost to influence the Council by his representations, and perhaps by influencing the Indians to make such representations before the Council as will tend to persuade them that it is best for me to stay. And their judgment must determine the matter. Not only has Mr. Woodbridge and others a friendship for me, and liking to my ministry, but it is greatly against their temporal interest for me to leave them.

As to Lucy's coming home, her mother will greatly need her, especially if we remove in the spring. But yet, whether your circumstances dont much more loudly call for her continuance there, must be left with you and her. She must judge whether she can come consistently with her health and comfort at such a season of the year. If she comes, let her buy me a staff, and after advice, and get a good one, or none. Mr. Effelsteen has promised her a good horse and side saddle, and his son to wait on her to Stockbridge. And I presume Mr. Fonda can let her have a horse and side saddle to Mr. Effelsteen's.

If you think of selling Harry, your mother desires you not to sell him, without letting her know it.

Timmy is considerably better, tho' yet very weak. We all unite in love to you Lucy and your children. Your mother is very willing to leave Lucy's coming away wholly to you and her.

I am your most tender and affectionate father,

Jonathan Edwards

Following this letter, twenty-one-year-old Lucy Edwards decided to stay with her sister at Princeton. The weather may well have affected her decision. It was when travelling in the Stockbridge area in the month of December that David Brainerd had more than once been in serious danger from exposure. Possibly it was the weather also which led to the delay of the Council meeting at Stockbridge until January 4, 1758. It was to be the last Council meeting in Edwards' life and we are indebted to Samuel Hopkins for a personal glimpse of what occurred. Edwards gave his view and was followed by Woodbridge who represented the Indians. It was Woodbridge's pleadings, as already noted, that Abigail Sergeant had considered decisive in his original appointment. But despite what must have been earnest speaking on the other side, the Council judged it Edwards' duty to accept the call to Princeton. 'When they published their judgment and advice, Mr. Edwards appeared uncommonly moved and affected with it, and fell into tears on the occasion, which was very unusual for him in the presence of others: and soon after said to the gentlemen that it was a matter of wonder to him that they could so easily, as they appeared to do, get over the objections he had made against his removal. But as he thought it right to be directed by their advice, he should now endeavour cheerfully to undertake it, believing he was in the way of his duty.'[1] In the language of the Princeton trustees, 'he came only after repeated requests'.

Given the urgency of Princeton's need, and the time of year which made a general immediate removal of his whole family impossible, Edwards left Stockbridge alone later in January. Recalling the farewell, seventeen-year-old Susannah, records:

My father took leave of all his people and family as affectionately as if he knew he should not come again. On the Sabbath afternoon he preached from these words, 'We have no continuing city, therefore let us seek one to come.' The chapter that he read was Acts the 20th. O, how proper: what could he have done more? When he had got out of doors he turned about, – 'I commit you to God,' said he.

Edwards set about his new work in a spirit which suggested nothing of the tears of January 4. And with Esther, her two children, and Lucy already at Princeton, he was not as lonely as he had been in the first months at Stockbridge. Certainly the Presbyterians were delighted at his coming to New Jersey. For David Bostwick, as for others, he was 'perhaps the greatest pillar in this part of Zion's buildings'.[2]

For his first sermon at Princeton Edwards gave out the text, 'Jesus Christ the same yesterday, and today, and for ever' > (Heb. 13.8), and when it concluded it is said that his hearers were surprised to discover that two hours had passed so quickly. Thereafter he preached each Sunday in the College hall, and introduced the senior class to questions in divinity for which they had to prepare answers later to be discussed in class – a procedure which met with an enthusiastic response. Speaking of these first weeks at Princeton, Hopkins writes:

During this time, Mr. Edwards seemed to enjoy an uncommon degree of the presence of God. He told his daughters he once had great exercise, concern, and fear, relative to his engaging in that business; but since it now appeared, so far as he could see, that he was called of God to that place and work, he did cheerfully devote himself to it,

---

[1] *Memoirs of Jonathan Edwards*, Samuel Hopkins, 1815, p. 185.
[2] Webster, p. 545.

leaving himself and the event with God, to order what seemed to him good.

When Edwards' new routine was interrupted by an in-noculation against smallpox on February 23, 1758, it caused no great attention. Smallpox being prevalent at the time, and having reached Princeton, it was judged advisable that as Edwards had never had the disease he should be inoculated. The vaccine took successfully and 'it was thought all danger was over' when postules in his mouth and throat began to prevent his swallowing. Unable now to drink sufficiently to prevent a secondary fever, his condition quickly deteriorated and recovery became increasingly unlikely.

A little before his death, in speaking briefly to his younger daughter, he said: 'Dear Lucy, it seems to me to be the will of God, that I must shortly leave you; therefore give my kindest love to my dear wife, and tell her, that the uncommon union, which has so long subsisted between us, has been of such a nature, as I trust is spiritual, and therefore will continue for ever. And I hope she will be supported under so great a trial and submit cheerfully to the will of God. And as to my children, you are now like to be left fatherless, which I hope will be an inducement to you all, to seek a Father who will never fail you. And as to my funeral, I would have it to be like Mr. Burr's, and any additional sum of money, that might be expected to be laid out that way, I would have it disposed of to charitable uses.'[1]

Shortly after leaving these messages for absent members of the family, 'he looked about and said, "Now where is Jesus of Nazareth, my true and never-failing Friend?"' Then when those at his bedside believed he was unconscious and expressed grief at what his absence would mean both to the College and to the church at large, they were surprised when he suddenly uttered a final sentence, 'Trust in God, and you need not fear'.

From Princeton, Edwards' physician wrote to Sarah Edwards on the same day, March 22, 1758,

This afternoon, between two and three o'clock, it pleased God to let him sleep in that dear Lord Jesus, whose kingdom and interest he has

---

[1] Burr, on his death-bed had ordered that his funeral should not involve pomp and cost.

been faithfully and painfully serving all his life. And never did any mortal man more fully and clearly evidence the sincerity of all his professions, by one continued, universal, calm, cheerful resignation and patient submission to the Divine will, through each stage of his disease, than he. . . . Death had certainly lost its sting, as to him.

The death of the fifty-four-year-old President, so soon after that of his son-in-law, was broken to the world in a Philadelphia newspaper of March 28. His old friend, Gilbert Tennent began a tribute with the words:

On Wednesday the 22nd instant, departed this life, the reverend and worthy Mr. Jonathan Edwards (formerly of Northampton, in New-England, but lately of Stockbridge), president of the College of New-Jersey; a person of great eminence, both in respect of capacity, learning, piety, and usefulness; a good scholar, and a great divine. . . . Divinity was his favourite study, in the knowledge of which he had but few, if any, equals and no superior in these provinces.

When the news reached Stockbridge Sarah Edwards was suffering so much from rheumatism in her neck that she could scarcely hold a pen, but brief lines written to Esther on April 3 epitomize the spirit in which she had sought to live with her husband for more than thirty years:

What shall I say? A holy and good God has covered us with a dark cloud. O that we may kiss the rod, and lay our hands on our mouths! The Lord has done it. He has made me adore his goodness, that we had him so long. But my God lives; and he has my heart. O what a legacy my husband, and your father, has left us! We are all given to God; and there I am, and love to be.

THE CONTINUING MINISTRY

The house at Kettering, England, where the Baptist Missionary Society was founded in 1792 – an event in the history of world missions which owed much to the writings of Edwards.

But this, with the rest of what I have offered on the subject, must be left with every candid reader's judgment, and the *success* of the whole must now be left with God, who knows what is agreeable to his own mind, and is able to make his own truths prevail – however mysterious they may seem to the poor, partial, narrow, and extremely imperfect views of mortals (while looking through a cloudy and delusory medium), and however disagreeable they may be to the innumerable prejudices of men's hearts:– and who has promised that the gospel of Christ, such as is really *his*, shall finally be victorious, and has assured us that the *word* which goes out of his mouth *shall not return to him void, but shall accomplish that which he pleaseth, and shall prosper in the thing whereto he sends it.* – Let God arise, and plead his own cause, and glorify his own great name. Amen.

> J E concluding *The Great Christian Doctrine of*
> *Original Sin Defended* (1.233)

It was the glory of this great man, that he had no love for innovation. . . . To the Scriptures he yielded the most profound reverence and the most implicit confidence.

> TIMOTHY DWIGHT on his grandfather;
> *Travels*, vol. 4, 324

23

 dwards, his father, and his son-in-law, Aaron Burr, had all died within a period of six months. Even so, the family partings were not complete. Esther Burr never received the letter from her mother with which we closed the last chapter. She died sixteen days after her father, < at the age of twenty-six, of an unknown cause, leaving her two infants, Sally and Aaron[1] as orphans. Esther's eldest sister, Sarah Parsons, at Stockbridge, wrote to Mary Dwight on April 18, 1758:

Dr Sister

I received your kind Letter by my Husband for which [I]return you my hearts thanks – but what or how to write or speak I know not. Last Saturday we had another Expre[ss] from Princeton which brought us the sorrowful Tidings that Dear Sister Burr was dead and buried yesterday week and no doubt have join'd the Company of our dear dear Friends lately deceased who have all got safe home to their heavenly Fathers House . . . she died of an accute Feavour, by Lucys account was much like the Feavour that carried my Sister Jerusha out of the World, lived but just a Week after she was taken, apprehended

[1]Aaron Burr, sadly the best-known of Edwards' posterity, spent his youth with his uncle, Timothy Edwards, and for a while, with his grandfather's friend Joseph Bellamy. In a career as a soldier, lawyer, and politician – becoming Vice-President of the United States – he lived 'without God'. Dying, virtually friendless, in 1836, Burr asked that he might be buried as near as possible to the *feet* of his father and grandfather in the Princeton burial ground.

she should die from her being first taken. . . . Oh how fast has she been ripening for that world she is now gone. . . . [1]

Jonathan and Sarah Edwards' own youngest child, Pierrepont, was now only eight years of age, but leaving him with the rest of the family, still in Stockbridge, Esther's mother journeyed to Princeton in the summer of 1758 and then to Philadelphia in September, to collect her two orphaned grandchildren who had been taken there following their mother's death. Arriving, apparently in good health, Mrs Edwards died of dysentery on October 2, at the age of forty-eight and was buried the following day in her husband's grave at Princeton.

The youngest of the Edwards' family, the delicate Betty, was then aged eleven. She was to die at the age of fourteen years in the home of her sister Mary in Northampton. Of the other girls, Sarah Parsons continued at Stockbridge and later at Goshen, Massachusetts, until her death in 1805. Mary Dwight died at Northampton in 1807, five years after the glorious revival at Yale where her son Timothy was President. Of her, Timothy could write, 'All that I am and all that I shall be, I owe to my mother'.[2] Lucy Edwards returned from Princeton to Stockbridge after the death of her father and sister, married a Woodbridge, bore nine children and died in 1786. In the words of her brother, Jonathan, she was 'hopefully a pious woman, exceedingly beloved by all her acquaintance'. Of all the seven daughters, it was Eunice – the twelve-year-old had visited sister Esther in Newark in 1756 – who lived the longest, dying in North Carolina in 1822, at the age of seventy-nine.

The three Edwards sons, Timothy, Jonathan and Pierrepont, all rose to prominence in public life. Jonathan succeeded his father in the work of the Christian ministry. He writes, 'Though I had, during my father's life, some convictions of sin and danger, yet I have no reason to believe I had any real religion till some years after his death.' Speaking of the Edwards family, Samuel Miller writes, 'Almost all his children manifested the fruit of his pious fidelity by consecrating themselves in heart and life to the God of their fathers'. At the

[1] *Burr, op. cit.*, pp. 302–3.
[2] *History of the Descendants of John Dwight*, B. W. Dwight, 1874, vol. 1, pp. 136 –137, 139.

time of the 'Edwards Family Meeting' at Stockbridge in 1870, one grandchild (a daughter of Timothy Edwards) was still alive at more than ninety years of age and sent a message to the gathering,

to say that God had fulfilled to her and hers the covenant which he made with her grandfather, even as he did to Abraham. She wants all her grandfather's descendants to study *more*, and put greater faith *in*, that covenant. . . . [1]

Much could be written of the influence exercised by Edwards' descendants, yet it was not primarily by this means that his life-work invested in the future. In the announcement of his death, Gilbert Tennent rightly foresaw that Edwards' own testimony would be heard in generations yet to come: 'It is a comfort to us, in the midst of grief, that this ascending Elijah has left behind him the mantle of so many valuable volumes, by which, though dead, he speaks with wisdom and warmth, in favour of truth and holiness.'

In his life-time Edwards had published possibly twenty-seven separate items. At death, his library, valued at £77, had contained some three hundred books, apart from his own published works. But there were also large numbers of his manuscripts, contained in 15 folio volumes, 15 quartos, and 1,074 sermon booklets (together valued at £6). Some of these manuscripts amounted to books which were partly prepared for publication. In other words, the potential of his future ministry was far greater than Gilbert Tennent knew in 1758.

It was Samuel Hopkins, supported by Joseph Bellamy, who took the lead in attempting to have more of Edwards' writings published. Sarah Edwards, stopping briefly at Great Barrington, in her hurried last journey to Philadelphia, had asked him to prepare an account of her husband and consequently the family had passed over all of their father's manuscripts into his hands. Hopkins and Bellamy were enthralled by the richness of these treasures. To the Rev. Thomas Foxcroft in Boston, Bellamy wrote on October 25, 1758, 'Mr. E. has left many excellent sermons and many volumes full of curious essays on the most important points', and Hopkins, referring to two

---

[1] *The Memorial Volume of the Edwards Family Meeting*, Boston, 1871.

particular manuscript works, 'Concerning the End for which God created the World', and 'The Nature of True Virtue', could say, 'I doubt not but that *hundreds* of subscriptions may be easily got for them in America'. He proposed that the sale of Edwards' works 'shall be for the benefit of his [Edwards'] two youngest sons'.

Foxcroft responded with enthusiasm to this news and promised 'faithfulness' in seeing any items through the press at Boston. As a result, by December, 1759, Hopkins had sent to Foxcroft the two treatises named above, plus a number of sermons about which he writes: 'I have selected forty-six volumes [i.e. notebooks] of manuscript sermons, which are, in my judgment, as good and suitable to be published as any which I have yet read.'[1] By April, 1761, Hopkins had finished his *Life of Edwards* and this also went to Foxcroft who had earlier proposed that it should be prefixed to the first volume of new material to be published.

A year after this, however, Hopkins complains sadly to Bellamy in a letter of March 24, 1762: 'Nothing is done toward printing Mr. Edwards's Life and Sermons. The sermons not transcribed; they depend much upon me to do it, while the sermons are at Boston! The printer writing for subscriptions, very few of which come in. . . . That on the *End of God* etc. is not transcribed yet. Nothing will be done. . . . '

A main problem was obviously the fact that the original Edwards' manuscripts were in no state to be printed. Bellamy had noted in 1758 that they would need to be 'written out in fair hand for the press'. Hopkins, in his enthusiasm, and perhaps assured that they could be transcribed competently in Boston, had sent them off too soon. For reasons unstated, a Mr. Searle, a friend of Edwards in Boston, could not proceed with the transcribing nor could Foxcroft who, in 1762, was sick. When, at length, Hopkins himself got to Boston in 1764 it was to find that the printer had set the type for no more than six of the forty-six sermons sent six years earlier and three sheets of the Memoir. Only now, it would seem, was anything energetically done. By December, 1764 the printer had seventeen sermons set and the next year, with one more sermon added, these,

---

[1] Further details on Hopkins' involvement with Edwards' manuscripts will be found in Hopkins' *Works*, vol. 1, pp. 215–18, 265–66.

prefixed by Hopkins' *Life and Character of Edwards,* were published. Despite the discouragement which he had already experienced, Hopkins writes in this volume:

> Mr. Edwards has left a great many volumes in manuscript, which he wrote in a miscellaneous way on almost all subjects in divinity. . . . If the public were willing to be at the cost, and publishing books of divinity met with as much encouragement now as it has sometimes, there might be a number of volumes published from his manuscripts which would afford a great deal of new light and entertainment to the church of Christ; though they would be more imperfect than if he himself had prepared them for public view.

At this same time in Boston, Hopkins finalized what remained to be done on the two treatises, 'The End for which God created the World' and 'The Nature of True Virtue' and these were also published as *Two Dissertations* in 1765.

The response to these two new publications under Edwards' name was so disappointing to Hopkins that he gave up the idea of preparing any more works for the press. In the words of his biographer, E. A. Park, he 'became satisfied that they would not be sold, and he therefore turned his mind to other subjects'. No reprint was to be required of his *Life of Edwards* in North America for nearly forty years.

This initial response to the attempt to further publicize Edwards' writings is worthy of some comment. For one thing it reflects the fact that Edwards was not regarded in his own age, in his own country, with the general esteem which he received at a later period. And in the eyes of the religious world at large he was scarcely regarded as an important author. As Thomas H. Johnson has observed, 'Among the lists of subscribers, often attached to the eighteenth-century editions of his treatises, the names of leading divines are strikingly absent. . . . Among Edwards' correspondents there are no prominent figures of church or state. Instead there are found almost exclusively lesser known Scotch Presbyterian ministers. . . . Even in England and Scotland it was not among the more fashionable clergy that Edwards was recognized as a powerful thinker. . . .'[1] Timothy Dwight, at the end of the eighteenth

---

[1] *The Printed Writings of Jonathan Edwards, 1703–1758: A Bibliography,* 1940.

century, speaks of 'the numerous complaints' made of his grandfather's writings in Great Britain and 'the numerous specimens of ill-nature with which he has been assailed'.[1]

Hopkins was certainly conscious of the prejudice against Edwards among 'fashionable clergy' on both sides of the Atlantic. In a letter to Foxcroft about the manuscripts which he had sent to Boston, he had said in December, 1759, 'Some have thought that if a way would be found out to get these two Dissertations printed in England (perhaps *without any name*) they would hereby be rendered more serviceable to mankind'.

Among contemporaries who were prepared to read Edwards was Ezra Stiles, President of Yale. In 1771 he speaks in his Diary of Edwards' *Two Dissertations* as having 'made a great noise in the world' yet in 1773 he could only estimate about forty-five ministers, out of five or six hundred in New England, 'who admire Mr. Edwards' writings'. Six years later Stiles gave up requiring his Senior Class to recite Edwards 'on the Will', and saw no prospects of any increase in readers of Edwards in the future. He wrote in his diary in August, 1787:

Edwards' valuable writings in another generation will pass into as transient notice perhaps scarce above oblivion, as Willard or Twiss, or Norton; and when posterity occasionally comes across them in the rubbish of Libraries, the rare characters who may read and be pleased with them, will be looked upon as singular and whimsical.[2]

Sympathy is due to Hopkins in the problems he faced with publishing Edwards in the 1760's and appreciation should be accorded for what he did achieve. But arguably, despite his best intentions, Hopkins was himself in part responsible for the failure to interest a larger number of his fellow-countrymen in Edwards' writings. Already, in the 1750's, Edwards had been charged by some with being too 'metaphysical and abstruse'. Hopkins, as a letter to Foxcroft on December 5, 1759, shows, recognized the danger that an early publication of the 'Two Dissertations' could increase that criticism: 'For this reason,'

---

[1] *Travels*, 4, p. 326.
[2] *The Literary Diary of Ezra Stiles*, Ed. F. B. Dexter, 1901, vol. 1, pp. 191, 363; vol. 3, p. 275. It should be said that the termination of the recitation of Edwards 'on the Will' was at least in part due to a decline in that method of instruction.

he writes, 'it has been inquired whether it is proper to have a number of practical sermons in the same volume and whether it would not be best to have a volume of "Sermons" published first; lest, if this should not find acceptance among common people (without whose assistance nothing of this kind can be done) it might discourage future publications of some things more practical.' In the same letter Hopkins expressed his own preference that Edwards' thirty sermons on 'A History of the Work of Redemption' be the first of further publications. But although these sermons were among the forty-six which he sent to Boston, the suggestion, as we have seen, was not acted upon and *Two Dissertations* came out very soon after the Edwards' *Life and Eighteen Sermons*. Perhaps Hopkins, impatient for action, and finding that some of the *Two Dissertations* had been transcribed when he reached Boston in 1764, overlooked the danger which he had rightly feared in 1759.

It was probably a mistake. Edwards' permanent and subsequently popular reputation as an author was to rest upon his books which had first been preached as sermons. As Warfield says, 'It was in his sermons that Edwards' studies bore their richest fruit'. In these works there were no novelties and the basic principles are clearly reformed and Puritan.

But in a few of Edwards' later works, particularly his *Inquiry on the Will* and the *Nature of True Virtue*, certain individual aspects of Edwards' thought appear and in connection with his concern to employ 'reason' or philosophy to buttress biblical truths. A theory of necessity or determinism is introduced to support the truth of divine sovereignty, and the unity of the human race (with its vital bearing on original sin) is supported by a philosophical idea of the continuity of creation. Further, Edwards' theory of virtue represents virtue as 'love to being in general' (a definition probably invented to counter the philosophical theory that morality is grounded in self-love) and another theory he advances (though not original to him) is the so-called distinction between natural and moral ability. As John L. Girardeau writes, 'Edwards was possessed of a wonderful metaphysical genius and of almost angelic saintliness of character, but that he was no exception to the law of human fallibility is proved by his paradoxical speculations in regard to the nature of virtue, the continuity of creation, the constituted identity of Adam and his race, and the tenableness of Berkeleian idealism.'[1]

These peculiarities and speculations in Edwards' thought were not introduced by him as 'new light' in theology. As Lyman Atwater correctly writes of Edwards' intentions: 'To set known principles in a stronger light, with new defences against new forms of antagonistic error, is one thing. To bring to light radically new truths, previously unknown or unregarded, is quite another.'[2] Edwards' individualisms are not to be found elsewhere in his works and it is clear that they were only introduced for a limited purpose in the few of his writings mentioned above. They are by no means characteristic of his teaching as a whole.

But Hopkins saw it differently. We have already noticed the advertisement which accompanied his *Life of Edwards* speaking of the possibility of 'a great deal of new light' from the publication of his subject's manuscripts. Thereafter Hopkins was to spend much time developing Edwards' few individual-isms into theories which were to become distinctive of a new school of New England ministers – 'the very New Divinity Gentlemen', as the unsympathetic Ezra Stiles called them in 1787. Prominent among these men was Jonathan Edwards Jr, who, while professing to state his father's thought more clearly, actually carried the departure still further. Impressed by the family name, many took at their face value the words of Edwards Jr, 'The disciples of Mr. Edwards . . . have since his day made considerable improvement upon former views'.[3]

Speaking of the peculiarities in Edwards' views which occur in the titles mentioned above, Lyman Atwater observes that these

might have attracted no special attention, and led to no important

[1] *The Will in its Theological Relations*, 1891, p. 19.
[2] *The Biblical Repertory and Princeton Review*, 1858, p. 598.
[3] In Edwards' *Works* 1:cxcii there will be found ten 'clearer statements' by Edwards Jr.. Atwater comments effectively on these, and marvels how he 'could have studied his father's writings and arrived at such misconceptions'. Happily there were those in New England who were not misled. We read of strict Calvinists, such as Jonathan French (1740–1809), being 'opposed to Hopkinsianism' (Sprague, 2, p. 44, and 3, p. 185).

results, as has often been the case with occasional eccentric views of great men, aside of the general track of their thinking. In this case, however, it was otherwise. These points were by subsequent divines worked out to their most extreme results, logical and illogical, in reference to the whole circle of doctrine, until they were themselves indeed generally repudiated, but not till they had been made instrumental in undermining many of the most precious truths, which Edwards put forth his chief strength in defending.[1]

Samuel Miller comments similarly on this deflection of Edwards' thought on the part of some of his followers:

No one contended with greater force or decision for the old Puritan theology than President Edwards. Yet, as a melancholy evidence of human imperfection, and of the consequences of a great man's aberrations, it stands confessed, that a departure, which seemed comparatively trifling, from the generally received creed, and philosophical speculations of the results of which their author little dreamed, have furnished the occasion for a multitude of the advocates of dangerous error, with more or less plausibility, to claim the authority of Edwards for their theological vageries.[2]

This process did not come to its full fruition until the 1820's and 1830's when, by C. G. Finney and others, the authority of Edwards was to be claimed for beliefs which were the opposite of those which he had taught. While it must be allowed, as Miller says, that Edwards himself was in part to blame for the outcome, the real damage began with Hopkins. The 'Hopkinsians' were side-tracked. They gave the impression that what interested them most in Edwards were aspects which could never give his writings a general appeal to the wider Christian Church. Speaking of these followers, Warfield writes, 'In their exaggeration of his rational method, without his solid grounding in the history of thought, they lost continuity with the past and became the creators of a "New England theology" which it is only right frankly to describe as provincial'.[3]

The very thing that was charged against a portion of Edwards' writings in the 1750's thus came to be associated with the general tenor of Hopkins' ministry. One of his hearers

[1] *Op. cit.*, p. 614.
[2] *The Life of Samuel Miller*, Samuel Miller Jr, 1869, 1, p. 299.
[3] *Studies in Theology*, p. 533.

recalls, 'I remember to have thought his preaching exceedingly dry and abstract, too highly charged with metaphysical discussion'. The same criticism was made of Jonathan Edwards Jr who was close to Hopkins: 'His own mind was so trained to philosophical disquisition that he seemed sometimes to forget that the multitude whom he was addressing were not also metaphysicians.'[1]

This being so, the close identification of Edwards' name with those of some of his disciples was not an aid to the sale of his writings. The label 'Hopkinsians' popularly applied to Hopkins and his followers, was, regrettably and erroneously, to be used interchangeably with 'Edwardeans'. Nevertheless, when allowance has been made for the extent to which this was prejudicial to Edwards' reputation, the explanation for the small interest in his writings in New England after his death has to be found in a more fundamental consideration.

The general spiritual scene in the later eighteenth century militated against interest in the doctrine which he had preached. Calvinistic convictions waned in North America. In the progress of a decline which Edwards had rightly anticipated, those Congregational churches of New England which had embraced Arminianism after the Great Awakening gradually moved into Unitarianism and universalism, led by Charles Chauncy.[2] And, for the most part, the separatist churches, which had dreamed of proving themselves the custodians of orthodoxy, also failed. In the words of G. L. Walker, 'The good in them was over-weighed with too much of what was not good to make success possible. . . . Mutual criticism, censoriousness, and extravagant employment of church discipline tore their churches in sunder.'[3]

Referring to the decline in Boston at this period, Samuel Miller (himself a New Englander) says that from about the 1750's and 1760's, that is, from the time of the death of Sewall, Prince, Foxcroft and other friends of Edwards who had

---

[1]Sprague, 1, p. 659. But it would be wrong to represent Edwards Jr. as an entire pulpit failure. The same witness says that 'a portion of his preaching' was sometimes 'irresistibly impressive'. An awakening in his pastorate at Schenectady in 1799 is recorded.

[2]See Conrad Wright, *The Beginnings of Unitarianism in America*, 1976.

[3]*Some Aspects of The Religious Life of New England*, 1897, pp. 116–17.

preached in the Great Awakening, 'the most precious and peculiar doctrines of the gospel were seldom preached by anybody'. He continues:

Soon after that race of ministers passed away, the War came on; the order of society was deranged; general laxity increased; and it so happened that some of the most erroneous ministers were high Whigs and greatly popular, and of course well adapted to secure a ready reception for their errors. Only let any set of pastors in the world forbear for fifteen or twenty years to preach the peculiar doctrines of the Gospel, and the way will be prepared at the end of that time to receive any sentiments which artful and popular men may be disposed to recommend.[1]

These spiritual conditions were undoubtedly the main reason for the disinterest in Edwards. In the words of the New Englander, E. A. Park, 'It is a humiliating fact, that several of Edwards' writings were sent to Scotland for publication, because our own community would not patronize them'.[2] Certainly in Scotland the disheartenment which Hopkins had experienced in the 1760's did not affect John Erskine whose faith in the importance and relevance of Edwards' writings was undiminished. In particular Erskine took on the task which no one had been able or willing to undertake in Boston, the transcribing and editing of Edwards' thirty sermons from 1739 on 'the History of Redemption'. Adjusting the material's sermonic form, he took personal responsibility for the publication with an Edinburgh bookseller in 1774.

Edwards' *History of the Work of Redemption* was savagely reviewed in at least one British journal. *The Monthly Review* described it as 'pious nonsense', 'a long, laboured, dull, confused rhapsody', by a 'poor departed enthusiast': 'It is merely an attempt to revive the old mystical divinity that distracted the last age with pious conundrums: and which, having, long ago, emigrated to America, we have no reason to

---

[1]Quoted by Sprague in his Memoir of Griffin, *Sermons of Edward D. Griffin*, 1839, vol. 1, pp. 101–2. The primitive orthodoxy of New England, writes Sprague, 'had been silently, and by almost common consent, driven into exile, and it came to pass at length that it was as much as a man's reputation was worth to appear openly as its advocate'.

[2]Hopkins' *Works*, 1, p. 217.

wish should ever be imported back again.'[1]

But the book was to become one of the most popular of all Edwards' works and the abuse did nothing to stop it reaching the hands of those for whom it was intended. In a prefatory advertisement Erskine writes of these sermons, 'They are in the general better calculated for the instruction and improvement of ordinary Christians, than those of President Edwards's writings where the abstruse nature of the subject, or the subtle objections of opposers of the truth, led him to more abstract and metaphysical reasonings' (1.532).

Future demand for Edwards' works in Scotland abundantly proved the rightness of Erskine's judgment. Whereas only one new Edwards' item was to appear in America before the end of the century, there were five more published in Edinburgh. Nor did Erskine restrict his energies in the promotion of Edwards' books to Scotland. It was a gift of such books from Erskine to English Baptists which moulded the thought of the men who from 1784 gathered in prayer 'for the general revival and spread of religion'. It was these Baptists of the English Midlands who re-issued Edwards' *Humble Attempt to Promote . . . Extraordinary Prayer* in 1789, and who sent William Carey to India in 1793. At least one volume of Edwards went with Carey on that historic voyage.

Somewhat strangely, perhaps, Edwards' works had another promoter in Britain long before these dates. As early as 1743, Edwards had criticized John Wesley for his deviation from orthodox Christianity (1.378), yet Wesley, from the time he saw *the Faithful Narrative* in 1738, was an admirer of Edwards' spirituality and of his defence of revivals. In abridgements, or as extracts, Wesley re-issued several of Edwards' best works, *A Faithful Narrative, Some Thoughts on the Revival, Religious Affections* and *Life of Brainerd*. Like Erskine, Wesley's judgment of priorities was right even if the liberties which he took in editing and abridging (with no leave from Edwards) are surprising by present-day standards. For besides popularizing Edwards, Wesley was also concerned 'to separate the rich ore of

---

[1] *The Monthly Review; or, Literary Journal*, LII (January to June, 1775), pp. 117–120. Quoted in D. Levin, *Jonathan Edwards, A Profile*, 1969, p. 251. British evangelicals, such as John Newton, received the same treatment from *The Monthly Review*.

evangelical truth from the base alloy of . . . Calvinian error'.[1]

Unacquainted as he was with New England, Wesley believed that the passing of revivals in that province was related to the prevalence of Calvinistic belief. By way of contrast, he considered that wherever his own beliefs prevailed there is 'no intermission, but the work of God has been continually increasing'. He writes in his Journal in 1755:

I was considering what could be the reasons why the hand of the Lord (who does nothing without a cause) is almost entirely stayed in Scotland, and in great measure in New England. It does not become us to judge peremptorily, but perhaps some of them may be these. . . . Many of them were bigots, immoderately attached either to their own opinions or mode of worship. Mr Edwards himself was not clear of this. . . . No marvel, then, that the Spirit of God was grieved.[2]

At other times, however, Wesley was willing to be 'peremptory': 'Is not Calvinism the very antidote of Methodism, the most deadly and successful enemy which it ever had?'[3]

But Wesley's assessment of New England was premature. When he died in 1791, many parts of North-East America were on the threshold of powerful revivals which were to be frequent for some forty years. Significantly, it was during this same remarkable period that Edwards' books now came to have the extensive circulation which Hopkins had come to regard as impossible. New editions of Edwards' published works were now called for, and in 1808–9 came the first North American edition of his collected Works, published at Worcester, Mas-

---

[1] The words are those of Wesley's biographer, Luke Tyerman, describing the purpose of 'A Christian Library', issued by Wesley between 1749–55, *Life and Times of Wesley*, vol. 2, p. 65.

[2] *Journal of John Wesley*, ed. Curnock, vol. 4, p. 123. It was Wesley's practice to distinguish between the 'essentials' of the Christian Faith and other beliefs ('opinions') upon which it would be 'bigotry' to insist. But while he blamed Calvinists for going beyond 'essentials', he himself *urges* his own distinctive beliefs such as universal redemption, falling from grace and sinless perfection, presumably upon the grounds that these beliefs must not be classed as 'opinions'. Of Brainerd, Wesley says, 'How much of his sorrow and pain had been prevented, if he had understood the doctrine of Christian Perfection! How many tears did he shed because it was impossible to be freed from sin!' *Letters of Wesley*, ed. Telford, vol. 5, p. 95.

[3] To Lady Maxwell, 1788, *Letters of Wesley*, vol. 8, p. 95.

sachusetts, in eight volumes.[1] Applied to *this* period, there is truth in Henry B. Parkes' words in the concluding chapter of his *Jonathan Edwards*, entitled 'The Blight upon Posterity', 'After his death his writings transformed half the people of New England from healthy human beings to would-be saints'. Parkes was writing long after the period when Edwards' works had such wide circulation but the Rev. John Todd, who lived at the time, gives us a glimpse of what these books came to mean to individuals:

> When a young student, I found a woman among the fevers of the rice-swamps of South Carolina who amazed and confounded me by her knowledge of theology. She was so far above me, that I felt myself to be nothing. The secret was, that she had for years lived upon the works of Jonathan Edwards.
>
> In the revival in Yale College in 1820, under the teachings of Asahel Nettleton, after many wrestlings of the spirit and intellect, I deliberately adopted the theology of this master in Israel; and have, as yet, never grown great enough or wise enough to change my opinions. A little later, down on Cape Cod, I met an old deacon, who, for profound and accurate theology, might have been a theological professor, and before whom I fairly stood in awe. He too, for years, had lived and grown upon a set of Edwards's works.
>
> Afterwards I had a parishioner who had read Edwards 'On the Affections' through six times; and he was a giant in theology.[2]

Without question, the foremost stimulus to this general reading of Edwards on the part of ordinary Christians was the doctrinal, fervent and experimental preaching which characterized this revival era of the late-eighteenth and early-nineteenth centuries. The truth preached, with little variation, was the same as marked Edwards' ministry and, without exception, the leading preachers, Bennet Tyler, Asahel Nettleton, Joel Hawes, Edward Payson, Edward D. Griffin, Lyman Beecher, and many others were all men who had read deeply in Edwards.

Beecher had followed Samuel Buell in the church at East

---

[1] A 10 vol. edition appeared at New York in 1829–30, while from 1843, the Worcester edition appeared in four volumes, with at least fourteen printings by 1881.

[2] *The Memorial Volume of the Edwards Family Meeting*, 1871, pp. 121–2.

Hampton, Long Island in 1799. In 1836 he could describe himself as 'steeped in Jonathan Edwards for more than forty years'. A letter to his son, George, who was training for the ministry in 1830 includes the following:

I was glad to receive your letter, and hear of your pleasant accommodations, both for exercise, for piety, and for study – especially that you are aware of the temptation of intellectual pursuits < to leave the affections to languish without constant care. It is our shame, and a deep evidence of the depravity of our hearts, that, during mental occupancy about God and divine things, the affections should run down. It is not so in heaven. . . . It need not, however, be so on earth to the extent which it is, as appears in the life and writings of Edwards, whose vigor of intellect, compass of thought, patience of investigation, accuracy of discrimination, power of argument, knowledge of the Bible, and strength of holiness, stand unrivaled. But for his piety, he might have been a skeptic more dangerous than Hume or Voltaire; and but for the command of his religion over all his powers, he might have been one of the most dangerous, as he certainly was one of the most original and fearless of speculators. But the attractions of his heart to God kept him in his orbit, and enabled him to go forth, and survey, and adjust the relations of the moral universe without becoming a wandering star; whose original investigation and deep piety, my son, follow. Next after the Bible, read and study < Edwards, whom to understand in theology, accommodated to use, will be as high praise in theological science as to understand Newton's works in accommodation to modern uses of natural philosophy.

Edwards and Fuller are the two best theological writers for a young man to study. But while Fuller, availing himself of his own powerful mind acting on Edwards's materials, has written with more conciseness and perspicuity than Edwards, he falls far below him in the ardor of his piety, and in his power of applying truth to the conscience. In this respect Edwards stands unrivaled. There is in his revival sermons more discrimination, power of argument, and pungency of application than are contained in all the sermons beside which were ever written. Study as models Edwards's applications. They are original, multiform, and powerful beyond measure.[1]

---

[1] *The Autobiography of Lyman Beecher, Ed.* B. M. Cross, 1961, vol. 2, pp. 177–8.
Buell, Beecher's predecessor, was the memorable preacher at Northampton in February 1742. He was inducted by Edwards to East Hampton in 1747 where there were 'four revivals' during his ministry – some, says Beecher, 'of remarkable power'. Beecher's sons did not follow their father's counsel and his daughter, Harriet Beecher Stowe, was one of the leaders among New

Any recommended list of books, given by orthodox preachers of this era, was always sure to include the name of Edwards. The seraphic Edward Payson writes in 1821:

> I aim to preach the truths of the gospel in a practical and experimental, rather than a dry and speculative manner. . . . The books which I have found most useful to me are Edwards' Works, Brainerd's Life, Newton's Letters, Owen's Treatise on Indwelling Sin, Mortification of Sin in Believers, and the 130th Psalm, and Thomas à Kempis's Imitation of Christ, translated by Payne. . . . Perhaps I ought to include, Baxter's Reformed Pastor and Saint's Rest.[1]

Edward Griffin, no less famed a preacher than Payson, spoke similarly. Dr Irenaeus Prime (the man who startled the Edwards Family Meeting at Stockbridge in 1870) recalled how as a youth of fifteen, he was at College in Williamstown at a time of general spiritual concern and awakening: 'A number of my fellow-students with me became seriously disposed to seek the salvation of our souls. We sent a committee to ask the president, Dr Griffin, to meet us in the recitation-room, and tell us what to do. He was so engaged, that he could not come that moment; but he sent a sermon, with the request that we would have it read by one of us in the hearing of all. Was it one of his own matchless, rhetorical overwhelming appeals? No: it was an old yellow volume of sermons by Jonathan Edwards. The one he commended to us was read; and I remember well that I was afraid at its close to walk across the floor, lest it should prove the cover of hell.'[2]

Happily Northampton itself not only shared in but contributed to New England's revived interest in Edwards. After a troubled vacancy the Church had succeeded in settling a minister by the name of John Hooker in 1753, the right hand of fellowship at his induction being given by Edwards' opponent,

---

England novelists who caricatured Christianity of the Puritan school. In *The Minister's Wooing* she made Samuel Hopkins the main character of a love-story, in the words of one reviewer, 'like Samson that he might furnish entertainment for the uncircumcised'. Probably these writers of fiction indirectly did more than Finney to discredit New England's orthodox Christianity.

[1] *Works of Edward Payson*, 1859, p. 251.
[2] *Op. cit.*, p. 141.

Robert Breck.[1] But fifty years later it was at Northampton that the second edition of Hopkins' *Life of Edwards* was published and in the years which followed there appear to have been several ministers at Northampton who were unashamed admirers of their predecessor. When one of these ministers, newly settled in Northampton, asked advice of Griffin respecting further studies, he received this characteristic exhortation:

It does appear to me that the most important object of all, and which ought for the present to engross your whole attention, is to bring that immense congregation, by your preaching, prayers, and pastoral visits under the influence – the dissolving and transforming influence – of powerful and repeated revivals of religion. As to scholarship, if it has not been attained before one has reached the age of thirty, and has entered on such a prodigious field of labor, it cannot be attained to any very high degree in connexion with such a conscience as yours. . . . I doubt much whether I would enter at present on any new plan of studies beyond those which are strictly theological. If you can prevail to imbue that great people with divine truth, and make the truth triumph where President Edwards fell, and bring them, by the side of Brainerd's grave, to pray as Brainerd prayed, you will have performed a work great enough for an angel's powers: you may then go to heaven, and the church will bless God that you ever had existence. Considering the history, and the magnitude, and the influence of your congregation, and the state in which you received it, few men have ever had such a work laid out for them; – it is enough to exhaust the powers of one mind. It is a charge ponderous enough 'to make the shoulder of an angel tremble'.

I would recommend it to you, my brother, to bathe your soul in Baxter's *Saints' Rest*, and to be much in prayer, and make yourself deeply acquainted with the Scriptures.[2]

The period of revival in North America, after lasting nearly forty years, terminated in the 1830's, and under the impact of influences not dissimilar to those which arose out of the Great Awakening. This time the leader of a new generation of separatists was Charles G. Finney who, opposing 'the tradition of the elders' (as he called orthodoxy), promoted 'new divinity' and 'new measures'. While claiming the support of Edwards, as already said, Finney opposed him at fundamental points

---

[1] Sprague, 1, p. 505, reports Hooker as being 'substantially a Calvinist'.
[2] *Sermons of Edward D. Griffin*, with Memoir, vol. 1, 1839, pp. 147–48.

including the nature of regeneration. Finney claimed that regeneration occurs by an act of the human will. Following the rise of Finney's influence, interest in Edwards was once more to decline and a broader and more superficial type of evangelicalism which was basically Arminian was to emerge in North America.

Charles Hodge, among others, has shown that Finney was endorsing the very error which Edwards had answered in his refutation of Taylor on original sin. The will has no self-determining power. Hodge stood with Edwards in his fear of the influence of Arminianism as 'derogatory to true religion'. Reviewing the influence of Finney's teaching, he writes: 'The depravity of the heart is practically represented as a very slight matter and the whole change necessary to constitute a man a Christian is represented as a mere determination of the mind. . . . The characteristic tendency of this mode of preaching is to keep the Holy Spirit and his influences out of view. . . . Conviction of sin is made of little account.'[1]

Hodge's words are a reminder that the real defence of Edwards against the 'new divinity' came from Princeton. Edwards hopes that the New Jersey village would long remain a centre for true Christianity were abundantly fulfilled. The most dependable reflections on Edwards' theology almost all came from such men as Hodge, Miller and Atwater – all teachers at Princeton Theology Seminary – and it remained so right down to B. B. Warfield who died in 1921. For upwards of a century-and-a-half, the place to which Edwards gave so much thought, and where his dust was to lie, remained a foremost preserver and propagator of historic Christianity.

*   *   *

[1]'The New Divinity Tried', *Theological Essays Reprinted from The Princeton Review*, 1846 (New York) and 1856 (Edinburgh). Concerning the claim that Edwards' writings support Finney, Hodge asks, 'We wish to know on what principle such statements can be reconciled with honesty'. But Finney himself, in his *Lectures on Revivals of Religion* (1835), sought to give this impression. When the American Tract Society abridged and edited reprints of Edwards and Flavel, the Presbyterian Synod of New York and New Jersey complained in 1845 that 'the doctrines of God's absolute sovereignty in saving men, in predestination, election, perseverance – of the nature and the extent of the atonement, of men's ability, and of infant baptism – are, in many instances materially modified, and in others wholly excluded'.

In Britain the early nineteenth-century resurgence of Edwards' publications not only matched that of North America but far exceeded it. Even John Erskine, who died in 1803, could scarcely have anticipated the flood of Edwards material to appear in British book-shops in the next forty years. An eight-volume edition of his collected *Works* was published at Leeds, Yorkshire, 1806–11, soon to be improved in a London edition of 1817, with two supplementary volumes of posthumous material added at Edinburgh in 1847. Undeterred by this edition already in print, another British publisher, rightly foreseeing the problems of the permanent marketing of such a large set, succeeded in packing more content than in the original eight volumes into a new two-volume edition of the Edwards' *Works* which came out in 1834. This edition was to go through ten printings by 1865 and is the one which remains in print today. Perhaps the most remarkable thing about this boom in the publication of Edwards' material is the fact that despite the availability of his collected *Works*, printings and reprintings of his individual books also multiplied simultaneously. For example, British printings of *The Religious Affections* appeared in 1810, 1812 (twice), 1817, 1822, 1825, 1827, 1831, 1833 (Welsh) and this does not include at least two printings of John Wesley's abridgement. In the same period Edwards' *Humble Attempt to Promote . . . Extraordinary Prayer* had printings in 1814 and 1831. His *Life of Brainerd*, already popular before 1800, was reprinted in 1808, 1818, 1820, 1821, 1824, 1826, 1829, and 1834, again excluding Wesley's popular abridgement. *A Careful and Strict Inquiring Into . . . Freedom of the Will* had its first nineteenth-Century British printing in 1816, followed by others in 1818, 1827, 1831 and 1840. *A History of Redemption*, already popular before 1800, now claimed many new readers in printings issued in 1808, 1812, 1816, 1829 (Welsh), 1831, 1832, 1835, 1838, with three more printings in the 1840's.

Such figures are indicative of the size of the interest in Edwards in Britain in the 1820's and 1830's. And, with the exception of *Freedom of the Will*, the reasons for this popularity were precisely the same as in the United States. The general Christian public had become his readers. James Bennett in his *History of Dissenters*, published in London in 1839, speaks of the principles of the Puritan fathers as 'highly valued by the present generation' and he gives this proof: 'Those writings of Charnock, Owen, Baxter, Watts, Doddridge and Edwards, were so voluminous that nothing but an extensive circulation could repay the cost. But of these expensive undertakings, the supply gave proof of the demand.'[1]

This demand for a writer long deceased is precisely what we noticed as occurring in Boston during the Great Awakening. Powerful biblical preaching invariably gives rise to serious Christian reading. In Britain during this period the reading of Edwards did much to inspire a new generation of preachers whose congregations, in turn, relished books which were in harmony with the Word preached. John Newton's words, already quoted, may be taken as representative of Anglican evangelicals. Leaders among the early nineteenth-century English Baptists were outspoken admirers of Edwards, none more so than Robert Hall (Carey's famous successor at Leicester) and John C. Ryland.

The same was true in Wales where Calvinistic Methodists had long regarded Edwards as the foremost exponent and defender of biblical views on revival. The biographer of John Elias compares him with Edwards,' both being doctrinal preachers, and Owen Jones, speaking of Elias' reading, writes, 'Dr Owen, John Howe, Jonathan Edwards etc were his chief authors'.[2]

In Scotland the influence of Edwards upon many preachers is even more directly traceable. Of John MacDonald, the foremost Highland evangelist of the last century, John Kennedy writes: 'There is reason to believe that the reading of President Edwards' works was the means of beginning the work of conviction which issued in his conversion to God'.[3] Meanwhile in Edinburgh, John Erskine's role as a promoter of Edwards was taken up with great effect by Thomas Chalmers who could say:

There is no European Divine to whom I make such frequent appeals in my class rooms as I do to Edwards.

I have long esteemed him as the greatest of theologians, combining,

---

[1] *History of the Dissenters*, vol. 3, p. 305.
[2] *Some of the Great Preachers of Wales*, 1885, p. 274.
[3] *The Life of John MacDonald*, 1849, pp. 263–4.

in a degree that is quite unexampled, the profoundly intellectual with the devotedly spiritual and sacred, and realizing in his own person a most rare yet most beautiful harmony between the simplicity of the Christian pastor on the one hand, and, on the other, all the strength and prowess of a giant in philosophy; so as at once to minister from sabbath to sabbath, and with the most blessed effect, to the hearers of his plain congregation, and yet in the high field of authorship to have traversed, in a way that none had ever done before him, the most inaccessible places, and achieved such a mastery as had never till his time been realized over the most arduous difficulties of our science.[1]

Chalmers' many students were to be extensively used both at home and overseas and the influence of Edwards is apparent in their lives. Perhaps the most notable instance of this was in the ministry of Robert Murray M'Cheyne. From the days of his first pastorate at Larbert, M'Cheyne preached for revival and believed in revival. 'It was here,' writes Andrew Bonar, his biographer, 'that he began to study so closely the works of Jonathan Edwards, – reckoning them a mine to be wrought, and if wrought, sure to repay the toil.'[2] The awakening during his subsequent ministry at Dundee in the early 1840's resembled what had occurred in Northampton.

Forty years later Edwards' Works were again falling into disuse on both sides of the Atlantic. In 1881 the aged Andrew Bonar visited Northampton and was 'much stirred up'[3] by the memories it evoked but his attitude was no longer representative of religious thought. In 1880, Oliver Wendell Holmes could speak of Edwards as 'a powerful thinker whose thoughts produced no lasting results'.[4] Thereafter, for more than fifty years, very few voices were to be heard in defence of Edwards' message. The opinion prevailed that his 'dogma' virtually prohibited any further usefulness for his writings. 'Of all the Americans of his day . . . none had more notable endowments for pure scholarship', says Thomas H. Johnson in 1931, 'yet none has left monuments so crumbled and overgrown'.[5] And

[1]From a letter to Dr Stebbins of Northampton, quoted in *The Memorial Volume of the Edwards Family Meeting*, p. 142.
[2]*Memoir and Remains of R. M. M'Cheyne*, 1892 edition (reprinted 1966), p. 35.
[3]*Andrew A. Bonar: Diary and Life*, 1960 reprint, p. 470.
[4]Quoted by Manspeaker, *op. cit.*, p. 97.
[5]*Ibid.*, p. 105.

again, 'That Edwards has not been generally read in these latter days (and that he probably will not be read in the future), is the fault of his subject matter.'[1]

Amidst all this early-twentieth century uniformity of thought there appears to have been only one doubter of its correctness among the best-known writers on Edwards. Arthur Cushman McGiffert was no Puritan but he had enough misgivings to raise questions in some minds whether, after all, Edwards' message is irrelevant for the modern world. In his *Protestant Thought before Kant*, 1911, McGiffert asserts of Edwards that 'his practical interest throughout was to humble man, to convince him of his total depravity and absolute bondage to sin, and so startle him out of his easy indifference and complacent self-confidence'. And further, in his *Jonathan Edwards*, 1932, the same author asks,

Has religious liberalism . . . failed where a philosophy of life has no business to fail? Has modern religion glossed over the stern facts of life with a saccharine sentimentality about the fatherhood of God? Has it taken the iron out of its ethic? Sin does not disappear just because it is not talked about or recognized.

It was words from McGiffert's first book which alerted D. Martyn Lloyd-Jones to find a second-hand set of the two-volume edition of Edwards' Works in 1929. Of these volumes he was later to say, 'I devoured these volumes and literally just read and read them. It is certainly true that they helped me more than anything else.'[2] Probably as much as John Erskine and Thomas Chalmers, Martyn Lloyd-Jones became the incentive behind a new generation of readers of Edwards. And once again, as faith in the historic Christianity of the Reformed Churches revived so did an appreciation of the doctrinal and spiritual values which Edwards represents. At the Puritan Conference, established at Westminster Chapel, London, in 1950, Edwards was to be a repeated subject for discussion and for addresses, and when the Banner of Truth Trust commenced publishing in 1957, with Westminster Chapel as its initial 'warehouse', three volumes of *The Select Works of Jonathan Edwards* were among its first publications. What had seemed

[1] *The New England Quarterly*, 1931, p. 356.
[2] *David Martyn Lloyd-Jones*, The First Forty Years 1899–1939, Iain Murray, 1982, p. 254.

impossible twenty years earlier was a reality. Edwards' Works had again found new and eager readers. Since 1974, the complete 1834 edition of *The Works of Jonathan Edwards* has again been available with between eight and nine thousand sets sold before the end of 1984.

In 1957, the same date as the formation of The Banner of Truth Trust, and entirely independently of each other, Yale University Press brought out the first volume of what was intended to be a definitive edition of Edwards. The motivation for this great project – which aimed to take in many unpublished manuscripts – was clearly different from the British venture. Yale seems to have envisaged Edwards for the University Philosophy Department and for the student of Colonial thought, rather than for the pulpit and the modern Christian reader. In a 'General Editor's Note', which introduced volume one of the Yale edition, Perry Miller wrote:

A generation or so ago, outside a restricted circle of professional theologians, Edwards was popularly known only as one who had preached a distasteful and happily outmoded brand of hell-fire and brimstone. There was, in fact, a general disposition to pass him over as an anachronism, as retrograde.

Miller was concerned that the reason for their new edition of Edwards' writings should not be misunderstood: 'This is not to imply that today the precise doctrines that Edwards maintained, have been or should be extensively revived; indeed it is quite beside the purpose of this edition to promulgate them'.

It is to be regretted that something of Miller's approach to Edwards has been reflected in the order in which the material has been presented thus far. A conviction of the importance of Edwards' *message* would have led to different priorities for although seven Yale volumes are now in print none of Edwards' individual sermons has yet been issued.[1] Nonetheless, in

---

[1] The Yale volumes issued to date are listed on p. 479. The general editorial policies of the Yale editors are explained by Thomas A. Schafer in 'Manuscript Problems in the Yale Edition of Jonathan Edwards', *Early American Literature*, 3 (Winter, 1968–69), pp. 159–171. It has so often, in the past, been the sermons which have awakened interest in Edwards. 'I have read some of Jonathan Edwards' sermons, which have left a deep impression on my heart,' wrote Andrew Fuller in his Diary on January 20, 1790 (*Complete Works of A. Fuller*, 1841, p. lii).

University libraries around the world, the text of Edwards is appearing in a more attractive format than has ever been seen before.

*   *   *

The propensity of Edwards' Works to regain attention and to re-assert their message is an historical fact worthy of notice. More than once, as we have seen, they have been forgotten and judged obsolete only to re-appear afresh with new power and significance. For Edwards himself such a phenomenon would not be surprising. Such variations in influence belong to the Christian Faith itself. The message is timeless. Edwards re-asserted, in eighteenth-century language, much that was best in the doctrinal and practical divinity of the reformed churches. He did so, not because of any adherence to the tradition of Calvinistic theology as such, but rather because he believed that theology to be scriptural. Only for that reason has it abiding and international relevance.

Herein lies Edwards' enduring strength. He was not an originator. He proposes no re-formulation of the doctrine and creed of the Protestant Churches. Rather he was ready to work from the basis of existing foundations. Whether in the Hampshire Association or among the Housatonics, he was content with the theology of the Westminster Confession and of the Shorter Catechism. His assessment of God's providential purpose in history was that the eighteenth century was not intended to be an age for new confessions and catechisms. These were already richly provided. What was needed was preaching, revival and missionary endeavour. It was a day for prayer and action, for seizing the opportunities offered by the new horizons of an expanding world.

But just because the eighteenth-century church was stronger in the realm of action than in doctrinal knowledge, Edwards has a vital role in securing continuity with the Christianity of the Reformation. The advance – and the new missionary age to dawn before the century closed – needed to be upon the basis of the doctrinal foundations already laid. Had Edwards not occupied the role of the foremost theologian of his century, the Christianity which was then revived might have been estranged from the Faith of the Reformers and Puritans. Edwards played a major role in conserving what was best in the past and in securing continuity for the future. 'He strove after no show of originality,' writes Warfield. 'He enters into the great tradition which had come down to him, and "infuses it with his personality and makes it live".' Thus to interpret Edwards, is to assert that he belonged to a tradition. His message and influence is not merely that of one great individual. Taken alone, Edwards can neither be rightly understood, nor rightly prized. Any assessment of his worth will always be determined finally by the assessor's view of the message and the tradition for which Edwards spoke.

There were, of course, those who conceived the needs of the eighteenth century to include the need for revision of traditional orthodoxy. They included such latitudinarian divines as Whitby, Warburton and Taylor, on the one hand, and such an inconsistent evangelical as John Wesley on the other. Wesley's respect for Edwards, as we have seen, did not include respect for his theology, and he attempted to make Methodism a movement for doctrinal change.[1] Given the success attending Methodist preaching, it was to be Wesley's type of Arminianism (and its more serious variant initiated by C. G. Finney) which posed the greater temptation to evangelical Christianity. The weakness of biblical evidence for the teaching which Wesley wished to substitute was half-hidden behind a charge that Calvinistic belief and evangelism are incompatible. 'Calvinism has been the greatest hindrance of the work of God', was Wesley's repeated assertion.

[1] On this subject, the anonymous author of an article entitled 'Evangelism of the Eighteenth Century' writes: 'When God wants men for a special exigency or a particular field, he brings them forward amply qualified for the work committed to their charge. These men . . . were not fitted either by nature or culture, or experience, for doctrinal reformers. And hence, we believe that Methodism was never commissioned for this specific work. We must be pardoned for any seeming want of charity, in declaring our belief that it travelled out of its legitimate sphere, when it undertook the work of reforming the creed of Christendom. Vast, far-reaching, and glorious, as have been the results of the Methodist movement, who shall tell us that they would not have been far greater and more glorious, had there been a strict and unwavering adherence to the doctrines so glowingly sounded forth by Whitefield, and others of their most distinguished founders?' *The British and Foreign Evangelical Review*, 1862, p. 30.

While George Whitefield's ministry was a powerful counter to this charge, in the long term it was Edwards' Works which were to be the more formidable and permanent obstacle to the success of Wesley's argument. No book did more to create concern for wider missionary endeavour than Edwards' *Life of Brainerd*. Gideon Hawley (his assistant at Stockbridge), who carried the book in his saddle-bag as he pioneered among the Iroquois, was only one of the first in a long line of Calvinistic missionaries. About the time Hawley died (1807), Carey and his associates in India were writing their 'Covenant' which included the words, 'Let us often look at Brainerd'.[1] John McDonald Jr, a next generation missionary in India, likewise regarded Brainerd as 'his favourite, and, in some respects, his model'.[2] Nor was it simply the example of Brainerd which counted. From the early 1780's it was Edwards' theology which was used to shape the vision of the Midland Baptists who led the way in the era of modern missionaries. Shortly before his death in 1815, Andrew Fuller, friend of Carey and first Secretary of The Baptist Missionary Society, dictated a letter to his old friend John Ryland which contained the following:

We have some who have been giving out, of late, that 'If Sutcliff and some others had preached more of Christ, and less of Jonathan Edwards, they would have been more useful'. If those who talked thus preached Christ half as much as Jonathan Edwards did, and were half as useful as he was, their usefulness would be double what it is. It is very singular that the mission to the East should have originated with men of these principles; and, without pretending to be a prophet, I may say, If ever it falls into the hands of men who talk in this strain, it will soon come to nothing.[3]

It may be said that the nineteenth-century argument against Calvinistic evangelism finally prevailed on the ground of ignorance of history as well as ignorance of Scripture. C. H. Spurgeon – the last great representative of the Puritan tradition until Martyn Lloyd-Jones – was not being heard by the Christian world at large when he protested:

---

[1]*William Carey*, S. Pearce Carey, 1923, p. 249. In re-reading Brainerd, says Carey, 'he soonest "caught fire"', 154.

[2]W. K. Tweedie, *The Life of John MacDonald*, 1849, pp. 263–64.

[3]*The Works of Andrew Fuller*, lxxxiv.

Did not Charnock, Goodwin and Howe agonize for souls, and what
were they but Calvinists? Did not Jonathan Edwards preach to
sinners, and who more clear and explicit on these doctrinal
matters. . . . In the history of the church, with but few exceptions, you
could not find a revival at all that was not produced by the orthodox
faith. . . . If you turn to the continent of America, how gross the
falsehood that Calvinistic doctrine is unfavourable to revivals! Look
at that wondrous shaking under Jonathan Edwards and others which
we might quote.[1]

The key to an understanding of Jonathan Edwards is that he
was a man who put faithfulness to the Word of God before every
other consideration. At critical points in his life, most notably
in not deferring to the 'advice' of Israel Williams in 1734, and
again in the communion controversy of 1749–50, he put the
truth first. He did this when considerations of personal interest
– 'my own reputation, future usefulness, and my very subsistence'. – all made the opposite course of action seem
expedient. It was this which Edwards rejected. For, at bottom,
Solomon Williams' case for retaining the *status quo* over
qualifications for communion was an argument for expediency.
Edwards' views, he complained, would lead to a small,
uninfluential church. But Edwards, while replying that it was
lack of holiness, not lack of numbers, which hindered the
advance of the church (1.474 fn.), was content to leave
influence and results with God. He knew that 'success' is not to
be judged in the short-term. The Christian's business is to
honour God, and in his own time God will honour his truth and
those who are faithful to it.

The history of Edwards' writings bears testimony to this fact.
Twenty years after the communion controversy the issue was
still in debate but the tide was turning. The Rev. Israel Holly
writing to a friend of looser views on the subject, said: 'If I was
to engage you in this controversy, I would say *Read Edwards*.
And if you wrote again, I would tell you, *Read Edwards*. For I
think it needless for any man to write after him, and fruitless for
any man to write against him upon this subject.'[2]

Edwards' convictions on church membership, writes

[1]C. H. Spurgeon, *Autobiography*: 2, 'The Full Harvest', 1973, p. 46.
[2]Winslow, from the *Historical Magazine*, 1867, p. 234.

[471]

Charles Hodge, 'gradually changed the opinions and practices of the Congregational churches throughout the land, and to a great extent those of Presbyterians also.'[1] Tracy gives the following illuminating information on the later influence of Edwards' doctrine:

Every Congregational church in New England, probably, has either adopted that doctrine, or become Unitarian. The future destiny of each of the churches seems to have depended more on its treatment of this question, than on any other single event. Those that were friendly to the revival, generally, but not universally, returned with Edwards to the ancient doctrine and practice, were thenceforth composed of members who made a credible profession of piety, and are saved. Those hostile to the revival, regarded that doctrine and practice as 'divisive', as 'uncharitable', as 'censorious', as 'an invasion of God's prerogative, to judge the heart'. They continued the practice of making no discrimination between men as converted or unconverted, and in most, but not all cases, the result is, that now, no man is excluded from their communion for any error in doctrine, or any immorality in practice; and in some of them, even the form of church membership is given up; the churches, as distinct from the congregations, no longer exist, and the ordinances are administered indiscriminately to all who will receive them.'[2]

The ministry of Jonathan Edwards is, very clearly, not yet concluded. He is being read today as he has not been read for over a century and in more countries than ever before. Such a recovery of truth has commonly been a forerunner of revival. For this let all Christians pray, and let it also be remembered that the Word of God never yet prospered in the world without opposition. There is no guarantee that men faithful to God will be recognizable by their numbers, their talents, or their success. But in due course, if not in this life-time, they will witness the fulfilment of the promise, 'for them that honour me I will honour' (1 Sam. 2.30).

[1] *Systematic Theology*, vol. 3, p. 569.
[2] *The Great Awakening*, p. 411.

APPENDICES

One

EDWARDS' PUBLISHED WRITINGS

(a) *During Edwards' Lifetime*

The following items are given in chronological sequence with a reference appended if they are available in the editions of Edwards' currently in print. *Works* refers to the 2 vol. Banner of Truth Trust reprint and J E, Yale, to the Yale University Press edition.

As a rough guide to those who are about to begin reading Edwards for the first time we would recommend that his writings be taken up in the order in which they were originally written and published.

1. *God Glorified in the Work of Redemption, by the Greatness of Man's Dependance upon him.* A Sermon [from 1 Cor. 1: 29–31] Preached in Boston, July 8, 1731. Boston, 1731. 8°, pp. iv, 25. (*Works*, 2, 3–7).

2. *A Divine and Supernatural Light, Immediately imparted to the Soul by the Spirit of God, shown to be both a Scriptural, and Rational Doctrine*; in a Sermon [from Matt. 16: 17]. Boston, 1734. 8°, pp. iv, 32. (*Works*, 2, 12–17).

(?) *Curse ye Meroz*: A Sermon [on Judges 5: 23], Boston, 1735.

Doubt exists over this item which S. E. Dwight says he could not find.

3. Part of a large Letter from the Rev. Mr. Edwards of Northampton Giving an Account of the late wonderful Work of God in those Parts. [Dated November 6, 1736. Appended to *The Duty and Interest of a People, among whom Religion has been planted*, to Continue Steadfast and Sincere in it, by the Rev. William Williams]. Boston, 1736. 16°, pp. 19. (J E, Yale, 4).

4. *A Letter to the Author of the Pamphlet called, An Answer to the Hampshire Narrative.* [Anonymous] Boston, 1737. 8°, pp. 84.

5. *A Faithful Narrative of the Surprizing Work of God in the Conversion of Many Hundred Souls in Northampton, and the Neighbouring Towns.* London, 1737. 12°, pp. xvi, 132. (*Works*, 1, 344–364; J E, Yale, 4).

6. The above, reprinted with corrections (see J E, Yale, 4) together with: *Discourses on Various Important Subjects, nearly concerning Salvation.* Boston, 1738. 8°, pp. vi, 286. (*Works*, 1, 620–689).

7. *Sinners in the Hands of an Angry God.* A Sermon preached [from Deut, 32: 35] at Enfield, July 8, 1741. Boston, 1741. 16°, pp. 25. (*Works*, 2, 7–12).

8. *The Resort and Remedy of those that are bereaved by the Death of an Eminent Minister.* A Sermon [on Matt. 14: 12] preached at the Interment of the Rev. Mr. William Williams. Boston, 1741. 8°, pp. 22. (*Works*, 2, 965–69).

9. *The Distinguishing Marks of a Work of the Spirit of God. Applied to that uncommon Operation that has lately appeared on the Minds of many of the People of this Land.* A Discourse delivered at New Haven [on 1 John, 4: 1], September 10, 1741. With Preface by Rev. Mr. Cooper of Boston. Boston, 1741. 8°, pp. xviii, 110. (*Works*, 2, 257–277 and J E, Yale, 4).

10. *Some Thoughts concerning the present Revival of Religion in New-England, and the Way in which it ought to be acknowledged and promoted.* Boston, 1742. 12°, pp. vi, 378. (*Works*, 1, 365–430 and J E, Yale, 4).

11. *The great Concern of a Watchman for Souls.* A Sermon [from Heb. 13: 17] at the Ordination of Jonathan Judd. Boston, 1743. 16°, pp. 50.

12. *The true Excellency of a Minister of the Gospel.* A Sermon. . . . Preach'd [from John 5: 35] at the Ordination of the Rev^d. Mr.

Robert Abercrombie. Boston, 1744. 8°, pp. 22. (*Works*, 2, 955–60).

13. *Copies of the Two Letters Cited by the Rev. Mr. Clap, in his late printed Letter to a Friend in Boston, concerning what he has reported, as from Mr. Edwards, concerning the Rev. Mr. Whitefield. With some Reflections on the Affair those Letters relate to.* Boston, 1745. 16°, pp. 16.

14. *An Expostulatory Letter to the Rev. Mr. Clap, in Reply to his late printed Letter, relating to what he reported concerning the Rev. Mr. Whitefield, as from Mr. Edwards.* Boston, 1745. 16°, pp. 16.

15. *A Treatise concerning Religious Affections.* Boston, 1746. 8°, pp. vi. 352. (*Works*, 1, 234–343 and J E, Yale, 2).

16. *The Church's Marriage to her Sons, and to her God:* A Sermon [from Isa. 62: 4, 5] Preached at the Instalment of the Rev. Mr. Samuel Buell. Boston, 1746. 8°, pp. 43. (*Works*, 2, 17–26).

17. *True Saints, when Absent from the Body, are Present with the Lord.* A Sermon [from 2 Cor. 5: 8] Preached on the Day of the Funeral of the Rev. Mr. David Brainerd. Boston, 1747. 8°, pp. 40. (*Works*, 2, 26–36).

18. *A Humble Attempt to promote Explicit Agreement and Visible Union of God's People in Extraordinary Prayer for the Revival of Religion and the Advancement of Christ's Kingdom on Earth.* Boston, 1747. 16°, pp. ix, 188. (*Works*, 2, 278–312).

19. *A Strong Rod broken and withered.* A Sermon Preach'd [from Ez. 19: 12] on the Death of the Hon. John Stoddard, Esq. Boston, 1748. 8°, pp. 29. (*Works*, 2, 36–40).

20. *An Account of the Life of Rev. David Brainerd.* Boston, 1749. 8°, pp. xxx, 316. (*Works*, 2, 313–458 and J E, Yale, 7).

21. *An Humble Inquiry into the Rules of the Word of God, concerning the Qualifications Requisite to a compleat Standing and full Communion in the Visible Christian Church.* With Appendix by T. Foxcroft. Boston, 1749. 8°, pp. vi, 136, 16. (*Works*, 1, 431–484).

22. *Christ the great Example of Gospel Ministers.* A Sermon [from John 13: 15, 16] preach'd at Portsmouth, at the Ordination of the Rev. Mr. Job Strong, June 28, 1749. Boston, 1750. 16°, pp. 28. (*Works*, 2, 960–965).

23. *A Farewell Sermon* [from 2. Cor. 1, 14] preached at the first Precinct in Northampton, after the People's publick Rejection of their Minister, and renouncing their Relation to Him as Pastor of the Church there, on June 22, 1750. Occa-

sion'd by Difference of Sentiments, concerning the requisite Qualifications of Members of the Church, in compleat Standing. Boston, 1751. 8°, pp. viii, 36. (*Works*, 1, cxcviii-ccvii).

24. *Misrepresentations Corrected, and Truth vindicated.* In a Reply to the Rev. Solomon Williams's Book, The True State of the Question concerning the Qualifications necessary to lawful Communion in the Christian Sacraments. Boston, 1752. 8°, pp. iv, 173 + 4. (*Works*, 1, 485–531).

25. *True Grace, Distinguished from the Experience of Devils*; in a Sermon [on James 2: 19] Preached before the Synod of N.Y. N.Y., 1753. 8°, pp. 42. (*Works*, 2, 41–50).

26. *A Careful and Strict Enquiry into the modern prevailing Notions of Freedom of Will.* Boston, 1754. 8°, pp. x, 294 + xiv. (*Works*, 1, 3–93).

27. *The Great Christian Doctrine of Original Sin defended.* Boston, 1758. 8°, pp. xviii, 388 + 7. (*Works*, 1, 143–233 and J E, Yale, 3). This title was with the printer at the time of Edwards' death.

(b) *Major Posthumous Publications*

28. *Sermons on Various Important Subjects* (annexed to his Life and Character, by the Rev. Samuel Hopkins). Boston, 1765. 8°, pp. viii, 279. (*Works*, 2, 130–256).

29. *Two Dissertations.* I. *Concerning the End for which God created the World.* II. *The Nature of true Virtue.* Boston, 1765. 8°, pp. vii, 191. (*Works*, 1, 94–142).

30. *A History of the Work of Redemption.* Containing the Outlines of a Body of Divinity. Edinb., 1774. 8°, pp. xi, 380. (*Works*, 1, 532–619).

31. *Practical Sermons.* Edinb., 1787. 8°, pp. viii, 401. (*Works*, 2, 104–256).

32. *Twenty Sermons.* Edinb., 1789 (Containing items 2, 16, 17, 19 and 25, listed above, plus 15 posthumous sermons which are reprinted in *Works*, 2, 51–103).

33. *Miscellaneous Observations on important Theological Subjects, original and collected.* Edinb., 1793. 12°, pp. iv, 476. (*Works*, 2, 459–510).

34. *Remarks on important Theological Controversies.* Edinb., 1796. 12°, p. iv, 480. (*Works*, 2, 511–603).
The last two titles were extracted from Edwards' private notebooks of 'Miscellanies'. Further extracts will be found in his collected *Works*, 2, 604–675 and in *The Philosophy of Jonathan Edwards*, From His Private Notebooks, Harvey G. Townsend, 1955.

35. *Charity and its Fruits.* [16 Sermons on 1 Corinthians 13, preached in 1738] Edited by Tryon Edwards, D.D. N.Y., 1851. 12°, pp. ix, 530. Reprinted Banner of Truth Trust, 1969.

36. 'Treatise on Grace', published in *Selections from the Unpublished Writings of Jonathan Edwards*, A. B. Grosart, 1865, and reprinted by James Clarke, Ed. Paul Helm, 1971, as *Treatise on Grace.*

(c) *Collected Works*

1. *The Works of President Edwards in Eight Volumes*, Edited by Edward Williams and Edward Parsons, Leeds, 1806–11. (Supplemented by two further volumes edited by R. Ogle, Edinburgh, 1847).

2. *The Works of President Edwards*, Edited by S. Austin, 8 vols., Worcester, Mass., 1808–9.

3. *The Works of President Edwards*, Edited by Sereno E. Dwight, 10 vols., New York, 1829–30.

4. *The Works of Jonathan Edwards*, 2 vols., London, 1834. The usefulness of this large but compact edition is illustrated by the fact that it was repeatedly reprinted for over forty years and remains in print today (Banner of Truth Trust, 1974).

5. *The Works of President Edwards*, 4 vols., New York, 1843–44. Reprinting, in close type, item 2 above (with additions), but contains less of Edwards than item 4.

6. *The Works of Jonathan Edwards*, General Editor: John E. Smith, Yale University Press, New Haven.

Vol. 1: *Freedom of the Will*, Edited by Paul Ramsey, 1957.

Vol. 2: *Religious Affections*, Edited by John E. Smith, 1959.

Vol. 3: *Original Sin*, Edited by Clyde A. Holbrook, 1970.

Vol. 4: *The Great Awakening*, Edited by C. C. Goen, 1972.

Vol. 5: *Apocalyptic Writings*, Edited by Stephen J. Stein, 1977.

Vol. 6: *Scientific and Philosophical Writings*, Edited by Wallace E. Anderson, 1980.

Vol. 7: *The Life of David Brainerd*, Edited by Norman Pettit, 1985.

Publication of this edition is continuing.

Two

THE EDWARDS' MANUSCRIPTS

Edwards left many notebooks and manuscripts containing material which, for the most part, he had not designed for publication, or, at least, not in their existing form. Originally with Samuel Hopkins, this material went to Jonathan Edwards Jr. ('Dr. Edwards') in the late 1760's. By his aid, John Erskine was able to get more of Edwards' writings to the press. But by the time of the death of Edwards Jr. in 1801 he was reported to have 'informed a very particular friend and relative . . . that he had selected from his father's manuscripts *every thing* which he supposed *proper* to be published' (*The Works of President Edwards in Eight Volumes*, vol. 1, 1806, p. 89). When John Ryland of England wrote to the aged Hopkins in 1803 concerning the whereabouts of the Edwards' material yet unpublished, the biographer of Edwards replied: 'I can give no information concerning the MSS of President Edwards which were in the hands of Dr. Edwards when he died. I had not seen him for a number of years before his death, and fear they have fallen into hands which will let them sink into oblivion. I have just entered on the eighty-third year and do not expect to live much longer' (*Works of S. Hopkins*, 2, pp. 757–8).

But, apart from the thirty MS sermons on Isaiah 51.8 which went to Scotland and were published as *The History of Redemption* (and thereafter disappeared), the Edwards' papers were safe and passed into the hands of Sereno E. Dwight, the principal editor and biographer of his great-grandfather. By the 1850's the MSS were with another great-grandson, the Rev. Tryon Edwards, who, with the publication of Edwards' *Charity and its Fruits* in 1851, proved that some of the best of the hitherto unpublished MSS had been overlooked. This was confirmed by the efforts of A. B. Grosart who, securing the loan of further MSS from Tryon Edwards, issued *Selections from the Unpublished Writings of Jonathan Edwards* in 1865. The most important item in this slender book was a *Treatise on Grace* of which Grosart says: 'This Manuscript was found by itself, carefully placed within folds of thick paper, and tied up with a silk ribbon. It proved to be arranged into chapters and sections, all paged; and, in short, precisely as now printed'. Grosart had crossed the Atlantic in the mid 1850's to confer with Tryon Edwards on the publication of a 'complete and really worthy edition' of Edwards' Works. This never materialized and in 1897, two years before his death, Grosart wrote: 'It was my privilege to publish for the first time a considerable selection from Edwards' unpublished MSS, and *the* disappointment of my life that a long-projected and prepared, and thoroughly adequate edition of his complete works, still remains an unfulfilled *desideratum* because this generation does not know its greatest and wisest and noblest men' (*The Sunday at Home*, 1897, p. 459).

Papers of Edwards, and relating to Edwards, left by S. E. Dwight, passed into the custody of Andover Seminary and other Edwards MSS were loaned to the Seminary during the lifetime of Professor E. A. Park (1808–1900). With Park's death and, it seems, the return of other material from Scotland, the great bulk of Edwards' MSS went to Yale where they have since remained and become, in the second half of this century, a prolific source for further studies on Edwards. After this long and chequered history, the majority of the MSS unpublished at the time of Edwards' death, have thus survived, the principal exceptions being those manuscripts which were discarded or lost after they had been transcribed and published.

Opinions vary over what of value remains to be published

from the original MSS. Interest among Edwards scholars appears to centre on the nine notebooks which make up his 'Miscellanies' and two volumes of this material, edited by Thomas A. Schafer, were projected by Yale University Press for 1970. To date they have not appeared, but it should be noted that much of Edwards' 'Miscellanies' is *already* in print. In the view of H. G. Townsend, 'It may be estimated that approximately three-fourths of the manuscripts has been published in more-or-less adequate texts' (*The Philosophy of Jonathan Edwards*, 1955, xvii). It may well be Schafer's editorial work which will be of principal interest, when, as it is hoped, the Yale edition of Edwards does bring out his 'Miscellanies'.

By far the most important of the material yet to be published is to be found in his MSS sermons and it is to be regretted that the current Yale edition, with seven volumes to date, has as yet provided none of his unpublished sermons. While it is understood that at least one volume is in preparation, Yale have no intention to print all that Edwards left in the form of fully-written sermons.

The sermon MSS are the only store of Edwards' material remaining unpublished which were obviously prepared for public use. Among MS material which he wrote for his personal record, nothing has been printed from the 900 pages of his interleaved study Bible (the so-called 'Blank Bible' in which he wrote from the early 1730's onwards) except some extracts given in the Grosart volume mentioned above. Some of Edwards' 'Notes' and 'Observations on the Holy Scriptures' have been published (2.676–816), but these are drawn from a different MS and are distinct from the entries in the study Bible. Of the Study Bible entries Grosart writes that they 'seem to us to be of a more richly experimental character than the others'.

Students of Edwards will value such of Edwards' notebooks as Yale are able to publish. One, 'On the Apocalypse', is given in vol. 5 of the Yale edition. Such material is of value, largely, for the guidance it gives to Edwards' methods of study and, sometimes, to developments in his thought.

Finally, of MS material yet outstanding, there has to be included the need for a volume of Edwards' correspondence. Such a work, well-edited, would certainly assist towards a better understanding of Edwards' life.

For further information:

F. B. Dexter, 'On the Manuscripts of Jonathan Edwards,' *Massachusetts Historical Society Proceedings* (second series), XV, pp. 2–16 (1902).

Thomas A. Schafer, 'Manuscript Problems in the Yale Edition of Jonathan Edwards,' *Early American Literature*, 3, (Winter, 1968–69), 159–171.

Three

A LETTER OF SARAH EDWARDS, 1750

The following statement, addressed to the Council meeting in Northampton in June 1750 to advise on the crisis between pastor and people, is valuable for two reasons: it is the only piece of writing of any length to survive from the hand of Edwards' wife and it deals with the saddest event in her husband's life. Her testimony is concerned to meet the charge that Edwards had previously hidden his real views in order to gain an advantageous settlement in the protracted parish differences over his salary. This testimony was published from a manuscript, 'handed down in the family of one of his lineal descendants', in *The Congregationalist and Christian World*, Oct. 3, 1903.

I, the subscriber, do testify and declare that above four years ago, not very long after Mr. Edwards had admitted the last Person that ever was admitted into this church who made no Profession of Godliness, He told me that He would not dare ever to admit another Person without a Profession of real saving Religion; and the same Time told me he had put something into his Book on Religious Affections by which the Country would know his opinion, and that He had done it on Design that They might have some Intimation of it.

[485]

And not long after, when riding out with him, (I being ill, and riding for my Health) He had considerable discourse on this subject, and spake much of the great difficulties that He expected would come upon Him by reason of his opinion. I asked Him what Course he intended to take. He said he knew not what. I asked Him if He would not publish something expressly handling the subject & vindicating his opinion: He replied, not unless He was forced to it, for He did [not] at all love openly to oppose his Grandfather in that manner: He said to preach against him would be looked upon as a great degree of arrogance (or to that purpose) and much more to print against Him. He chose rather for the present to content Himself with giving some occasional Intimations of his opinion, that People may be thinking of it; as (said He) I have already done in my Book on religious affections; when that Book comes out all my People will know that I am of that opinion, and added, I am still looking & inquiring into this matter and 'tis possible I may hereafter see otherwise.

He often touched on this matter in discourse with me before his Books on religious Affections came out; But when these Books came abroad He said to me that He wondered that He heard nothing of the People's taking notice that He differed from Mr. Stoddard. He very often said that He did think it probable that the People would never yield to his opinion; but yet from Time to Time expressed a full determination not to go on in admitting members without a credible Profession of Godliness any more, unless He should receive other Light, and often signified that when He should begin to have Occasion to act on his Principles, or when any offered to come into the Church, that made no pretense to Godliness, & He should be obliged to refuse, then the Tumult would begin.

And sometimes when we talked of the Probability of Col. Stoddard's disliking my[1] opposing the opinion & Practice of his Father, He always said to that Purpose that let that be as it would, it was his full determination to go on no longer as He had done, unless He had conviction offered. I several Times heard Mr. Edwards say that He thought it his best way to improve his Time in endeavoring to get Light, 'till He was obliged to act, and that He chose to give some intimations of his opinion before He had occasion to act, lest when He came to refuse any one that offered Himself to join with the church, giving as a Reason of it that He had changed his opinion, It should be suspected that this was not the True Reason, but that this Refusal was indeed from personal Prejudice.

I often heard Mr. Edwards speak freely of his forementioned opinion, and his Resolution to proceed no further &c, before his

[1] The original MS reads 'my' but it would appear to be a mistake for 'his'.

Family & before others, both Town People and Strangers, before Col. Stoddard's death, & before his salary was settled, and never as a secret Thing or a Thing that He desired would be kept so; nor had I ever any Imagination that He desired it should be kept secret; and therefore both I & my children often freely spoke of it when we had Occasion. I often heard Mr. Edwards speak of these Things to Mr. John Brainerd; and particularly of the Probability of its ending in a separation between Him and his People.

I heard him once speak of these Things very freely and fully about four years ago, when Mr. Buel & Mr. Osborn of Long Island & Lieut. Phelps & Mr. Noah Parsons of this Town were present; & while he was discoursing of it, Noah Lyman came in & Mr. Edwards did not at all forbear on that account but still went on freely uttering the same things. I remember He once talked of it to Col. Dwight before his salary was settled, who never had I suppose, at that Time Intimated any favourable Thought of his opinion. He once before Col. Stoddard's death talked largely of the matter in my hearing with Mr. Burr of Newwark, Mr. Strong, now settled at Portsmouth, being present. He told Mr. Burr that He should be glad to see otherwise if He could, for as his Judgment now was, He could proceed no further in our Former way; tho' it was not unlikely that his Refusal might be a means of Throwing him out of Business, & bringing Him & his Family to Poverty. Mr. Burr then said to Him 'If the case be so, you had better run away from these difficulties and accept the Place of the President of N-Jersey College.' Mr. Edwards replied He must not run away before He was called, for these difficulties were not come upon Him yet.

I remember Mr. Edwards once in talking to some Gentleman of these matters Expressed Himself thus, that the difficulties He had a Prospect of appeared to Him like a Bottomless ocean, He could see no end of 'em. I once asked Him whether it was worth his while to strive to have his salary settled seeing He thought it probable that this difficulty would end in a separation between Him & his People; He answered, there were so great difficulties, arose through the salaries being unsettled that if he tarried but a year or two longer He chose to have it done. I can further testify that to my observation, Mr. Edwards's being of this opinion was publickly talked of abroad, three years ago the last February, and that I then heard it openly talked of at Hartford & New Haven, & being enquired of about it there, spoke of it freely my self. I also once talked freely of it to Elisha Pomeroy going to Boston with Him before Col. Stoddard's death.

Northampton, June 17th. 1750
SARAH EDWARDS

Four

AN ANECDOTE ON WHITEFIELD AND 'THE WITNESS OF THE HOLY SPIRIT'

After 25 years at Great Barrington, the pastoral charge of Samuel Hopkins was terminated in 1769 and the following year he became pastor of the First Congregational Church at Newport, Rhode Island. It was here, on August 3, 1770, that he welcomed George Whitefield – whom he had first heard with delight thirty years earlier – to his parsonage. The preacher remained in Newport for five days, dying elsewhere in New England on September 30.

The following anecdote is from Patten's *Reminiscences of Hopkins*, as given in *The Works of Samuel Hopkins*, vol. 1, p. 87:

'While Mr. Whitefield was at Newport, he was invited, with Mr. Hopkins and others, "to breakfast with a religious family, about five miles from town. On their way, Mr. Whitefield said to Mr. H., "I am sorry that you New England ministers employ so much of your time in controversy. [A remark often repeated since Whitefield's time.] I wish you would devote your attention more immediately to the conversion of sinners." Mr. H. replied, "I have not published so large a pamphlet in the way of dispute as yours against Mr. Wesley." [A fit reply, to which Whitefield rejoined,] "O, the doctrine of Mr. Wesley was so contrary to the faith, and so dangerous, that a regard for the cause of Christ compelled me to attempt its refutation." "The same motive," said Mr. H., "may have influenced others; it certainly did me in what I have written." [An apt retort.] After a considerable pause, Mr. Whitefield said, "Is it not surprising, and much to be regretted, that good Mr. Edwards should deny the witness of the Spirit?" Mr. H. replied, "I did not know that he had. What do you understand, sir, by the witness of the Spirit?" Mr. W. paused in apparent study for a definition. Mr. H. said, "Do you mean by it an impression on the imagination, by some immediate communication from the Spirit, that your sins are forgiven, and that you are a child of God?" "No," said Mr. W., "that does not express my opinion." "Do you then mean," said Mr. H., "an influence of the Spirit of God, exciting such a love for God and Jesus Christ, such clear views of their character, as that the subject of it knows from experience and from Scripture, that he is a child of God and an heir of salvation?" "This," said Mr. W., "more accords with my views." Yet this," said Mr. H., "is that witness of the Spirit for which Mr. Edwards pleads, in distinction from the former, which he represents as a species of enthusiasm."'

John Erskine, a friend of Whitefield's, writing in 1748 of some changes of views on the part of the latter, says: 'Now he scarce preaches a sermon without guarding his hearers against relying on impressions, and telling them that faith, and a persuasion we are justified, are very different things, and that a holy life is the best evidence of a gracious state'. Quoted by John Gillies, *Memoirs of the Life of George Whitefield*, 1772, pp. 177–8.

On assurance by 'an immediate testimony of the Spirit of God' see John Owen, *Works*, 6, p. 594.

INDEX

Index

as known by S. Hopkins: 180
et seq.
her character, conversion and
religious experiences:
193–9
her husband's salary: 278
helps to nurse Uncle John:
313
her portrait requested: 368
a serious illness: 379
her death: 446
her letter of June, 1750, on the
dispute about reception at
the Lord's table: 485–7
Children: Elizabeth: 313, 446
Esther: *See* Burr, Esther
Eunice: 403, 446
Jerusha: 148, 182, 304,
309–10, 403*n*
Jonathan: 377, 394–5, 446,
452, 454
Lucy: 148, 403, 439, 441, 446
Mary: 148, 401, 405, 446
Pierrepont: 353, 446
Sarah: *See* Parsons, Sarah
Susannah: 403, 410, 440
Timothy: 148, 410, 437, 445*n*,
446
Edwards, Tryon: xxviii, 138*n*
Effelsteen, Mr.: 439
Eldership in churches: 16, 344–6
Elias, John: 464
Elizabethtown (NJ): 123
Emerson, Joseph: 185
Enfield: 168, 169*n*, 171, 217
Erskine, John: xv, 291–2, 307, 309,
346, 355, 356, 363, 368, 378, 379,
390, 391, 455, 456, 463, 464, 466,
490
Essay concerning Human Understanding
(J. Locke): 64
Ewing, John: 407

Faust, Clarence H.: xxix, 44, 322*n*,
348*n*
Fay, James: 173
Finney, Charles G.: 453, 461–2, 469
Firmin, Giles: 128*n*

Finley, Samuel: xix, xxii
Fish, Joseph: 220
Flavel, John: 68, 142*n*, 226
Fonda, Mr.: 439
Foote, W. H.: 211*n*, 406*n*, 414*n*
Fourfold State, The (T. Boston): 211
Foxcroft, Thomas: 207, 447, 448,
450, 454
France, New England at war with,
285, 387 *et seq.*
Freehold (NJ): 124, 432
Frelinghuysen, Jacobus: 132
French, Jonathan: 452*n*
French Prophets: 204, 242, 245
Fuller, Andrew: 467*n*

Gay, Ebenezer: 281, 282
Peter: xxi, xxv*n*
Gee, Joshua: 208
Giger, G. M.: 136
Gillespie, Thomas: 291, 292, 325,
362, 381
Gillies, John: *See Historical Collections*
Girardeau, John L.: 451
God glorified in man's Dependence: 108
Goen, C. C.: 109, 118*n*
Goodwin, Thomas: 471
Gordon, Adoniram Judson: 308
Goshen (Connecticut): 217, 446
Grafton: 172
Grange, Lord: 293
Great Barrington: 391, 447, 489
Green, Ashbel: xv
Jacob: 284
Griffin, Edward D.: 455*n*, 458, 460
Grosart, Alexander B.: xi, xxviii,
139, 189, 191, 279*n*, 319*n*, 367*n*,
386
Groton: 224, 244
Guide to Christ (S. Stoddard): 129, 131
Gurnall, William: 215
Guthrie, William: 128, 215
Guyse, John: 114, 117–8, 121

Hadley: 20, 196, 315, 324
Hall, David: 160, 220, 327, 348
Robert: xvi, 464
Samuel: 27

Index